# The Service

## The Memoirs of General Reinhard Gehlen

Translated by David Irving

Introduction by George Bailey

## WORLD PUBLISHING

TIMES MIRROR
NEW YORK

*Dedicated to my colleagues*
*in the Service*

Published by The World Publishing Company
Published simultaneously in Canada
by Nelson, Foster & Scott Ltd.

First printing—1972

First published in a shorter edition by
v. Hase & Koehler Verlag, Mainz, Germany
ISBN 0-529-04455-2
Library of Congress catalog card number: 73-183092
Printed in the United States of America
Designed by Jacques Chazaud

**WORLD PUBLISHING**
TIMES MIRROR

# CONTENTS

[ v

head of Foreign Armies East. I reorganize the branch. Cooperation with the Abwehr.

The Russian reserves. How we calculated the enemy strength. How we investigated the enemy's raw material situation. The growing signs that Stalingrad would be a turning point. Reports from our agent in Moscow. My bitterness that our warnings were ignored. Intelligence tactics in the East. Hitler's preparations for Citadel and our warnings of Russian countermeasures ignored. Our suspicion falls on Martin Bormann.

We could have defeated the Russians if the war had been fought on a political level too. Clausewitz had pointed the way. Our troops were welcomed by the Russians at first. Our commanders recruited Russian volunteers as auxiliaries. The capture of General Vlasov and the launching of the Vlasov movement. Hitler thwarts our plans, and Himmler takes them over as his own late in 1944—too late.

Hitler's reluctance to listen to unpleasant facts. He turns the Abwehr over to Himmler. Deteriorating military situation in the East during 1944. The collapse of Army Group Center, June 1944, and the failure of the bomb plot against Hitler. General Guderian's difficulties in persuading Hitler to accept my reports as accurate. Soviet invasion of January 1945 and the flight of my family from Silesia. A Churchill document is fed into our hands. I propose a ring of forest fires to defeat the Russians. The bridges are left unburned. My staff begins to plan for the future. Russians plan to bombard the Americans. The odyssey begins and we hide out in the mountains.

PART TWO   THE PARTNERSHIP

Return from Washington to Germany, 1946. Negotiations with General Sibert, and an agreement is struck between us.

What my colleagues had done during my absence. We build the Gehlen organization. The kind of men we picked. Our relations with our American partners. We are found a new headquarters, at Pullach outside Munich. Problems with American financing and military customs. We are transferred to CIA control in 1949. More money problems cost us valuable staff. Contacts with Adenauer and his government. The BfV is established; my objections to the appointment of Otto John as its head. Headquarters at Pullach, and security measures I had to take. Further meetings with the Bonn authorities.

Sefton Delmer exposes our organization in the press. The 1953 troubles in East Germany, and the Communists begin their counterattack on my organization. Ernst Wollweber, the East German secret service chief. My security measures. The Geyer case. The loss of an agent leader, kidnapped by the East Germans. The case of Wolfgang Höher. The American-controlled sabotage organizations. The case of Walter Gramsch. The private secretary of the prime minister, and the deputy prime minister we brought over to the West. My report to the EDC committee. The Soviet white book attacking us. Operation Uranus. The case of Emil Bahr. Links with the German press.

Relations with the federal government. Internal security of the state. The Otto John affair, 1954. A military intelligence office is set up. The Gehlen organization is regularized. Links with the CIA. My memories of Allen Dulles. Modes of transfer of the organization to federal control discussed. The need for intelligence services to be free of government interference. My channels of communication to the Russians. Stars and Stripes hauled down outside Pullach.

PART THREE    IN SERVICE OF WEST GERMANY

The nature of intelligence services, and their reputation. Difference between agents who act out of idealism and those who work for money. The emergence of secret intelligence services. Intelligence services must report objectively and not actively influence government policy themselves. The shortcomings of intelligence predictions. Effectiveness versus accountability. How other countries manage their services.

How the BND worked. The limitations we imposed on ourselves. The Hungarian revolution. The Suez crisis. Khrushchev's secret speech in Moscow. Wollweber's dismissal. Berlin crisis of 1958. The role of the U-2 incident. The Bay of Pigs. The erection of the Berlin Wall. The shocking confessions of KGB agent Stashinskyi.

Political assassination discussed. Why did Bonn not protest either the Stashinskyi affair or the kidnapping of Antoine Argoud? The Heinz Felfe affair and how it affected us. The value of lie detector tests. The *Der Spiegel* affair causes a rift with Adenauer. The Cuban missile crisis. Relations with the French and SDECE. The British intelligence service characterized. Renewed crisis over Berlin. Playing off the Arabs against the Jews. Erhard replaces Adenauer. A television team at Pullach. One of our men in Moscow is nearly eliminated.

My views on the fighting in Vietnam. Khrushchev goes into oblivion. The overstated importance of Red China. Ulbricht's visit to Cairo. Insurrection in Indonesia. The need to keep our three intelligence services separate in Germany. We predict the Israeli attack on Egypt, June 1967. Soviet aid in the wake of the Arab defeat. My presidency of the BND comes under fire from the civil servants. The suicide of my deputy, and my own retirement.

PART FOUR   THE FUTURE OF THE WEST

The ideological premises of Communist foreign policy are unchanged. Semantic distinctions in Communist meanings of words like *coexistence* and *ideology*. The role of "disinformation."

*Chapter Fourteen*

WORLD COMMUNIST OPERATIONS AND INFILTRATION   305

What are the present international organizations acting as fronts for Communist infiltration and subversion? The work of the various Communist parties. The dual role of Communist diplomatic missions. How the innocent and simpleminded are taken in. Instances of "disinformation."

*Chapter Fifteen*

TWENTY-FIVE YEARS OF SOVIET POWER POLITICS   333

Review of postwar events in light of Communist ideology and aims—the pattern remains the same. The alarming increase in the power of the Soviet Union. The attempts to establish popular front governments. The fiction of the "peace-loving" Soviet government. The role of the Middle East as pivot of the Soviet flank attack on Europe. The Berlin notes of 1952. Soviet policy in the Khrushchev era. The August 1970 Soviet-German treaty. The use of Berlin as a lever. The basically aggressive nature of Soviet foreign policy. The East German people look to Bonn for succor. The situation once Mao Tse-tung and Tito have departed. The likelihood that Russia and China will overcome their differences. Not Brezhnev, but Shelyepin will be the new dictator. My predictions for the coming two decades.

# Introduction

hen I visited General Gehlen in his home on Starnberger Lake not long ago, the first thing I noticed in his living room was a portrait of the elder Field Marshal von Moltke. In this portrait Moltke cuts an almost ludicrous figure; his *Pickelhaube*—the ceremonial Prussian helmet with the spearhead sticking out of the top—is too big and the collar of his uniform too wide for the rather scrawny neck of the old fellow (Moltke did not retire until he was eighty-nine). He looks uncomfortable and altogether unsoldierly. That was just the point, said my host. Moltke was indeed unsoldierly, he did not at all conform to the type of the Prussian officer. Instead, he was the typical General Staff officer in that he was atypical. For the General Staff sought and cultivated the unorthodox, the unconventional, the unusual officer, in the hope of thus acquiring original thinkers and bold, untrammeled spirits. How was this?—against the background of the Prussian military tradition of absolute discipline, of "cadaver obedience," a group of nonconformists, a clique of head-strong and (often enough) eccentric individualists, as witness Moltke's violent falling out with Bismarck over the conduct and purpose of the Franco-Prussian War. Yet so it was, and so it remained until the destruction of the German government in 1945: it was altogether fitting that the plot against Hitler should have been hatched and engineered by General Staff officers.

The Prussian General Staff evolved from the impact of the French Revolutionary and Napoleonic wars on Germany. The military historian Behrenhorst remarked that instead of being a country that had an army, Prussia was an army that had a country which it used as a billeting area. It is true that until the middle of the nineteenth century the Prussian army was the only organization that held the scattered provinces of the monarchy together. But the Prussian army was the dynastic projection of the House of Hohenzollern. As such, it owed only one allegiance—to the person of the monarch, a tradition that was to have disastrous consequences when that allegiance was transferred to the person of the head of state, whoever he happened to be—and particularly when he happened to be Adolf Hitler.

The Prussian officer was by no means only a military man: he was first and foremost an official of the Prussian state. He was an administrator, technician, engineer—he ran the state. When an army runs the state it becomes of necessity more than an army. It is all the more understandable, then, that the army should have been for a long while almost entirely in the hands of the landed aristocracy, the Junkers. When Gerhard Johann Scharnhorst, the founding father of the General Staff, appeared on the scene at the end of the eighteenth century, all the generals and regimental commanders of the Prussian army were titled. Some time after, when commoners predominated in the officer corps, they affected the manners and adopted the morals and outlook of the aristocrats.

Because it was the prerequisite of Prussia's rise to power, militarism was the inevitable product. Frederick the Great transformed a tin-pot marshland kingdom of two million souls into a world power almost overnight. The rape of Silesia "made" Prussia.

But to take Silesia and, more importantly, to keep it, Frederick had to incur the undying enmity of all Europe, especially since he followed the invasion of Silesia with the invasion of the "neutral" kingdom of Saxony. Militarily, the invasion of Saxony was justified because of Prussia's impossible geographical position in the center of Europe, surrounded as she was by land borders (moreover, by flatland borders); even the natural barrier of the sea to the north was breached by the Danish peninsula. The central position of Prussia made it necessary for her to be able to defend herself against all her neighbors simultaneously. It is not just that the best perimeter defense is a perimeter offense—the *only* perimeter defense is a perimeter offense. The encircling enemy must be struck before he can properly set himself to strike. The policy of striking first and finishing quickly was dictated by self-preservation. Thus, in his own day Moltke was forced to the conclusion that the initial deployment of troops was of decisive importance.

Prussia's precarious geographical position (like Israel's today) brought with it an inflation of military means. It is impossible to give notice of the revaluation of currency, because the valuation takes place at the moment of notice. Similarly, mobilization in nineteenth-century Europe became tantamount to a declaration of war, particularly since mobilization involved deployment for attack. An attack from a deployed position imposed the aggressor's concept of the war on the enemy and in all likelihood decided the final issue then and there. Hence, as Moltke concluded, the side that mobilized first started the war, not the side that fired the first shot, an argument the Israelis thoroughly understand. For this was the philosophy, recurrent throughout the ages, of preventive war, or of the preemptive strike, to cite its modern nuclear strategic form.

Perhaps the immediacy of the global nuclear threat has laid the foundations for a better understanding of what Anglo-Saxons long regarded as the exaggerated sense of urgency in the Prussian makeup. The logical extension of such a congenital conviction of immediate danger threatening from all sides was the General Staff planning, the painstaking, minute—"to the smallest detail"—projection and preparation of future wars, an activity that made the

General Staff infamous in the West (the East had a better instinctive grasp of such things). It was one phase of this activity, the surveying of possible future fields of battle, that sent Moltke to Turkey. His official mission was to act as instructor to the Turkish army and as military adviser to Hafis Pasha in the struggle against Kurds and Egyptians; his unofficial—that is to say, his real— mission was to put Anatolia and its surrounding territory on the map. Moltke notes in his memoirs that vast areas of Turkey were still uncharted, having been left blank on the Reichhardt map, while other areas had been falsely charted. "In the observation of the breach of the Euphrates through the Kurd mountains," writes Moltke in 1837, "my immediate predecessor was Xenophon."

But there was something else that followed logically from Prussia's exposed position: the compulsion, and compulsion it was, to unite all the Germanys in order to create the unified striking force which alone was capable of mounting an effective perimeter defense-offense. As Moltke told the recalcitrant South Germans in the Customs Parliament in 1868, "With the best of good will, the South German states for the present can offer only a coalition, while all around us we see nothing but large and unified armies. We, too, and for this reason, wish for an inner fusion, but we wish it less out of North German or Prussian interests than out of the general German interest and quite especially out of your own interest." Moltke went on to say that Prussia could wait until the South Germans finally saw the light. But this was a white lie. Writing to his brother in the same year, he put it bluntly: "Without outside force, such a thing will not come to pass; sooner or later we are going to have to do battle for it." The Franco-Prussian War, which Prussia waged with the South German states against France (time was when France waged war with the South German states against Prussia), was in more than one sense directed primarily against the South German states themselves, for only by this means—short of an outright war of conquest—could they be incorporated into a Germany unified under Prussian hegemony.

It was Prussia's success in the war against Austria in 1866 that secured Moltke official recognition and provided him (and hence the General Staff, by way of the precedent he set) with direct access to the sovereign as special adviser. It was only natural that German military intelligence should grow out of the General Staff. Nor was it happenstance that after the collapse of Germany in 1945, one of General Gehlen's primary motives in arranging the continuance of his organization under American sponsorship was the desire to provide a haven for a number of General Staff officers in something like their professional function. Indeed, in something very like their professional function. The similarity between General Staff work and intelligence work, particularly as the latter has developed in the last twenty-five years, is great and still growing. Indeed, and this is one of the main points of General Gehlen's account: ever since World War II, intelligence agencies of the larger nations have been gradually superseding conventional diplomatic institutions. This is because the work of maintaining or expanding positions of influence abroad cannot be done only by diplomatic means. The global positions of both the United States and the Soviet Union are built on systems of military alliances. As a result, the primacy of the military establishments of the superpowers in foreign affairs is unquestionable. The fact that the Soviet Union has invaded (or reinvaded in the case of Hungary) two of its European satellites in the last sixteen years should not obscure Soviet preference for managing such crises by political rather than military means. The significance of the fact that it could not salvage the Czechoslovak situation politically, let alone diplomatically, can hardly be exaggerated. But its inability to do so placed all the more emphasis on intelligence work and particularly on intelligence as political action in a foreign country. The expulsion by Great Britain of 105 Soviet "spy-diplomats" illustrates the fusion and the confusion of the two fields of activity. As General Gehlen puts it, an intelligence service operating abroad is the most important instrument for the provision of the basic materials of a country's foreign policy. It can also be, as he shows in this book, the most important instrument for the implementation of foreign policy. An intelligence agent can do things a diplomat cannot and must not do. He need not be disavowed by his government if he is caught red- or black-handed; he is never so much as acknowledged by his government in the first place. Ideally, the intelligence agent should blend with the environment of his area, so that if he makes mistakes they will appear to be natural and not excite suspicion. The activity requires a great deal of adaptability and perceptiveness. But above all, and this is the one absolute involved, intelligence work requires trust-worthiness. In the necessary absence of controls, in the concomitant necessary presence of unusual discretionary powers in the hands of individual operatives, the only practical basis for proceeding is trust.

Now the extension of trust to anyone and for whatever reason is a naive act. It is for this reason that intelligence operatives and their superiors so often appear naive in their doings and attitudes when these are exposed or presented to the public. The foundations of trustworthiness within a group have always been assumed to be like-mindedness and, hence, similarity of background. In Great Britain, whose intelligence service was acknowledged to be the best in the business, such likeness of outlook and background was (and, decreasingly, still is) symbolized by the old school tie. In Germany, it was the officer corps, particularly the Prussian officer corps, that provided the guarantee of common ethical grounding. The British service had its comeuppance with the defection of Guy Burgess and Donald McLean, followed by the disastrous exposure of Kim Philby as a lifelong double agent for the Soviet Union. As for the Prussians, when they made a virtue of necessity they made a necessity of virtue. That virtue, by any of its many names— loyalty, faithfulness, devotion, obedience—coincided ominously with the old Teutonic first virtue, *Treue*—fidelity.

I say "ominously" because wherever need places so high a premium on the presence of a virtue, there its absence or (worse still) its sudden disappearance becomes all the more devastating. Surely this is why German history is fraught with famous and infamous instances of betrayal. Betrayal is the German leitmotiv, beginning with Arminius and extending through the stab-in-the-back legend as an explanation of Germany's defeat in World War I.

*Treue* was based on the fact or myth of ethnic homogeneity—

if the "fact" was a myth then the myth was a fact—the "blood-likeness" of the tribe. When Bismarck proclaimed the German Empire at Versailles, he began with the words, "The German people, united in its tribes . . ." Since the end of the Middle Ages Germany has been the arena of the great religio-ideological struggles of the West. Time and again, the land on which the Germans domicile has been divided by the battle lines of foreign as well as domestic armies. Time and again, the allegiance of the German tribes has been divided by conflicting faiths. German history is the concatenation of attempts to preserve or restore ethnic homogeneity by institutional means, particularly by institutionalized religion. "The God of the Germans" was a racial god for this reason. This need for an institutional harness for the German ethnos was one of Luther's larger motives in taking the steps that led to the Reformation. The same consideration turned the Counter-Reformation into a campaign to destroy German ethnic homogeneity. It would be impossible to exaggerate the importance of Protestantism as the informing spirit of Prussia: the number of Prussian leaders who, like Clausewitz, were sons of Protestant clergymen is something like legion. And it is too often overlooked that while Bismarck did not succeed in uniting all the Germanys, he did succeed in uniting all the Protestant Germanys in a German empire.

It was this German habit of combining the religious and the political that provided the Swiss diplomat and historian Carl J. Burckhardt with the prophetic insight, quoted in General Gehlen's preface to this book, that communism is a new religion whose significance and dynamism makes it comparable to Islam as a historic force. For in the ethos of the proletariat Marx had in fact discovered and developed an alternative to the ethnos of folk tradition reinforced by institutionalized religion. In the search for another stuff that would hold a body politic together he had in fact produced an effective substitute for race—class. This accounts, I think, for the virulence of the long struggle (it has now, perhaps, entered its decisive phase) between Christian conservatives and Socialists-cum-Communists in Germany. (This is not to equate socialism with communism; communism is to socialism as fascism is to conservatism.) The history of Prussia and the Prussianized German Empire and its transient successor states is the history of the consolidation and decline of Protestant Christianity and the rise of socialism. For socialism, like Protestantism, is a German invention. It is the same struggle that has divided Germany once again and is now in the process of subdividing the division; for there is in fact a split within the split, the new fissure traveling from the controversy over how to heal the old one. I think Americans can best comprehend Prussians by comparing them with the Pilgrim Fathers, and by comparing the Prussian tradition with the American puritan tradition. It was not, surely, just happenstance that John Foster Dulles, the son of a Protestant minister and himself steeped in Protestantism, instinctively understood and sympathized with the cause of German reunification.

In West Germany the struggle is between the Christian Democrats and the Social Democrats. As this book attests, the struggle has lost nothing of its classic vehemence. In East Germany, "the first workers' and peasants' state on German soil," the Communist leadership has seen fit to introduce and assiduously cultivate the trappings and uses of Prussian military tradition—a thing the West Germans neither desire nor would dare to do. But something must be done. General Gehlen writes against the background of the apparent breakdown of tradition and the great traditional institutions of Germany: the church, the university, the army, indeed the state itself. Small wonder that General Gehlen is alarmed; he is a specialist in the salvaging and safeguarding of institutions. It is a matter of record that he was preeminently responsible for the rescue of the only German organization to be rescued, surviving both the nightmare of the Nazi terror from within and the holocaust of perimeter attack from without, and maintaining continuity virtually unbroken. This was done by seeking, finding, and securing the sponsorship of first an enemy army and then an enemy government for the continuation of his organization's activity as before, against the same enemy and the sponsor's formal ally. This could not have been done had it not been preceded by a correct assessment of what the real situation at the war's end would be. The assessment was made many months before the event, continually reconfirmed and constantly prepared for. This was contingency planning and preparation par excellence, the application of order-of-battle techniques to a peacetime situation: the procurement of information on the deployment of enemy strength, the estimation of his resources, and, above all, the assessment of his intentions. General Gehlen takes pride in his achievement and in the recounting of it. His pride is pardonable. It was an altogether extraordinary achievement; his account of it makes the most informative book on intelligence I have yet read.

GEORGE BAILEY

# Preface

If—finally unburdened of the duties of working life—one at last wins the leisure to survey his own career, with its ups and downs, its straights and its inevitable diversions, one thing soon becomes clear: in every career there are the usual milestones; but interwoven throughout this canvas of the generally valid, which will be much the same from one personality to the next, there will be traces of the unique and the singular. It is these traits that in fact mark out that personality for what it is.

As a young officer I stubbornly refused to learn a foreign language beyond what I had picked up in school, so that there could be no risk of my being posted to military intelligence work within the General Staff, let alone to the secret service itself. Like probably every one of my comrades in the long history of the German General Staff, I yearned for the day when I would be given an active command of my own. Yet it was precisely in this dreaded field of endeavor that I was fated to find my métier and, I say with gratitude, my fulfillment—analyzing the enemy's position and working with the intelligence services.

In the significant events of a person's life we can see reflected the broad trends of his epoch: we can detect the zeitgeist, the spirit of the age, just as we can recognize the scars left behind by the particular circumstances of his era—such as war, expulsion from his native soil, national collapse, and defeat. But we can also see something of the inner bearing of the man, something that stamps him as a soldier, and, moreover, as a General Staff officer. In my own view the mundane events of my life are not worth committing to the pages of this book. My education at home, my graduation, my entry into the Reichswehr, my commissioning as a lieutenant at the end of 1923, and then my service in various positions in the line and at staff level—there is little there that would distinguish my career from that of a thousand other General Staff officers. I do not expect others to be interested in my life until my appointment on April 1, 1942, to head that branch of the army's General Staff known as Foreign Armies East (*Fremde Heere Ost*).

It is this, the latter segment of my life, that prompts me— and, I would claim, justifies me as well—in publishing my memoirs. Through no effort of my own, from that day on my life took a turn that was both unique and singular. From April 1, 1942, onward I was in a position of extreme responsibility, exerting a growing influence on intelligence work that was to be of great importance for the security of my country.

* * *

The essence of secret intelligence service, apart from an all-embracing knowledge, is the ability to follow and project historical trends into the future. The reader may regard the following letter of the Swiss diplomat and historian Professor Carl J. Burckhardt to Hugo von Hoffmansthal, written as early as 1925, as an impressive example of this kind of gift.

> My dear, honored friend,
> Are you not sometimes astounded that the so-called statesmen of our times perceive so little of what is really happening?

Everybody still keeps staring at Germany, as though that is where all the world's events are to be decided, as though that is the source of all our dangers; one learns nothing of what is happening beyond this hypnotic phenomenon called Germany, with its incitements to horror, anger, or disgust, and we learn nothing of what is happening beyond the curtains suspended over Germany's frontiers.

It seems like only yesterday that we had the Treaty of Brest-Litovsk, with Russia ordered back to within the frontiers it had occupied in the middle of the sixteenth century. The territories ruled by the last of the czars in the west and south, and the whole of the Ukraine, were forfeited, while independent states were founded in the Transcaucasus: Armenia, Azerbaijan, and Georgia emerged, the whole of Siberia was an entity of its own. But already all this has been reconquered. Only Poland—rebellious, Catholic Poland—remains a sovereign state, until the next earthquake comes, and with her the diminutive, defenseless Baltic provinces.

In Siberia the Red armies were able to operate without hindrance, while the Ukraine and the Transcaucasian regions were regained by annexing them to the Bolshevik church. The Japanese withdrew three years ago from the Far Eastern republic founded in 1920, and their forced departure enabled it to link up with the RSFSR*; now Russia stood on the shores of the Pacific once again. Remarkable, that in the whole Anglo-Saxon world, in Britain, in her dominions, and in the United States, this world-shattering, historic fact aroused far less attention than this or that happening on the banks of the Rhine, or within the artificially created frontiers of isolated German Austria, or than anything concerning Czechoslovakia in particular. What a sense of political proportion! Czechoslovakia, the republic of a Beneš!

Can you really believe for one moment that when the chips are down this republic will be able to withstand the enormous pull of this Slav and Marxist magnetism, this drive to world federation? Pan-Slavism, with the driving dynamic force of a new religion! Can anybody seriously believe that the poor and the deprived, or the Asian hordes robbed of their former religious bonds by rationalist missionary schools

---

* *Rossískaya Sovétskaya Federatívnaya Sotsialistícheskaya Respúblika,* Russian Soviet Federated Republic—TRANS.

will be able to resist the promises of this new twentieth-century gospel—promises which can be cashed in here and now? Evidently it is assumed so, for people gaze as though hypnotized at this little patch called Central Europe, they rile the Germans who are in the throes of national disillusion, having lost a war, and who have long ceased to be a world power, if indeed they ever were one. They provoke them with their mistrust and mesquin treatment until in the end all their national penchant for overreaction, for striking out, for fatalism, once more gets the upper hand. And yet it would be so simple to invigorate the present moderate governors of this country by offering them generous and accommodating policies. Instead we cast about for ways to compromise them, one after the other, and of putting them in impossible positions as far as their political position at home is concerned, until in the end only blind anger and the characteristic German injudiciousness and political clumsiness will remain, available to the first demagogue to come along, unleashing a popular frenzy which the West will then regard as the supreme world danger per se, as an exceptional menace to us all, while the real menace bestirs itself in fact beyond this German facade, between the Baltic and the Pacific Ocean, on a geographical scale such as mankind has never seen before. Federation, founded on a universally pervasive weltanschauung acting in the service of a nationalist imperialism, is an irresistible process of crystallization. Compared with this, what chance has something as unattractive in the eyes of the world at large as German revisionism, or as the expansionist dreams of Germany?

To me, the solution of the present German problem seems to lie in granting the moderates within the Reich sufficient tangible success to consolidate their position. In Germany, it is only external success that will enable the moderates to retain control of the affairs of state. The inclination toward extreme solutions is a German characteristic, as we have learned from the Reformation and from the philosophical revolution of the nineteenth century. It is a constant that ought to be particularly familiar to us in the West, just as we are familiar with the character of a relative with whom we are obliged to live and to a certain extent we learn to take it into account. But Russia is in large part an Asiatic power, and there is much of the incommensurable about her. Russia, as the center of the gospel movement, is gaining strength as once did the Arab world inspired by a Mohammed. It is a matter of facing up to the mightiest power generator we have ever known. It is not a matter of embarking on academic or emotional discourses on the value or otherwise of bolshevism. That has nothing to do with the issues of modern foreign policy. Bolshevism is but one of the many forms that socialism can adopt, a vastly more effective form than one whose genesis cools off halfway. We are all living in an age of socialism now. There are differences only of degree. That is why the Russian phenomenon cannot be regarded as a theoretical exercise any longer; it is the greatest reality of our age, and as such it can be of interest to us only insofar as this is a reality that is furnishing unimaginable reserves of strength to a nation struggling for world domination with every means at its disposal.

Germany and Japan are the natural opponents of any Russian expansions. But the West—the British empire and the United States—who in the long run is most threatened by this expansion, is doing all in its power to weaken Germany and Japan. The renunciation of the British-Japanese Treaty (is it three years ago already?) seems to me to be as portentous a capitulation to completely secondary North American interests as it is short-sighted. Japan, I might add, is a far surer factor with regard to Russia than Germany, where memories of old alliances directed against France will always rankle—memories of the wars of Frederick the Great and of Tauroggen. It is too easy for most countries to think in terms of apparent historical analogies, and it is far harder to recognize that all the circumstances have changed.

It seems to be a characteristic of democracies that they project all their own domestic infatuations and passions into the field of foreign affairs, where they can easily cause the most frightful harm.

Enough for today. Please accept the warmest good wishes of your respectful friend,

CARL J. BURCKHARDT

That was a letter written nearly fifty years ago. It shows how clearly and accurately a capable politician can perceive the developing trends of history in advance. How much more possible it must be to do so over a shorter time span, if one has at his disposal a comprehensive knowledge of the kinds of factors determining a given situation and, moreover, future trends.

To achieve this painstaking result, a purposefully organized and trained apparatus of high-grade specialists is required. These specialists must be so closely attuned to one another that they can correctly recognize the individual factors that condition a situation and put them into proper perspective. The job also demands a solid general knowledge and an absolute cognizance of one's own situation, that of one's partners, and that of real and potential enemies. Such is the task of the foreign intelligence service. As the British, for example, have found out, this service must be regarded as the most important instrument for assembling the basic materials of foreign policy.

In the Anglo-Saxon world, as in the Soviet Union, there is no debate as to the need for such a service or the special character forced upon such an agency by the uniqueness of its task. Particularly in Britain, working for it is not at all regarded as disreputable; rather, it is a gentleman's business, and one that enjoys the trust of the entire population. It is not a backstairs trade or a James Bond adventure. In Germany, alas, the importance of such a high-grade instrument has never been truly recognized by large segments of the populace. This was shown most recently by the publication in 1971 of a series of articles in *Der Spiegel* on the Federal Intelligence Service I created. The many major and minor errors aroused some doubt as to the seriousness with which the articles were meant to be taken, but this does not detract from the fact that in no other country of the world would it be possible for such a tasteless and inaccurate account—with countless indiscretions and falsehoods—to have been published about a government agency. After all, an intelligence service needs a measure of screening from public scrutiny if it is to do its job properly. Only the parliamentary subcommittees concerned with the various supervisory functions should have any powers of inspection.

This attitude may give rise to misunderstandings, particularly in this age of "absolute" freedom of the press. But the consequences otherwise may well be that a twilight aura begins to surround the intelligence service, and this can only be harmful for its already thankless work. The lack of understanding can have such repercussions that the very accomplishment of its job is called into question, and the objects it is set are not attained. From my years of experience and from repeated exchanges of views with leading members of other intelligence services, I know that in stating these bald facts I am neither exaggerating nor alone. This, more than anything else, has persuaded me to commit my memoirs to paper, as far as they relate to the development of the German intelligence service since 1945.

At the same time, I wish to express with these pages my gratitude to my many civilian and military colleagues in the service. To all of these men, more than to any others, there applied in essence the Schlieffen dictum that "General Staff officers have no names." Without their permanent and understanding assistance, all our efforts would have been in vain, and my work, in particular, would have been without success.

# The Service

# From Hitler's Bunker to the Pentagon

s a brigadier general of the German army and chief of one of its most important intelligence branches, it had never occurred to me that late in August 1945 I would find myself seated with a number of my former staff officers in an American Air Transport Command DC-3 flying the standard of a three-star U.S. Army general on my way to Washington, D.C.

We must have seemed an unlikely bunch of civilians to be crossing the Atlantic at that time. We had been given only three days to obtain the necessary civilian clothes to exchange for our Wehrmacht uniforms and to lay hands on such suitcases as we could before departing for the United States. On no account were we to be recognizable as former soldiers, for the Russians particularly had begun to ask their former allies where General Gehlen was. Fitting us out in plain clothes was no easy matter in a Germany pulverized from one end to the other by air raids and the general ravages of war. I had to beg and borrow to obtain the most urgent

[ 1

items from my friends. It was an even taller order to get suitcases at such short notice, and in the end we had to improvise with the most motley collection of receptacles. Colonel Stephanus, one of my intelligence officers, had had to ram his few effects into an empty violin case. Perhaps people who saw us took us for members of a string sextet—unless they had happened to see us embark on this transatlantic flight on the personal aircraft of General Bedell Smith, Eisenhower's chief of staff. The charade remained successful, despite one curious incident: when we touched down in the Azores for a brief refueling in mid-Atlantic, we found the local community had drawn up an honor guard to welcome Bedell Smith, whom they obviously assumed was aboard the plane. None of us had ever been to the United States, but though we were curious as to what lay ahead, the mood was anything but one of exhilaration.

Thirty-six hours of flying lay ahead. I reflected on the events of the last few months. It was five months or more since I had last seen Hitler. On February 27, 1945, Colonel General Heinz Guderian, the army's chief of staff, had taken me with him to the Bismarck Room of the Reich Chancellery in Berlin, where the führer still held his war conferences. The last German offensive in the West had collapsed, and he had returned to the Reich capital in January to direct the defense against the Russian onslaught in the East. Hitler had long planned to strike at the exposed northern flank of the Soviet invaders from Pomerania, on the Baltic coast. But I had warned him in my intelligence summaries that there were clear indications that the Russians intended to thwart this by acting first to cut off the Pomeranian forces altogether from the Reich. On February 24, my prediction had been confirmed. Russian tank forces had knifed through our Pomeranian line almost without effort, and they were poised to advance on Danzig and the Baltic sea. In a desperate move, Hitler ordered Army Group Vistula, commanded by the SS chief Heinrich Himmler, to defend at all costs the road and rail links with Danzig—the very corridor of land over which he had ostensibly gone to war in 1939. I reported to Hitler the unvarnished facts about the Russian tank strength opposing Himmler—figures we had pieced together over the previous weeks from prisoners of war and deserters. Then I returned to my barrack headquarters in the woods at Zossen, to the south of Berlin.

I had also suggested to Hitler that we use amplified phonograph records of tank tracks, marching feet, and the other sound effects of massive reinforcements arriving to persuade the Russians that we had built up a particularly powerful and impregnable line of defense between the river Oder and Berlin. There was little else that we could offer. We had called up our last reserves, and in the final fighting for Berlin even youngsters would be put in uniform to man bazookas against the Russian tanks. Hitler adopted the "sound effects" idea, issued the necessary orders on March 5, 1945, and ordered my dismissal as chief of eastern intelligence a month later. There is nobody less popular than a prophet of misfortune whose predictions have been proved true in every detail.

Now I was in a plane bound for Washington. It had taken some time to persuade the Americans that they would be needing an eastern intelligence service. After going into hiding in the Bavarian mountains for the first uneasy weeks after the final collapse, I had surrendered to the Americans on May 22 along with four of my principal staff officers. Early that Tuesday morning, we had set out from our mountain hut, with our knapsacks on our backs, for the nearby town of Fischhausen on Lake Schliersee, where the Americans had set up their town headquarters. I well recall my feelings—a grim humor at the situation as I, a brigadier general who had played a not unimportant part in the war, had to turn myself over to a young American first lieutenant in the Counter Intelligence Corps (CIC). But there was no going back now. The town commandant was understandably quite agitated when a general and four staff officers suddenly reported to him. We were unable to enlighten him as to just what a catch he had made, since he could speak no German and we no English.

He excitedly telephoned his superiors, and they told him to send us one at a time to headquarters at Wörgl. I went first—loaded into a military police jeep and delivered to the CIC unit commander at Wörgl. He interrogated me in the presence of a uniformed female secretary who took notes on everything I said. I remember being somewhat disappointed that his main questions were concerned less with my former specialization as chief of the army's eastern intelligence branch than with the situation in Germany under Adolf Hitler.

I was then sent on to Salzburg to Counter Intelligence Corps headquarters, but the military police officers driving me evidently could not locate the building. After driving me back and forth for some time they finally bundled me into an inn, in the taproom of which there was already another prisoner. The other prisoner was soon taken away, and I was left alone, while a sentry stood guard outside, armed to the teeth, with a machine pistol at the ready should I try to get away.

After three days had passed and nothing had happened, I suggested to an American officer who came into the deserted inn that it was high time that I was taken to the corps' headquarters, but it was heavy going to make ourselves understood. When at last he realized what I was talking about, he burst out, "We forgot all about you!" and promised to look into the matter at once. Some time later, the military police returned and ordered me to pack my bags. I was put into a jeep and driven off to Augsburg, 150 miles away, where the U.S. Seventh Army had its big interrogation center.

The center was a compound consisting of a large number of small but attractive detached and semidetached villas. They were divided into four or six apartments of two or three rooms each— the ideal accommodation for prisoners awaiting interrogation since we were unable to contact each other to compare notes if we wished. Until now I had met only American officers. Almost without exception, these men viewed the situation in accord with official U.S. propaganda. They believed the Soviet Union would eventually develop out of its Communist phase into a liberal state. Stalin was always referred to as "Uncle Joe." Not one of my interlocutors had shown the slightest recognition of the real expansionist aims of the Soviet government.

I was held for about three or four weeks at this disappointing Augsburg camp, while my interrogating officer, who was evidently a German émigré, gradually satisfied himself that I was not a particularly valuable prisoner. He could not have been less interested in the Soviet threat. He was concerned only with domestic German affairs and episodes; or, alternatively, he would ask me about purely organizational matters and personalities, and on these scores I said little. But wheels must have been whirring within wheels somewhere, for one day my door was flung open and a voice bellowed, "Get packed, get packed!" and I was off again. I was loaded into a truck with various other officers, most of them complete strangers to me, and we drove for many hours in the general direction of Stuttgart and Frankfurt.

When we reached Wiesbaden, I was told I was a Gestapo general, and despite my indignant denials I was thrown into Wiesbaden prison. Here the American personnel were uncharitable, to say the least. For a time I even feared from their manner that there would be violence. But as I was being marched down a corridor, I found myself suddenly face to face with my old chief, General Franz Halder, who had been sacked as chief of staff by Hitler in 1942. With his granite face, pince-nez spectacles, and close-cropped hair there could be no mistaking him. Overwhelmed by spontaneous joy at this unexpected reunion, we slapped each other on the back and congratulated each other. The Americans were sufficiently impressed by this display to moderate their attitude toward me from that moment on. Halder belonged to that unfortunate group of civilians and officers whom the Americans had liberated from various concentration camps only to incarcerate them again themselves. Most of them belonged to the conspiracy to take Hitler's life, of July 20, 1944. At Wiesbaden I also caught sight of Hermann Pünder, the pre-1933 state-secretary in the Reich Chancellery, Nikolaus von Horthy, the former regent of Hungary, and Admiral Dönitz, whom Hitler had appointed his successor.

I was housed together with them at Villa Pagenstecher, part of the main interrogation center run by the U.S. Twelfth Army Group under its G-2, Major General Edwin L. Sibert. So I had not been "shelved" at Augsburg, as I had at first feared. At Wiesbaden there were a number of civilian and military prisoners whom the Americans evidently considered important for political or military reasons.

On the first morning after my arrival there I was led downstairs into the garden, where a Captain John Boker invited me to join him on a bench in the sunshine. He was smartly dressed and of cultivated manners. He was perhaps thirty-five, and in his bearing and demeanor every inch an officer, as we understood the term in Germany. (I later learned that he did in fact have some German blood in him, being a third-generation American of German ancestry.)

I know more about Boker now than I did then. During the previous few weeks he had handled the German air force intelligence group commanded by Lieutenant Colonel Holters. This group had surrendered to the U.S. Third Army and had been sent to an interrogation center where Boker had formed a small special unit to work with them. That was where Boker had gained his first unflattering impressions of the CIC and of the army's document collection groups, which were interested only in shipping documents back to the United States without any instinct for exploiting the German personnel who had previously been working on the documents. Boker had taught German army organization and tactics at Camp Ritchie, and before that he had been assigned to an interrogation center outside Washington which I was to come to know better myself. One of Boker's friends from Camp Ritchie had told him that if he could fill a quota of fifteen tons of captured documents he could accompany the shipment back across the Atlantic. With that kind of pressure on, he was clearly going to have to act fast if we were not going to lose our main documents. Captain Boker was the first American officer I met with expert knowledge of Russia and with no illusions about the way political events were turning. He had formed his own ideas about the future.

In retrospect I can see that meeting him was one of the most crucial stages in the development of my plans. Our meetings retained their official character for only a relatively short time. After our initial reserve toward one another had been overcome we became close friends and have remained so to this day.

We had a long talk that morning about the political and military situation. He asked detailed questions about my former work, which I answered only partially. After he left I spent the night thinking things over, deciding whether to lay my cards on the table. Buried in various secret locations* in the Bavarian mountains I had the most important files and indices of my former intelligence branch. I had an organization in embryo which I was prepared to offer the Americans for intelligence work against the Soviet Union. Was this the moment to reveal this to my captors? When I next met Boker, at first I did not show the full hand. We circled each other warily in several further conversations, while I put out such feelers as I could to him, gradually disclosing my own ideas about the future and my ambitions and intentions. I assumed that he was perhaps keeping his superiors—Bedell Smith and Sibert—fully informed on our talks and that he was instructed to lend me a sympathetic ear. At any rate, with each day that passed, he became increasingly frank in his remarks.

I now know that at that time Captain Boker was acting on his own when he listened to my plans for the reconstitution of my wartime group. There were still too many hostile officers—people with blind hatred of the Germans. This was understandable enough, but there were also U.S. military officers who believed they could co-operate with the Russians. There existed highest-level directives to the effect that any German documents concerning the Soviet Union, and any German officers and personnel involved in "eastern area activities," were to be turned over to the Russians. Boker feared, he later told me, that if he had reported our existence too early to Frankfurt and the Pentagon, we might have become exposed to these hostile forces, and then we would have been beyond salvation. Instead, he discussed the problem with the commanding officer of his interrogation group, Colonel W. R. Philp—an officer of whom I still have the fondest memories. Boker had formed an unusually close relationship with this colonel, and the colonel gave him carte blanche to form his own completely independent section to deal with us, reporting only to him.* (Boker and Philp suspected that

---

* Boker tells me he selected only five men for his special unit: Lieutenants John Zorek, Franz Brotzen, and Ulrich Landauer (all German-born linguists of impeccable background); Lieutenant Paul Comstock, of Oklahoma, who had political connections in the U.S. Senate which might prove useful; and Master Sergeant Benjamin Greenwald, from the German section at Camp Ritchie.

there was a Russian infiltrator in the interrogation organization at their level.)

Boker and I agreed that I should send for a small number of my former colleagues from the other prison camps, so that the Americans could judge for themselves the specialized knowledge that we had. I signed a number of letters for him and gave him the names of the seven officers I had picked so that he could identify them from the prisoner of war lists and have them transferred to Wiesbaden. Boker secured Philp's permission to go out in the field and bring them in himself to avoid going through regular channels which might have attracted attention to these prisoners. He himself collected Gerhard Wessel, who had succeeded me in April, and Major Hiemenz from the camp at Bad Aibling, and drove them to me in his open jeep. I had also listed Colonel Stephanus, Major Hinrichs, Major Füner (a Russo-German we dubbed "Papuschka"), and two others. It took several days to collect them all. When he returned, Boker told me with a grin that at first he had spoken to each of my men without showing them the letter in which I authorized them to cooperate with him. Without exception, they had been completely unreceptive until he had produced the letter. Boker made no secret of how much this had impressed him.

At about the same time, Boker had our names removed from the prisoner of war lists that were in circulation. He was concerned because the Russian liaison officers had access to these lists, and our joint effort could still end in tragedy. As my officers arrived at Wiesbaden he had them housed without official registration in the Villa Pagenstecher, and no access was permitted to us except by Boker's unit. As for our hidden archives of wartime intelligence documents, some had remained undiscovered in the fields where they lay buried. I sent out my men from Wiesbaden, and these caches were retrieved. Others already had been found by American military units, and Boker was able to locate them—though not without some difficulty, in view of the discretion involved—in a document collection warehouse near Frankfurt. His unit produced a blanket requisition from Frankfurt army headquarters to have an entire section from the warehouse delivered to two of his officers.

They drove over in a two-and-a-half-ton truck and returned with a vast load of documents and a printing press, only part of which belonged to my group. The printing press, with its boxes of forged stamps and other paraphernalia, had formed part of a Russian "line crosser" outfitting section. It had been used to forge German pay books and other papers.

Thus the first step had been taken. A small number of my closest colleagues was once again at my disposal, and my files and archives had been reassembled under one roof. We were in a position to negotiate. My talks with Captain Boker returned repeatedly to the same point: the collapse of the East-West alliance could only be a matter of time; a conflict of interests was bound to break out between East and West and this would jeopardize the safety of Europe and of the United States. So how could we reach agreement as rapidly as possible on suitable terms for collaboration? Neither of us had any doubts about the problems which lay ahead.

Boker feared that my group might still be broken up for individual interrogation by various agencies and that our documents would be removed and sent directly to Washington. Even if after some months we were reunited, he felt that our morale would have suffered so much that even the loyalty my officers displayed would not prove strong enough.

\* \* \*

I had proposed to Boker that our intelligence potential should be put to work for the United States quite independently of the U.S. Army's G-2 military intelligence, but in collaboration with it. But Boker was aware that there was no provision or policy whatsoever for the utilization of German personnel of any kind for what amounted to espionage against America's Russian allies. Indeed, there was considerable opposition to such a plan, as he was in the process of finding out. On the other hand, the G-2 service did not conceal its ignorance of "Uncle Joe" and his vast empire; so our offer must have been a sore temptation, as we deduced from our talks with the G-2 officers. It would save them a mass of organizational effort and afford them access to information and expertise that would take them years to collect under their own steam: Soviet military manuals, the complete order of battle of the Red Army, digests on Russian industrial and economic strength, not to mention an existing espionage network behind the Iron Curtain.

But uppermost in the Western public's mind was still the image of the Soviet Union as a friend and ally in victory, a nation of benevolence and democratic intentions. And had not the Americans fought this war to stamp out "Prussian militarism"? How could American public opinion be expected to tolerate their officers collaborating with former German officers and members of the German intelligence service, in view of the hideous crimes committed by the Nazis—crimes which among other things had resulted in Eisenhower's policy of nonfraternization? Ambassador William C. Bullitt, a close confidant of President Roosevelt, was to write in 1946 that Roosevelt had died in the knowledge that he had used Beelzebub to drive out the Devil, and that the United States was now facing its most serious danger. But, I recall, Bullitt added that it would take about five years for this fact to sink in in a democracy. Nor was he proved wrong in his prophecy. While the American attitude toward the Soviet Union was shaken by the entry of Russian troops into Persia at the end of 1945, it was not until the Korean War that the American public opened its eyes to reality.

Captain Boker decided to influence Colonel Philp to bring General Sibert over to our side. Sibert's aide was a Colonel Sapieha, who was already a realist as far as America's future relations with the Russians were concerned. But, more importantly, Philp was a close friend of Sibert, and an artillery colonel. Boker came to me and asked us to prepare the best report we possibly could on Russian artillery. This was to be a pièce de résistance to climax a dinner party his unit arranged to present us to the colonel. We also wrote a detailed report on the "line-crossing" activities of Russian agents at the end of the war, which had been on such a scale that there could be no doubt but that this would soon be a major source of trouble for the Western Allies. For Boker this was the point of no return. He later told me that Philp had been so impressed by the professional nature of our reports that he had immediately taken up the question of our future with General Sibert. There was no way around this if Sibert was to be convinced of our integrity and our desire to serve the West unselfishly; but this attention also meant that we were now exposed to the hostile glare of the other Allied agencies who only now learned of our presence in Wiesbaden.

For a long time our future was in the balance. Given the political situation in August 1945, it was understandable that nothing could be decided at once. Perhaps it was not a decision that could be made by the American commanders in Europe anyway. Boker told me years later that it soon became apparent that the Pentagon wanted to have all our documents sent over to Washington, but not us. There was absolutely no desire to have us continue working. But he had been able to persuade Sibert's headquarters that these documents should not be separated from the experts concerned, and that we must be persuaded to cooperate. Sibert, in fact, would have liked us to stay right where we were and keep the documents as well, but this was overruled by the Pentagon.

That was how I and a handful of my colleagues came to be sitting in General Bedell Smith's personal plane, flying to Washington at a time when the Russians were still dealing as allies with the other three powers in London over plans to prosecute the war criminals. I left Wessel in Europe with Boker's Lieutenant Comstock to act as my locum tenens in my absence. The agreement we had struck remained in force—he was to undertake no active operations for the Americans without my written authority. But short of that, he was to try to maintain contact with any of our former colleagues who might prove useful in the future—men such as Lieutenant Colonel Hermann Baun, who had controlled our espionage activities in the Soviet Union. Clearly, one reason for shifting us to America was a desire to reduce the risk of an indiscretion in Europe. By now we had all been deleted from the American prisoner of war lists—with the curious result that as late as 1949 the Counter Intelligence Corps still had me on their wanted lists. On the other hand, our shift to Washington would enable negotiations and discussions to be conducted in a more conducive atmosphere than the turmoil of war-torn Europe.

* * *

Our plane came in low over the Potomac river and landed at Washington's National Airport after thirty-six hours of flying. It was parked at the end of the field and surrounded by sentries. We were met by a U.S. Army captain who was to be responsible for us at first and by a uniformed official of the Department of Agriculture who was looking for any contraband plants we might be trying to import into the United States. He was totally uninterested in the possibility that we might be bringing anything of greater value for the West with us. To our disappointment Captain Boker, who had developed into a sort of Faithful Eckhardt as time had passed and who had accompanied us in the plane, took leave of us at the airport. He did tell me, however, that he would try and see me again the next day. Kohler escorted us cordially to an arrival lounge. There we had to undergo a medical examination. Sitting on a bench with thermometers stuck into our mouths, we looked for all the world like a row of sparrows on a twig.

Something about this reception made me vaguely uneasy. We were led out of the airport building and loaded into a van with no windows and just one barely adequate ventilating slot. I could see that my traveling companions were equally taken aback by this transport and all it seemed to imply. As the van started its journey I tried to work out where we were heading by sensing the van's change of direction and timing each stretch of road between. When it finally stopped we were about fifteen miles south of Washington by my calculations. I guessed we were in Alexandria, Virginia, and this later turned out to be about right. We were at Fort Hunt interrogation camp, although it was not identified to us for security reasons. The American soldiers referred to it only as P.O. Box 1142. The ugly building was surrounded by a barbed wire fence and guarded by four watchtowers; we dubbed it "Truman's Hotel." In it there was an adequately furnished room for each of us—but with one feature that struck us all as odd: there was no doorknob inside the room, so the occupant could not get out if he wanted to.

This was virtually solitary confinement, and it lowered our morale with a vengeance. The strain on our nerves increased as nothing happened to interrupt the monotony over the next few days.

I was hard put to keep up the spirits of my colleagues. Captain Kohler tried to gloss over our new predicament by suggesting that all this—the cell-like rooms, the barbed wire, the watchtowers—was being done in the interest of our security and safety. There was a further disappointment on the day after our arrival when Captain Boker came to see me. "I am sorry," he said, "but I won't be able to take care of you anymore, General. After tomorrow Captain Waldman will be at your service." He did not seem to be too pleased about being taken off the case. As he did not enlarge on this announcement (perhaps he was not permitted to), it only increased our uncertainty.

* * *

Captain Eric Waldman arrived the next day. We went for a long stroll and talked, putting out cautious feelers and trying to find out more about each other. He seemed reliable and frank enough as a man. While he betrayed some reserve in consequence of the tragic fate of his family in occupied Europe, this by no means ruled out all prospect of his cooperating with us. We later became firm friends. For many years to come he was to make a strong contribution to the success of our idea, and in many other ways he also helped the youthful Federal Republic in West Germany wherever he humanly could. (His endeavors have since been recognized by the award of Germany's Federal Service Medal.)

Captain Waldman made it clear to us that the present somewhat harsh arrangements were the result of certain "special circumstances." And he asked us not to lose heart; he would set things right as time went on. We gathered that this was an interrogation camp established for the exploitation of particularly important prisoners of war. The camp's commandant was an exceptionally ambitious officer, and he was piqued by the fact that we had been withdrawn from his tender mercies as far as exploitation was concerned. Every day, Waldman collected us from outside our accommodation block and drove us off (once to the Pentagon) for detailed conversations with experts of the War Department's G-2 division working under General George V. Strong. This provoked the camp commandant to try to get our goat by inflicting various petty infamies on us, such as the unaccustomed style of accommodation, in the hope that we would retaliate by refusing to cooperate with "the Americans." Once the Pentagon had lost interest in us, he hoped we would be returned to his exclusive control, and *he* could then take the credit for exploiting our brains and abilities.

When I learned this, I realized there were squabbles between various factions in America no less than those that had hampered us in Nazi Germany. For the people in the line of fire—in this case us—it could be highly uncomfortable, but there was nothing to do but grin and bear it. After some time Captain Waldman managed to get us different accommodations. We were given three little rustic cabins in the woods with no fence of any kind and with complete freedom to move around on parole within certain geographical limits. In these huts we lived in twos and threes, and the limits were sufficient for us to move around in almost complete liberty in the free time that was given us.

My professional mistrust prompted me to comb the three huts for hidden microphones, as I did not want the Americans to profit from every word we spoke in private. As expected, I found a microphone concealed in quite ingeniously contrived locations in each hut, so the next day I complained to Captain Waldman. I assumed these "bugs" had found their way in with his knowledge, and I suggested that for security reasons alone it seemed inappropriate to permit listening devices to be operated against us, since the other end was probably monitored by some NCO who might well jeopardize our plan by revealing our true identities on the outside. Waldman was furious about the microphones. "It's incredible," he exclaimed. "I'm going to find out who's responsible for this!" It turned out that the camp commandant had ordered the bugs installed to keep an eye on Captain Waldman. No doubt he hoped to glean enough information in this way to compromise his rival for good.

I now know that after Boker had brought us across the Atlantic he reported to the Pentagon, where no one understood that he had reconstituted a working intelligence organization of potentially great importance. The Russian section of the army's G-2 branch then took over from him, and they confirmed at once that we were essential to the future security of the United States. But for policy reasons it was out of the question to develop our organization—the most that G-2 could do was to interrogate us in minute detail and exploit our documents. Given the circumstances, it was very fortunate that Waldman was a good friend of Boker's and committed himself to our preservation as a group with the same enthusiasm, for the Pentagon made it very clear to Boker that unofficial visits to us at Fort Hunt were frowned on. He retired from the army a frustrated man, visiting us once more in our quarters shortly before Christmas with little tokens—mostly pocket knives his firm had manufactured. We later sent him a card to which were sewn a number of foreign coins as a token purchase price for the knives. We did this so that, as the superstition goes, "our friendship would not be cut."

* * *

We were repeatedly visited by experts from the War Department who wanted to get an idea of our plans and capabilities. The director of one of these study groups was Colonel Lovell (who was later unfortunately killed in action in the Korean War). Before World War II he had been military attaché in Berlin, and he used to tell people how correctly he had been treated while interned by our Wehrmacht while awaiting repatriation to America after Pearl Harbor. He assured me he would do his utmost to see we were not handled one bit worse in America. I learned to appreciate him as an upright American soldier with whom it was possible to talk frankly about everything. Their expert on Russia was also a particularly capable man, benefiting from an excellent judgment on all Eastern affairs.

The work that was required of us consisted of answering questionnaires on the Soviet Union's armed forces and of writing studies based on the material made available to us. As time passed we were handed more and more material for evaluation and analysis, and the results we turned in gradually convinced the Americans that we were capable of everything we claimed.

It was during this phase that I briefed those of my colleagues I had kept in the dark about my plans for the future—namely of creating an Eastern intelligence service on German soil using the same management as before, but with American backing. I well remember the astonishment some of them displayed. Only their good breeding and their trust in me kept them from speaking their minds to me there and then. Even at the end of 1945, when conversation with our American hosts came around to these same proposals, there was still an evasive reaction. Apparently they still balked at the political hurdles that would have to be overcome. We were told we would have to wait until public hostility toward Germany had simmered down and the split with the Soviet Union had become more acute. The public had to come to grips with the Soviet problem first; otherwise, in a democratically governed nation like the United States, there would be the most awkward outcome in both domestic and foreign politics.

As late as December 1945 the Americans would go no further than offering to sanction counterespionage work on a restricted scale by a unit directed by Hermann Baun, if I would agree. I gave them my approval, as this was the thin end of a wedge which would make it possible for us to enlarge the scope of our operations later on. At this time, Baun was being held by the CIC at a camp at Oberursel, a former Wehrmacht interrogation center not far from Frankfurt. The CIC knew nothing of the overall plans that were being laid at the Pentagon in connection with myself. One consequence of this was that Baun at first believed the CIC was granting him permission to start up operations on their own initiative as a result of the proposals *he* had made.

The Russians themselves were responsible for the final adoption of my plan. The foreign ministers of the Four Powers had agreed in London that all foreign troops should be withdrawn from northern Persia by March 2, 1946. But during October 1945 the first indications reached Washington that the Russians were in fact sending in additional troops. Reading the leading articles in *The New York Times* and the Washington *Post* we could see American public opinion inching round to outright hostility toward Moscow.

The final blow was struck in February 1946, as Russian troops occupied northern Persia in violation of the London agreement. The dramatic about-face in American public opinion still took us by surprise, but it was explained to me in an idiom I still remember: "The Americans don't like to be taken for suckers." Now, at last, the people saw that the Soviet Union was a leopard which could never change its spots: this was a Communist state which would never change to a peace-loving nation differing only in form from the Western democracies.

The attitude toward us changed. All at once we were offered a more detailed and fundamental level of cooperation. We were allowed to drive into the city of Washington, accompanied only by an American officer to interpret for us, for it was taking us longer to learn English than we had thought. From our pay as prisoners of war we were able to make small purchases, and we were shown around Washington to see the sights and learn its history. Captain Waldman displayed a real concern for all our problems throughout this time. The months we spent together in Washington established a degree of mutual confidence between us that was to pave the way to the final success of our joint effort. By the middle of 1946, all the preparations had been made.

On July 1, 1946, we embarked on a liberty ship, a troop transport, for our return voyage to Europe, and we berthed at Le Havre a week later. The weather had been magnificent for the entire crossing. Our good friend Captain Waldman had preceded us to Germany by one month, but he was to remain with us there for a long time to come as both friend and counselor. Cramped though the confines of the troop transport were, we soaked up the sea air and the sunshine. We enjoyed the good food and spent the evenings on deck watching the films put on for the prisoners of war and crew. For the other prisoners outside our group there must have been an agony of doubt and uncertainty as to what lay ahead of them. But our own morale could not have been higher: we were coming home to Germany, and we were on the threshold of a great new task.

## Part One

---

# Foreign Armies East

## CHAPTER ONE

# Initiation

On April 1, 1942, I was appointed head of Branch 12 of the German army's General Staff. This branch was known as Foreign Armies East (*Fremde Heere Ost*), and it was primarily concerned with gathering intelligence on our Soviet enemies. It was my first position of direct responsibility for any kind of intelligence work. My appointment resulted from the chief of staff's desire to see a change in the leadership of the branch. He was dissatisfied with my predecessor, and we were on the threshold of launching a major offensive in Russia toward the Volga and the Caucasus. Part of General Halder's motive for selecting me may have been that I had served as his personal staff officer from the end of 1939 until early 1940 and that I had subsequently worked on the planning for the new Caucasus offensive in the operations branch right up to the date of my new appointment. I was therefore familiar with our objectives and military dispositions and with our intermediate and long-term aims on the eastern front.

For the first twenty years of my career as an officer, however,

I had had virtually no contact with intelligence work. My first interest in the possibilities it afforded had been aroused in the years before the Munich crisis of 1938, during which I had served first in Branch 1 of the General Staff (plans and operations, under Colonel Hansen), then in Branch 10 of the General Staff (fortifications, under Colonel von der Chevallerie), in which we were concerned with the theory and planning of German lines of fortification. This made it necessary for us to investigate what the other side was up to. Once I had to tour the frontier between Silesia and Czechoslovakia together with a Lieutenant Colonel von Riesen to reconnoiter the Czech fortification works. Riesen was an officer of Admiral Canaris's Abwehr organization,* attached to Military District 8 in Breslau (he traveled under the code name Schneider). We spent some days with the photographic units on the frontier, obtaining long-range shots of the Czech installations using a giant telephoto lens of about 1,000-millimeter focal length. By this means we secured information on the thickness of the concrete at the sites even at ranges of twenty miles and more. This journey kindled my first interest in such work. (And a decade later, when I became head of the "Gehlen organization" in occupied Germany, I adopted the code name Dr. Schneider in memory of the lieutenant colonel who had performed this service, since he had by then passed on to a place where code names are no longer of any consequence.)

In the course of my work at the War Department Building in Berlin's Bendlerstrasse, I established contact with figures who were already legendary, as well as those who were later to become notorious. Among the former, I valued most highly my acquaintance with General Ludwig Beck, Halder's predecessor as chief of the army's General Staff: he was constantly looking for new methods and military tactics, emulating General von Seeckt in this respect. (Seeckt had contended that in an armed conflict Germany could have no hope of victory unless she could force her enemy into a

---

* The intelligence service controlled by the Oberkommando der Wehrmacht (OKW, the high command of the German armed forces). The reader is hereafter referred to the Glossary (pp. 381–86) for explanation of unusual terms or abbreviations.—TRANS.

fluid and mobile warfare from the start.) Beck was aware of the possibilities of technology in modern war. He was modern in outlook and immediately supported introduction of the costly new assault gun after it was demonstrated to him, even though he could afford only one detachment in each division to be equipped with such weapons. He hated the Nazis and went out of his way to avoid them; he had only one personal meeting with Adolf Hitler, and that lasted only a few minutes.

My recollection of the leading Nazis is only fragmentary. Heinrich Himmler once invited me to lunch alone, sounded me about my organization, and discarded me. In June 1938, I had my one and only meeting with Hermann Göring, too. He had been ordered to inspect the army's fortification work along our western frontiers, and I was attached to the tour as fortifications specialist to the staff of General Adam, the commander in chief in the West. The construction program had originally been planned on a magnificent scale by the War Department for eventual completion by 1964 as a permanent barrier in the West. But by mid-1938, of course, little of this program was completed. Göring made no secret of his criticism. Adam was normally a sanguine and receptive general, but after two days of Göring's onslaught he walked out, leaving me, a thirty-six-year-old army captain, to represent the War Department's point of view. No sooner had I opened my mouth to answer Field Marshal Göring's criticism than he interrupted me, referred to me as "young man," and silenced me. Afterward I spoke to his deputy, General Milch (one of the more upright and capable personalities in the Luftwaffe), and asked him to make it clear that as I was the only War Department officer present I must be listened to. Milch must have spoken to Göring about it, because I was given a proper hearing after that. I later spoke to Halder (who was on the point of succeeding Beck) and told him I thought Hitler's orders to Fritz Todt, the engineer, to take over the fortification work from us was an ominous development. But it was symptomatic of the führer's deep-seated mistrust for the General Staff and our specialized knowledge. He once said, "If I want a project to run smoothly, I always give the experts a wide berth."

Undoubtedly Hitler was characterized by a degree of misplaced genius, but it was that type of genius that is brilliantly successful in peacetime and crumples when it is confronted by the serious burdens of war. He was completely without scruples.

Adolf Hitler lacked the training to understand fully military factors and strategic possibilities, but he nonetheless remained convinced of his genius as a warlord until the very end. He was supported in this belief by those of his subordinates who had emerged from the party. It was rooted in the fact that the first military decisions which Hitler adopted against the considered advice of his officers—the occupation of the Rhineland, the assimilation of Austria, the two Czech crises—and the initial campaigns of World War II—in Poland, Norway, and France—were met with unqualified success; and thereby confirmed his predictions and apparently disproved the caviling prognoses and calculations of General Halder.

Thus, events at first served to strengthen Hitler's unjustified self-confidence and to throw the General Staff into sharp relief as a pack of pessimists and defeatists. But Hitler tended to base his decisions on the assumption that his enemies would act illogically; and this was a gamble which someday was bound to fail. Instead of weighing carefully each step he took, he began a dangerous poker game and shut his eyes to the fact that sooner or later he would be dealt a losing hand. Even in 1939 he did not deserve to win. Our forces were nowhere near ready for war, and if the Allies had shown resolution in their political and military actions when war broke out, there would have been at most a short period of armed conflict followed by the defeat of Germany, a defeat which seemed certain from the outset. This claim may seem farfetched, but in support I would mention that the army's entire stock of heavy-artillery ammunition—apart from heavy-field-howitzer ammunition—consisted of 812 trainloads and that even by the summer of 1939 no significant production of this ammunition had commenced. At the end of the fighting in Belgium and northern France in early June 1940, there was only enough ammunition left for the light field howitzers. Our stocks of heavy-artillery ammunition—including that of the heavy field howitzers—were virtually exhausted.

Major Hasso von Etzdorf, a diplomat who was attached to my branch as liaison officer to the Foreign Ministry, once summed up Hitler's unrealistic logical processes with a bitter parody of the title of one of Schopenhauer's studies, "The World as Will and Imagination." Etzdorf described Hitler's world as "the world of will without imagination."

* * *

From November 10, 1938, until the outbreak of war I was battery commander in the 18th Artillery Regiment. When the Polish campaign began in September 1939, I was posted as operations officer to the 213th Infantry Division, a *Landwehr* ("reserve") division in which the average age of the "troops" was forty-five and one of the regimental commanders was no less than sixty-seven. I was one of the three active officers temporarily assigned to this division. Apart from some fighting around Modlin, in which we acquitted ourselves with dignity, the campaign ended with little excitement for us. In October 1939 the General Staff recalled me to the fortifications branch at its headquarters in Zossen, south of Berlin, and I stayed there—apart from tours of inspection along Germany's eastern and western frontiers—until the eve of the German attack on France and the Low Countries.

General Halder detailed me to act as Field Marshal von Brauchitsch's liaison officer with the Sixteenth Army, and to General Hoth's armored group; and then during the second phase of the French campaign I acted as liaison officer to General Guderian's armored corps, which played a crucial role in the final collapse of France. Following this, for three months I accompanied General Halder as his adjutant, while Hitler went through the motions of preparing to invade the British Isles.

From the very start I had the clear impression that Hitler did not take Operation Sea Lion seriously, and this impression was strengthened from observations I was able to make as Halder's adjutant and, after October 1940, as head of Group East in the War Department's operations branch under Colonel Adolf Heusinger. There were certain clues in Halder's behavior that led me to conclude that Hitler regarded the entire Sea Lion plan as nothing more than a highly elaborate but very effective means of deceiving the Russians as to his real strategic intentions in the East —a decision Hitler had evidently reached sometime before I was given Group East. Not even the army group commanders were privy to Hitler's real plans.

Unpopular though this view may now be, I must state that I have no doubt that Hitler's decision to invade the Soviet Union was correct, because it was inevitable. While Moscow had no firm plans to attack us before the Polish campaign of 1939 (in which Stalin aided Hitler), by the time we attacked Russia in June 1941 the picture was very different: it was clear that Stalin had resolved to postpone his attack on his former ally only so long as was necessary to see us bleeding to death and exhausted after a conflict with the Western Allies. Then he would have grinned and attacked us as well, in the knowledge that the capitalist powers had meanwhile torn themselves to pieces too. He might have waited until 1943 or 1944, but my colleagues in Group East of the War Department and I were convinced he was going to attack sooner or later. The advanced state of the Soviet Union's preparations for an offensive war support this conviction. For example, the echeloned, in-depth deployment of their divisions at the time of our attack indicated that they were putting together a powerful land force for an attack on us. The structure of their industrial economy led to similar conclusions as well. But if Hitler was correct in making this decision, what was wrong was the manner in which he conducted the Russian campaign. In this connection, I might add that the führer nurtured something like a love-hate relationship with Joseph Stalin. When he was in difficulties, Hitler sometimes asked himself out loud, "What would Stalin do in a situation like this?" It was perhaps in emulation of Stalin that Hitler instituted the arrest of the relatives of certain conspirators in the assassination plot of July 20, 1944.

\* \* \*

Among the conspirators who later paid with their lives was Admiral Wilhelm Canaris, head of the OKW's Abwehr intelligence organization. While I was Halder's adjutant I came into frequent contact with the admiral, for he had to pass through my office to reach Halder's. I soon learned, however, that my presence was not desired —for reasons of privacy as much as of security—and I tactfully withdrew. When I became head of Group East, working on the planning of Operation Barbarossa—Hitler's attack on Russia—one of the proposals I made was for Abwehr units to be attached to the assault troops taking part in the attack, a suggestion Canaris warmly endorsed at a conference I attended in his offices late in 1940. Although I was only a major, he was always charming, receptive, and genuine. Later, our relationship deepened into one of great mutual trust and proximity.

That Canaris's character is shrouded even now in mists of ill repute is a fate he shares with many other figures of the intelligence world both in Germany and abroad. He has been criticized by authors who obviously cannot have been acquainted with him. Canaris has been repeatedly accused of procrastination, lack of resolution, and doubtful conduct. The "disclosures" of certain treason cases have tended to leave stains on his reputation; but for my part I am convinced that none of these vague and all-too-superficial histories has done the admiral justice.

In addition to his deep-seated religious feelings and his impeccable conduct as an officer, Canaris was endowed with intellectual traits not seen in officers since the first half of the nineteenth century—traits that had helped officers like Roon, von der Goltz, and Count Yorck von Wartenburg, as well as Clausewitz and Moltke, to spectacular achievements in sciences other than the purely military. Moreover, unlike many officers, Canaris knew how to think in global terms. This was how he was able to predict political trends with uncanny accuracy. Admittedly, he did not always find the right audience—men who were as ready and willing to listen to his prophecies as were Fritsch, Brauchitsch, Beck, and Halder. But this was a fate he shared with more than one of his colleagues. It was hardly surprising that as war broke out in 1939 he had taken a very pessimistic view of the outcome and that the mantle of a Cassandra had lain heavy on his shoulders.

Canaris was a convinced opponent of the Nazis. Like General Beck he suffered deeply from the internal conflict wrought by the military oath he had sworn in God's name and by his opposition to the regime. The fact that Germany was caught up in a life-and-death struggle and that, in the event of defeat, Germany as a whole would have to suffer and not just the Nazis only intensified this inner torment. I recall a long private talk I had with Canaris in 1942 in which he discoursed at length on the concepts of treachery and high treason, arriving at the conclusion that only the latter could be justified, even given the exceptional circumstances of the war Germany's leaders were now fighting. But Canaris added that the perpetrators had to recognize that only one thing would guarantee justice to the conspirators—that the plot must succeed. And they also had to realize that until success was achieved they and their relatives would be exposed to grave risk. He acted accordingly, gathering into the Abwehr numerous figures endangered because of their political beliefs, rescuing them from the grasp of the Gestapo; and he set the seal on his beliefs—after hideous torture, as we know from the survivors of Flossenbürg concentration camp —by execution on April 9, 1945.

Admiral Canaris absolutely rejected political assassination as a means; his religious convictions enjoined him from even considering such methods.* I remember well the occasion when he indignantly informed me that Hitler had assigned him to the job of assassinating Winston Churchill. He had turned the job down, he said (just as he did when ordered to eliminate the escaped French general Giraud). I can therefore state with certainty that Abwehr II, the sabotage branch headed by General Lahousen, was employed only for destroying or crippling vital military objectives in the enemy's rear. The Soviet KGB and its predecessors did not share these compunctions: the organization was responsible for the liquidation of unwanted individuals in addition to espionage and sabotage activities.

Canaris's Abwehr organization collected not only military but

---

* This is confirmed by an entry in General Erwin Lahousen's diary of February 2, 1943: Canaris refused to sanction a sabotage attack on Russian military headquarters, since he had "on principle expressly forbidden Abwehr II [i.e., sabotage] attacks directed against individual personages."—TRANS.

political intelligence as well. This was channeled through the OKW
—to which his agency was subordinated—to various authorities
such as the Foreign Ministry and the War Department. He himself
had a number of very high-level personal political contacts abroad,
and he used to pay frequent visits on them. Even during the war he
maintained his excellent contacts in the Spanish and Portuguese
governments. One consequence of this was that in 1940 he was
sent to Madrid to persuade the Spanish to declare war. He told me
at the time that he thought the total effect of any Spanish declaration of war would be minimal, a view General Halder shared.
Canaris believed it would bring Germany fresh burdens rather than
relief; and, quite apart from that, it would slam one more door
between us and the rest of the world, which to an intelligence chief
was a matter of personal importance. He was very relieved at the
failure of his mission.

* * *

The latter part of 1940 was taken up with preparing for our
invasion of Greece, which was planned for the spring of 1941,
using Bulgarian territory as a jumping-off place. After the führer
directive had been issued for that operation, we turned our detailed
attention to the coming Russian campaign. I myself was preoccu-
pied with logistic problems, the details of reserves and transportation, and, later, with the basic objectives of the army groups.

Hitler launched his invasion of Russia on June 21, 1941. In
its early weeks, it was obvious that we had caught the Russians off-
balance, and there was jubilation at Hitler's headquarters as the
front line advanced further and further into Soviet territory. Within
our army's General Staff, a special branch had been set up under
Colonel Eberhard Kinzel to control intelligence on the Russian
front and contiguous areas. Kinzel, however, found it difficult to
get along with General Halder, as entries in Halder's diaries indicate, and he failed to adapt his intelligence organization to keep
pace with the rapid war of movement that characterized the early
months of the campaign. The outcome of Halder's dissatisfaction
with Kinzel—as I have mentioned—was that on April 1, 1942, I

was appointed to succeed him as head of Foreign Armies East.

The general military situation by early April 1942 was this: we had succeeded in stabilizing our front line in the important sectors held by Army Groups Center and North, where the front had been dangerously weakened during the disastrous winter months. The setbacks there had led to considerable loss of ground, and much equipment had been lost in the retreats. But far worse was the effect of the winter crisis on the German soldier, who after two years of victorious advance had for the first time experienced a setback, if not an outright defeat. Even though the real culprits were the severe weather conditions together with an initial shortage of winter equipment and greatly reduced divisional strength, there were bound to be dangerous psychological results.

But it was not only for psychological reasons that we had to regain the initiative as soon as possible. There was a real military threat: the Soviet counteroffensive which began in November 1941 (and came as no surprise to Foreign Armies East) showed that Stalin was not adverse to switching strength from the Far East to relieve the pressure on his western front if need be. Moreover, the winter fighting had displayed the Russians' capacity for improvisation. Any respite we gave them now would disproportionately add to their fighting strength, which had declined severely during the summer of 1941. If we could not take the offensive the conflict would be indefinitely prolonged, and with it would emerge the danger of war on two fronts. We could not expect the intervention of strong American forces to be delayed later than 1943. Thus, by the start of 1942, Hitler faced a situation similar to that confronting the Supreme Army Command during the Great War in the spring of 1917.

During my tour of duty in the operations branch we had the job of determining where and with what units our new offensive ought to be mounted. We concluded that, despite every effort on its part, the Wehrmacht and its supporting armaments industry would not be able to replace manpower and equipment losses fast enough to justify launching an offensive along the entire length of the eastern front from the Crimea in the south to Leningrad in the north. But we believed that the divisions left confronting Britain in the west would probably get by in 1942 without needing reinforcements. We would therefore have to limit ourselves to smaller offensives—recapturing the ground lost during the winter, particularly in the Crimea and at Kharkov, and capturing Leningrad to neutralize the Baltic and strengthen our land contact with the Finns.

We concluded that we ought to use the remaining divisions to attack the Russians in places where they would have to stand and fight. In the opinion of the chief of staff, General Halder, our attack ought to be centered on Moscow. In addition to the psychological effect, the capture of Moscow would even then, in 1942, deprive the Soviet empire of its political nerve center and main transportation center. While it would not make it wholly impossible for the Russians to continue the fight, it would certainly hamper them considerably. There were bitter arguments with Hitler on this issue, since he insisted on an offensive in the direction of Stalingrad—to eliminate the Volga as a waterway—and the Caucasus. Hitler's argument was that the capture of the oil fields there would decide the war: without them, Germany's fuel supplies would dry up within six months. This prediction turned out to be wrong, for even without the Caucasian oil fields we were able to keep fighting for two and a half years more.

* * *

Even during the French campaign of 1940, Halder's relationship with Hitler had not been without friction. In the summer of 1941 it had been placed under further strain by Hitler's obstinate demand for the main military effort to be shifted to the south, at Kiev. His decision did indeed result in the greatest encirclement action ever fought, the Battle of Kiev, in August 1941, in which nearly two million Russian prisoners were taken. But this modern Cannae remained a local victory upon which were to follow the winter catastrophe outside Moscow and the failure of the 1941 campaign.

The controversy over this new 1942 campaign exacerbated this conflict until it became unbearable for either of them, and it resulted in a final parting of their ways on September 24, 1942. I recall one remark Halder made to me which vividly illustrates the feeling at the end between Hitler and his principal strategic adviser: "I will just keep contradicting Hitler until he gets rid of me. He won't listen to the voice of reason anymore." (Hitler always refused his senior officers' requests to be relieved of their commands.)

As the Caucasus oil objectives showed, economic considerations conditioned Hitler's decisions—not the demands of war or the requirements of foreign policy, all of which spoke against the launching of sweeping operations into the Soviet hinterland. The insoluble problem of logistics once we had crossed the river Don to the south, where there was only a single railroad track and poor highways, also argued against starting such an operation; but Hitler cast all these misgivings to the winds.

This was why it was vital for us to identify, confront, and destroy the enemy at the onset of the offensive. The General Staff branch entrusted to me in April 1942 had to be able to brief our supreme command as completely, precisely, and rapidly as possible on the enemy situation and on the enemy's strategic and tactical intentions.

I was now head of Foreign Armies East, the intelligence branch responsible for the entire eastern front. I moved into Colonel Kinzel's office at the headquarters of Foreign Armies East immediately. It was a large hut in the middle of the General Staff encampment on Lake Mauersee, southwest of Angerburg, in East Prussia. It was a small compound made up of wooden and brick huts in the depth of the forest, invisible to any aircraft that might pass overhead, and only a half-hour's shuttle-train journey away from Hitler's main headquarters, the "Wolf's Lair," at Rastenburg. The huts were all well equipped, and kept at a comfortable temperature by a main heating plant for the whole compound. An ultramodern communications center enabled us to contact Wehrmacht units anywhere in occupied Europe within seconds. My office was in the hut directly opposite General Halder's living and office quarters. Its center was filled with a big map table, and my own desk was in an alcove at one end, illuminated by powerful lamps that caused any-body who came within range of them to perspire.

In peacetime, the branch's job had been to build up the most comprehensive picture it could of the defense and armaments poten-tial of the eastern countries under its surveillance. This was done in conjunction with other agencies both inside and outside the army's General Staff. The branch had circulated reports to keep officers and men adequately informed on conditions they must expect—for example, geographical or meteorological data. Of particular value was any data we could gather on the so-called fighting quality of each enemy unit—the beginning of what we now refer to as a psycho-political appreciation of the enemy. The information we had filed on the Soviet fighting man in this respect during peacetime was to be wholly confirmed during the first year of the Russian campaign: we had predicted that the Russian soldier would be tough and frugal, and that his modest material needs would enable him to fight on long after the battle itself was lost. We anticipated, too, that indoctrination would affect the officer corps but not the bulk of the recruits, and this also proved correct. Moreover, we correctly predicted that when Soviet defeats occurred the desertion rate would increase.

We were not concerned solely with the Soviet Union, however. During the early war years under my predecessor, we were re-quired to provide digests on the armed forces and equipment of all the Scandinavian countries, and on Czechoslovakia and the Balkan countries as well. We reported regularly on their fortifications, their attitudes toward Germany, and their internal political situations. In addition to compiling the order of battle reports on the regular eastern armies confronting us, we had to conduct intelligence work against the growing partisan activity in Yugoslavia.

During the early part of my office, the branch was ordered to include the gathering of intelligence on a powerful new enemy, the United States. I recall that the American secret rearmament plan, of which only eight copies existed, came to our attention as early as the spring of 1942, simply through our careful sifting of the Amer-ican press. The U.S. general Wedemeyer (who had attended our staff college in Berlin from 1936 to 1938, and who was perhaps one of the most outstanding American strategists of World War II) told me in 1960 that nobody had ever established how this top secret document came into the hands of the press. At the time he was the principal general staff officer in the U.S. Army's operations branch. In the course of the affair he suffered probably the most nerve-wracking hours of his life, but he finally emerged from the investigation without a stain on his name. He made it clear to me that the investigation indicated that the leak was somewhere in President Roosevelt's immediate entourage.

In the middle of June 1942, I was able to give Halder a bulky report we had compiled on American strength and strategic intentions for the coming year, with photographs of U.S. tanks and landing craft, details of the U.S. Army's expansion plans, and a discussion of the shipping tonnage available for transporting American troops. At the time, we concluded, lack of shipping space would rule out any danger that the Allies could mount a full-scale second front that year. In the report we quoted an Abwehr source in the British embassy in Lisbon which pointed (correctly) to the Allied intention of intensifying the bombing of Germany and of carrying out minor landing operations on the French coast. A few days later, I was able to circulate a detailed report on the U.S. Army in which I noted that a "European theater of operations" had been activated under Brigadier General Eisenhower. I went on to emphasize, that "in the near future we must take into account the fact that American forces will appear in moderate strength at first."*

Our principal intelligence target was of course the Soviet Union. In peacetime, in order to build up an exact picture of the Russian units, we had used every possible source of information— the files of the Abwehr, the dispatches of our military attachés, the reports circulated by the Foreign Ministry. Of course we had also exploited the available nonsecret publications, even though these

---

* From a report among my Foreign Armies East files in the Federal Military Archives, Freiburg (File H3/420).

were subject to stringent press censorship. By careful analysis we could often extract valuable facts to extend our knowledge beyond that obtained from secret sources. Despite the difficulties imposed on him by the Soviet Union's extensive counterespionage and by Hitler's absolute prohibition against espionage activity in the Soviet Union after his pact with Stalin was signed in 1939, my predecessor Colonel Kinzel had already succeeded in building up a relatively accurate picture of the Russian defenses, order of battle, and mobilization measures and of Moscow's strategic planning. It was on the basis of this information that our Barbarossa campaign plan had been developed and adjusted to meet each changing circumstance. Kinzel had also instituted detailed surveys of Soviet manpower and industrial reserves, and I found these reports of particular value when I took over. As we became more deeply embroiled in the conflict with Russia, we extended the activities of our staff and task force. We assembled thousands of files on Soviet armed forces and NKVD units and compiled intricate card indices on high-ranking Soviet officers. Maps were drawn indicating communications networks, radio links, poison gas depots, principal lines of advance, and the location of NKVD agents. Finally, we made detailed comparisons between German and Russian units of similar size.

* * *

Seven days after I took over Foreign Armies East, I reported in detail to General Halder on the Russian forces' rate of reinforcement and their aircraft movements over the previous month, and then I discussed with him the way I proposed to work in the future. He told me, with some emphasis, that he expected not only a thorough estimate of the daily situation, but also a long-term appreciation of the enemy's strategic intentions and capabilities. This was an important innovation. In a note appended to a collection of these appreciation reports, I explained in December 1944:

> At the beginning of the campaign against the Soviet Union, Foreign Armies East did not issue any written appreciation reports on the situation, as the enemy's command showed

that it was totally dependent on German operations and was incapable of any strategic initiative of its own. Apart from its verbal reporting, therefore, this branch was able to limit itself to issuing daily digests until the beginning of the winter of 1942.

When the Soviet command managed to regain the initiative on some sectors of the front at the beginning of the winter of 1941–42, the branch began to issue a daily "Report on Enemy Trends," in which some attempt was made to go into an appreciation of the enemy's probable intentions.

As the war progressed, however, it became necessary for the appreciations of enemy plans—which had previously been discussed verbally each day with the chief of the General Staff—to be set down in writing.

From April 11, 1942, onward, therefore, a "Brief Appreciation Report on the Enemy Situation" was prepared each day and circulated to the authorities concerned (chief of the General Staff, chief of the operations branch, intelligence officers at army group level, Luftwaffe operations staff).

In addition to these, we prepared a "Comprehensive Appreciation Report on the Enemy Situation" at various intervals (usually four to eight weeks) so that as the war went on our command would have material on the actions to be expected of the enemy over long periods of time.*

After a short time as head of the branch, I realized that there was much room for improvement if Halder's wishes were to be met, and that a number of organizational and psychological problems would have to be overcome. The main psychological problem was the traditional lack of regard for the military intelligence branch, particularly for intelligence procurement. I was originally not entirely innocent myself in this regard.

The effects of such an attitude were evidenced by the small number of active officers in military intelligence in peacetime. The army's organization scheme of January 1939 shows only seven officers in Branch 12 (Foreign Armies East). At army corps level there was the Ic/AO officer—the joint military intelligence–counterespionage officer—usually a young army captain on a posting

---

* File H3/1662.

to the General Staff. The peacetime organization made no provision for an enemy intelligence expert at divisional level; in wartime, this position was usually occupied by a reserve officer (who often performed amazingly well). Of course, the disdain for this work was wholly unjust, as the enemy intelligence expert, especially in the higher echelons, had to think with two brains at once if he was to perform his assignment properly. It was not enough to know the precise military units and equipment opposing him; he had to be able to forecast the enemy's intentions, and this called for a subtle empathy with the enemy's mentality and a detailed knowledge of the enemy's command tactics. He then had to be able to put all his facts convincingly to his superiors, acting the role of devil's advocate. This was not without its difficulties, for the staff intelligence officer was usually junior in both age and rank to the Ia (operations officer) and chief of staff in his echelon.

Soon after taking office, I therefore proposed to General Halder that the Ic (military intelligence) officer should be given the same rank and seniority as the Ia, which was that of a principal officer; this request was granted, particularly in the higher levels like army groups and armies. While the Ia continued to be the primus inter pares, the military intelligence officer at least had the same rank. The result was an increase in the latter's influence; his words were treated with greater respect than before, and he could add more weight to his appreciations of the enemy's intentions.

The second deficiency in my view was the inadequate cooperation existing between Foreign Armies East and other important intelligence agencies, particularly Admiral Canaris's Abwehr. For example, the Abwehr repeatedly forwarded to me information of considerable interest, but their evaluation of it left much to be desired.

This deficiency was not caused by any negligence or lack of interest on the German side. Hitherto the war's course had seen the initiative in German hands; each campaign had in turn resulted in rapid and overwhelming victories for German arms. It was therefore natural, as I indicated in my December 1944 note, for the attention of the organs of military intelligence and tactical com-

mand to be primarily focused on the events of the day and the immediate future. There was little the Abwehr could contribute to this
kind of work, simply because of the time it took to communicate
the results of its investigations. During this period of fast-moving
operations we were largely reliant on forward intelligence and
reconnaissance by the combat units themselves. This satisfied our
needs, although in retrospect I am amazed at the accuracy of the
results we obtained from such primitive material. The failure of the
summer campaign of 1941 ended that phase. The enemy had
gained the initiative—at least for the time being—and we were
confronted for the first time by the need to develop a long-range
analysis of the enemy's capabilities and strategic intentions, if we
were not to run up against unpleasant surprises.

It was in this situation that I took up personal contact with
Canaris and persuaded him to extend the areas in which we could
collaborate. He was formally head of the OKW's Foreign and Intelligence Office (*Amt Ausland/Abwehr*). The former section attended
to the affairs of our attachés in friendly and neutral countries. The
latter section, the Abwehr, was subdivided into three branches:
Branch I—espionage, under Colonel Piekenbrock; Branch II—
sabotage, under Colonel Lahousen; Branch III—counterespionage,
under Colonel von Bentivegni. The Abwehr had its own intelligence
network, operating as did the British service largely with free-lance
agents of proved reliability. But Canaris had no organization for analyzing the intelligence data he received: the raw report was circulated to those who seemed most likely to be interested, with the result
that any piece of intelligence depended for its effect solely on the
sound judgment of its recipient. In the absence of any systematic
process of analysis operating in conjunction with the other sources of
material at the Abwehr's disposal, some items might be grossly
overrated by the recipient, and others wholly ignored. (It was the
lesson I learned during my collaboration with Canaris's Abwehr
system that moved me, when I set up the Gehlen organization after
1945, to establish an efficient section of analysts inside the organization; and I did what I could to dispel the heresy that secret
services should concern themselves solely with secret sources, and

pay no attention to the freely available, "open" material available from newspaper stands and book stores throughout the world.)

Canaris, of course, was not without difficulties of his own by 1942. The destruction of many of his networks in countries that became our enemies with the outbreak of war made his agency's work harder, but not impossible. In the United States the FBI had closed down virtually every German contact; but as I have said, the garrulous newspapers and magazines of that nation made it possible for him to bridge the gap until he could rebuild his networks there. A further difficulty confronting him was that since 1933 the Nazi party in the guise of the so-called Foreign Organization (*Auslandsorganisation*) and Himmler's SD (*Sicherheitsdienst,* "security service") had been attempting to establish rival networks in a manner that verged frequently on the dilettante. Canaris was in a weak position, as the OKW's chiefs did not give him the support he needed.

The Reich Main Security Office (RSHA, in which the Gestapo, criminal police, and SD were unofficially combined in 1936, and which Himmler formally established on September 27, 1939), in particular, had struggled to get control of espionage and counterespionage. In 1933, Hitler had granted the request of his defense minister that the Defense Ministry alone be responsible for counterespionage and countersabotage operations to protect the state and its national economy and armed forces. But by 1935 it was plain that Himmler and his trusty police chief Reinhard Heydrich were not inclined to heed Hitler's ordinance. Thus, 1935 had seen the creation of Special Bureau Stein, which conducted investigations into suspected treason cases on behalf of both the Gestapo and SD and the armed forces. It was built into the RSHA as an ad hoc bureau, with the express aim of encroaching on the Abwehr's preserves. The Abwehr's response was to turn its scrutiny onto Stein himself, but he fled abroad and, using the code name Pfeiffer, tried to work for the Poles and British (without enjoying much success). These clear inroads into his authority caused Canaris to get together with Dr. Werner Best of the RSHA. Together, they hammered out a basis for collaboration, the "Ten Commandments" of 1936, which established guidelines for the cooperation of the Abwehr with the Gestapo and SD, and clearly set out their individual responsibilities.

Two years later, the SD's carefully camouflaged foreign intelligence service was refashioned into Branch 6 of the RSHA, and this was taken over by Walter Schellenberg* in June 1942. In May 1942, or about a month after I became head of Foreign Armies East, a new agreement was reached between the SD and the Abwehr, allegedly based on a ten-point program drafted by Schellenberg. The negotiations were conducted by Canaris and Colonel von Bentivegni on the one side and the head of Branch 4 of the RSHA, Heinrich Müller, on the other. It was only now that the SD's espionage activity abroad became legal, and Canaris had to concede it permission to undertake military intelligence work abroad as well. In a way, this concession was the beginning of the end for the Abwehr, and heralded the take-over two years later of the whole intelligence service by Himmler's RSHA. Without doubt, Walter Schellenberg was the driving force behind the SD's struggle for ascendancy in espionage and sabotage operations. Canaris always warned me that Schellenberg was a dangerous adversary; but he was a man of clever and winning ways, and many people spoke of his knack for intelligence work. I heard that he had gotten along well with Canaris's man during the years of cooperation between the Abwehr and the state police authorities; but all that changed when Schellenberg became head of Himmler's intelligence service. Canaris, high-principled as he was himself, probably took Schellenberg's loyalty for granted.

* * *

I saw that my first task was to establish closer contact between Canaris's Abwehr networks and the various military commands. In peacetime, apart from informal contacts within the Defense Ministry, the Abwehr had been linked to the military commands only at

---

* Schellenberg, born January 16, 1900, was deputy head of Branch 6 of the RSHA from 1939 to 1942, when he became its head. He conducted many political intelligence missions abroad, was sentenced to six years' imprisonment by an American tribunal at Nuremberg in 1949, and died in 1952.

the military district (*Wehrkreis*) level, in the person of the Ic/AO officer. With mobilization, even this tenuous link went by the board, as the Ic/AO now had to act purely as the enemy intelligence officer at the forward headquarters of the army corps concerned.

Canaris's organization operated highly mobile forward intelligence and reconnaissance units under three control stations (code-named Walli I, Walli II, and Walli III), each with a different kind of mission. I requested him to place his Abwehr units on the eastern front under my control, with the exception of the Walli II units (i.e., the sabotage commandos), which I wanted nothing to do with in view of the overall situation. I told Canaris I would not interfere in any way with the running of the Abwehr units, or their upkeep, but we had to find some faster way of getting their data to the fighting commands. It was typical of his unlimited readiness to cooperate that he agreed to my request without a moment's hesitation.

My first step was to transfer the control station Walli I from it present site east of Warsaw to Nikolaiken, about twenty miles from the main field headquarters of the army (OKH) at Angerburg, so that the contact between the secret intelligence units and my branch, Foreign Armies East, would be as immediate as possible. Walli I, commanded by Major Hermann Baun, controlled the agents and special reconnaissance units operating along the whole eastern front; Baun himself was an undersized, brown-eyed, Russian-born German who spoke accent-free German and Russian like a second mother tongue. He remained in control of my intelligence procurement operations until the end of the war, and beyond. The new organization I introduced provided a rapid flow of intelligence data from the front line to our branch along two parallel channels: the first followed the military chain of Ic officers at each command level, and the second the Abwehr chain, with crossovers at each level. A frontline intelligence unit would report to the Ic officer at army level, and simultaneously to the Abwehr's forward reconnaissance command at army group level. The latter would then collate these reports and report in turn to the Ic at army group level and to the Abwehr's overall control station under Major Baun, Walli I. In the first instance, Baun then

reported to my branch, using both the reports of the forward reconnaissance units that had reached him in this way and also the results
of his own Abwehr operations. Canaris's agency, for its part, received copies of all the reports reaching Foreign Armies East.
Finally, to speed the communication of reports, I ordered that the
preparation of the daily intelligence summary was to begin simultaneously at every level; the result was that each Ic was usually able
to hand his commanding officer a complete intelligence summary by
evening.

An example will make this clearer. Hitler had directed that in
the coming spring offensive the breakthrough into the Caucasus
come first and foremost. On April 10, 1942, in my first brief report
to General Halder, I stated that the Russians would probably also
concentrate their main effort in the south, although it was still not
clear whether they would adopt a passive defensive strategy, or
would try to stall us by a surprise counterattack. A few days before
von Manstein launched the German offensive on May 8, Foreign
Armies East received the following signal from the Abwehr: *

> WSEA 1530 30 April 1942. 23.30hrs =
> To Foreign Armies East, Section 1. =

> Secret. Abwehr unit reports April 13: member of Central
> Committee, Nossenko, has told editor of newspaper *Pravda*
> in conversation from Kuibyshev that in the last joint session
> of the Central Committee's Presidium with the High Com-
> mand it has been decided to snatch the operational initiative
> from the Germans before they can launch their offensive. It
> was decided to go over to the offensive with Red Army first
> on occasion of Mayday festival.

> 3979/42 secret.

> BAUN, *Major*

This report had taken a long time to reach us, it will be
noticed. I showed it to General Halder on May 2. By then there
were other indications that the Russians were planning to spoil our
attack. And, indeed, before we could start the planned second phase

---

* File H3/1500.

of our Caucasus offensive, the Red Army launched a sudden and concentrated assault at Kharkov on May 12. Thanks to the War Department's and the General Staff's determination not to lose the initiative, however, the following sixteen days saw an encirclement action at Kharkov which ended with two Russian armies destroyed and 240,000 prisoners in our hands.

* * *

To accomplish everything General Halder expected of us, it proved necessary to expand the staff of my branch and change its structure. From about twenty-five officers attached to Foreign Armies East at the time I took over, it expanded to about fifty by the end of the war. As principal assistant (Ia, or operations officer) I took Lieutenant Colonel Baron Alexis von Roenne. Von Roenne was a tall, fair-haired, bespectacled Balt, with the superior air of a schoolmaster addressing pupils on a matter which was far beyond their comprehension; he could be very sarcastic to those he considered his intellectual juniors, but he was a fanatical enemy of the Bolsheviks and spoke a fluent and cultivated Russian as well as passable French and English. I subdivided the branch into three groups: Group I was under Major Heinz Danko Herre,* a tall, athletic officer with fading blond hair, who, like von Roenne, was a highly qualified, Russian-speaking staff officer; this group was responsible for the daily enemy intelligence digest. Group I was again subdivided into one subgroup for each of the army groups on the eastern front. Group II, under Major Kühlein, dealt with long-term assessment of the enemy's position. It assembled information from other agencies and analyzed the facts necessary for an evaluation of every aspect of the enemy's capacities relating to war (e.g., manpower, arms production). The

---

* Herre was born on January 23, 1909, in Metz, and had acted as chief of staff to a mountain corps in the Ukraine; he succeeded von Roenne as my Ia early in 1943 and then played a leading part in the activation of the Vlasov divisions. He rejoined my organization on January 10, 1946, as my personal assistant, acting as chief of the evaluation section from 1953 until June 30, 1958; he then took over as chief of operational intelligence procurement from Colonel Lothar Metz (who had succeeded Kühlein in that position) until May 1964, when he was posted to our Washington embassy as the Federal Intelligence Service's representative there. He resigned the service on February 1, 1971, with the rank of brigadier general.

group owned a magnificent library of books and documents from all over the world and kept permanent files of statistics which were brought constantly up-to-date; after the German defeat in 1945, this collection formed the starting point for my colleagues and myself when we established the Gehlen organization.

Group III, which was run by a Captain Petersen under the supervision of von Roenne, consisted of our experts on Russia. They were a remarkable group, shrouded in an air of conspiracy, and with a penchant for throwing drinking parties on the most tenuous of pretexts; they had an ill-deserved reputation for sloth, but in fact their accomplishments were many. Most of them were Baltic Germans or Germans who had been born in Russia; they knew the terrain and to them Russian was a second mother tongue. Among them were many outstanding Russian experts, for instance Wilfried Strik-Strikfeldt, a forty-five-year-old former czarist officer born in Riga, who had fought against Germany in the Great War. The group was responsible for all translating and the considerable Russian interpreting work in the prisoner interrogation camps, for example. Russian military manuals and documents were translated and circulated to our own field commands; on one occasion, in July 1943, we captured a Smersh* counterespionage manual advising Russian units how to detect "parachutists, radio operators, saboteurs, and other German espionage agents." It was translated by Group III, and we modified our tactics and forged documents accordingly.† The commanding officer of Group III controlled the interrogation camp maintained by Foreign Armies East at Lötzen, East Prussia. Altogether, the group was of particular importance since there were few experts on the Soviet Union in Germany, and our own leaders had to be kept well advised on everything connected with the Russian enemy.

Within a few weeks the new system was working well. During the course of the day, the intelligence data and digests arrived from

---

* Contraction of Russian *smert shpionam* ("death to spies"), a counterespionage organization which worked with and watched the Red Army from 1941 to 1947, and whose functions are today carried on under the Soviet Ministry of Internal Affairs.—TRANS.

† File H3/732.

all the army groups on the eastern front. The dispatches from Major Baun's office, Walli I, were rushed over from Nikolaiken by an NCO dispatch rider on a motorcycle (Baun himself was rarely seen at Angerburg). These were processed by the individual groups within my branch in preparing the evening intelligence digest we were to issue. Many of the incoming reports had to be checked back on; and we had to issue follow-up orders to the reporting units at the front. Out of these incoming reports we gradually digested an over-all picture of the day's main events and established a basis for an assessment of the enemy's probable situation and intentions, even before we received the appreciation reports composed at army group level. The constant exchange of ideas between our branch and the Ic officers at army group level in the course of the day was of great importance. This was also the case for the exchanges between our branch and Major Baun and our comparison of ideas with Halder's operations branch. By the time the military intelli-gence reports began to arrive from the army groups during the afternoon, the respective subgroup heads had already been able to form views of their own which they compared with the new arrivals. In the evening, about an hour and a half before Halder called his main 10 P.M. situation conference, I summoned a branch confer-ence in my room, attended by Major Herre, head of Group I, and the heads of all his subgroups. Herre reported to me the latest news from the army groups, from aerial reconnaissance, from radio monitoring (these reports were always very bulky documents indeed), and from Walli I, and the details were discussed with his subgroup heads. About a dozen officers clustered around the map table in my room, as each subgroup head reported on his own army group and outlined his views on that group's intelligence report. On the basis of this briefing, I then decided on the general line to be adopted by our over-all daily intelligence digest to be issued by Foreign Armies East. Un-der considerable pressure, this document was then produced, usually two or three pages long, and each evening I took it with me when I went to the main conference called by General Halder as chief of staff.

All the General Staff branches concerned with the strategic

situation were represented at Halder's conference: the heads of the operations, Foreign Armies East, organization, and rail transport branches; the quartermaster general (for logistic problems); the chief of army signals (for communications); and, on some occasions, representatives of other branches. The head of the operations branch usually opened the proceedings, followed by myself as head of Foreign Armies East, and then, after the others had also reported, Halder would decide on the orders and other measures to be issued. At about nine o'clock the next morning there was a further situation conference in my own office after the night's batch of incoming reports had been processed. This was followed immediately by a ten o'clock situation conference called by Halder, similar to the evening one but shorter, based on the situation maps freshly printed during the night. He would then take this information with him to the main, midday conference called by Hitler at the "Wolf's Lair."

Obviously speed was of the essence if our intelligence digests were to be of any value to the field commanders. (If this was true for offensive operations, it was even more so when the enemy had seized the initiative.) I believe that the new organization and system I introduced met this vital requirement. From the daily digests we also produced a comprehensive report on the enemy's situation, as I have mentioned, at intervals of one or two months. This long-range digest then formed in its turn an important basis for comparison with the current daily digest: any distinct divergence from the pattern established in the long-term digests acted as an early warning that the enemy was up to something. It was a warning system which would have been very difficult for the enemy to deceive. Any palpable increase in the rate of sabotage incidents, or an increase in partisan activity, or a sudden concentration of espionage operations in certain areas acted as an immediate alarm signal to my branch. We reacted by issuing orders for intensive intelligence effort in the particular sectors of the eastern front concerned. Armed reconnaissance units crossed the lines and pulled in Soviet prisoners; and our monitoring units eavesdropped on the enemy's radio traffic near the front lines (the radio communications of the particularly officious Soviet military police units were always rewarding listening in this respect).

So, in achieving our results, neither I nor my colleagues resorted to black magic. It was application, thoroughness, expert knowledge, and speed that made our intelligence digests so valuable for the war. This did not mean that our reports were always in accord with Adolf Hitler's wishful thinking. I myself briefed him on only four occasions; the rest of the time it was usually the duty of the chief of staff (first Halder, then his successors Zeitzler and Guderian). I can only confirm how manfully my superiors battled with this man, trying to reverse decisions that were obviously wrong. But given a man of Hitler's obstinacy, they were the kinds of decisions that frequently only the force of destiny could alter. Again and again, Hitler dismissed the warnings contained in our reports as "defeatism" and hinted that we were trying to sabotage his plans. The chief of staff always did what he could to shield me from such outbursts, which might otherwise have resulted in my peremptory dismissal. My own few meetings with Hitler all passed placidly enough, but Guderian frequently got the rough edge of his tongue. I well recall one occasion when Guderian went to Hitler's headquarters at the end of the unsuccessful Ardennes offensive in January 1945, a few days before the Soviet invasion of Germany proper began. When he returned he vividly described how the führer had thrown my charts and situation report to the ground and had suggested that I belonged in a lunatic asylum.

CHAPTER TWO

# Stalingrad
# and
# Citadel

One vital question mark hung over the first half of 1942: how many new divisions could the Russians still create from their reserves? My predecessor had assembled a file of unmistakable indications that the flow of reinforcements to the front was drying up, and he had tried to determine whether this was because the Russians had no fresh manpower reserves available or whether this indicated they were secretly creating fresh units some-where to hold in reserve for the summer operations.* There were many indications from the interrogation centers and from radio monitoring that workers were being recruited from industry to fight at the front; and in February 1942 a friendly intelligence service supplied us with the resolutions of the Presidium of the Supreme Soviet, proclaiming something similar to the total war announced by Goebbels in Germany one year later.

---

* File H3/420.

Late in May 1942 I presented my own conclusions on the Russian reserves position to General Halder, and by the following month we had enough information to make a reliable estimate of the size of the reserves. This was an interesting example of the use of both secret data and readily accessible statistical information published by the Soviet Union itself. In its January 1939 population census the Soviet Union had a total population of 170 millions, but natural population growth and the annexation of large parts of Europe had by 1942 swollen this to 199 millions. In the course of our operations, we had overrun the most densely inhabited area, with about one-third of the entire population of the Soviet Union, some 66 millions, of which up to one-third had probably been evacuated or drafted into the Russian armed forces. In our calculations we took into account the fact that the Russian nation was at that time a young one, with almost half the population younger than twenty (in Germany less than one-third of the population was under twenty), but we found that the high mortality rate and the general ravages of war among the older age groups offset this factor. Thus, on the one hand a relatively high proportion of the Russian people was of military age, a proportion which would increase in the years that followed; but on the other hand there could be less recourse to the older age groups than was possible in Germany. The percentage of women in Russia was also unusually high, over fifty-two percent, which provided a greater incentive to use female labor in industry. On this purely statistical basis the Russians could have had only about 17 million men under arms, since experience showed that any given country can mobilize at most ten percent of its total population.

From our interrogation camps and captured documents we knew that Russia had called up all able-bodied men from eighteen to forty-five years of age (of the 35.4 million men, 28.4 million were able-bodied); there were also indications that in some places forty-six- and forty-seven-year-old men were being recruited. Using our own experience in Germany as a basis for calculation, we could assume that 11 million men at most had been placed in "reserved" draft categories in Russia, and that this figure was probably closer to

9 or 10 million in view of the lost territories. By this method also, we arrived at an estimate of about 17 million able-bodied men available to the Soviet armed forces.

From these 17 millions had to be subtracted the losses since war broke out. Our armies' reports, and estimates of our allies, assessed these at 430,000 dead and invalided in the war with Finland from 1939 to 1940; and the losses since our own attack on Russia had brought the total to 7,530,000 dead, permanently invalided, or taken prisoner up to May 1, 1942. This would leave 9.5 million men in the Soviet armed forces. These were believed to be distributed as follows: of 7,800,000 active troops, about 6,000,000 were in the army,* 1,500,000 in the air force, and 300,000 in the navy. On paper, therefore, the Russians had a manpower reserve of up to 1,700,000 able-bodied men, but for various reasons these could only be made available gradually to the combat units, and several thousand men had to be tied down in the supply, training, clothing, and logistics echelons.

There were ways in an emergency in which Russia could theoretically find the manpower to raise new divisions, and we would no doubt learn more as the year progressed. But we had to bear in mind that with Russia we were dealing not with a central European country, but with half of Asia, a territory thirty-two times the size of Germany, covering about one-sixth of the earth's surface. We could safely assume that it would not prove possible for Moscow to tap more than a fraction of these manpower resources. My predecessor had somewhat optimistically concluded in March that the Soviet reserves were "virtually exhausted," and added:

> Only a meager reserve is available over and above the armed forces already existing, and in view of the prevailing conditions in Russia one must be skeptical as to whether this reserve can be built up to the theoretical estimate.
>
> The Russians will never again be able to throw reserves into the scales as they did in the winter of 1941–42.

---

* This estimate was confirmed by intelligence from a reliable source: in late March 1942 Stalin said, "I have to meet the needs of a six-million-man army." The statement of a foreign diplomat independently revealed the same figure.

In June 1942 I did not see any prospect of the springs of Soviet manpower drying up, for the ruthlessness with which the enemy was prosecuting the war was such that we had to expect Moscow to reinforce the front line without regard for the effects on the national economy, on arms production, or on the supply of foodstuffs. Thanks to their not unexpected talent for improvisation, and to the endemically rigorous qualities of the Soviet state, Moscow had succeeded in mobilizing several million men in new divisions. They had put them into uniform, given them the rudiments of training, and they had conveyed them over great distances into the front line. Thus, we now found just as many Red divisions confronting us, despite their disastrous losses at Kiev, Vyazma, and Bryansk, as there had been when we launched our attack, and the Red Army appeared to be maintaining its frontline strength of 4,500,000 attained in January 1942. As for the Soviet air force, we noticed that it had shifted its main focus to our Army Group South, which indicated that the Russians were either planning a major offensive there themselves, or were anticipating a German offensive.

I concluded my June 1942 appreciation with the words,

> It is clear that the enemy has suffered major losses in the defeats of these last twelve months. The fighting so far has shown the German soldier to be justified in feeling he is superior to the enemy, and we have seen that where an assault is launched in force, success is guaranteed. But the enemy's numerical superiority in manpower and equipment must not be underestimated. If we are to carry the impending operations in the East through to final victory, we shall have to make a supreme effort.*

Far more crucial to the Soviet position were its dwindling supplies of vital raw materials. I endeavored to make this plain in a paper delivered to our staff college late that summer.† With the loss

---

* This June 1942 paper is still in my possession. By way of comparison with the Soviet armed forces, the German figures were: army, 4,100,000; air force, 1,800,000; and navy, 430,000. (These figures represent our forces on all fronts—the East, West, and North Africa.)
† "The Economic Potential of the Soviet Union," September 7, 1942 (among papers in my possession).

of the Donets coal-producing region, Russia was entering a major industrial and transportation crisis: by 1942, had war not broken out, total Russian coal output would have reached about 200 million tons a year, but now they would not obtain more than 80 million tons. The railroads had traditionally swallowed half the coal output, and the industrial regions along the central and northern reaches of the Volga, including Moscow, and of the Urals and Siberia took the rest. The coal output of the remaining fields in the Urals, Karaganda, and Kuznetsk would probably be adequate for the eastern industrial zones; but the coal supply for the remaining western industrial zones was critical, having to be shipped by rail over distances of more than 1,500 miles from Karaganda and Kuznetsk. Several steel mills in Kuibyshev had had to close down in March 1942. Shipping on the Volga was without fuel, and the railroad system was beginning to show signs of strain. With the loss of the coking plants in the Donets region, coke output was down to about forty percent of Russia's prewar output, and this in turn was affecting iron and steel production. Iron ore production would reach only 13 million tons instead of the planned 40 million, pig iron only 7 million instead of the planned 22 million, and steel only 8 million instead of 28 million tons.

Soviet arms production was also likely to suffer from other raw materials shortages. We knew that the output of manganese ores in the Urals and western Siberia was inadequate for the local steel industry, and that manganese was having to be transported north from Chiatura in the Caucasus. But the Caucasus was the objective of our summer offensive, and its capture would have a severe effect on Soviet steel production. Furthermore, the second richest veins of tungsten and molybdenum in Europe (after those in Portugal) were also in the Caucasus (at Tyrny-Auz in the Elbrus mountains south of Pyatigorsk), with a 1941 output of 700 tons of tungsten concentrate and 450 tons of molybdenum concentrate. These ores were also processed in the Caucasus—the smelting works were located at Sestafoni in Georgia. We calculated that the loss of ferrous alloy production at Sestafoni would reduce high-grade steel production for the arms industry by at least thirty percent. As far as petroleum production was concerned, we did not expect the loss of the Caucasian oil fields to have much effect on Soviet fighting capacity until mid-1943, as there had been extensive stockpiling in central Russia. Similarly, Russia had devoted considerable effort to developing independent sources of natural and synthetic rubber. We had overrun her most important plantation areas for natural rubber, and two of the three original synthetic rubber factories had been evacuated, but four or five more were known to be opening up, and we believed the Soviet Union could meet all its war needs with a probable output of 80,000 tons a year.

Finally, we also had to take into account the increasing rate of deliveries of arms and materials from the United States. The transportation of large quantities of war equipment such as trucks, antitank and antiaircraft guns, shells and bombs, together with tanks and aircraft had built up initially through Persia. From November 1941 onward, however, the Allies had been making increasing use of the Arctic sea route to Murmansk. According to prisoners captured during attacks on the Allied convoys, the ships carried foodstuffs, tanks, aircraft, aircraft engines, guns, and ammunition. By July 1942 the Allies were estimated to have shipped no fewer than 2,800 tanks to the Soviet Union, and our intelligence suggested that about thirty armored brigades had put in an appearance on the eastern front equipped with British and American tanks. The Russian troops were not very happy with the quality of these tanks, as they were inferior to the Soviet T-34 in every respect, and with their narrow tracks their cross-country performance was poor; moreover, their engines could not comfortably digest the low-grade fuels common in the USSR. British and American aircraft had also been severely affected by oil freezing in the sub-zero temperatures; the Russians considered their own makes far superior.

* * *

By this time, Hitler's major offensive toward the Caucasus was well under way. Voronezh had been captured, our armies had advanced along the Don, and the Volga had just been reached south of Stalingrad. In my view, our forces would shortly succeed in overrunning the oil fields of the Caucasus and consolidating our position on the Volga before winter set in, although we had to expect strong resistance. As early as July 12 the Russian high command had created the Stalingrad Front under Marshal Timoshenko, and on the fifteenth I briefed General Halder on the new Russian forces appearing in the eastern front and on agents' reports that the enemy was preparing for a determined defense of Stalingrad itself. On the following day Halder and Heusinger discussed with me the probable scale of the coming battle, and to what extent time was in our favor.* As our armies, principally the Sixth Army under General Paulus, advanced further and further toward Stalingrad that summer, General Halder and I had cast anxious eyes on the lengthening left flank along the Don, and Halder repeatedly warned of the possibility that Moscow would launch a counterattack on this flank, most probably across that part of the Don that extended between the Khoper tributary and the great bend at Kremenskaya, for this sector was held not by hardened German forces but by our Rumanian allies.

Even if the coming operation was insufficient to destroy the Red Army or bring about an early collapse, the physical occupation of the vital Caucasus region and the blocking of the Volga as a Soviet waterway would cause untold harm to the enemy's economy. But ahead lay yet another Russian winter in which the enemy could rely on his superiority in winter combat to inflict such manpower and equipment losses on us that we would have to dismiss all thought of renewing the German offensive in 1943, particularly in view of our obligations in other theaters. I warned that we should be on the lookout for numerous enemy formations specially trained for mobile warfare in winter, and we should expect violent partisan activity in the rear of our armies. It was by no means impossible, I stated in September 1942, that given the sparseness of our front line, these Russian tactics might produce crises like those of the previous winter.

---

* Halder notes in his diary that day, "We shall have to prepare for and perhaps even commence this battle while we are still fighting the battle for Rostov, north and south of the Don."

* * *

By the time the Soviet counterattack began on November 19, 1942, which was to lead eventually to the Stalingrad disaster, my branch Foreign Armies East had predicted ten days in advance precisely where the blow would fall and which of our armies would be affected. The Stalingrad tragedy marked the turn of the tide in the eastern campaign; it heralded the ultimate defeat of the Third Reich. Since the complete file of our branch's "Brief Enemy Situation Reports" is available, our claim to have given good warning is more than substantiated.

Between October 25 and November 9 incoming reports yielded a persistent impression of a weak but steady flow of reinforcements to the front facing the Rumanian Third Army, although it was not until the latter part of this phase that Soviet intentions became clear to us. We soon received reports about the arrival of further troops at Serafimovich, a town on the Don about 100 miles northwest of Stalingrad. There was heavy transport and loading activity along the railroad line leading to it—our reconnaissance aircraft could see lights moving at night—and extensive traffic crossing the Don at Kletskaya, about twenty miles closer to Stalingrad (it was from Serafimovich and Kletskaya that the first Soviet counterattacks were launched). On October 29, I took my latest report across to General Zeitzler, the new army chief of staff; Zeitzler, a bustling, stocky, bald-headed, dynamo of action, had replaced the exhausted General Halder a month before. My report said, "There is nowhere any sign of preparation for a major attack, but the entire area needs continued intensive observation." Two days later I repeated this view but added that there was an increased impression that there might be localized attacks on the Rumanian position at Serafimovich, to which I added on November 2: "In connection with the increasing troop movements west of Serafimovich, we must expect there to be continued reinforcement of the enemy confronting the Rumanian Third Army, and possibly even an attack. We must await further indications."

At the same time, we observed the corresponding withdrawals of troops and equipment from neighboring Russian formations—

particularly the Sixty-fifth and Twenty-first Armies—to build up the sectors from which the Soviet attack would begin. On November 2, I reported the first indications of this from radio monitoring reports. On the following day I cited a number of specific instances where air reconnaissance had observed tanks and field artillery at locations just north of Stalingrad along the German front, disappearing and then reappearing a few days later near Serafimovich. "There emerges an increasingly clear picture of preparations for an attack on the Rumanian Third Army, though they are still in their early stages," I wrote on November 3. "We cannot yet be certain whether the object is an attack designed to lure our forces away from Stalingrad, or an operation with a much broader objective." At the time I tended to favor the former possibility.

It was clear from the active reinforcement of Stalingrad and the heavy Soviet air raids on our positions there that the enemy had by no means given up the fight for the city, I added on the fourth; and I mentioned for the first time that there were indications that the Russians were planning further major relief operations from Beketovka, just south of Stalingrad. The reinforcement of the Soviet forces in Serafimovich at the expense of their front line between the Volga and the Don continued over the next few days. Our air reconnaissance detected between 2,000 and 2,500 vehicles moving north of Kletskaya, and we were able to identify the new Russian rifle and armored divisions concerned. Finally, on November 10, I warned, "The appearance of the Soviet headquarters for the southwestern front somewhere to the northwest of Serafimovich indicates that a major enemy attack operation is in sight."

From "Max," the office controlling the Abwehr agents in Moscow, I had received the following signal a few days earlier:

On November 4 Stalin presided over Council of War in Moscow, attended by twelve marshals and generals. Following basic principles were laid down at this council:
   (a) operations to be executed cautiously to avoid heavy casualties;
   (b) loss of ground is unimportant;
   (c) it is vital to salvage industrial and public-utility instal-

lations in good time by evacuation, which explains orders issued for dispersal of refineries and machine-tool factories from Grozny and Makhachkala to New Baku, Orsk, and Tashkent;

(d) rely only on oneself, don't count on getting aid from allies;

(e) take sharp measures to prevent desertion, either by better propaganda and rations or by firing squads and tougher GPU supervision; and

(f) all the planned attack operations are to be executed before November 15 if possible, insofar as weather permits. These are primarily from Grozny toward Mozdok; at Nizhni-Mamon and Verkhni-Mamon in the Don basin; and at Voronezh, at Rzhev, south of Lake Ilmen, and at Leningrad. The necessary troops are to be brought out of reserve and up to the front line.

Events over the following months showed that this report must have been genuine.

But what use are the best intelligence reports if one's own forces are too weak to withstand the enemy, or the warnings are not heeded? By November 11 it was clear that the flow of reinforcements to the Russian front at Serafimovich and Kletskaya was slackening off, and on the twelfth I stated in my written report to General Zeitzler:

> In front of Army Group [Don] the enemy's attack intentions, which we have long suspected, are gradually becoming more clearly defined: in addition to establishing two main groups of forces which we have detected opposite the two wings of the Rumanian Third Army—where the enemy can now be said to be ready to attack—there are growing indications that forces are being concentrated still further west, primarily in the Kalach area (we have intercepted radio traffic between the Russian Sixty-third Army and six or seven unidentified formations and detected the probable insertion of the First Guards Army; rail traffic to Kalach is possibly transporting sections of the Fifth Tank Army; and we also have Abwehr reports of reinforcements arriving at Kalach) and possibly in front of the Hungarians as well.

I warned emphatically, "While it is not possible to make any overall assessment of the enemy situation with the picture as uncertain as it is at present, we must expect an early attack on the Rumanian Third Army, with the interruption of our railroad to Stalingrad as its objective so as to endanger all German forces further to the east and to compel our forces in Stalingrad to withdraw. This will thereby reopen the river Volga as a waterway." That the railroad from Morozovsk to Stalingrad was the objective of the attack had been confirmed by a captured Russian officer. I added that it remained to be seen whether we should also expect a major Russian offensive across the Don against the Italian Eighth and the Hungarian Second Armies (possibly with Rostov as its goal) at staggered intervals after the impending attack on the Rumanian Third Army, or whether the Russians would launch simultaneous but somewhat more limited operations against the Italians and Hungarians. While the Russian troops confronting the Rumanian Third Army continued to take up their assault positions (according to a deserter, three new tank brigades were being brought into the line opposite the Rumanian Sixth Army Corps), I reported on the eighteenth that a simultaneous Russian attack from Beketovka, south of Stalingrad, could not be excluded.

\* \* \*

At five the next morning, November 19, 1942, the Soviet offensive began, precisely where we had predicted: from the bridgeheads of Kletskaya and Serafimovich, under the overall command of the Russian southwestern front. On the following morning a second offensive began from Beketovka, just south of Stalingrad. I reported that day, "While it is so far not possible to investigate the tactical situation in the breakthrough locations in detail, it appears probable that a major crisis is now upon us, particularly in consequence of the breach effected in the Rumanian Fifth Infantry Division. We must expect these attacks to be pressed southward, using the forces held in reserve in the rear for this purpose." On the twenty-second, the two arms of the Soviet pincer movement met at Kalach, encircling our Sixth Army in Stalingrad and a number of lesser formations—250,000 of our finest troops, with 100 tanks, 1,800 guns, and over 10,000 vehicles. The rest of the tragedy belongs to history.

Understandably, I was bitter about the outcome. A few days after the last shots were fired in Stalingrad and the starving remnants of Paulus's gallant army had gone into captivity, I wrote a summary* of the lessons to be learned and the causes for the defeat:

Any retrospective look at the events since mid-November is bound to be overshadowed by the fact that all of them—with the exception of the first moves in the offensive against the Rumanian Third Army—have resulted from a sequence of basic command errors on our side, as to whose extent and effect the *military* authorities were perfectly aware from the moment they were committed. It is not within the scope of this survey to discuss the reasons why these errors were nonetheless made.

Leaving aside the failure of our allies, the Russians can credit their great victories to the fact that they have applied standard German command principles: Zhukov as military commander enjoys complete freedom within the framework of the task assigned to him; the Russians have adopted German tactics and German strategic doctrines. In the meantime, we have borrowed from the Russians their earlier system of rigidly laying down the law on virtually everything and going into the tiniest details, and therein lies the blame for our defeats. German military leaders who can think and act independently are discouraged—indeed both such qualities can lead to court-martial. Thus we have forfeited one of the fundamental requirements of a successful and versatile military command. We have become benumbed, and are incapable of strategic action. . . .

This introduction was clearly recognizable as a criticism of Adolf Hitler's leadership. I continued by reviewing the military trends we had witnessed since November and emphasizing that we had always correctly identified the enemy's intentions well in advance. I summarized the mid-November offensive on the Rumanian Third Army and our own Sixth Army as follows:

* "Thoughts on the Situation," February 10, 1943 (A copy of this report is among my personal papers).

After General Halder [Zeitzler's predecessor as chief of staff] had repeatedly warned of the possibility that the enemy would launch an offensive across the Don between the Khoper River and the great bend, at the end of October and early in November we identified the first indications of the impending offensive, which was later to result in the encirclement of the Sixth Army. From November 9 onward our intelligence digest indicated that a major offensive was being prepared against the Rumanian Third Army, and at about the same time we repeatedly warned of preparations to attack the Italian Eighth and the Hungarian Second Armies, and Voronezh. On November 21 we underlined the enemy's intention of isolating the Sixth Army, and three days later the Sixth Army was indeed encircled.

For the sake of history it must be recorded here that . . . the General Staff was adamant that only the immediate withdrawal of the Sixth Army could save it from annihilation and release the forces that would almost immediately become necessary for the bitter fighting in which Army Group Don became engaged. It was as early as this that—at least in our intelligence digest—we pointed out that only the virtually immediate withdrawal of Army Group A behind the Don (a bold decision, but one characteristic of German staff training), while retaining a bridgehead east of the Taman Peninsula, would leave us with any chance of using these forces to crush the Russian offensive across the middle reaches of the Don, and to retain the initiative for a fresh offensive to the south. At the time, it was objected that ground conditions in winter would prohibit any such operations; but subsequent developments have refuted that objection with a vengeance. Ludendorff also managed to "operate" in winter, in Poland.

The story had been the same with the Soviet offensives against the Italian Eighth Army on December 16, which had finally sealed General Paulus's fate in Stalingrad, and the assault on the Hungarian Second Army four weeks later. Again we had given adequate warning as I pointed out in my February 1943 survey.

* * *

With the Russians, as I was always at some pains to stress, we were dealing with strategic and political brains of high caliber and cunning. For example, early in February 1943, it was learned that Soviet agents we captured were under strict orders to play down Russian military capabilities when we interrogated them.* And again, their military objectives were well calculated, as we learned from an Abwehr report we received from a recently dispatched agent who had established contact with a Western Allied military mission in Moscow. From time to time, as I shall mention again, the Allies considered it in their own interest to show us some of the cards the Russians were dealing to them. In this case, the Soviet authorities had given the mission a statement on their military objectives. This was in reply to a Wehrmacht communiqué which had stressed that Moscow had attained none of the strategic objectives it had set for its offensives of the winter of 1942–43. The Russian statement read,

> The principal Russian strategic objective is not one of regaining lost territory or pushing the enemy back to the west; rather, the Russian war leadership intends to crush the German army's striking power. This aim can be realized only if Germany's war-making potential—and that means her military equipment—is destroyed. This is the objective of every Russian operation. For this reason, it is of no consequence whatever to the Russian command how many "hedgehog" defense positions the Germans establish in the Soviet rear, or how many of her soldiers Germany sends to their doom.
>
> While the deep Russian strikes may seem to be ambitious or bold operations, or may even seem to have been launched solely with the aim of brushing up the war maps where possible, in reality the aim of these operations has always been to seize the main German supply dumps and destroy them. Conditions on the eastern front call for a completely different kind of warfare from that in the rest of Europe. On the western front the German army command can place its munitions dumps and other depots hundreds of miles behind the front and still keep its combat units rapidly supplied in an emergency by means of motor transport, thanks to the excellent and extensive highway networks there. On the eastern front the supply dumps are obliged to remain comparatively

---

* File H3/286.

close to the fighting front. The frequent and sudden weather changes, with dense snowfalls or sudden thaws, could otherwise result in a unit being cut off from its supplies at a crucial moment when the enemy has launched a surprise attack on it.

This is why the Russian High Command has concentrated on the German army's supply bases in the Caucasus, at Stalingrad, and in the Don bend, and after its careful investigations were complete it committed the Soviet attack formations accordingly. The collapse of the German front on the Don, at Stalingrad, and in the Caucasus is mainly a consequence of the successful threat of the Russian spearheads into the heart of the German army, which then suddenly found itself deprived of sufficient supplies for relatively long sectors of its front. The enormous quantities of German war equipment which have already been captured or destroyed by the Soviet forces are therefore the "Russian strategic objective." For the Russians, a small village in which a large munitions dump has been located is more important than any city, however magnificent the winter quarters it might seem to offer the German troops.

In countless publications Germany has repeatedly stressed that this war is primarily an industrial war. In logical progression from this, the Russians are fighting their war against German war industry on the eastern front. In the summer of 1943, we shall see that the Soviet military command has achieved a crucial victory by eliminating a significant part of the enemy's heavy and light arms and equipment.

It was no easy task to see through the increasingly sophisticated Russian tactics of deception by now. Faked radio messages had initially been easy to detect by sending out reconnaissance aircraft to photograph the areas concerned. But the enemy became more devious—they began faking tank tracks across muddy fields by using rollers or other vehicles.

They had learned a lot from their defeats of 1941. From a captured Russian general we found out that Stalin had established a committee under General Shaposhnikov, his army chief of staff, to investigate the causes of Soviet military unpreparedness. We apparently learned nothing from our errors: rival decoding organizations were maintained by Göring's Luftwaffe, by the OKW, by the Foreign Ministry, and by the navy (a chaotic situation which I was able to prevent in postwar Germany until my retirement).

Such decoded material as Foreign Armies East did receive during the war was of great value, particularly for assessing the true conditions behind the enemy lines. For example, in 1942 the OKW forwarded to me such items as a lengthy cable from the Yugoslav ambassador in Kuibyshev (to which city the diplomatic corps had been evacuated from Moscow) to his exiled foreign ministry in London, reporting at length on the Soviet agricultural plight. At about the same time, we were reading the cables of the American ambassador to the State Department in Washington, reporting on Soviet labor problems and arms production. From decoded Turkish intelligence cables we were extracting information on Russian armored brigades.* (On other occasions the Turkish foreign minister supplied us with information of interest to us about Russia.) The army's own radio-monitoring units also picked up tactical signals from which we could identify the movements of units behind the enemy lines, their supplies of tanks and assault weapons, and whether particular units were preparing to attack or digging into defensive positions. Our cooperation with General Fellgiebel, the chief of army signals, was particularly good.

Apart from the Abwehr agents themselves, our most important sources of intelligence were captured prisoners and Soviet army documents. Soviet newspapers (and those of the Western Allies) and Soviet radio also yielded worthwhile information from time to time despite every effort at censorship. Even the letters the Soviet soldiers received were rewarding reading; by a stroke of luck, Army Group South captured no fewer than 8,000 sacks of Soviet forces' mail in the middle of June. I ordered a small army of interpreters to screen every single letter, particularly with regard to Soviet morale, region by region. On July 7, 1943, the first detailed analysis was shown to Zeitzler, and he showed it to Hitler. The letters showed that a food crisis was about to grip the Soviet population,

---

* Files H3/420, H3/68.1, and III.H395.

that black market trading was flourishing, and that the civilian population was suffering appalling hardships in support of the fighting front. The report cited some examples of the human tragedies reflected in the captured letters, and commented pointedly: "These were no 'subhumans,' the people who wrote these letters."*

Accurate though our strategic predictions had proved to be, I was still dissatisfied with our tactical intelligence system. In December 1942, I called a conference of the Ic officers at army and army-group levels, together with my own Group I. I outlined methods by which I planned to speed up the inflow of intelligence reports from the front and the subsequent outflow of these reports from my branch. At that time, the system of forwarding aerial reconnaissance reports was a constant source of worry, as they usually reached my branch untimed, undated, and so late as to permit at best a retrospective survey of events. The daily reconnaissance reports forwarded by the army-group Ic's were of great importance, but they did not always arrive soon enough for us to digest them in time for the führer's conference. To speed up the process I introduced a new system of telephoning reports through, so that the verbal reports from the reconnaissance units reached the air intelligence officers at army-headquarters level by 7:00 P.M. each day. Thus, the night's reports reached the OKW and General Staff by 7:00 A.M. I also insisted that these verbal reports be made regularly and on time, whether or not all the facts were known; an incomplete report was better than none when my Group I began its editing work each day. I insisted on the same procedure with the reports on the enemy's artillery strength, since if these reached the General Staff on time they provided a valuable parameter for assessing the enemy's strength, particularly with regard to whether he was regrouping or creating new units. I introduced a system of ten-day reports on the enemy's artillery situation. They were initially greeted with some skepticism, but later widely accepted for the valuable statements that they were.

\* \* \*

---

* H3/644.

The Soviet winter offensive ended late in March 1943, with our victorious battle for Kharkov. Hitler now needed a major offensive victory to turn the tide on the eastern front, and he picked the tempting Russian salient at Kursk, where he could both capture large quantities of Russian equipment and troops and shorten his own front by some 150 miles. On April 15 he issued his orders for the offensive, which was code-named Citadel. It was to place the initiative for the coming spring and summer campaigns firmly in German hands again—"The victory at Kursk must act as a beacon to the world." Hitler proposed to launch the attack late in May, as soon as his tank divisions were refreshed. Over the weeks that followed, his armored divisions gathered in the Orel bend, waiting to attack. But now Hitler repeatedly postponed the date, first for one reason, then another, while the Russians, who were fully aware of our intentions, took the appropriate measures and prepared a daunting system of defenses extending some 150 miles back from the front line. With each week that passed our prospects of success lessened; whereas initially the War Department and my own branch had been confident of victory at Kursk, by late June we were confident of defeat.

My branch reported in compelling detail on the Soviet defensive preparations.* On April 17 we received from a reliable agent the information that six days later Stalin was summoning his sector and army commanders to Moscow to discuss the "indications of a German offensive." Another reliable agent reported on the twenty-seventh that an incomplete rifle division, a tank brigade, two tank battalions, and two field artillery regiments had arrived at Valuyki from Saratov (Valuyki was opposite the starting point for the southern pincer arm of Citadel); and that every day tanks, engines, and tank guns were leaving the tank factories at Kazan and Gorki, bound for the sector of the front in the vicinity of Kupyansk, Kursk,

---

* A detailed history of the predictions of Foreign Armies East in the months before Citadel was launched would be impossible in this book. The reader's attention is drawn therefore to three studies on the operation by General Gotthard Heinrici in *Wehrwissenschaftlicher Rundschau*, 1965, pp. 463–86, 529–44, and 582–604, where many of my reports are quoted; and to the official history published by a federal government agency: Ernst Klink, *Das Gesetz des Handelns: Die Operation "Zitadelle," 1943* (Stuttgart: Deutsche Verlagsanstalt, 1966).

and Orel (i.e., the Citadel area). On April 28 an untried agent reported that the Russians expected their enemy would soon mount a major offensive in the area between Kharkov and Kursk. From such Abwehr reports there was no doubt that the Soviet high command had learned of our intentions and was taking the necessary countermeasures.

By the time Citadel was finally launched on July 5, it was clear that we had lost the advantages of both strategic and tactical surprise. I had taken every opportunity, as the files of Foreign Armies East show, to warn the German command against the plan for this major offensive. Since Hitler refused to be dissuaded, on July 3 I wrote an emphatic warning of the likely outcome, under the title "Appreciation of the Enemy's Moves if Operation Citadel is Carried Out."

> Once Operation Citadel begins the enemy can either restrict his countermeasures to the Citadel operational area, blocking our attack—if necessary by bringing up reserves from neighboring areas—by remaining generally on the defensive apart from minor counterattacks. Or, if the enemy considers the overall war picture warrants such action, he will launch the offensives he has already prepared against Army Group South and Army Group Center, while still blocking Citadel. In view of their degree of readiness to attack, and with regard to the situation in the Mediterranean,* the latter appears the more probable of the two alternatives, although we cannot exclude an initially limited reaction to Citadel. We therefore have to expect that, probably soon after our offensive begins, the Russians will mount strong diversionary attacks and counterattacks in those sections of the front held by Army Groups South and Center where we have detected their preparations to attack.

I added that if the Russians should unexpectedly concentrate their countermeasures on the Citadel area and the front line in the immediate vicinity, we would have to expect them to move considerable reinforcements to Kursk from other areas if the fighting

---

* Where the Allied invasion was expected any day, and eventually occurred on July 10, five days after Citadel.

continued very long. But we considered this most improbable, for we were certain that the Russians would try to thwart us by promptly launching spoiling attacks elsewhere to relieve the pressure on Kursk, and follow this up by developing counteroffensives toward the lower Dnieper and toward Orel.

On July 4, the very eve of Citadel, I repeated my opposition in even more emphatic terms:

> From the point of view of the general war situation, there is not one ground that could justify launching Operation Citadel at the present juncture. The prerequisite for victory in the offensive is twofold—we should have numerical superiority and the advantage of surprise. At the time originally planned for the launching of the offensive, both conditions were met. But now, from what we see of the enemy situation, neither is met. For weeks the Russians have been just waiting for our attack in the very sector that we have picked for the offensive. And with their customary energy they have done everything in their power—constructing line upon line of fortifications one behind the other, and moving up the necessary forces— to halt our offensive as soon as it begins. Thus there is little likelihood that the German offensive will achieve a strategic breakthrough.
>
> Taking into account the total reserves available to the Russians, we are not even entitled to assume that Citadel will cost them so much in strength that they will later be incapable of carrying out their general plan at the time they choose. On the German side, our reserves, which will become so desperately necessary as the war situation develops (particularly in the Mediterranean!), will be tied down and thrown away uselessly. I consider the operation that has been planned a particularly grave error, for which we shall suffer later.

The German offensive began next morning, with about 2,000 tanks and 1,800 aircraft starting the pincer movement toward Kursk; the going was heavy, the rate of advance was slow, and the Russians doggedly defended every inch of the ground. We later captured an enemy document listing all but one of the divisions we had marshaled for the offensive. On July 10, in the Mediterranean, the British and American forces invaded Sicily, and on the twelfth precisely the move Foreign Armies East had anticipated occurred: the Russians launched a counteroffensive toward Orel, with a simultaneous counterattack by strong forces at the southern end of the Kursk salient. On the following day, with some 17,000 Soviet troops killed, and 3,300 of our own, Hitler ordered Operation Citadel stopped. That day I congratulated my staff on the bitter fulfillment of our prophecies:

*The Head,*
*Foreign Armies East*                 *Headquarters, July 13, 1943*

The course of the fighting on the eastern front these last few days has once again confirmed precisely every detail of the intelligence picture of the enemy we produced despite formidable obstacles that were put in the way of our assessment of the enemy's distribution of forces. The chief of staff [Zeitzler] expressed particular commendation for this a few days ago.

I know this excellent result is the consequence of the hard work and magnificent cooperation of all this branch's staff and experts, and of the support it enjoyed from the other agencies such as air intelligence, the controller of signals reconnaissance, and Walli I.

I wish to thank all the staff and to express my hope that they will continue to do the job assigned to us with the same effort and enthusiasm.

GEHLEN*

Operation Citadel was the last German attempt at a strategic offensive in the Russian campaign. With its failure the tide of the war in Russia finally turned against us. The German army was forced onto the defensive and never regained the initiative. Foreign Armies East continued to do its duty, to reconnoiter the enemy's positions and strength and to obtain the necessary facts for the command decisions, as well as we were able. We produced intelligence digests and showed which enemy moves we considered most prob-

---

* H3/463.

able. But the more our predictions were confirmed by subsequent events, the less Hitler as supreme commander was inclined to heed our reports which were shown to him by Zeitzler.

* * *

By this time, I had come to the conclusion that the Russians had an excellently informed source working for them in the German supreme command. Canaris and I repeatedly observed quite independently of one another that the enemy was receiving rapid and detailed information on incidents and top-level decision making on the German side. Admiral Canaris came to my headquarters at Angerburg one day and in the course of a lengthy conversation indicated whom he suspected to be the traitor, although I believe that, even so, he knew more than he told me. It was a personality about whom I had had my own doubts for some time. The secret was carefully preserved by the Russians, both then and afterward, and I fully believed it myself only years after the war, when I came into possession of certain information as head of the Gehlen organization in West Germany.

What Canaris told me concerned the fateful role in which Hitler's closest confidant, Martin Bormann, was cast in the last war years and in the postwar epoch too. Bormann, who had been Hitler's personal secretary since early 1943, and chief of the Nazi party organization ever since Rudolf Hess's flight to Scotland in May 1941, was Moscow's most prominent informant and adviser from the very moment the campaign against Russia started. There is no foundation whatever for the allegations which have been made from time to time to the effect that Bormann is alive and well, living in the impenetrable jungle between Paraguay and Argentina, surrounded by heavily armed bodyguards. He crossed to the Russians in May 1945 and was taken back to the Soviet Union.

At the time, I believe, Canaris lacked proof. Our suspicions were largely confirmed when, independently of one another, we found out that Bormann and his group were operating an unsupervised radio transmitter network and using it to send coded messages to Moscow. When the OKW monitors reported this, Canaris demanded an investigation; but word came back that Hitler himself had emphatically forbidden any intervention: he had been informed in advance by Bormann of these *Funkspiele,* or fake radio messages, he said, and he had approved them. This was the sum of our knowledge at the end of the war. Canaris and I both realized it was out of the question to put watchdogs on Bormann, the most powerful man next to Hitler in the Nazi hierarchy. And neither of us was in any position to denounce the *Reichsleiter* with any prospect of success. The disdain Hitler had shown for my own intelligence summaries, however right they had later proven, was one factor, and the increasingly exposed position of Canaris and the Abwehr was another. The smallest slip would have put an end to our investigations, and probably to us as well. Canaris described to me his grounds for suspecting Bormann and told me what he assumed to be the reasons for his treachery. He would not exclude the possibility that Bormann was being blackmailed, but he was inclined to see the real motives in the *Reichsleiter*'s immense and insatiable ambition—he was tortured by complexes toward the milieu in which he found himself, and driven by the ambition to succeed Hitler when the day came. We now know of course how cunningly Bormann succeeded in bringing first Göring and then Goebbels into discredit with Hitler, for they were his great rivals.

It was not until after 1946, when I headed my own intelligence organization, that I had an opportunity to look into Bormann's mysterious escape from Hitler's Berlin bunker and his subsequent disappearance. Some time later I received conclusive proof of Bormann's postwar movements. During the 1950s I was passed two separate reports from behind the Iron Curtain to the effect that Bormann had been a Soviet agent and had lived after the war in the Soviet Union under perfect cover as an adviser to the Moscow government, and has died in the meantime.

## CHAPTER THREE

# Wooing
# the
# Russians

𝕴 still believe that we could have achieved our 1941 campaign objectives had it not been for the pernicious interventions of Adolf Hitler, the most fundamental of which resulted in the Battle of Kiev. The consequences of military victory would have been a matter for conjecture, since Hitler's goal was the conquering of lebensraum, and this implied the total destruction of the Russian state. We in the General Staff on the other hand had come around to envisaging a more moderate and realistic political solution, in which a Russia would continue to exist. We had realized that this vast country, rich in manpower and raw material resources, could in the final analysis only be conquered—or, rather, liberated from communism—with the help of the Russian peoples themselves, and this is how even after the setbacks of the winter campaign of 1941–42 we could still have succeeded had the war been intelligently directed. We could have won the Russians over because of their instinct for national self-preservation alone—quite apart from their pent-up hatred of communism in general and the Stalinist system in particular. But Hitler refused to believe this whenever the possibility was put to him.

It is in Hitler's failure to exploit the psychological potential of the Russian peoples, most of whom had shown the greatest warmth toward us in the opening phases of the campaign, that we can see the real mistake he made. We can see it again in the brutal way he imposed his satraps Koch, Sauckel, and Kube on the conquered Russian provinces and converted the people's frustrated hopes into blind hatred of the Germans. These mistakes counted more heavily against us than many a strategic blunder, because Hitler had stirred up moral feelings.

Unlike the wars of earlier times, modern wars are basically wars between peoples. The wars of the eighteenth century were fought between the armed forces of the combatant states. Modern wars are fought by the people as such, who must bear the necessary sacrifice and involve themselves body and soul in their cause. In particular, the modern world is divided into two diametrically opposed ideological camps—the "free world" and "international communism"—and from this there springs a more intense and fundamentally emotional aggravation of the otherwise purely military conflict. Hitler and Stalin always emphasized the ideological aspect, and even Eisenhower titled his memoirs *Crusade in Europe,* in deference to the convictions of many British and Americans. I do not believe the near future will see any change in the respective roles of war and ideology, nor do I believe politics (and hence wars) can ever be divested of their ideological character. However ugly the prospect may be, there always will be wars in the years to come. The teachings of Mao, of Ché Guevara, and of Giap tell us so, as does a study of the work on military strategy by Marshal of the Soviet Union Sokolovski, which reflects the official attitude of the Soviet Union toward war and politics.

It is this extension of war to every facet of human activity that obliges us to see its essentially political character, as the military strategist Karl von Clausewitz demonstrated in his famous thesis *On War.* While political goals shape war and influence it from one moment to the next, it is the soldier's duty to insure that he will not be confronted with insoluble tasks by his political leaders (as happened in June 1941). Political leaders should do what they can at every stage to ease the soldier's task by bringing both political and psychological weapons into play. This was the victory that we, the General Staff, aspired to with the help of Russian officers and men recruited from among the prisoners in our hands; and this was what we were denied by our political leaders. In retrospect we can only agree that it is a matter for regret that Hitler (unlike Lenin, who is known to have studied Clausewitz from the numerous marginalia that have survived in his hand) did not follow the master's teachings more closely and act accordingly.

Clausewitz stated that war is only a continuation of state policy by other means:

> War . . . is an act of violence intended to compel our opponent to fulfill our will. . . . Violence, that is to say, physical force (for there is no moral force without the conception of states and law), is therefore the *means;* the compulsory submission of the enemy to our will is the ultimate *object.* In order to attain this object fully, the enemy must be disarmed, and disarmament therefore becomes the immediate object of hostilities in theory. It takes the place of the final object, and puts it aside as something we can eliminate from our calculations.*

After going in greater detail into the aims, objects, and motives of war, Clausewitz comes to the following conclusion:

> The war of a community—of whole nations, and particularly of civilized nations—always starts from a political condition and is called forth by a political motive. It is therefore a political act. Now if it was a perfect, unrestrained, and absolute expression of force, as we had to deduce it from its mere conception, then the moment it is called forth by policy it would step into the place of policy, and as something quite independent of it would set it aside, and only follow its own

---

* General Karl von Clausewitz, *On War,* trans. Colonel J. J. Graham (London: Routledge & Kegan Paul, 1956), vol. I, bk. I, para. 2.

laws. . . . War in the real world . . . is not an extreme thing which expends itself at one single discharge; it is the operation of powers which do not develop themselves completely in the same manner and in the same measure, but which at one time expand sufficiently to overcome the resistance opposed by inertia or friction, while at another they are too weak to produce an effect; it is therefore, in a certain measure, a pulsation of violent force more or less vehement, consequently making its discharges and exhausting its powers more or less quickly—in other words, conducting more or less quickly to the aim, but always lasting long enough to admit of influence being exerted on it in its course, so as to give it this or that direction, in short, to be subject to the will of a guiding intelligence. Now, if we reflect that war has its root in a political object, then naturally this original motive which called it into existence should also continue the first and highest consideration in its conduct. Still, the political object is no despotic lawgiver on that account; it must accommodate itself to the nature of the means, and though changes in these means may involve modification in the political objective, the latter always retains a prior right to consideration. Policy, therefore, is interwoven with the whole action of war, and must exercise a continuous influence upon it, as far as the nature of the forces liberated by it will permit. . . .

We see, therefore, that war is not merely a political act, but also a real political instrument, a continuation of political commerce, a carrying out of the same by other means. All beyond this which is strictly peculiar to war relates merely to the peculiar nature of the means which it uses. That the tendencies and views of policy shall not be incompatible with these means, the art of war in general and the commander in each particular case may demand, and this claim is truly not a trifling one. But however powerfully this may react on political views in particular cases, still it must always be regarded as only a modification of them; for the political view is the object. War is the means, and the means must always include the object in our conception.*

In the summer of 1941 the destruction of the Soviet forces was the objective whose attainment would have created the neces-

---

* Ibid., paras. 23 and 24.

sary conditions for the realization of the political end, namely Hitler's political intentions. Without question, this objective had not been attained. On the contrary, severe crises had been mastered only with the greatest difficulty and with the loss of virtually irreplaceable manpower and equipment, not to mention the loss of territory. Hitler wanted desperately to regain the initiative in 1942. He initiated the operational thrusts toward Leningrad and the Caucasus on the basis of economic necessity. Thus his ends were not primarily political; economic considerations, instead, influenced his selection of military objectives. This could still have been justified à la Clausewitz if the offensives would have permanently weakened the enemy and cost them the war or—as Clausewitz sets out in Book Eight—if the capture of these focal points had created an improved climate for a negotiated peace. But that was far from Hitler's mind.

As early as the spring of 1938 General Ludwig Beck, Halder's predecessor as chief of staff, had pointed out in a study for Hitler that his policies would inevitably lead to world war involving the United States, and that equally inevitably Germany was bound to emerge as the loser in the conflict as she simply was not strong enough. This was directly in line with Clausewitz's thinking, "that the tendencies and views of policy shall not be incompatible with these means, the art of war in general and the commander in each particular case may demand. . . ."

During the planning of the Russian campaign the commander in chief of the army, Field Marshal von Brauchitsch, and his chief of staff also expressed to Hitler their concern about launching a campaign with limitless objectives deep into Russia because of the sheer logistical problems, if for no other reason. Hitler however was apparently convinced he could smash all Russian resistance within a few weeks. He refused to involve himself in any discussion on the detailed objections raised by his advisers. Even the output of replacement personnel, which would have sufficed to replace the losses in a blitzkrieg type of war at most, seemed adequate to Hitler. General Halder's criticisms, which were shared by the commanders of the three army groups, were confirmed only too rapidly by the events in Russia. Despite magnificent achievements and colossal initial victories, the German Wehrmacht was unable to inflict a decisive defeat on the Red Army during the first one or two months, and the enemy was able to continue his resistance, hurling more and more fresh divisions into the fight. After Moscow recognized that the Japanese were not going to attack Russia in the Far East, a number of Siberian divisions also appeared at key positions along the eastern front.

The General Staff had planned to direct its main effort against Moscow, as the center of Russian transport communications and political life (which was, of course, a military rather than political objective). But as a result of Hitler's whims the campaign was diverted in support of Army Groups North and South; and while this intervention, which deflected southward sections of the main spearheads attacking Moscow, admittedly led to the great encirclement action at Kiev which yielded some two million Russian prisoners, it contributed little to the main objective of the Russian campaign. Our assault spearheads managed to reach the outskirts of Moscow, but then lacked the strategic and tactical reserves to carry the operation through to final victory.

Hitler left nobody in doubt as to the political target he had set himself. He wanted once and for all to liquidate the Bolshevik menace and—as he had already indicated in *Mein Kampf*—to win the lebensraum he needed for his people in the East. Obviously, in his public proclamations he laid greater emphasis on the former argument, and with equal fervor German propaganda proclaimed the liberation of Russia from communism as the purpose of the war.

As I have said, the military command was from the outset skeptical of the prospects of totally smashing the Soviet state with the limited military means at our disposal, even if we were convinced of the superiority of our own personnel. The inadequacy of the means was all too obvious to us. On the other hand, Hitler's prewar policies had always proved right, and the General Staff's military doubts, based on a cautious appraisal of the situation, had always proved wrong: the occupation of the Rhineland, the annexation of Austria, the incorporation of the Sudeten territories, Munich, the invasion of the rest of Czecho-Slovakia, and the passive reaction of the Western powers during the Polish campaign—all had proved Hitler right and us wrong. He therefore prohibited the generals—sometimes in abusive language—from voicing political objections. Never had the primacy of politics (and wrong politics, at that) been demonstrated more forcefully than during the Third Reich. The military leaders had to bow to Hitler's edicts in 1941; now, at last, events had proved us right.

\* \* \*

The political objectives of the campaign—indistinctly formulated as they were—became less and less credible once the military objective, the complete subjugation of the Soviet forces, was not achieved. First the autumn rains and then the winter laid their unimaginable burdens on our troops, already exhausted by four months of fighting. Casualties and equipment losses had long passed a level at which they could be sustained.

It was therefore natural that the various branches and sections of the General Staff began to seek ways of salvaging the Soviet campaign. All the discussions came to the same conclusion: a suitable political line must be adopted which would awaken positive expectations for the future among the Russian peoples and enable us to activate them in the fight against Stalin and his system. Soldiers have often been accused of regarding war as purely military, a matter of guns and bullets. But this is not always the case, for in 1938 Hitler had to complain, "Instead of having to put brakes on my generals, I find I am having to whip them to go to war!" By early 1942, it was clear that the soldiers were increasingly in favor of giving the political element full rein by formulating appropriate war aims designed to secure the active cooperation of the Russian population. As time passed, moreover, Reichsminister Alfred Rosenberg, who headed the Ministry for Occupied Eastern Territories, showed that he shared our views.

Hitler rejected all such suggestions and showed no inclination whatsoever to contemplate a political solution. He was incapable of weighing the available means against the end he had set.

He opted exclusively for force and led the German people to their ruin in so doing. It was at this time that the propaganda slogan "Führer command—suffer us to obey" was modified by public rumor to a bitter parody, "Führer command—if we obey we suffer."

I would like to stress that it was the soldier—and those in the higher echelons of command were particularly conscious of this— who recognized first that Hitler had wholly surrendered the primacy of politics to the supremacy of the absolute military decision. We believed that political forces should have been brought into play to relieve some of the burden on the fighting man and to inject some kind of political purpose into the campaign against the Soviet Union. This was the only way that might still lead to a satisfactory political end—to collaboration with a Russia liberated from communism and allied by friendship to Germany.

There was such a possibility because the Russian people had suffered grievously under the terrors of Stalinism before 1939. I need only recall the purge of the kulaks, the interminable economic chaos, the purges in the Red Army—partly in connection with the Tukhachevsky affair—the decimation of the party's cadre, and the repression of the national minorities: all these were elements in our favor. The persecution of the Russian Christians also left behind permanent and bitter scars on the deeply religious Russian peoples, as we discovered again and again. When Strik-Strikfeldt interrogated the son of Stalin soon after his capture, the prisoner told him: "The one thing my father dreads is the emergence of a nationalist regime opposed to him. But that is a step you will never take." The interrogator asked why, and Stalin's son replied, "Because we know you have not set out to liberate our country, but to conquer it."

Our troops were celebrated by the Russians everywhere they arrived, whether in the northern or central regions of Russia, in the Ukraine, in Bessarabia, or elsewhere; they were greeted by the local population as liberators and garlanded with flowers. Entire Red Army formations of up to regimental and even divisional strength laid down their arms; the numbers of deserters in the first months, quite apart from the millions of prisoners of war, exceeded our wildest expectations. Colonel Herre used to recount how as acting chief of staff of a mountain corps he had watched the reactions of the Ukrainian townsfolk to the Germans as "liberators" from Soviet oppression; Herre had sent on one occasion for the senior town citizen and asked if he could supply a score of able-bodied Russians for guard duties in the motor pool. Within an hour, over fifty Russians had mustered in the school which was his headquarters. As Herre's corps advanced, it adopted this method in every town.

In the three Baltic republics of Lithuania, Latvia, and Estonia —which had only been occupied by the Russians in 1940—memories of their own national independence were still quite fresh. Lithuanians, Latvians, and Estonians had therefore immediately offered help to the German liberating armies in the hope of thereby restoring their countries' independence. Ukrainians, Caucasians, and tribes of Turkish origin believed that in addition to being liberated from Stalin's yoke they would see their own nationalist aspirations fulfilled—even if these did not always go so far as many of their former leaders, now living in exile, would have liked. After twenty years of arbitrary injustice and terror, the reestablishment of elementary human rights such as the dignity of man, liberty, justice, and the sanctity of property united every inhabitant of the Soviet empire (insofar as he was not directly working for the Moscow system) in a common readiness to support the Germans. What could be more natural for us than to exploit this readiness?

By extending an honest offer to the Russian peoples and following it up in the appropriate way, it would have been possible to unleash a war of liberation which almost certainly would have ended in a rapid and satisfactory conclusion of the Russian campaign. Our military commanders in the field had already made a start in this direction, more from a healthy instinct of self-preservation than for any political motives. As we could not replace all our losses rapidly and the endless Russian expanses made increasing demands on our manpower, our commanders recruited Russians, Ukrainians, and other nationals as auxiliaries and volunteers for various types of duty. These *Hilfswillige* voluntarily acted as drivers, ammunition carriers, cooks, and interpreters, and the like. The number of such auxiliaries could never be exactly determined, since the individual commanders would frequently avoid reporting precisely how many they had. By mid-1943, however, there were about 320,000, of which a large number were actually fighting alongside our troops. The Eighteenth Army alone had 47,000 "Hiwis."

In addition, there were other signs of a Russian initiative which we could put to political use against Moscow. In the German-occupied city of Smolensk, for example, a committee of Russians had come together and offered to set up a Russian nationalist government and recruit a Russian army of liberation of about a million strong to fight against Stalin. Recognizing that the enemy situation called for a clear overall political line, Field Marshal von Bock and other commanders gave initial support to the Smolensk committee's proposals. But these proposals were turned down by Hitler, as were similar suggestions put forward by the Lithuanians, Latvians, and Estonians. Army Group Center also argued in favor of replacing its personnel deficiencies by recruiting 200,000 Russian auxiliaries. Brauchitsch described this proposal as being of decisive importance; but it was never put into effect, as both he and Bock were relieved of their commands for other reasons in December 1941.

I recall having a number of discussions with Halder and other leading General Staff officers in the winter of 1941–42. We agreed that there was an urgent necessity for the clear formulation of *political* war aims, together with a radical alteration in our occupation policies toward the Russian population. Under the pressure of events, the frontline commanders also called for an immediate solution. Those of us directly involved in these discussions anticipated that the worsening military situation would force Hitler to modify his views and that consequently there would be a change in the current occupation policies. With Halder's approval we therefore took every step necessary to speed up such a decision. Those of us who were most concerned in this controversy were the heads of the operations branch (Heusinger), of Foreign Armies East (myself), the quartermaster general (Wagner), and several others.

This group's first action was to regularize all the native auxiliary and volunteer units and to regulate their victualing, pay, and position vis-à-vis the German troops. An order was drafted permitting our divisions on the eastern front to recruit and feed about 3,000 to 4,000 native auxiliaries each (previous actions of this kind had resulted from the individual initiative of the field commanders). This was a great help in that while our German personnel losses could never be entirely recouped in quantity or quality, the fighting fitness of the divisions in the front line would remain sufficient to continue the battle, assuming there were a number of changes in our political and military policies. By the beginning of 1942, however, Hitler had still not agreed to modify his political objectives along the lines I have described. Far from it, for by the spring he had decided on his vast offensive towards the Volga and the oil fields of the Caucasus, and this had run into strong military opposition, as I have described. If this campaign were to continue, our long supply lines to the front—which had been under constant threat since the winter from partisan warfare—would inevitably become overextended. If the Russians were to make a stand and hold us, we would lose even more men and material; but if the enemy were to withdraw, taking all his forces and equipment with him, we would have to pacify and secure enormous areas. And since the existing Russian population in the areas we occupied continued to outnumber us, this task could be performed only if we could gain their friendship and recruit from among them.

* * *

In the early summer of 1942 the Russian Lieutenant General Andrei Andreyevich Vlasov had fallen into our hands on the eastern front near Volkhov. Vlasov was one of the Soviet army commanders who had successfully defended Moscow against the German onslaught, commanding the Twentieth Army under Zhukov's overall leadership. Soviet propaganda had made his name and face famous throughout the Red Army, which made what was to follow all the more painful for the Moscow leaders.

We soon learned that it was Vlasov's dream to lead a Russian national army of liberation into the Soviet Union. In September 1942, while still a prisoner of war, he put his name to a proclamation released as a leaflet over the Russian lines, appealing to the officers and men of the Red Army. Tens of thousands of them answered the call and surrendered to German units within a few days. All this confirmed just what the Soviet experts of my branch, Foreign Armies East, had reported and suggested to Chief of Staff Halder; Colonel von Roenne's group—particularly Captain Strik-Strikfeldt—contributed most to these suggestions. The success of the Vlasov proclamation was not without its impact on the senior officers who had at first been somewhat reserved toward this approach. Thus, the conviction grew that General Vlasov, who certainly never went out of his way to flatter the Germans and never left any doubt but that he was collaborating with us only for the sake of Russian national independence, might be the man to fight for and build a new and different Russia with German aid. I later met him myself. He made a very forthright and reliable impression; his voice was firm and clear, and his language betrayed a fine intellect. Above all, his military ability was testified to by his experience in the battles for Kiev and Moscow.

Hitler, however, lacked all sense of reality. He was either unable or unwilling to deviate from his faulty political and military intentions for the conduct of the Russian campaign. Neither Halder nor Zeitzler was able to change his views. Hitler saw Vlasov at most as a propaganda tool to weaken the Soviet armed forces; promises might be given to him and to deserters who came over to join him, but on no account should these promises be kept.

The German officers who negotiated with Vlasov faithfully reported Hitler's attitude to him. But they nevertheless persisted in their efforts to make common cause with him in fighting both Stalin and the ignorance of the Nazi leaders, as they believed this to be the quickest route to peace and the ultimate liberation of the Russian peoples. After much hesitation, and despite overwhelming doubts, Vlasov agreed. From this alliance between German and Russian officers there emerged what was to become known as the "Vlasov movement." The movement was only one tragic stone in the mosaic of the war, and it is a matter for conjecture whether, had it flourished, it could have saved Germany from the ultimate total defeat once the United States was ready to intervene in strength.

Vlasov was transferred to the High Command (OKW) in Berlin in October 1942 and shortly thereafter released from prisoner of war status. He was given the opportunity to collect a staff of fellow workers. Hitler had placed no restriction on this OKW propaganda effort, since one of the slogans under which the Russian campaign had been launched was already "the liberation of the Russian peoples." The German field commands and the Russians themselves had at first believed in this slogan until early in 1943, when they found out how wide was the gulf between propaganda and reality. From this propaganda headquarters Vlasov and his staff were able to appeal to the Russian population on both sides of the front line—to the public, the volunteers, the prisoners of war, and the eastern workers—some 80 million people all told. We received the clearest indications that even the Soviet marshal Konstantin Rokossovsky was only awaiting the right moment to come out openly against the Stalin regime. It looked like a tremendous step in the right direction.

When we approached the Foreign Ministry with our view that the war could be won only if the Russian people actively threw in their lot with us, Count von der Schulenburg, our former ambassador in Moscow, and his counselor, Gustav Hilger, took up the cause and championed our proposals. However, they encountered either complete lack of sympathy or a paralytic terror of undertaking anything that was without the permission of Ribbentrop and Hitler, let alone anything diametrically opposing their orders.

At the same time, both Colonel von Altenstadt (of the quartermaster general's branch) and I drew up studies stressing the necessity of psychological and political warfare in the East. We called for new methods of dealing with the partisan plague. The studies were highly praised and widely discussed and entirely without effect. Hitler personally issued orders for the ruthless liquidation of all partisans, regardless of whether they were willing to surrender or desert to us or not. These orders resulted in a further escalation of the partisan conflict, and a renewed embitterment of the population toward everything German. Strik-Strikfeldt delivered a lecture entitled "The Russian Character," which, in contrast to

Hitler's views, must have appeared almost revolutionary; but I had it duplicated and distributed to every division on the eastern front and to the prison camps (which came under the quartermaster general) as well. The document called for an understanding of the Russian mentality, and its general tenor was that the Russian must be won over for our cause. If we could not win him, we would have

## THE COMPOSITION OF THE EASTERN TROOPS (1943)*

|  | Infantry, Cavalry, or Artillery Units of Battalion Strength | Labor, Guard, or Training Units of Company Strength |
|---|---|---|
| Eastern volunteers | 51 | 10 |
| Turkish tribes in Russia | 33 | 11 |
| North Caucasians | 13 | — |
| Volga Tartars | 12 | 1 |
| Cossacks | 24 | 1 |
| Armenians | 8 | — |
| Azerbaijani | 11 | — |
| Georgians | 11 | 2 |
| Estonians | 4 | — |
| Finns | 1 | — |
| Lithuanians | 3 | 6 |
| Far Easterners | 1 | — |
| Greeks | 1 | 1 |
| Ukrainians | — | 2 |
| Russians | — | 2 |
| Latvians | — | 2 |
| Kalmucks | 3 | — |
|  | 176 | 38 |

to rule by brute force. If we were to win him, we must set an example in word and deed. This was of course all aimed primarily at the eyes and ears of our German troops.

In the autumn of 1942 Colonel Stieff and Major Count von

* From Burkhard Müller-Hillebrand, *Das Heer 1933–1945* [The Army 1933–1945], vol. III (Frankfurt-am-Main: E. S. Mittler, 1969).

Stauffenberg of our organization branch approved the activation of a Russian propaganda section. Thus, there was officially born the Russian Leadership Center at Dabendorf, a prison camp south of Berlin, ostensibly still purely a propaganda exercise. There Russian officers and propaganda workers were trained, a skeleton officer corps was established, and Russian newspapers were printed. There also, in conjunction with the OKW's military propaganda unit and Foreign Armies East, the political and military objectives for a Russian liberation movement were worked out. At the suggestion of the head of the operations branch, an official command post of "general in command of volunteer units" was activated by Halder in conjunction with his organization branch (under Stauffenberg). The first incumbent was General Heinz Hellmich, who had been in Russian captivity in World War I. His successor was General Köstring.

As a result of the work of these various officers, of Vlasov's own work, and the initiative of our frontline commanders in the East, by early 1943 we had between 130,000 and 150,000 "eastern troops," organized into 176 battalions and 38 independent companies. At that time, as a result of a policy decision higher up, there was no amalgamation of these into larger formations. (See the chart on page 86 for a breakdown of our eastern troops as of early 1943.)

* * *

As early as August 1942, von Roenne and Colonel von Tresckow (chief of staff of Army Group Center) had decided to resuscitate the Smolensk committee. But when Hitler heard of it he forbade the plan, and the committee was permitted to exist as a fictional body only. Vlasov's staff and the OKW's military propaganda section drew up a proclamation for the Smolensk committee, and this was signed by Vlasov and General Vasily Malyshkin at the end of October 1942, ready to be broadcast in millions of leaflets on both sides of the Russian lines as the Stalingrad battle approached its terrible climax. The proclamation moldered for many months in a drawer in Rosenberg's ministry and does not appear to have been brought to Rosenberg's attention until the disaster of Stalingrad was over. Not until February 12, 1943, did he authorize its distribution, and that same evening Captain von Grote ordered the printing of the millions of leaflets. This lack of action wrecked the General Staff's plan to test the effect of coupling military and political initiative in the Caucasus campaign.

Under the pressure of military events, we did finally succeed in forcing a conference at Rosenberg's ministry in December 1942 to discuss the whole problem; the Wehrmacht was represented in strength at the conference and spoke out unmistakably for completely new political objectives in Russia. Most of them seemed to believe that Rosenberg, a Baltic German, was himself the father of Hitler's Russian policies. Rosenberg was clearly impressed by what he heard at the conference and promised to support these proposals to Hitler, although he was still unwilling to deviate from some of his own ideas, which tended toward dividing the Soviet Union into separate national entities such as the Ukraine. Rosenberg's subsequent discussion with Hitler was a complete failure, as Hitler waved aside all his arguments with a few well-chosen and final words.

Colonel Martin, head of the OKW military propaganda section, persuaded Goebbels to agree to a meeting with Vlasov to discuss a new manifesto composed for the Russian peoples. Goebbels had already recognized that the menacing trend in the war demanded nothing short of an about-face in the Third Reich's attitude toward Russia. It was characteristic of the petty jealousies prevalent at the top that Rosenberg now flatly forbade Goebbels to interfere in his affairs; and by the time Vlasov finally saw Goebbels it was already 1945, and much too late.

* * *

In the spring of 1943, General Vlasov visited the eastern front at the suggestion of Foreign Armies East. At the end of February he paid a two-week visit to units of Army Group Center, and in April he spent some days with Army Group North. He made speeches to the Russian battalions and to the local Russian population and was received everywhere with open arms. After many grim experiences the Russians now saw in him the only token of a future freedom, the guarantee of a better future. They no longer trusted the Germans as they had a year before. Keitel however found Vlasov's "brazen" conduct in delivering speeches outlining Russian nationalistic policies quite intolerable. On April 18 he ordered Vlasov's return to prison camp and threatened that if he continued his conduct he would be turned over to the Gestapo. We managed to prevent the worst excesses against him, and it was all we could do to salvage the beginnings we had made with our Russian liberation movement.

We had managed to convince General Zeitzler that our ideas were right, and he approved a major propaganda operation designed to step up the Russian desertion rate at the same time as we launched our next big offensive, Operation Citadel. We code-named the operation Silver Lining, and trained 1,500 officers and propaganda workers specially for it at the Dabendorf training camp. A key element of the operation was that the deserters had to be "welcomed" where possible by Russian reception teams. A special leaflet was designed with a facsimile of my signature instructing all our troops to treat deserters particularly well and find out if they wished to join the "Russian Liberation Army." Citadel was planned to commence at dawn on May 6; so on the evening of May 3, we issued the code word *Silver Lining:* the 18 million leaflets were to be released over Russian lines as the offensive began. There was a last-moment panic when we learned that *Silver Lining* was a long-existing Luftwaffe code word for commencing poison gas warfare, but this caused no real problems. As it turned out, Citadel was postponed for two months, and our Silver Lining operation, which began without the accompanying military offensive on the night of May 6, went off at half cock. It resulted in hundreds of deserters, but not the many thousands we had confidently expected.

When Hitler learned that the Russian nationalist policies propagated by Vlasov were threatening to get a firm foothold among the Russian auxiliaries aiding the German cause, he called a conference with Keitel and Zeitzler on June 8, 1943, at the Berghof, in Berchtesgaden, and destroyed all our hopes. "One thing has to be prevented," said Hitler, "that anybody on our own side gets any wrong ideas. We have to draw a clear distinction between the propaganda we broadcast to the other side and what we really propose to do."

Hitler persisted in his stubborn opposition to the plan for a real army of Russian troops under Vlasov's command, and he prohibited any concrete promises to them on the future of Russia after the German victory he even now expected. He permitted the phantom propaganda army, using Vlasov's name, to march on for propaganda reasons; and we could tell how much anxiety this caused Moscow, for we rounded up many Soviet agents parachuted behind our lines with explicit orders to infiltrate that army at all costs and to bring Vlasov back dead or alive into Communist hands. Moscow produced several anti-Vlasov leaflets, but faced with the dilemma of releasing them by the million from the air and giving Vlasov still wider publicity in the Soviet forces, they chose instead to have squads of agents in key areas distribute them by hand.

In the end Vlasov was denied success. We had sensed from the autumn of 1943 onward that the Russian liberation movement was at an end. Hitler decided to disarm all the foreign units and turn them over to the labor service, alleging that their desertion rate was too high. Within a few days, Colonel Herre, who had been appointed chief of staff to the general of volunteer units, countered Hitler's order with clear proof that the accusations leveled at his volunteers were untrue. The desertion rate was no greater than in any German unit, he pointed out; and he stated that there was nothing out of the ordinary that could have justified Hitler's order. Against this had to be set the fact that in view of the military and logistics problems, any dissolution of the foreign units would have catastrophic consequences for the German eastern front. Even Keitel showed he had doubts in this respect. In mid-October the decision was modified so that the foreign units were instead transferred to the western front, and Hitler waived the order that they were to be disarmed by force.

This decision of Hitler's proved once again his inability to understand warfare as Clausewitz did. Through this order, the General Staff lost its sole means of introducing psychological warfare into the conflict on the eastern front. The transfer of the foreign units to the western front from the end of 1943 onward was further proof of the insincerity and hollowness of Hitler's *Ostpolitik*. In any case, since he had not managed to persuade our allies the Italians, Rumanians, and Hungarians to defend their fatherlands on the Don and the Volga, how could he expect the Caucasians to fight any better if they were assigned to the Atlantic wall! They rightly interpreted this as a lack of confidence in their reliability and as proof that the Germans lacked the will to cooperate with them.

\* \* \*

From early 1944 onward we had other worries on our minds. Himmler and his SD began to take an interest in the Vlasov movement. He sensed in this movement a rival to the non-German divisions of the Waffen SS, the so-called volunteer divisions; above all, he saw it as an obstacle to his plans to settle and administer a Slav colonial empire in the future. All this meant that Foreign Armies East, the OKW's military propaganda section, and the Abwehr frequently had to restrain the SS from interfering. A veritable "war" broke out on several fronts, which was ultimately at the expense of our effort in the east.

Himmler's attitude unexpectedly changed in August 1944. Unabashed by the fact that he was the brain behind the "subhuman" theories of the Third Reich, and that the year before he had still referred to General Vlasov as "a traitor" and "a Russian swine," the rapidly deteriorating war situation now forced Himmler to adopt the exact line that my staff and I had long been preaching, and which the SD had fought against tooth and nail. Despite Rosenberg's protests (in which Rosenberg had the support of Keitel), Himmler sanctioned the creation of a "committee for the liberation of the Russian peoples," with General Vlasov at its head. At first, he promised the general ten divisions under his direct command; the figure was later reduced to three. Himmler also undertook to raise the status of Russian prisoners and the eastern workers within the Reich to the same level as those of other nationalities.

But this was all happening far too late. Born of opportunism and despair, the Vlasov army was doomed to failure from the start. On February 10, 1945, the first two (and only two) Russian infantry divisions, numbers 600 and 650, were formally handed over to Lieutenant General Vlasov by General Köstring, who had succeeded Hellmich as general of the volunteer units. The ceremony was attended by SS officials and party representatives and by Colonel Herre, on my behalf. The Russian flag was hoisted next to our own, and these divisions' arduous path into their fatherland began. Vlasov's attempt to salvage them from the ruins of the Reich and to transfer them to the Western Allies were thwarted by the Allies themselves, since the Yalta agreement bound all belligerents to surrender Allied prisoners to their countries of origin. Thus, he and his followers found themselves treading the bitter road into imprisonment and eventually onto the gallows of their own country, which they had wanted to liberate from the yoke of Stalinism.

If I survey the tragedy of the Vlasov movement now, after an interval of twenty-five years or more, I am bound to admit that, given Hitler's manic ideas, the movement was doomed to failure from the start. All the effort Germans and Russians alike had invested in the movement had been for nothing. For countless Russians and their friends, like General von Pannwitz (one of the divisional commanders),* it meant being branded as "traitors." The lesson I learned was that the psycho-political element cannot be suppressed in modern politics or warfare; and if it is not promptly and completely taken into account, or if the nature of modern war is misunderstood, then however great the means that are provided by a country for its armed forces, they will be wasted, and all sacrifice will be in vain. While Clausewitz could write of war as "a continuation of politics by other means," Lenin followed this dictum with a rider of his own: "Peace is only a continuation of war by other means."

Politicians are not the only ones whom this concerns, but officers as well; and they should not just take an interest in the political implications once armed conflict has actually broken out, but during the years of peace that precede the conflict.

---

* In 1945, Lieutenant General von Pannwitz commanded the Fifteenth (Cossack) Cavalry Corps.

## CHAPTER FOUR

# Defeat
# and
# Surrender

itler had always declined to bother himself seriously with
unpleasant facts and figures, and this tendency increased
after the unsuccessful attempt on his life in 1944. He was
interested only in hearing what fit in with his own train of thought
and was thrown completely off balance by the slightest contradiction. Even officers of a naturally contentious disposition like Halder
and Guderian found it difficult to put conflicting opinions to him
without being instantly interrupted. As I have already mentioned, I
conferred with him only rarely—four times in all. Had I regularly
accompanied the chief of staff and head of the operations branch
into Hitler's war conferences, my dismissal would have probably
occurred much earlier than it did.

Except for when Hitler ordered me to attend the meeting,
Zeitzler or Heusinger took my intelligence digests with them into
the conference room and incorporated my findings into their own
remarks. On the occasions when I did attend, I always stated my

opinions forthrightly and unambiguously, while at the same time trying to speak in a language that Hitler's peculiar mind would understand. At the first two meetings Hitler had listened to me with interest. But the more the war situation turned sour, the less he was inclined to heed his intelligence service.

The wartime chief of the British Imperial General Staff, Lord Alanbrooke, refers frequently in his diaries to comparable difficulties he had with Winston Churchill. But whereas Churchill was an enthusiastic amateur strategist, to the horror of his colleagues, and extremely stubborn in arguing his ideas, unlike Hitler he was ultimately open to persuasion. He rewarded his colleagues for sticking to their guns with his friendship and enduring loyalty. When someone argued persistently with Hitler that his plans were wrong—and worse still, was proved right by events—Hitler soon found ways of getting rid of him. Admiral Canaris was a case in point. When an Abwehr agent defected to the British from Turkey early in 1944, thereby compromising "Cicero," a famous Abwehr agent in Ankara, Walter Schellenberg cleverly fed the details to Hitler through Himmler's liaison officer at the führer's headquarters. As he had been suspicious of Canaris for some time, Hitler seized this as a pretext to strip the admiral of his espionage organization. On February 12, 1944, he ordered:

1. A uniform German intelligence service is to be established;
2. I put the reichsführer SS [Himmler] in charge of this German intelligence service; and
3. Insofar as this affects the military intelligence and counterespionage service, the reichsführer SS and the chief of the OKW are to take the necessary steps after due consultation.*

At first Colonel Georg Hansen was assigned to head the Abwehr's intelligence arm; and from June 1 all Abwehr functions were transferred to the RSHA under Himmler and Schellenberg. Thanks to Keitel's intervention as chief of the OKW, we were fortunately able to retain all frontline intelligence work on the eastern

---

* File H3/1539.

front purely under the aegis of the army (in other words, it remained in my control). We appointed Colonel Buntrock, head of our frontline intelligence section, as liaison officer with the RSHA; he was an expert on military intelligence, and I had complete faith in him. In his new capacity, he was directly subordinate to Keitel. Schellenberg, however, was dissatisfied with our success in retaining these units and tried very hard to get complete control of military intelligence work and our frontline intelligence organization, which was controlled by Major Baun. The senselessness of such a step should have been obvious to him. The Ic officers and the reconnaissance units reporting to them were parts of the military command structure. Had the Schellenberg proposals been put into effect, they would have meant the end of any kind of organized military command, as they would have destroyed one of the essential elements for making command decisions—the rapid, immediate, and conscientious provision of intelligence on the enemy. The war came to an end, however, before Schellenberg could achieve his aims. (I have always maintained that the active intelligence-procuring agency needs a firm guiding hand, and that a correct assessment of the military situation can only be based on a steady flow of intelligence. In other words, it is often necessary for intelligence procurement to be directed to particular assignments; and it is equally necessary to avoid jumping to conclusions supported by an inadequate intelligence foundation. At the time I could hardly have suspected that this mutual interplay of the procurement and analysis sides of intelligence work would decide the pattern of Germany's intelligence service after her defeat.)

* * *

By the spring of 1944 the military situation on the eastern front was so gloomy that I supplied our long-term intelligence digests only in sealed envelopes to other leading members of the General Staff and to Major Baun. I had to ask them not to show the reports to anybody else and to return the documents to me, "in view of the way the enemy position is viewed therein."

By March 28 we had assembled enough Abwehr material to

report that the Soviet offensive would be conducted without respite on every sector of the eastern front, and that the Russian command had been given the following objectives: they were to occupy Estonia, Latvia, and Lithuania; they were to advance through Rumania to Hungary, Bulgaria, and Yugoslavia; and they were to occupy what had once been Poland. We knew all the details of Marshal Zhukov's military plans, and of his anxiety lest the Germans launch a counteroffensive from Galicia; and, moreover, we knew in detail of the orders issued to Marshal Koniev and General Malinovski. In my summary issued two days later, on March 30, 1944, I opened with the words:

> The present situation on the eastern front is overshadowed by the anticipated general enemy offensive against our Army Groups A and South. As it proceeds, a more menacing situation than ever before has emerged on the eastern front, and in the not too distant future this may result in far-reaching political, military, and economic repercussions on the rest of the war in Europe.

I recommended that the only prospect of regaining the initiative lay in bold command decisions taken without regard to the loss of ground they might involve. I predicted that, by occupying the Balkan countries, Poland, and the Baltic states, the Russians would try to obtain by the end of 1944 a position on the very frontiers of the Reich.*

Hitler refused to sanction the necessary strategic withdrawals. He hung on to the Crimea until early May, when he was forced to order his troops to abandon their positions there. By early June the Soviet armies had advanced to the frontiers of Poland, and all the indications were that they planned a major offensive against Army Group Center, commanded by Field Marshal Busch, which was defending Poland and East Prussia. On June 13 I warned that the enemy had recently started introducing fresh strength into the areas facing the army group: "Particular attention should be paid to the areas southeast and east of Bobruisk, on both sides of Chausy,

---

* The report and appendices are in file H3/1531.

along the highway northeast of Orsha, and on both sides of Vitebsk." These were the precise sectors of the front that were to be breached a few days later; the only information we could not ascertain with certainty was the date. I suggested, "According to various items of information, there are at present increasing indications that the offensive will begin between June 15 and 20." But I added that Russian security was so good that we had never yet managed to predict the actual date and hour of an attack.*

The Soviet offensive began early on June 22, supported by 4,000 aircraft. Within a few days the German front line had caved in, and within a month the Soviet armies were on the very frontiers of East Prussia. As I had also predicted on June 13, a second phase of the Soviet offensive began a few days after the first, with a general attack on Lemberg (Lvov).

\* \* \*

A few days after the Soviet offensive began, on July 1, 1944, I was stricken by severe blood poisoning and hospitalized at the field hospital at Angerburg; after a short sojourn there, I was transferred to a hospital in Breslau. It was this that probably resulted in my being "overlooked" by the Gestapo when their witch-hunt after the unsuccessful bomb plot against Hitler began. I played no active part in the conspiracy, but it would be untrue were I to deny I knew that one was afoot. Some months before, my colleague General Heusinger had hinted to me about the elements of the conspiracy in enough detail for me to gather what he was talking about. I regarded my own small task as being to insure that the military intelligence organization was staffed only with officers upon whom we could count in such an emergency, and I asked Colonel Kleikamp of the personnel branch to make sure that I alone decided who was appointed to Ic posts in the near future. I was also aware of the opposition within the army to Hitler. In the winter of 1941–42 I had a visit from the later General von Tresckow, who was at the time operations officer of Army Group Center and whom I knew well from staff college. Comparing notes on the military situation,

---

* File H3/1662.

we both reached the conclusion that the campaign (and that meant the war as well) was bound to end in defeat, not because it could not be militarily or politically won, but because of Hitler's continued interference, which resulted in such elementary blunders that defeat was inevitable. We saw only one solution: Hitler would have to go. At the time, we had broken off this dangerous train of thought somewhat dismayed at our own presumption. We had, after all, sworn oaths of allegiance to Hitler, and we had grown up in the old Prussian officer tradition.

After Heusinger hinted to me that wheels were now moving, I discussed the actual tactics with my old regimental comrade General Hellmuth Stieff, who was by now head of the General Staff's organization branch. I stressed the importance of keeping the circle of accomplices as small as possible and of preparing the coup d'état with extreme care if it was to succeed. Another of the conspirators, Colonel von Freytag-Loringhoven, called on me at the field hospital at Angerburg about three days before July 20 to warn me that the plot was now under way.

Germans—and here one is probably entitled to generalize—do not make the best plotters. I believe it was Lenin, sitting in his sealed railway car in which the Germans transported him from Swiss exile back to Russia in 1917, who fumed: "If the Germans want to start a revolution, they buy a platform ticket first!" My friends paid for the failure of the conspiracy with their lives. Freytag-Loringhoven committed suicide, Stauffenberg was shot, and Stieff was hanged. Colonel von Roenne, who had transferred from my branch to take command of Foreign Armies West, was hanged in October for the part he had played. Fortunately Colonel Wessel, my chief assistant, smashed open my filing cabinet at Angerburg and destroyed all the incriminating documents he found in them, particularly my correspondence with General Halder (who, like Heusinger, was incarcerated for many months in a concentration camp after the failure of the plot).

The ethics of the plot have subsequently exercised many minds and resulted in much moralizing by both participants and bystanders. My own view is clear; I have always believed that high treason is high treason. It can be morally justified, however, by an exceptional national emergency, the only circumstance imaginable to me. Together with those of my friends who took the ultimate risk, I would accept that Hitler's pernicious leadership provided such an emergency. Given the rigidness of the Allied demand for unconditional surrender, however, it is difficult to see how the putsch could have succeeded in absolute terms. The plotters were certainly aware of this. A few weeks earlier, Colonel Hansen—who had originally headed the southeast section of Foreign Armies East for the first few months of my office, and trusted me implicitly—had come to see me at our headquarters in Angerburg about a very delicate affair. He confided to me that he (as Piekenbrock's successor in charge of Abwehr espionage) had arranged to meet an "emissary of Churchill" on a lonely road somewhere in southern France, and was going to put to him the all-important question of whether the British government would be prepared to negotiate an armistice with a new German government if Hitler were overthrown. Hansen returned some days later, having met the emissary as planned; I had never before seen him looking so dejected. The emissary had stated that the British position was that there could be no exception to the doctrine of unconditional surrender, and he was not empowered to talk about anything else. Hansen was executed with the rest of the plotters.

* * *

For many years my colleagues and I had trained ourselves to see things through the enemy's eyes—to think as he would think and calculate his intentions. From the start we had sensed the growing Russian confidence in final victory, and now we could only agree that this confidence was justified. Early in October 1944 I told my more intimate colleagues that I considered the war was lost and we must begin thinking of the future. We had to think ahead and plan for the approaching catastrophe. These thoughts and discussions occupied us for many months, during which the burden of everyday work still had to be done. I was aided to an increasing extent by my deputy and successor (both in April 1945 and in May 1968) Lieutenant Colonel Gerhard Wessel.

These dangerous internal conferences were aided by the solidarity of my staff, which had withstood many a crisis before. We were screened from hostile and curious fellow officers by the fact that we could rely unconditionally on each other. The older General Staff officers were by and large hostile toward the regime and its ideology. This was not the case, however, with the rising generation of officers, particularly with the recently appointed "National Socialist leadership officer"—Hitler's emulation of the Soviet commissar principle—which each unit and section now had to have. I had selected Major von Kalkreuth to act as our "commissar," and when he protested to me that he could not reconcile this with his Christian ethics, I replied that that was precisely why I had chosen him. It had not escaped my attention that the war was taking its toll of many young officers' personal sets of values, and that the political indoctrination was resulting in either boundless national socialism or an equally unbridled fatalism at the General Staff's headquarters. I recall that one of our female staff was a particularly fervent Nazi, until we gave her official clearance to listen to and monitor the British radio broadcasts. By the end of 1944 she had lost all her enthusiasm for Hitler.

Guderian had done what he could to build up our military strength on the eastern front, but in the late summer of 1944 Hitler announced his plans for a major offensive in the Ardennes to his senior advisers, and large segments of Guderian's carefully built up defenses were dismantled to provide the forces Hitler needed in the West. The Ardennes offensive began on December 16, while the Russians patiently waited with their own onslaught. Guderian and I could see it coming, and using our well-tried intelligence methods, we knew exactly where and with what strength the Russian blow would fall. Particularly valuable were the maps my branch prepared showing the lines of communication between the Soviet agents on our side of the front line and their controllers in Russian territory. On December 24 Guderian took these reports to "Eagle's Nest," Hitler's western headquarters at Ziegenberg; but Hitler not only rejected his demand for massive reinforcement of the eastern front at the expense of this futile offensive in the West, but even dis-

missed our intelligence picture of the Soviet buildup as "pure bluff."*
On the thirty-first Guderian again warned Hitler in person that the
eastern front was in danger of collapsing like a house of cards; Hitler
indicated that he felt the eastern front was strong enough to cope with
any Russian offensive. On January 8, 1945, I handed General
Guderian a further appreciation of the situation drawn up by my
branch. I recommended that we evacuate East Prussia if the rest of
the eastern front—and that meant Berlin—was to be held: "The loss
of East Prussia will hurt less than total defeat." I believed that the
Soviet offensive would commence on or about January 12.

On January 12, 1945, the Soviet invasion began with an offensive by Marshal Koniev's First Ukrainian Front, followed by the
Third White Russian Front on the thirteenth, and the First White
Russian Front under Marshal Zhukov and the Second White Russian Front under Marshal Rokossovsky on the next day. Within a
few days the whole eastern front was in flames from the upper
Vistula to East Prussia. The most horrifying reports of Russian
atrocities began to reach us. Early in December a Ukrainian deserter had reported to one of my frontline units that in a Red Army
briefing session in Warsaw he and his comrades had been told that,
on Stalin's orders, robbing and looting were strictly forbidden in the
occupied Polish territory, and they were to adopt a friendly attitude
toward the Polish population, but that the Soviet troops were permitted to do what they wanted on German soil. My own family and
the families of many of my colleagues were now in the path of this
cruel Russian colossus.

Hitler had strictly forbidden officers to evacuate their families
to the West, but I could not stand by and leave mine to their fate.
Besides, it was vital for my future mission to know that they were
safe in the West. But it was a simple matter for an intelligence
organization to forge the necessary movement papers, with the
faked signature of the gauleiter of Silesia. General Vlasov's troops
helped them to load what they could onto some trucks; and on
January 21 my wife left Liegnitz, in Silesia, in a car driven by

---

* Contrary to the version given in other accounts, I did not accompany Guderian
to Ziegenberg on any occasion.

Major Baun—with our four children, the youngest under three, packed in the back. A small truck followed with their servant and some cases that were later robbed at Oberstdorf. They drove to Reichenbach, in Silesia, where the Vlasov units were billeted on an estate. The next day they continued westward to Dresden, were Baun's wife ran a small hotel. The city was already filling with refugees, so they left again for Thuringia, where I had some relatives living at Rossbach, near Naumburg. It was fortunate that they did not stay in Dresden, for a few nights later the city was devastated by an Allied saturation raid in which over 100,000 civilians died, including the luckless wife of Major Baun. Baun himself had collected the files and archives of Foreign Armies East and drove several truckloads of them to Naumburg, where they were stacked in the empty wine cellars of the vineyards. There I thought that both my family and the files would be safe from Russian hands.

Apart from these natural worries about our families, we were unconcerned about what fate held in store for us personally. This was hardly surprising, for we had managed by good intelligence work to obtain shortly after the Teheran and Yalta conferences full details of the Allied plans for destroying and partitioning Germany. We did not have much hope that the enemy coalition would fall apart immediately after the war (a vain hope that was widely believed in the front lines). But on the other hand we could not accept either that this was the end for Germany; and it was this stoicism that encouraged me to apply my mind to the problems of the postwar period and what my duties to Germany then should be. Obviously, once our intelligence network had been broken up it would be difficult, if not impossible, to reconstruct an efficient secret service for many years. Moreover, the longer the reconstruction took, the easier a Communist enemy would find it to penetrate the new service. It might have seemed a pointless and illogical exercise to many in early 1945, but to me it was clear that if a new German intelligence service was going to emerge in the postwar period, there had to be as little interruption as possible. It was obvious to me that the future German government would need such a service. From the personnel angle this would be possible only if we could resume our work immediately following the war, using my existing intelligence staff and my leading colleagues as a nucleus.

There were considerations of foreign policy that also argued in favor of salvaging as much of our intelligence organization as possible: the face of communism had changed only in outward appearance, but its aims remained the same. Stalin had mobilized the energy of the Russian people by appealing to their patriotic instincts and by encouraging an imitation Soviet nationalism. Hitler's senseless *Ostpolitik* and his attitude toward the Russians had been grist for the Soviet dictator's mill. All our experience taught us that Stalin was not going to abandon his aims now but would pursue his expansionist plans still further. His goal would continue to be the world revolution that was going to "bring the blessings of socialism to all mankind." My staff and I anticipated that the need to defend the West would sooner or later force the West to make common cause with us against communism. Just when that would be, of course, we had no idea.

\* \* \*

We were strengthened in this conviction by a political appreciation drafted by Churchill, which reached us by devious means in February 1945. Perhaps I should indicate here that it is the duty of every sophisticated intelligence service to keep open a channel of communication with the enemy's intelligence service. Perhaps it may sound strange that while I was able to keep such channels active during the Third Reich—although it might have cost me my neck— I was unable to do so during the latter days of my work in the Federal Intelligence Service. Such contacts can often be of great advantage. I have already mentioned the channel we established to the British Military Mission in Moscow during 1943. It was through an even more direct channel that the British MI6 (a military intelligence organization) supplied us a copy of Mr. Churchill's political intelligence appreciation of February 1945. When it landed on my desk at Zossen I saw that Churchill's analysis viewed our position far too favorably in the East but that it was entirely accurate in its picture of Soviet potential and intentions. The document indicated that the British did not share the optimism of their American allies on "Uncle Joe's" democratic qualities; and it revealed that they had few illusions about the future development of Poland and the Balkan countries, including Hungary, into Soviet satellites. I now believe MI6 supplied this document to us so that we might enable them to warn the British cabinet how exaggerated was the British estimate of our ability to withstand the Russian onslaught in the East. I informed General Guderian of the existence of this explosive document, and with his approval filed it with no further action. It was destroyed at the end of the war.

On February 15 the first sections of my branch, Foreign Armies East, transferred by railroad from Zossen to Reichenhall, in Bavaria. Ten days later I signed a further long-term summary of the enemy's intentions in which I examined the probable main directions of the coming Soviet offensives and the implications to be drawn from Marshal Zhukov's appointment as the supreme commander of the forces operating against us. "While hitherto the Soviet strategic command has been guided almost exclusively by military considerations," I pointed out, "it is now coming increasingly under the influence of political considerations. In this connection we can clearly discern their endeavor to seize the appropriate positions of strength, regardless of any agreements reached in the Teheran and Yalta conferences, in order to confront their allies with a fait accompli as far as possible." I considered the object of the coming Soviet operations to be the destruction of our armies in the East and the rapid occupation of the central German industrial area around Leipzig and Halle. All the intelligence we received indicated that the primary thrust was to be expected from the sector between Görlitz and Schwedt, although there was still no indication as to when the Russians would resume their westward drive. While we were awaiting that moment, I turned over in my mind the various ways in which the Russians could be checked, and one unorthodox manner occurred to me: on March 3, 1945, I sent Guderian a note on the possibility of using huge forest fires as a weapon of war.

Between 1866 and 1939 there had been a number of forest

fires in that area—our files contained all the information I needed. My proposal was to find ways of setting fire to the 400 miles of forest front, particularly in the area between Görlitz and Guben. Pine forests were ideal, especially after a long period of drought. This, and a minimum wind-force of four, might be expected late in April or in August, while the combination of pine forest and the appropriate conditions was not at all likely to be found in southern or northern Germany, so the Russians could not retaliate in kind. I explained, "Every major forest fire has shown that once it really gets going it is impossible to stop even with enormous fire-fighting effort." I proposed, "To achieve our object of annihilating the enemy's equipment and personnel, the fires must be started in such a way that the enemy has no chance of escape (a ring of fire)." My branch calculated that fires like these could be started with relatively modest means—some 360 sorties by FW-190 fighter-bombers releasing incendiaries along a hundred-mile line. I asked for an order from the führer to prepare for such an operation, but that was the last I ever heard of it.

Another opportunity for stemming the Soviet invasion occurred when we examined air reconnaissance reports which showed that only four railroad bridges crossing the river Vistula from east to west were still intact. On March 24 I advised Göring's operations staff, "Luftwaffe attack on Vistula bridges at Cracow, Deblin, Warsaw, and Thorn is urgently needed. Enemy supplies for Neisse and Oder fronts dependent on the bridges at Warsaw and Thorn." On the twenty-sixth General Koller, the Luftwaffe's chief of staff, put this proposal to Hitler, but only reluctantly, for the special aircraft that would be needed had been earmarked for an ambitious plan for a strategic air attack on the entire western Soviet electricity supply. Hitler decided, "In that case I would prefer to dispense for the time being with the attack on the Vistula bridges; they can be done later." In desperation I called the attention of the SS—who controlled the sabotage units operating behind Russian lines—to the four bridges. "Their destruction or damage would bring very real relief to our troops," I cabled them. The reply reached me the next day: "Planning re one of the bridges listed is in hand. Execution of operation

depends on fuel allocation, aircraft allocation, and various personnel matters." I see I wrote on this reply, "That means we can't
expect any action for the next six months!"* The Vistula bridges
were still intact when the great final Soviet offensive on Berlin
started a few days later.

There could be no doubt as to what faced Germany. From one
of our intelligence units we obtained a report on a leaflet handed
to every Red Army soldier which contained Stalin's Order No. 5, instructing that the German people were to be annihilated, all German
factories and property to be destroyed, and the "German beast
stamped out in its kennels." On the western front, a copy of the
Allied plan for postwar Germany, a brown-covered, inch-thick
folder with the code name Eclipse, fell into our hands. To our
amazement, the partition that was proposed for postwar Germany
made Berlin a Four-Power enclave in the heart of a Russian-con-
trolled zone, and Thuringia, where I had believed our precious
Foreign Armies East archives were safe from the Russian invasion,
was clearly assigned to the Soviet Union.

In what was to prove my final intelligence digest, early in April,
I indicated that the impending loss of both Königsberg, the capital
of East Prussia, and Vienna would release fresh Russian strength
against us, and that massive troop reinforcements were pouring
into the area between Küstrin and Frankfurt-an-der-Oder for the
final assault on Berlin. The digest was put before Hitler by Guderian's successor, the infantry general Krebs. Hitler dismissed it as
"absolutely idiotic" and defeatist, and on April 9 I was relieved of
my position as head of Foreign Armies East. Lieutenant Colonel
Wessel succeeded me as acting head.

* * *

Meanwhile, I had ordered my family and the files of Foreign Armies
East evacuated from Thuringia. They were loaded aboard two
trucks, and the documents were brought out of their hiding place
in the wine cellars at Naumburg and loaded up too. Near Leuna,

---

* File H3/653: and I added, "Preserve! Very important!"

the two trucks ran into an air raid, but they fortunately escaped damage. Later that night, near Hof, they were halted by an SS unit and forced into a nearby SS barracks for their load and papers to be examined. Under the circumstances this exposed them all to a danger hardly less acute than the one they had so recently escaped in the air raid on Leuna. But the two skillful drivers—including Lieutenant Baun, the son of our frontline intelligence section's chief —were on their toes. They found a second gate unlocked at the rear of the barracks, and through this they drove the two trucks out and all escaped. My family found temporary accommodations in an industrialist's country house at Cham, a provincial capital near the Czech border, in the Bavarian forest. The truckloads of secret files and documents continued southward in safety to Berchtesgaden and nearby Reichenhall, where part of Foreign Armies East was waiting for them.

It was at this country house, Gutmanning, that my wife and I celebrated her forty-first birthday on April 17 with a modest party appropriate to the grim circumstances. I invited all my former colleagues, officers, and men, and a number of the female staff. During the first days of April, I had gone with Wessel to pay a private visit to Lieutenant Colonel Baun, controller of the Walli organization, at Bad Elster, some sixty miles north of Cham. In the hotel there, I briefed Baun on my plans for the future. My view was that there would be a place even for Germany in a Europe rearmed for defense against communism. Therefore we must set our sights on the Western powers, and give ourselves two objectives: to help defend against Communist expansion and to recover and reunify Germany's lost territories. (The latter objective would of course find little acclaim from the victorious nations.) But I felt that the common defense interests of the Western powers must inevitably lead them to recognize that without Germany all Europe was lost. This was why we could realistically expect them to show an interest in exploiting our intelligence service for espionage work in the East. Given the total defeat that was now approaching, it was probably utopian to entertain any notion of rebuilding the service immediately after the war ended, as the Allies would destroy every organization sponsored by the Third Reich. But the attempt was still worthwhile so that someday a future German government could take the organization over, using our present staff as the expert nucleus.

Of course many questions arose. We could not know when a postwar German government would be set up. And it was questionable in April 1945 whether we could succeed in establishing with one of the three Western powers a working basis that would prove acceptable to a later German government. We could not work purely as mercenaries for a former enemy if we were not to burden the future intelligence service with the psychological stigma of having been a quisling organization. I therefore later tried to establish a degree of formal legality for our plans; in the last weeks of the war I outlined the plans to General August Winter, deputy chief of the OKW's operations staff, and secured his blessing for them (since he was the only OKW authority I was able to reach).* After the war I chanced to meet Grand Admiral Dönitz in the prison camp at Wiesbaden. Dönitz was formally Hitler's successor as head of state. He also approved my plans.

During the Bad Elster stage in our planning, shortly before my dismissal, the question naturally arose which of the three Western powers would be the best partner for us. I discussed it at some length with my principal assistant, Lieutenant Colonel Wessel. Through Lieutenant Colonel Baun, using the channel to which I have referred earlier, we sent an offer of our future services to the British secret service. Baun received no acknowledgment, but from events in the Bavarian mountains some weeks later we gathered that it had been received by the British. Taking everything into consideration, it seemed more expedient to make our approach to the American military forces. I suspected that once the shooting stopped the Americans

---

* Winter confirms this in a memorandum in the Gehlen organization's files, dated July 18, 1952. In the conversation at Königsee near Berchtesgaden, I told him that one result of unconditional surrender would be that our priceless files on the Soviet Union might either fall into Russian hands or be destroyed or vanish into low-level Allied agencies which would not appreciate their value. Winter noted that I proposed withdrawing with these files and my top associates into the mountains until the hue and cry died down, before offering our services to the West, as in this way we would be serving our fatherland as best we could: "For my part, I wholeheartedly approved of General Gehlen's proposals."

would probably recover a sense of objectivity toward us more rapidly than their European allies, and subsequent history bore me out on this point.

Baun was a first-class intelligence procurer who not only knew how to give his contacts worthwhile assignments and proper leadership but looked after them properly as well. He worked mainly with Russian volunteers and was able to maintain contacts in the heart of Moscow until the very end. He agreed at once to make the necessary preparations as far as his networks were concerned, and I told him what I wanted. His adjutant took part in these discussions, but no other people were taken into our confidence. From early April 1945, his headquarters, Walli I, was in the Algäu—a province which was overrun by the Americans at the end of the month and later occupied by the French. At the arrival of the Allied forces, Baun and his staff transferred in plain clothes to a prearranged rendezvous, while most of his intelligence workers went underground and waited to hear details of their future employment. He secured his files in a similar manner to those of Foreign Armies East, putting the most important files on microfilm, and burying them or hiding them in various locations.

During the last few weeks of the war events came thick and fast, making our preparations no easier. On April 12, my colleagues insisted on holding a small farewell party for me to mark my departure from Foreign Armies East. Three years had passed since I had taken the branch over and started to build it up. It was a gloomy celebration, for nobody knew what now lay ahead of us. That our prognosis on the coming great conflict between East and West was shared by Moscow was shown by intelligence reports now reaching us. In mid-April we learned that a group of Soviet agents had been parachuted behind our lines near Berlin on the night of the seventh with instructions to prepare for the entry of Russian troops into Berlin on about the twentieth. "They also had the assignment of reconnoitering British and American preparations for attacking the Russians, and they were particularly instructed: 'in the event that Berlin is captured by the British and Americans, the agents are to destroy all their papers, but on no account identify themselves as agents.' "* The implications were obvious, and they spoke even more loudly from the statements of a Russian prisoner captured southwest of Küstrin on the eve of the final attack against Berlin, led by Marshals Koniev and Zhukov on April 16:

> Big offensive will begin on April 16 at latest. Artillery bombardment first, 300 or 400 rounds per gun. Attack with 100 tanks per regiment. Prisoner speaks of new assault tanks with 180-millimeter gun and of new 180-millimeter heavy mortars. Object of the offensive is to beat the Americans to the capture of Berlin. Russian officers anticipate clashes and offensive engagements with Americans; they will have to drench the Americans "by accident" with an artillery bombardment, so that they get a taste of the Red Army's lash. Troops have been ordered to put their uniforms in order and wash and shave every day to give a cultivated impression.†

It was a depressing situation, but perhaps it was the very gravity of the hour that enabled my former staff and me to perceive that whatever fate might hold in store for us, we would try to remain together and work in harmony as we always had in the past. In mid-April I began my own preparations. I scouted around for suitable hideouts in the Bavarian mountains, and supervised the microfilming and burying of the branch's files. The whole branch reassembled at Reichenhall in full working order, with the exception of a small group under Major Scheibe, which had been detached to the northern command staff of the OKW in Holstein, near the Danish border.

In view of my dismissal, there was one minor snag to be overcome. I had earlier expressed to the director of army personnel, General Burgdorff, a desire to command a combat division, and he now assumed that that was still my ambition. I asked him to post me instead to the generals' reserve, "to enable me to train my successor," Colonel Wessel. I also claimed that Heinrich Himmler had a special job for me. Since Burgdorff was a pious

---

* File H3/215.
† File FHO/2.

Nazi, my claim sufficed and he released me to the generals' reserve in the War Department. To give substance to my claim, I telephoned Schellenberg and asked him if Himmler would be interested in a detailed study of the rise and fall of the Polish underground resistance, to see if we could learn anything from the Polish experience that might be of use to us in the ordeal we might well be about to face. Schellenberg phoned me back not long afterward to confirm that this was a subject which would particularly interest Himmler. Over the next eight days I completed on the basis of our documents a very bulky study on the Polish resistance. I concluded that there was no point whatever in Germany's adopting similar underground methods if we were defeated or reached armistice with our enemies. Major Hiemenz agreed to drive to northern Germany to deliver the document to Schellenberg for Himmler. I drove with him as far as Cham so that I could see my wife and children, who had been joined by Frau Hiemenz. Then I returned to Reichenhall. As it turned out, I was not to see my family again until July 1946, and much would have happened to me before then.

* * *

On April 28, 1945, our odyssey began. We buried our documents in scattered locations near the Wendelstein mountain, in Algäu province, and at Hunsrück. Since we correctly assumed that we could not prevent some of the hiding places from being unearthed, we tried to duplicate the caches as far as possible so that we would have at least one set of everything at our disposal when we came to set up shop again. We arranged to split up into three groups, which were to hide in the Alps until the hue and cry accompanying the end of the war died down—perhaps three weeks. These groups would then report to the nearest American unit and go into captivity. Since the Americans would probably try to capitalize on our expert intelligence workers, each group was instructed to refuse any kind of cooperation until they had been shown written orders to that effect signed by me.

I detailed one of our reserve officers, Chief Forester Weck, to find and prepare three hideouts in the Alps—mountain huts which were to be hard to find, but easy to reach with provisions and with a good supply of water. The huts were to be situated so that we had a good view of all roads of approach but could escape unobserved if danger threatened. Weck did his work well, finding one hut near Fritz-am-Sand, not far from the village of Reit-im-Winkel, on the Austrian border. The second hut was Wild Moss Lodge, on the Wild Kaiser slopes, and the third was Elend Lodge (a corruption of the Old German *Ödland* "barren ground"), near Lake Spitzing.

I packed my belongings and left for the easternmost of our assembly points, the hut at Fritz-am-Sand. But hardly had I arrived when I learned that Himmler had issued orders for the liquidation of General Heusinger and myself, so I decided prudence was the better part of valor, and moved to the westernmost hideout, the Elend Lodge, instead, as too many people had learned of my intention of hiding at the other. While I was on my way I picked up a radio message from Baun, who had settled with his intelligence procurement section in the Algäu. He asked me to rendezvous briefly with him at Hindelang to give him further instructions. Instead of my usual Horch automobile, I took an elderly DKW for the rendezvous on the other side of the mountains. My old staff officer from the Polish campaign, Captain G——, accompanied me. As we drove up the mountain pass we ran into retreating sections of one of our divisions which had been in combat. They had been heavily outnumbered by American forces as they tried to defend the mountain passes. It was fortunate that I had chosen the smaller car for, short though this stretch of highway was, it took time and effort to fight our way through the traffic jams. It was dawn before we reached the southern foothills of the mountains, and there our way was barred by the combat troops, who told us that the mountain highways were all blocked either by fighting or by demolished bridges. So we had to turn back without having established contact with Baun's group.

It was on the return journey that I asked to be set down

somewhere below the Elend Lodge, not far from the so-called Zipfelwirts, an inn right on the Austrian frontier. I left the road and climbed upward through a valley off to one side. The climb was tougher than I had expected. There was deep snow, and it was heavy going. Weck had warned me more than once that there were scattered SS units around the Elend Lodge, who had at one stage wanted to take over the hut themselves. That was why I considered it better to use this side valley for my approach. I must admit that had I known at the beginning how arduous it is to climb in snow without path or road, I would not have made the attempt. The climb took me many hours, or so it seemed, and as I climbed my thoughts circled endlessly around the events of the past few weeks and the uncertainty that lay ahead. My sober and doubting intellect reproached me, as I toiled my way upwards, that our enterprise could hardly be more utopian. But my resolve remained unshaken by this inward skepticism. These mental processes did however have the effect of passing the time during what had seemed at first an interminable ascent. I was finally redeemed by the sight of open snow ahead as the forest came to an end. A gently sloping snowscape unfolded ahead of me, in the middle of which nestled a large, low-roofed, wooden hut, with broad eaves, a tall brick chimney, and a veranda. This was the Elend Lodge. A wisp of smoke curling up out of the chimney informed me that it was occupied, and as I approached I found my comrades and colleagues from the group I had dispatched to this hideout waiting for me—six officers and three of our female assistants.

It was important for our plan that we should not be captured too soon. We had to bear in mind that despite the Americans' reluctance to climb into the mountains, they might still institute a search for us. On the other hand we did not expect any search during the hours of darkness. So as dawn broke each day, one section of our group would climb higher into the mountains, while the three girls and the two younger officers who could not manage the difficult climb because of their injuries stayed below and kept guard on the lodge. We usually climbed to the Auer

Ridge and set up camp about a mile southeast of the Red Wall, in a terrain that was partially open and windswept, and partially covered by green forestation. We passed the days studying the countryside and rejoicing in the first signs of green shooting up gradually through the snows. Had we not been burdened with uncertainty about the future, had this not been May 1945, this mountain sojourn would have been a beautiful and idyllic respite, memorable for the stimulating conversations we conducted sitting in the sunshine as much as for anything else. I myself had known this country since 1921, when I had been at infantry school here and learned to ski on these slopes.

As dusk fell each evening, we would set off down the mountain slopes again. Before we reached the Elend Lodge we would check to make sure our comrades had hung out a tablecloth on the washline as the signal that all was clear. A few days after the capitulation, three civilians appeared at the lodge during our absence, looking for me by name. We suspected that they were German-speaking members of the British secret service, a suspicion that was later confirmed. No doubt this was a result of the signal we had sent to London via Baun some weeks before. Somewhat less placid was the visit paid by a small American infantry unit, which carried out a textbook raid on the lodge, raking it with machine-gun fire before storming it and searching it from top to bottom. They subjected the fortunately uninjured occupants to a thorough interrogation and took the three female staff and the two young officers with them down into the village where they were put through a further grilling. They then asked their captives where they would like to be discharged to, and all asked to be permitted to stay at the Elend Lodge for the time being. When we returned that evening from our mountain encampment, we found the tablecloth on the line and our five loyal comrades waiting for us. They proudly showed us their discharge papers from American captivity, bearing the provisional address "Elend Lodge." It was an unexpected stroke of good fortune, for it enabled us to keep at bay other people interested in requisitioning the hut for themselves.

Chief Forester Weck acted as liaison man between us and the other groups. He had exchanged his Wehrmacht uniform for that of a forester and was able to move about freely in consequence. Somewhat later in May, with the thawing of the snow and the warmer nights, we had to abandon our practice of leaving the hut each morning and returning in the evening, since the danger of being raided by night was now just as strong as by day. We set up a permanent camp of carefully camouflaged tents in a fir-tree glade south of the Auer Ridge, and here we passed another week of fine weather. These days of living in the arms of nature were truly enchanting. We had grown accustomed to the peace, and our ears were attuned to nature's every sound.

Meanwhile, Weck had not been inactive either. From the forestry office he obtained the key to a secluded and almost inaccessible hut near the Maroldschneid Ridge (it was so well hidden that despite the clearest directions it took us a long time to find it). The hut was at the crest of a steep rock face, densely surrounded by forestation on the other three sides, but with a magnificent view across the mountains. We enjoyed every minute of these last days of freedom to the full. The chamois which we encountered all about us were a particular delight, and they gradually lost all fear of us.

By now it was the end of the third week in May, and high time for us to put our plan into action. It was time to go down into the valley and report to the nearest American unit. The parents of one of our men, Major Schoeller, lived at Fischhausen, on Lake Schliersee. He suggested we spend the Whitsun holiday there, and report next day to the Americans. We decided to make our way down from our hideout along the northern face of the Maroldschneid Ridge, cross the Ruchen Heads, the Red Wall, and the Taubenstein slopes to the east of Lake Spitzing, and then follow the highway down to Fischhausen. We were to keep off the actual road and walk about halfway up the slopes west of it, through Neuhaus. It was important to stay as high up the slopes as we could, so as not to fall into the hands of one of the numerous patrols moving about lower down. We were determined not to be taken prisoner. We wanted to surrender on our own initiative to the Americans. It was all part of the plan.

Under other circumstances, our mountain trek would have been an unforgettable and wonderful experience, but for us this was still almost war. The evening before, we had stripped off our badges of rank and exchanged our red-striped trousers— symbol of the General Staff—for others, so now we were heading like countless other stragglers in a generally westward direction. The view from the Taubenstein mountain, which all five of us— the two injured officers were left behind—reached together, was superb. Then we split up and set off again at ten-minute intervals. Near the Lower Schönfeld Alp there was a French mountain unit; we could see them through our binoculars. We had no choice but to cross this valley if we were not to spend the night on the bare mountain. But the little French unit was lying there at ease, its mules grazing and the soldiers scattered among the dozen or so houses. As I approached the houses, a window opened and a somewhat curious French mountain infantryman looked out. I walked steadily on, greeted him with a "Bonjour, Monsieur!" and went past him; he returned my salutation and closed the window, evidently satisfied.

Soon after, we passed the northern end of Lake Spitzing, not far from the mountain railroad station. Here too we had to take care, for the road was frequented by American jeeps and military police patrols. By evening we were safe in the house of Major Schoeller's parents at Fischhausen. Three days later we would be in the hands of the American intelligence service; and three months hence, we would be in an American DC-3, flying the Atlantic to Washington.

# Part Two

## The
## Partnership

CHAPTER FIVE

# Gentlemen's Agreement

week after we sailed from the United States, our liberty ship berthed at Le Havre in northwestern France. It was July 1946. In Nuremberg the war crimes trial was coming to an end; Europe was swept by hunger and devastation; and the cold war was just beginning between East and West. Captain Eric Waldman, who had arrived at USFET's G-2 section* from Washington in June, was waiting for us at dockside, and got my small group off the boat even before the American soldiers were able to disembark. We were driven in a number of cars to Orly Airport, outside Paris; I went in a U.S. Army reconnaissance car alone with Waldman, who briefed me about everything that had happened at USFET's G-2 that would be of consequence for the implementation of our combined intelligence project. From Orly we were flown to Frankfurt in a special plane.

Our new home was to be at Oberursel, which had become

---

* That is, the military intelligence section of United States Forces, European Theater.

famous as a Luftwaffe interrogation center during the war. The chief of USFET's G-2, Brigadier General Edwin L. Sibert, was now using the compound for the same purpose. For the time being, we were regarded as a study group. Three houses in the compound were placed at our disposal; they served as both office and living quarters. The American liaison team, consisting of Captain Waldman and a new arrival, Lieutenant Colonel John R. Deane, was housed separately in a fourth building, the so-called Blue House. A few days later we also saw Captain John Boker again, who had returned to a staff post at USFET.

A formality came first: we were discharged from prisoner of war status so that we could move around at will, bound only by the need to return to our place of employment. The first few days were taken up with conferences with the two American officers on the question of how best to organize our work and how American and German aims could best be reconciled. The American Colonel William Russell Philp, who was now in command of Oberursel, would supervise the work and furnish logistic support. There was never any suggestion that this should be an all-American affair, nor that I was in any way betraying Germany in dealing with the forces of occupation. It may seem now of purely academic interest, but this was precisely why, before leaving Germany, I had secured the formal approval of General Winter and Admiral Dönitz for my future collaboration with the Americans in the interests of Germany.

The cluster of houses in which we worked was surrounded by barbed wire; but this time it really was for our protection, to keep out unwanted visitors. The American zone was overrun by Russians, probing around for all sorts of reasons; General Eisenhower had adopted a lenient attitude toward this, hoping (in vain) for some kind of reciprocity from them. An added advantage of the barbed wire was that it made our section look like part of the main Oberursel prison camp, in which there was the most motley collection of mainly political prisoners. It was excellent camouflage and did not depress us in the least. I was able to see my wife and children again after a year's separation, and my staff were also able to see theirs.

* * *

Soon after our arrival, General Sibert came to see us. He was now the military intelligence chief on the staff of the commander of United States forces in the European theater (i.e., G-2, USFET) and one of the few senior Americans to have seen the coming East-West conflict from the outset.* He was a man of great moral courage, and this deserves to be recognized. He had been the target of a lot of ill-informed criticism for having failed to detect Hitler's preparations for the Battle of the Bulge in December 1944; I have always held that no logic could have indicated that a sane military leader would commit thirty-five divisions in the manner Hitler did that winter. Now that Sibert agreed to take my organization under his wing, he said to us in effect, "If anything goes wrong, God help all of you!" Sibert and I went over every aspect of the new organization; he fully understood why I felt bound to impose certain conditions on our cooperating with the Americans.

As far as the political ambitions of the Communist bloc looming in the East were concerned, Americans and Germans were now sitting in the same boat, and we had to think in terms of a common defense effort. This, if nothing else, justified our working together; it was for the diplomats and politicians to attend to the rest. There was no escaping the future as we saw it, and the events of the last twenty-five years have confirmed that we were right. I had gone over much the same ground in my very first talks with Captain Boker at Wiesbaden and with the authorities in Washington, and yet again in the negotiations with the American liaison team here at Oberursel, so my remarks cannot have been much of a novelty for General Sibert, though I dare say I put them to him in a pithier form than the summaries he had received.

My later discussions with General Sibert in Oberursel ended with a "gentlemen's agreement" which for a variety of reasons we never set down in black and white. Such was the element of trust that had been built up between the two sides during this

---

* Sibert was later a major general and chief of staff to General Mark Clark in the Korean War.

year of intensive personal contact that neither had the slightest hesitation in founding the entire operation on a verbal agreement and a handshake. This unconditional trust was absolutely crucial to our success in the years that followed.

I remember the terms of the agreement well:

1. A clandestine German intelligence organization was to be set up, using the existing potential to continue information gathering in the East just as we had been doing before. The basis for this was our common interest in a defense against communism.
2. This German organization was to work not "for" or "under" the Americans, but "jointly with the Americans."
3. The organization would operate exclusively under German leadership, which would receive its directives and assignments from the Americans until a new government was established in Germany.
4. The organization was to be financed by the Americans with funds* which were *not* to be part of the occupation costs, and in return the organization would supply all its intelligence reports to the Americans.
5. As soon as a sovereign German government was established, that government should decide whether the organization should continue to function or not, but that until such time the care and control (later referred to as "the trusteeship") of the organization should remain in American hands.
6. Should the organization at any time find itself in a position where American and German interests diverged, it was accepted that the organization would consider the interests of Germany first.

The last of the six points may raise some eyebrows, since it might seem that the American representatives had gone overboard in making concessions to us. But this point demonstrates better than

---

* I later learned from Sibert that the small sum of money involved came out of the general funds for support of G-2 activities in USFET.

any other Sibert's great vision: he recognized that for many years to come the interests of the United States and West Germany must run parallel.

This was the key to our success—that from the start we had concluded an agreement that was strong enough to withstand all the difficulties and problems that were to beset it in the years that followed. I stand in admiration of Sibert as a general who took this bold step—in a situation fraught with political pitfalls—of taking over the intelligence experts of a former enemy for his own country. It was very much to the credit of everybody concerned with our "trusteeship" on the American side that they were able to find the right psychological basis and climate of mutual trust for this unique venture to be launched.

The political risk to which Sibert was exposed was very great. Anti-German feeling was running high, and he had created our organization without any authority from Washington and without the knowledge of the War Department. I understand that he informed his opposite number in the British zone, Major General Sir Kenneth Strong, of our existence, but he asked him not to inquire too closely into the matter for fear that the press might discover our activities.

## CHAPTER SIX

# The Gehlen Organization

$\mathcal{T}$hose of my former officers who stayed behind in Europe had not been idle in the months before my return from the United States. Shortly after my flight to Washington, Lieutenant Colonel Wessel established contact with Hermann Baun, who had been through much the same as we. He had surrendered to the Americans as we had arranged in our discussion in the empty hotel at Bad Elster a month before the war ended; he had also been shipped back and forth across Germany, finally ending up not far from Wiesbaden, in the CIC interrogation center at Oberursel.

The regime there was very strict, as the center also housed a number of suspected war criminals for interrogation purposes. Baun bore with this situation, as did his colleagues, displaying a characteristically grim humor; and eventually he told the CIC he was willing to work for them as we had arranged. I have already described in the Prologue to these memoirs how during my talks in Washington at the end of 1945 I had agreed to the resumption of active operations on a trial basis by Baun and our other former colleagues left in Germany. Two considerations had been uppermost in my mind at the time. First, we had to convince the justifiably skeptical Americans that, apart from our document files (which the natural process of obsolescence would render valueless in time), we could offer them other intelligence of a topical and worthwhile nature, which would be all the more impressive in a Germany torn by chaos, her communications constricted by interzonal frontiers, and with millions of her citizens forced to migrate aimlessly the length and breadth of the nation. Second, the passage of time would make it harder with every week that passed to recruit the nucleus of workers we needed. Once they had been discharged from captivity and swallowed up into civilian life, we would probably never manage to find these experts again, given the prevailing conditions of catastrophe.

Wessel learned from the Americans that I had agreed to a resumption of operations; Baun was put in the picture by the CIC at Oberursel. Unfortunately, neither Wessel nor I knew at the time that Baun had not been told the whole story by the CIC, as they had been kept in the dark as to my existence and the plans that evolved in Washington, and they remained in this state of ignorance until 1949.* We later found out that Baun had proposed his own plans for a practical intelligence operation to the Americans. His proposed organization was not dissimilar to Admiral Canaris's Abwehr between 1933 and 1941. What he wanted was an independent intelligence-procurement agency under his leadership which would work as and where he saw fit, handing over its information to a totally independent second agency for analysis and evaluation. This was in flat contradiction to the plans that had been approved in Washington, and I certainly could not have supported him, if only because it would have made it easy for the Americans to play off one agency against the other. And as much as I valued Baun's

---

* According to another source, Baun entered in his diary late in March 1946, "General Sibert authorizes resumption of work of I (espionage) and III (counterespionage) category."—TRANS.

experience, there would be no guarantee that the Americans would be passed only such information as I would personally be willing to take responsibility for. My own experience of certain Abwehr reports during the war made me very uneasy in this respect. The existence of two parallel organizations would also prove an unnecessary complication when the time came for a new German government to take us over, quite apart from the fact that it was this biaxial structure that had yielded such a large and damaging crop of command errors during the war.

Nor did the Baun plan reflect the way the American authorities in Europe envisaged our work. They showed a marked preference to deal with me after my stay in Washington was over. While Washington had—after protracted negotiations—given its general agreement to our starting work, the actual terms of this joint operation remained a matter for General Sibert: his was the head that would roll if the experiment went wrong or if there was a political scandal. This was another reason why he and his colleagues preferred to work with one German, who would take responsibility for the whole operation, and who was, moreover, the senior ranking officer of the former Foreign Armies East staff. A further factor was that, to the Americans, Baun was a man of complex personality. He had been born in Odessa and had spent the formative years of his childhood there before his family returned to Germany. He had grown up bilingual, and had absorbed the Russian mentality. As with so many other foreign-born Germans who had spent years in Russia, there was something of the Russian soul in him, that emotional, sentimental and immeasurable something that distinguishes the Russians from other peoples; but the other side of this attractive coin was his extravagant and uncontrollable imagination, which made it hard for him to pass sober judgment on hard facts, and which caused him to waste too much time chasing will-o'-the-wisps. This, and his years under Canaris and the Abwehr put a natural barrier between him and the Americans who had to deal with him, and inevitably roused certain misgivings in them which were sometimes not entirely justified.

It was largely because the CIC had not been able to put Baun fully in the picture that when we came to discuss our detailed organization plans in August 1946 Baun was reluctant to subordinate himself wholeheartedly to me, even though the outline of our future joint effort with the American army had been broadly mapped out by then. I was planning to put Baun in charge of my espionage section, and Wessel in charge of the analysis section. Had the proper degree of frankness been displayed to Baun by the Americans, it would doubtless have spared us much of the later unpleasantness that arose. Of course it cannot be ruled out that the Americans may have considered it in their interests initially to have two irons in the fire, given the somewhat obscure situations at that time. And there were certainly some officers in USFET's G-2 branch who were less enthusiastic about identifying themselves with the joint operation than Colonel Philp, Captain Boker, and Captain Waldman. The fact that we did not secure a formal agreement with the American secret service (by then, the CIA) until much later* shows just how unstable the situation was despite the goodwill shown by both sides.

The difficulties facing Wessel and Baun early in 1946, when they had first started their attempts to rebuild an intelligence organization, were largely the result of the postwar chaos in Europe. But the remarkable feature was that not one of those whom they approached to act in one capacity or another for them let them down. Although virtually every German refugee from the East had lost everything he possessed, again and again over the years we found among these homeless expellees people who were willing to risk everything for us, even if they had in the meantime found other employment. It made no difference what their personal politics were. There were allegations that it was this loss of livelihood and property that made working for us attractive, and that the organization we were building up was nothing more than a bunch of desperados and adventurers joined together to learn a new and murky trade. This kind of accusation was repeatedly leveled at us by Communist propaganda from the Soviet zone until about 1954,

---

* See p. 143.

and in some cases it was even picked up by the mass media of the West. The truth was that we had nothing of value in the ordinary sense that we could offer our workers in return.

Our existence was a closely guarded secret; to be successful and guard against infiltration by the enemy we had to remain a secret, too. So our typical worker's return to normal life as a regular citizen was blighted from the start: for security reasons he could not mention his work to his relatives; he had no government protection, because the German state as such had ceased to exist, and the protection the occupation authorities could offer him was less than marginal. The jurisdiction of the United States authorities was restricted to their own zone, even after the economic fusion of this with the British zone and the formation of the bizone late in 1946. On top of this, initially only USFET's G-2 section knew of our existence, a state of affairs we wanted to last as long as possible; so for a long time our operatives were at the mercy of the ultrasuspicious organs of other American security agencies, particularly the ever-watchful CIC and the military police. Many are the songs we could sing on that score! The pay was meager—my own salary being only about 1,200 marks a month in 1952.

In the years before the West German currency reform of June 1948 our working capital was in the form of U.S. dollars, at first sight well worth having but in fact bound up with innumerable difficulties for us. For example, we were not allowed to cash dollars at banks, in order to avoid having to answer awkward questions about where they came from; so we had to try and change them with the assistance of our American friends—otherwise we could not have obtained the German currency to keep the organization on its feet. In short, it took a lot of idealism after six years of war, captivity, expulsion, and the many other personal privations from which no German had been spared, for any man to agree to work for us.

* * *

The first trial intelligence-procurement operations had started early in April 1946, and the results had met with the Americans' approval. We were not able to "awaken" some of our agents in the Soviet Union who had become dormant with the end of the war; and, in fact, the original network was to play a smaller part in our rebirth than has been suggested in some publications. Baun made a start in that direction, but I felt it was better to concentrate on recruiting fresh agents while we could, as we could not be sure which of the old ones had been won over by the Russians. Those that we could trust were "awakened" by prearranged signals, but in the state of disorder existing in postwar Europe it was comparatively easy for our people to be sent deep into the Soviet Union to establish personal contact. Of far greater value, however, were the files and indices we had maintained on the Russian military units.

Meanwhile, after the July 1946 conference with General Sibert had resulted in the "gentlemen's agreement" referred to above, espionage operations proper had begun. Our first requirement was the creation of a small but efficient "brain" for the organization, followed by a somewhat larger operations staff to control the espionage work and a reliable analytical section. This vital spadework took up much of our time, eager though we all were to get started, since we lacked many of the things we needed. We had little space to work in, no technical equipment such as radio transmitters and receivers, and we urgently needed a larger staff. But we had lost contact with many of those who had been working on intelligence during the war. We also had to recruit enough clerical personnel for our purposes. But beginning again from scratch like this did have its advantages: it is far harder to take over a large existing organization and try to convert it and modernize it than to create one from nothing, benefiting from all the experience gained in the past. Wessel and I wanted only one thing, to form a nucleus for a single, future German intelligence service that would profit from all we had learned from the services we had witnessed or worked in during the war and prewar years.

Where there is a multiplicity of foreign intelligence services there can only be rivalry, overlapping, and security risks—for they offer the enemy's intelligence organs ideal opportunities for penetrating them from within. I therefore planned to use the years that followed until a new German government came into being in creating a uniform intelligence service capable of carrying out every kind of espionage work against the enemy: it would unite under one agency diplomatic intelligence, economic intelligence, military intelligence, and counterespionage. Clearly such an agency could only emerge in the future as a civilian body, if for no other reason than the sheer size of the task. Accordingly, we essayed to recruit high-grade civilian personnel in addition to the former army officers at our disposal. For example, we took on former members of the foreign service, former civil servants, and the like, provided that they had had a clean slate in the Third Reich and had done nothing reprehensible since then.

The speed with which we could set up the new organization was bound to depend on the space, funds, and equipment placed at our disposal. But to the Americans we were still something of an experiment; so improvisation and makeshift characterized the first trial runs of the "Gehlen organization," as we soon came to be known to our friends. Despite this, we still had to show worthwhile intelligence results, if we could, to convince the Americans that there was a future in us.

The original differences with Baun were settled, at least for the time being. In addition to getting him an efficient operations staff for his work on the intelligence procurement side, to speed up this in-flow of reports, we had to find him accommodations near our organization's headquarters. We finally found room for him at an inn at Schmitten, fifteen minutes by car from Oberursel where we were; our headquarters stayed in the Blue House cluster of buildings there. We initially accommodated our analytical section there too, but later on we removed it to Kranzberg castle, where there was room for it to expand later on.

We soon established good relations with the American liaison team—Colonel Deane and Captain Waldman. It was Waldman who bore most of the brunt of the cooperation with us. I have already emphasized how much we owed to him. Even when his superiors showed little sympathy, he committed himself wholeheartedly to our cause, putting up with the personal disadvantages this involved him in without a murmur. Colonel Deane was an outstanding active service officer, who had distinguished himself in combat but had had little to do with intelligence work for some time. A number of minor difficulties resulted from the colonel's lack of experience in intelligence affairs. When, for example, I tried to impress him with the need for us to obtain false identity cards, his first retort was an astonished, "That's against the law!" It took some effort on my part to persuade him that it was not a true violation of the law and that the use of fake identity cards is common practice in intelligence circles. After I had gradually succeeded in convincing him of certain other peculiarities of our trade, this trusty officer swung around to our side and threw the full weight of his personality behind us. Thus we gained a second mentor in addition to Waldman; and that is why I have always followed the later career of the colonel, who is now an influential general in the United States, with a particular sense of gratitude.

More serious were the difficulties that arose during this period with Hermann Baun, whose concept of the organization remained very different from my own. He tended to regard our job purely from the intelligence procurement angle and overlooked the political need to limit ourselves strictly to what we were capable of and to what was desirable as well. Nonetheless, he attempted to carry out his own plans rather than mine, and this disinclination to accept the fact that I was in charge led to increasing friction. In April 1947 I therefore found it necessary to replace him as chief of intelligence procurement, but since he had otherwise served me well I put him in another responsible job; I did not "elbow him out" as was subsequently claimed in various publications. His successor was Colonel Hans Dillberg,* a loyal staff officer with great vision, particularly on the organizational side. He had picked up a lot of experience in a prominent position in intelligence procurement during the prewar period, and later he had worked extensively in military intelligence as well. Under his expert management, our intelligence procurement advanced by leaps and bounds.

---

* Dillberg was the code name used by this officer at headquarters; it was not his real name.

\* \* \*

It is difficult to describe the exceptional problems confronting us in 1947 and 1948. What is now the Federal Republic of West Germany was at that time occupied territory, partitioned into three zones, with all passenger and goods transport under strict allied surveillance. Even on our own side of the demarcation lines we had to operate under a cloak of conspiracy which would scarcely have been possible without American aid. It was no rare occurrence for one of our workers to be seen acting suspiciously near the zonal border and to be arrested by the CIC or the British security forces. We then had to secure his release with the help of the American liaison team, but without disclosing his real job—no easy undertaking. Our officials setting out from Bavaria to our regional office (*Aussenstelle*) in the American enclave at Bremerhaven in northern Germany had to fill their cars with spare gas tanks, for if they ran out of gas on the way they could expect no mercy from the British or French occupation authorities. Railroad connections were bad; telephone lines were indistinct and overloaded, and tapped by the Allies anyway. The economic situation was a catastrophe. But our organization was gradually expanding and its mouths had to be fed. It did not help matters that our operational bases were distributed across the entire length and breadth of western Germany and had to be given realistic "fronts" as camouflage. Our workers were not able to give the authorities any information on their circumstances if they had to report in connection with personal affairs or family matters. Nor was it possible until our transfer to federal control in 1956 to register them in any state insurance program, as officially there was no employer, a headache that persisted for us long after we had been transferred to the West German government.

Every piece of our equipment, from typewriters to radio transmitters, had to be supplied by the U.S. Army. Here too there was a great danger of our being exposed, with all the undesirable consequences that would imply, so we often had to put up with long delays. The problems facing us in establishing links by courier, post, and telephone across the Iron Curtain were equally formidable.

That we succeeded in solving all these problems seems a miracle to me even now.

We restricted our investigations at first to purely military questions. This was inevitable, as we had rebuilt our organization on the existing foundations of the forward reconnaissance units (*Frontaufklärungseinheiten*) we had used on the eastern front. It soon became clear however that along with the growing estrangement between the former Allies, the Americans' interest in purely political problems increased. By the end of 1946 we were already keeping an eye on political trends behind the Iron Curtain. From that, it was a logical progression to embrace espionage on Communist economic affairs and arms technology as well. In this latter field, which the orthodox American services had begun to watch only comparatively recently, we were able to communicate particularly important results to them. My own concept of a uniform intelligence service, which I had based on the experiences assembled by Group II (i.e., long-term appreciation studies) of Foreign Armies East during the war, was clearly right, if these early results were anything to go by.

\* \* \*

In the autumn of 1947 we unfortunately lost both General Sibert and Colonel Deane. The latter was replaced by Colonel L——, who with the best will in the world failed to see eye to eye with us and unwittingly jeopardized the entire joint operation. He was a good soldier—even as a full colonel he still regularly practiced parachute jumps—but he regarded his as a position of command, with authority over us Germans too, an attitude totally at variance with the gentlemen's agreement I had concluded with Sibert. He knew only one military relationship: he gave the orders and we had to obey them; it was a creed he had practiced his entire military life. We were servants of the U.S. Army—therefore we had to toe the line. His attitude caused a lot of friction; he was not the best of partners for myself, as head of an organization which had by then already expanded to a considerable size, employing several thousand men. I am sure he did his best to work in harmony with us;

but the differences of opinion multiplied, and they began to affect our work.

One achievement must be chalked up to this colonel, from the few months before he was moved to another position. By now, we were literally bursting our accommodations at the seams. He managed to secure for the organization a small estate at Pullach, a village some five miles south of Munich. At the time, it housed the Anglo-American Civil Censorship Division; but he had it moved out, and the Gehlen organization settled into this compound in December 1947. The twenty-two houses in the compound had originally been built as the Rudolf Hess estate, and designed for use as a reserve headquarters for the War Department, in a tree-shaded setting on the banks of the little Isar River. Although considerably expanded, the site still serves as the headquarters of the Federal Intelligence Service (BND) in Germany. The American liaison team moved into the biggest building, which had housed Martin Bormann's former offices, in Heilmann Strasse (the road running through the compound, which was now blocked off at each end); I moved into a small ground-floor office in one of the houses opposite. The camouflage drab painted on the roofs and walls was gradually removed, the buildings renovated, and the gardens put in order.

The move to Pullach brought enormous relief to our cramped headquarters staff. For security reasons, we all brought our families to live within the Pullach compound as well. (My own wife and children had been permitted to join me at Oberursel in July 1946, after my return from Washington.) The presence of our families made it necessary in turn for the headquarters to become self-sufficient: we had our own school, our own kindergarten, and all the other things necessary for us to restrict to a minimum our contact with the outside world. The local village believed that the compound housed German civilian internees. The Americans were not enthusiastic about the need for our families to be brought within the compound, but the presence of several wives who were not tied down by small children—including several with academic degrees —resulted in an immediate and worthwhile addition to our labor force. The discipline of the German families living under overcrowded conditions within the compound was particularly commendable; in retrospect the decision was undoubtedly correct, because our personnel were thus spared the burden of living apart from their families, in addition to the other deprivations that belonging to my organization involved. Of course everyone was allowed complete freedom of movement and could leave the compound whenever he liked; but no one was allowed to make any contacts within a certain radius or to shop in the neighborhood. To destroy temptation at its root we opened our own food store, which still serves the BND's tenants within the compound.

* * *

The move took place at a time of a crisis of confidence within the organization. It had been caused by the fact that we were not always able to meet the needs of our personnel for better accommodations and to provide the equipment appropriate to the job, including vehicles, radios, and other technical equipment. The U.S. Army's provision of office equipment and the necessary funds for our continued existence also left much to be desired. An official budget had been negotiated with the American authorities, but again and again it proved quite inadequate. On all these matters there were lengthy and tedious negotiations, and for the most part I had to conduct them in person. It is difficult to give an adequate impression of the numerous trivial questions which had to be dealt with—matters that I frequently had to push through in what was almost unarmed combat. I see from my records that in 1948 alone I had to submit to the Americans no less than four long lists of urgent and explicit requests.

Our field workers of course knew little or nothing of this constant fight on their behalf, so I could well understand their grumbling. The U.S. Army liaison team did what it could to satisfy our demands, but the army suffered from bureaucracy and insisted on our following the proper "service channels." And since those channels led from Pullach to Frankfurt and from Frankfurt to Washington and all the way back again, the process was long and time-consuming.

The disputes with Colonel L—— finally culminated in my flatly refusing to obey an order he issued in March 1948, since it would have cost the organization its hard-won independence. I told him bluntly that the management of the organization was my affair and mine only, as had been laid down in the gentlemen's agreement with Sibert, and that I would therefore accept no "orders" which directly interfered with the internal affairs of my organization. I might be prepared to accept recommendations; but I would not consider myself bound to accept them, I added, unless I felt they would serve the mutual interests of Germany and the United States. At this he withdrew his "order."

This episode and other similar instances of a lack of intelligence-mindedness in Colonel L—— finally obliged me, for all my respect for this soldierly and distinguished officer, to ask for his replacement by an officer better versed in our affairs. The negotiations were not particularly easy, since the American authorities were at first inclined, however much they agreed with me, to put their prestige into the scales on the colonel's behalf. But they finally recalled him in August 1948. He was replaced in December of the same year by Colonel Philp. The change occurred at a particularly fortunate time, for the following eight months were to see my organization laboring under great strains. These were primarily the result of the currency reform in West Germany, but there appear to have been certain domestic budgetary difficulties for the Americans as well. Philp reconciled the two positions and kept the collaboration going more than once, setting a great example of how much depends on one trustworthy and reliable personality if different nations are to cooperate in intelligence work.

* * *

The proof that the Americans valued our work highly was that they came to us with more and more missions to fulfill. This meant we had to recruit more and more workers; and this in turn brought us a number of organizational headaches. My own position was that for an organization like ours to start producing results virtually from the first day, we would have to make do with a minimum of red tape. The lack of funds forced this on us too: what money we had was there to produce results, not to finance a large and extravagant superstructure; there was always the risk that such a body would tend to follow Parkinson's Law and finally become an end in itself. This was a tendency which I was determined to defeat from the start.

In any case, even by 1948 there could be no certainty that the organization was a permanent fixture, and for this reason too I felt I had to keep the number of permanent employees as small as possible. Also, the smaller the superstructure, the easier it would be to keep under surveillance; and the greater would be our chance of detecting "leaks" rapidly.

In intelligence the most delicate leadership problems are always those posed by the procurement sector. The old and well-tried military code that "orders have to be obeyed" has little pertinence in the field of intelligence procurement. The agents, in particular, and their immediate superiors—the last links in the chain, at the extreme periphery of the organization—must often act independently. Frequently, they alone are in a position to judge whether and in what manner an assignment can be accomplished. The same goes for the intermediate links as well, for they are often called on to make snap decisions involving a high degree of responsibility and initiative. So, in general, assignments have to be issued in the shape of broad directives, and it then boils down to a question of mutual trust whether one link in the chain can rely on the next to act in the appropriate manner. In addition to political insight and a talent for organization the head of the procurement section should have an ability to improvise which enables him to seize sudden opportunities or overcome unexpected obstacles. He must also possess a strong element of psychological insight and an ability to control his men firmly enough while still giving them enough rein.

One seldom finds among one's colleagues anyone even approaching this ideal. The proper solution is therefore to try for a constant upward flow of officers and for regular personnel changes at intervals of about two to six years. Dillberg was the first of my senior colleagues to whom I applied this maxim; I replaced him as chief of the procurement section after about a year. He must be credited for having injected great impetus into the job; but there are times, particularly in the early years of an organization, when too much impetus can be positively harmful, particularly where security is concerned. It can be a hindrance during the vital running-in period that any new machine must undergo.

I replaced Dillberg at the time of the first Berlin crisis, so I had to find a successor who was cautious and who would conduct the business of intelligence gathering with due deliberation. My choice fell on one of the older generation of former Abwehr officers, Herr Schack,* whose intelligence experience went back to well before the war. He was just my type of man, exceptionally thorough and deliberate, the kind who reached decisions (whether on security affairs or on matters of command) only after he had inspected every possible angle. Even so, I recognized that Schack could not fill the post forever. I left Schack in control of procurement for a relatively long time; he did good work, and this deserves to be underlined, because he was already well on in years when he accepted the job.

Strange though it may seem, this was a time when we feared the Allied fiscal authorities more than the long arm of Soviet counterespionage agencies. The June 1948 German currency reform brought us particularly severe monetary problems. During the reign of the reichsmark, our budget had been solidly based on our dollar allocation, a currency of real value on which we could depend; but although the disappearance of the dollar and the postwar bartering of cigarettes and other commodities was a blessing for the national economy, it was a disaster for the Gehlen organization. Forthwith our allowance was paid to us in the new deutschmarks. Our overall American allowance was cut back anyway; and coupled with the artificial rate of exchange we were given (1 dollar to 3 marks, versus the official rate of 1 dollar to 4.20 marks), we were suddenly receiving 70 percent *less* than before. To add insult to injury, the deutschmark was for a long time regarded with hesi-

---

* Schack was the code name by which he was known at headquarters; it was not his real name.

tancy by the public, and its value sagged markedly. The outcome was that for months our organization did not have enough funds to make ends meet; we could only have met even our most urgent commitments if the Americans had increased their subsidy by at least 50 or 100 percent, and even this would have left a serious gap to be plugged. It was a bitter experience after so many years of work.

It must be remembered that at that time we were not an official government agency, backed by all the resources of the state. We were an independent organization being financed by such funds as the U.S. Army could spare for us. The need for efficient camouflage alone forced us to lead something of an underground existence; and in the midst of this financial crisis, we had to do what we could to keep our heads above water. I set up a special section for raising the funds we needed to continue. With the $125,000 that remained to us, we purchased as much cocoa as we could from American stocks, and sold it around Munich—particularly in the notorious Möhlstrasse black market area—at a profit so large that we more than tripled our original outlay. If our operatives were caught, their special American passes provided for their immediate release. The American authorities connived wholeheartedly in this, as they had no option. But the general shortage of funds was so crippling that other field units frequently had to discontinue important sources they had built up; or agent leaders were forced to take new commitments upon themselves, underwriting costs out of their own pockets in the dim hope that everything would somehow turn out all right. Of course it was hard to make them understand how it was that the wealthy United States was suddenly unable to part with more money for us; but the negotiations on this problem were taking time because the domestic currency reform in Germany had taken the American authorities we worked with as much by surprise as us, and no kind of advance planning had been possible.

On the other hand, the German public's willingness to help was very great in 1948. We received much financial assistance at Pullach from wealthy industrial circles, partly in the shape of loans and partly in the form of valuable goods; and in due course I established under General Horst von Mellenthin* a "special connections" section whose responsibility it was to maintain touch with government and industry. (Unfortunately, West German industry was reluctant to go beyond purely financial assistance. When we suggested to certain firms with major contracts behind the Iron Curtain that they employ key members of our organization to provide them with a legitimate cover, almost all refused.) Above all, it was the individual *people* who came forward—people who owned little or nothing themselves, but were fired by a great and idealistic desire to help. I was often deeply moved by the positive disposition toward us that we encountered everywhere at that time—an era which is usually characterized today as one in which only material considerations were of any consequence. It was the little things that showed how closely the public identified themselves with our cause: to a man, the villagers supported me when I moved with my family to my present house near Starnberg, after they gradually learned who I really was. They regularly misdirected strangers who inquired the way to my secluded villa; and when one car driver asked a local druggist, within minutes he had telephoned to warn me of the stranger. When we did our shopping in the town of Starnberg I was cordially addressed as Herr Gehlen by the shopkeepers—but only if there were no strangers in the shop.

Only one thing could rescue us from our chronic financial crisis—the rapid transfer of the Gehlen organization from U.S. Army control to the special coordinating agency the U.S. government had set up in 1947, the Central Intelligence Agency. We confidently expected the CIA to have a much broader horizon in consequence of its global assignment to collect and collate political, economic, and military intelligence. It would surely recognize the possibilities inherent in close German-American collaboration over intelligence work, and it would have a realistic idea of how much this kind of operation costs.

From as early as November 1948, therefore, we were involved

---

* Mellenthin had headed the War Department's attaché branch during the war, and had later commanded an army corps; in the late fifties he became my deputy at Pullach, as predecessor to Worgitzky.

in negotiations with the CIA's representatives. Their first job, obviously, was to find out as much as they could about the kind of work my organization was performing. This took some time—to our increasing embarrassment, for by now we were in the jaws of an increasingly uncomfortable dilemma. By February 1949 our financial position had become so acute that I found myself obliged to warn the U.S. Army liaison officer attached to us that if the crisis persisted much longer, I would have to prune the organization I had built up, and this would inevitably lead to a reduction in our efficiency. Soon afterward, I repeated this position in a letter to the G-2 at SHAPE. I went so far as to offer my resignation, and recommended that in view of the imbalance between the modest means placed at our disposal and the tasks we were expected to perform, the Gehlen organization should be disbanded. This cannot have fallen on deaf ears, for only shortly before this time our Operation Bohemia had succeeded in penetrating and smashing the entire Czech spy network operating in West Germany. Our Esslingen office had persuaded two Czech intelligence officers to defect, and they had driven across the border in two cars loaded with a mass of files and details on the Czech networks, enabling the American authorities to move in and destroy them without trace.

At this time a very accommodating Department of the Army colonel happened to be visiting us. He at once recognized what the problem was, but explained that the American defense budget as a whole was in some difficulty as a result of the Berlin crisis. (It was the period of the costly Berlin airlift forced on the Western powers by the Soviet blockade.) He entreated me not, on any account, to disband or cut back our organization, as we were doing such valuable work for the Americans. He gave his word that something would be done to help us. So the goodwill of the American allies was without doubt as fervent as ever; the real cause of the crisis was red tape, a phenomenon with which we in Germany were only too familiar.

* * *

An intelligence service is a highly sensitive instrument. The moment there is any kind of upset at the top the tremors are sensed by every link all the way down the chain even if the actual details do not become known lower down.

The effect of the five-month financial crisis I have described was to increase the general uncertainty in which our organization had to operate. It was not until the late spring of 1949 that our talks with the CIA finally reached a positive outcome; the terms were formally settled in English on May 13 and in German on the twenty-third, in a new gentlemen's agreement that this time was put in writing. On July 1, the beginning of the new American fiscal year, the CIA took over responsibility for us. But even then our difficulties were not really over, for the cracks could not be papered over as easily as that.

The CIA appointed a liaison staff to replace that of the U.S. Army; civilian clothes now took the place of the familiar American army uniforms. The CIA liaison staff chief, Colonel M———, turned out to be a particularly straightforward and forceful personality. There were some initial snags before mutual confidence was established, but after that the colonel did all he could to keep things moving and to help us. Even so, our financial problems continued to dog us for many months. We resolved to make a virtue of necessity and start a long-term shake-up in the organization to refine it to the $n$th degree. Fortunately, the experienced CIA men were less interested in getting immediate results than in building up a really worthwhile and efficient organization. My admiration for the individuals on that early CIA liaison staff is boundless: they recognized that their own parent organization was considerably younger than ours, and clearly regarded their job as being to learn as much from us as they could. There is not one member of that CIA liaison team who has not now reached a high position within that agency.

We began the rationalization process late in the summer of 1949. It yielded a crop of problems which were all interrelated in one way or another. First, we had to take steps to adapt the organization to its reduced circumstances without any loss of efficiency; second, the organization had to be restructured to conform by and large with the regular procedural and administrative methods of the CIA; and third, we had to start preparing for a policy meeting with the new West German government, which had been founded in September. If the government agreed to take over our organization as a nucleus for a foreign intelligence service of its own, as we hoped, then our administration would have to conform with German standards too.

Throughout this period Colonel M—— positively radiated confidence and reliability. In harmony with his proposals we stream-lined the organization until by October 1949 we could show that we were putting our funds to better use than ever before: we merged offices, scrutinized every salaried position, and shortened the links in our communications and courier networks. At the same time, we remodeled our administration along the lines of the German gov-ernment agencies, insofar as we could without conflicting with the usages of the CIA.

An intelligence service cannot always be run with the same procedures adopted for other government agencies. Most govern-ment agencies have a purely administrative function; but the prime task of an intelligence agency is procuring and evaluating informa-tion—the administrative, technical, and financial aspects of the agency are of less moment. Experience shows that excess red tape inevitably impairs the efficiency of secret services (as well as of armed forces) and finally suffocates them altogether. To combat excessive bureaucracy is, therefore, one of the most important duties of the head of the intelligence service. (That is why at least one Western government has found it preferable to have intelligence experts with ancillary civil service training administer its secret service rather than civil servants who are expected to grasp the ramifications of intelli-gence operations.)

It is also of fundamental importance to preserve the flexibility with which the agency can apply its technical and financial means, so that it can put its operational decisions into effect quickly. Gov-ernments are therefore faced in principle with two alternatives: either they can force their intelligence agency into the straitjacket of the existing civil service regulations, or they can make an excep-tion for it. In the former case, while the organizational pattern so fervently desired by civil service authorities will have been achieved, there will be a significant reduction in the agency's effectiveness. In the latter case, the vital mobility of the intelligence service will be enhanced without any consequent loss of control over the application of public funds. Every major country has opted for the second alternative; so did all West German governments up to the time the Socialist coalition was formed in Bonn late in 1969. I will return to this problem below.

Without going into tedious detail here, it will suffice if I say that the Gehlen organization adopted the same financial practices as those that the earlier Abwehr had established with the approval of the Reich Audit Office. We kept detailed accounts of all personnel and capital expenditure, just as any other government department would; but the minutiae of intelligence service costs were represented by one lump sum, for which our operational leaders had to account internally in detail. These secret accounts were scrutinized by special inspectors who reported only to the head of the organization. With minor modifications, this procedure was also approved by the Federal Audit Office in Bonn when we were later transferred to the federal service.

* * *

Life was not a bed of roses with the CIA at first. Their bureaucratic attitude toward the financing of our organization, and in particular their "project" system, resulted in our shelving major operational plans for long periods since the question of whether or not we would be provided with funds for them could only be decided at CIA headquarters in Washington. The essence of the project system was that the probable outcome of every operation and its requirements in time, manpower, and money had to be submitted for clearance in advance. By the time clearance arrived at Pullach from Washington, the whole plan was usually long out of date.

Our Abwehr experience led us to prefer a system whereby the operational decisions and the allocation of resources were left to our upper command echelons alone; these would be given operational funds of their own and general guidelines and directives (except for instances where I reserved the right to make final decisions myself).

These infuriating and repeated delays, along with further friction connected with our transfer from the U.S. Army to the CIA, resulted in yet another crisis of confidence within our organization. The mood is well illustrated by a letter I received from one of my outpost leaders, Ritter, in October 1949:

> I want to inform you personally of the situation in my unit. The whole political and economic situation, the attitude of the Allies over the devaluation of the deutschmark, the impotence and pitiful plight of our present government and of Germany in general, can hardly be said to give us much enthusiasm for our work. On top of this there is the very real uncertainty about the organization's final relationship to the present government. Will the organization be German or an all-American affair? We can be excused for beginning to suspect that the latter will be the case, since our friends are insisting on more and more information on what we are doing, in more and more detail, down to the very lowest levels; or is this just a false impression created by the tendency of those who have survived the *Chistka** to give themselves a raison d'être by stepping up the paper war and reeling out more red tape?
>
> It may well be that the provision of funds, fees, rewards for information, and subsistence payments have been covered until January 1, 1950, but the fact is that they are neither so generous as to be enough to work properly with, nor so inadequate that we can put our pens down with a clear conscience and do nothing; because nobody knows for how long, or at what rate, these funds will continue to flow to us, and this makes any kind of proper planning utterly impossible. If I could be sure that this financing would remain at this level for the time being, I would cut my unit by a third or a half so as to be able to pay those that are left a better rate and be able to ask more of them in consequence.
>
> I never did think much of this idea of financing the "projects" and getting advance clearance for them from Washington, and I have put up as few projects as possible myself; unfortunately, my fears that at least three months would pass before the projects were approved has proved only too true; indeed the reality is far worse. *Five* months have elapsed since I submitted my first plans, and not one has yet been

---

* Russian for "purge," a perhaps overdramatic word for the reduction of U.S. military personnel that became necessary in Europe at this time.—TRANS.

approved. Meanwhile, most of the men we earmarked for the projects have gone sour or lost confidence in us; unfortunately, these were our best people, people who took the mission seriously. Those that are left are the ones who took things less seriously, and who have no sense of urgency. A further factor is that these operations were mostly planned on the assumption that they would be put into effect in summer, or in autumn at the latest. The men stipulated these conditions themselves—after all, there is some difference between undertaking an assignment in the East in summer and in winter. Even if these projects are given immediate clearance, by the time we have given the men a refresher course it will be winter, and more than one will then have second thoughts.

The result of all this is that our American friends could hardly get a worse impression of us, because of the many projects we submitted perhaps only a vanishingly small percentage will ever be carried out. (I intend to make this point to Mr. St—— as well when he visits me on October 21 with Herr W——.) The main thing is that I want to avoid any suspicion that I only submitted those projects to fleece our friends of their money.

Given the prevailing situation in our organization I am coming around to the view that it would be better to get out now while the going is good. But as my own unit has been built up on the basis of personal trust alone, I would prefer not to go until I can be sure that those of my colleagues who still wish to carry on with their work will be in good hands. This is a crisis of confidence which extends far further up the organization than the earlier ones. It is of course impossible to conceal completely one's own sense of insecurity in one's dealings with one's colleagues; and often one does not wish to anyway, because it would be doing a disservice to people who put their trust in me.

I am putting the position bluntly to you, just as it is; and I am not wearing my heart on my sleeve in any way; the letter is for your eyes only, and I will leave it to you to decide how best to use it. . . .

This letter painted the situation in much the same colors as I had already heard it described by other members of the organization. I had a private talk with Ritter, informed him of the difficulties

I was having with our American friends, and warned him they would certainly last for some time yet. Unfortunately he was not happy with the assurances I gave him, and he resigned from the organization some time later. I deeply regretted the loss of this experienced and likeable intelligence officer.

His letter and subsequent resignation were not without effect on our American partners. Colonel M——— intensified his efforts on our behalf and began an intensive investigation of various ways to make our position easier.

* * *

A month before this letter, on September 12, 1949, Dr. Konrad Adenauer had formed the first postwar government in West Germany, and Germany was once again able to act as a state, as a nation of independent substance. This was of more than academic interest to us at Pullach: in line with the agreement we had concluded with the Americans three years before, it was now time for us to start thinking in terms of approaching the new German government. Even though its absolute sovereignty was still to be recognized, we were under an obligation to inform the government of our existence, if nothing else, particularly since the gentlemen's agreement stipulated that a reconstituted German government should have the right to decide on our future.

As early as mid-August 1949, on the day of the first elections for the Federal Parliament, I briefed a certain Bavarian minister whom I assumed would have good contacts on our work with the coming German government. One result of this was that I was enabled to shore up our contacts with the Bavarian authorities, particularly with their prime minister and his minister of the interior. On October 12, 1949, I made my first personal contact with the Bonn government, visiting Ritter von Lex (who was at that time a *Ministerialdirektor* and later rose to the rank of state-secretary in the Federal Ministry of the Interior); and it was through him that I established contact with the then minister, Dr. Gustav Heinemann (who is at the time of writing West Germany's president). Through Lex and Dr. Hans Globke (the *Ministerialdirigent* in the Chancellor's Office), I submitted to Adenauer a memorandum with my proposals for a future foreign intelligence service; I do not know how he received my ideas, but on November 14 I again traveled to Bonn for meetings with the vice-chancellor Franz Blücher and with Heinemann and Herbert Blankenhorn of the Chancellor's Office, and the exchange of views on the Gehlen organization lasted about an hour this time. We discussed the organization's history and its achievements so far, and finally I was able to expound the ideas I had been mulling over in my mind ever since the end of the war—ideas which could be expressed in the form of concrete proposals for the first time. The frank discussions went off exceptionally well, and I drove back to Pullach in a satisfied frame of mind.

I began to feel that the selfless sacrifices of my colleagues had not been entirely in vain; at least I was happier about the future than I had been twelve months before. The German government had begun to take an interest in us. Discreet though my approaches to Bonn had been, however, they aroused misgivings in our American partners. Colonel M—— went so far as to forbid me to have anything further to do with the German government officials; this was in an edict of December 21, 1949, the result, I assume, of orders from Washington. I was instructed that the future of the organization was a matter for the Americans alone to decide, presumably to prevent me from treading on the toes of our future allies. Since this American veto flatly contradicted the terms of our agreements, I tacitly declined to bow to it.

Over the next few months there was some improvement in this delicate situation, as the Americans no longer prevented me from pursuing my contacts with Bonn. Presumably the American authorities recognized that since they could not prevent this association indefinitely it would be better to sanction it and satisfy themselves with "keeping informed" on the progress of our contacts. Early in 1950, I established the first official contact with Globke, who later became state-secretary in the Chancellor's Office. I got on well with him from the first moment, and gained the impression that he had no doubts as to the importance of the Gehlen organization.

It was clear to me that he wanted to keep contact with us strictly reserved to his own office.

Globke promised us all the technical assistance we needed, and asked us to do what we could to help the security authorities in West Germany during the period of their organization, for previously the maintenance of public order and protection against the growth of extremist organizations had been exclusively in Allied hands. I discussed the details of the kinds of aid we would be rendering with the Ministry of the Interior and with its state-secretary, Ritter von Lex.

\* \* \*

It was not until September 20, 1950, that I had my first opportunity to meet Konrad Adenauer in person. I was called to see him at the König Museum, a science museum in Bonn which temporarily housed the federal government and Adenauer's office until the Palais Schaumburg was ready for occupation. Globke was also present. In the twelve years that followed until our temporary estrangement over the *Der Spiegel* affair, I came to recognize in Adenauer one of the greatest German statesmen of this century. My relationship with him developed over the years into one that went beyond the merely professional, into something approaching unquestioning mutual trust. I remember on one occasion when I had to report to the chancellor on a certain security affair within the organization, he asked me, "Tell me, General, is there anybody you can still trust?" To this I replied, "Where there is no trust, Chancellor, there can be no intelligence service." And I added, "But we call it a 'watchful trust' "—a qualification which caused him visible amusement.

Of course I prepared for my first encounter with him, with all that it meant for the organization's future, with some care. I was curious to see whether he was the old fox and oversimplifier he was supposed to be, and whether the authoritarian paternalism his admirers credited him with would make any real dialogue possible between us. On the other hand, I was not coming to Bonn empty-handed: after all, we were the first German postwar organization, and our roots extended back to even before the establishment of the Anglo-American bizone. I felt too that my own reputation as a "legendary personality"—however little I felt like one myself—might rouse his own curiosity to see me.

Adenauer welcomed me with a warmness and openness that cast my doubts to the winds. I did not even need to impress the basic need for a foreign intelligence service on this old man—in fact over the years that followed he and Globke manifested an unusual degree of understanding for the difficulties facing my organization. The chancellor at once recognized the value of the instrument being offered him, and indicated he would seize the opportunity while he could. I informed him that I also proposed to advise the leader of the Socialist opposition, Dr. Kurt Schumacher, of our existence and to ask for his backing as well. The difficult mission of a foreign intelligence service could only be accomplished if it was recognized to be strictly nonpartisan in nature, by both government and opposition. Adenauer at once agreed.

I left the König Museum confident that Adenauer would give us all the help we needed; here, I was convinced, was an outstanding German who was willing to put everything into the fight for the supreme goal that we at Pullach had set ourselves as well—the restoration of our afflicted fatherland.

I had already made Dr. Globke's acquaintance during my various earlier visits to Bonn. To work with him was so pleasant and stimulating that I would not willingly have dispensed with the years of our joint effort before his retirement in 1963. I was glad to do what I could to defend him from the vicious Communist smear campaign that was later mounted against him—an infallible indication of the true value of this man for West Germany. Four years older than myself, he was the epitome of the old German civil servant type; he was the kind who would serve without fear or favor. He was not what we would call an *éminence grise;* but he did endeavor to remain in the background, while religiously obliging the various federal authorities to accept the policies of his master, Dr. Adenauer. He had the entire machinery of the new government at his fingertips, and an infinite understanding for the complexities of foreign policy. It was this sense of judgment that enabled him to recognize at once the benefits to be derived from backing the Gehlen organization.

I called on Dr. Kurt Schumacher on the day after my visit to Adenauer; the Socialist leader was probably one of the most tragic figures I ever met—his right arm had been shot away in the Great War, his left arm almost paralyzed, and his left leg amputated above the knee during an enforced stay in a concentration camp. He had with him his deputy Erich Ollenhauer, his confidential secretary Annemarie Renger, the vice-president of the parliamentary assembly Professor Carlo Schmid, and Fritz Erler, a leading Socialist deputy. Schumacher wholeheartedly identified himself with Adenauer on the principle that ours must remain a nonpartisan organization—in other words that we must have the support of all the political parties except the Communists. It would clearly be unfortunate if such a sensitive instrument was to be passed from one set of hands to another each time the government in Bonn changed; the uncertainty among our staff—of which I had witnessed more than enough over the last two years—would be intolerable. It would cripple the organization and achieve nothing but an upward gravitation of political opportunists into the higher echelons. I felt confident that I would be able to see eye to eye with Schumacher on any matter of importance. When I left him, he assured me his party would underwrite our work as well, and that it would support our later transfer to federal control.

*　*　*

By now responsibility for internal security had been largely transferred to German control. On April 14, 1949, the three Western military governors had forwarded what came to be known as the "Police Letter" to the Bundesrat, or Upper House. This authorized them to set up an office for collecting and disseminating information on revolutionary activities directed against the future Federal Republic; but the new body would not be equipped with any kind of police powers. The provinces of North Rhine-Westphalia and Lower Saxony had already established agencies for this purpose on Allied instructions. Shortly after my visits to Adenauer and Schumacher, a law was passed formally establishing the Federal Office for the Protection of the Constitution (BfV);* this legalized the temporary beginnings made at the provincial and federal level, uniting all internal security under one authority controlled by the minister of the interior.

For some weeks the question of whom to appoint chairman of the BfV was discussed within the ministry. State-Secretary Ritter von Lex offered me the job; it was a difficult decision for me, but after much reflection I accepted, only to be told a few days later that my name had been turned down in favor of another. In a way I was relieved, because the job of a glorified policeman would not have appealed to me much; but I was less than enthusiastic about the man on whom the final choice had fallen: Dr. Otto John, a forty-one-year-old lawyer, who took up the appointment in December 1950. The Ministry of the Interior invited me to release a good officer from my own organization to act as John's lieutenant. I gave him Colonel Albert Radke, a very conscientious officer who at once put the BfV first, as soon as he was transferred.

I admit that I felt many misgivings when I heard that Dr. John's name was being canvassed for the BfV appointment, and I made no secret of this in Bonn. I verbally suggested to Lex that the appointment would be more than tactless in view of John's "past": he had fled from Germany to Madrid and London after the bomb plot failed, in 1944, and had then worked there for our enemies; he had worked under a man like Sefton Delmer for "Soldiers' Radio Calais," broadcasting hate propaganda against our troops; wearing British uniform, he had interrogated many prominent German officers as prisoners—including several under me at Pullach—who would now be expected to work with him. Even more disturbing for me personally—and I would be expected to work in harmony with him—was that Otto John had collaborated with the British team prosecuting Field Marshal von Manstein, one

---

* The law establishing the BfV (*Bundesamt für Verfassungsschutz*) was enacted on September 27, 1950.

of the finest soldiers of this century. I would not go so far as to say, "Once a traitor, always a traitor"; but I felt the position called for a man of character—a character different from John's. My more deep-seated objections, which I did not mention to Bonn, were that John was unsteady and rootless, he was not a professional in this field, and his alcoholism made him a potential security risk.

My objections were discounted. The British authorities, particularly Sir Ivone Kirkpatrick, spoke well of him, and my American colleagues raised no objection themselves. Otto John announced his intention of paying his first courtesy visit to us at Pullach not long after. General Mellenthin, my deputy, advised all staff that three themes were taboo during the visit: John's pre-1944 resistance work, his collaboration with Sefton Delmer, and his participation in the Manstein prosecution. To everybody's astonishment, however, at a social gathering in our guest house in Munich that evening John himself brought the three forbidden topics up. He tried to suggest that he had gone out of his way to help Manstein during the trial, but without success. My own impressions of John as a person were unfavorable: his eyes were pale and watery, his manner vague and undecided. In intelligence work one rapidly acquires a certain *nous* for the indefinable, and John made us all uneasy. We gave him a thorough briefing on the political situation, and as he left, Colonel Herre, my personal assistant, expressed to me his own verdict in a pungent American phrase, as was his custom: "I wouldn't trust that man as far as I could throw him."

The work of Otto John's office and my own organization inevitably overlapped, particularly where our own "III F" (counterespionage) work was concerned. Claiming that de jure East Germany was an extension of his German "beat," John, in time, extended his counterespionage channels way behind the Iron Curtain. We received the BfV's reports and digests, and we aided them all we could with the material supplied to us by agents we had emplaced within the Soviet and East German espionage headquarters, but I made no use of the liaison officer the BfV had seconded to Pullach, and I kept John himself at arm's length. I see from my personal papers that in July 1951 I again recommended to Dr. Globke that John's appointment be delayed or canceled, in view of a certain "morals incident" involving a Pullach officer and—a phrase indicative of our extremely delicate position as a German intelligence organization—"in view of the strong suspicion that John is working for the British intelligence service."* Dr. Adenauer seems to have shared some of my misgivings, for he began to send us the BfV's reports for a second opinion, and he received John himself only very rarely indeed.

At about the same time, yet another intelligence agency came into being. In October 1950 an office was set up under Minister Theodore Blank as "Government Commissioner for the Reinforcement of Allied Troops in Germany," as a forerunner to a West German defense ministry.† Blank's security adviser, Gerhard, Count Schwerin, appointed a former lieutenant colonel of the Abwehr, Friedrich Wilhelm Heinz, to set up a military intelligence service for the "Blank Office." I will not devote much space here to Heinz. He was more of a politician than a soldier, an adventurer who had set up a free-lance espionage office after the war in conjunction with a dubious Dutch intelligence officer—who later unsuccessfully blackmailed him over his questionable contacts with Wilhelm Zaisser, head of the East German secret service, and committed suicide. Particular suspicion was aroused by an incident in which he claimed he was kidnapped in West Berlin by Communist agents and taken to the eastern sector for questioning by the Soviet security service. We checked his statements against the detailed plans and maps in our possession at that time of the MVD headquarters at Grunau (from various sources we had pieced together such accurate plans that we even knew which Russian officers sat in which rooms), and we reported to the German authorities and to the Americans that his version was highly improbable. Heinz was finally "retired" in October 1953 after an affair involving a false question-

---

* The memorandum on this July 1951 conference is among my personal papers.
† Another duty of the special connections section headed by General Mellenthin (see page 141) had been to keep tabs on the most reliable former General Staff officers, so that when the day for the reactivation of West Germany's armed forces arrived, we could at once supply the appropriate authority with detailed lists of which former officers were to be trusted, and which had developed a postwar leaning to the East.

naire (he had apparently promoted himself to full colonel). Two of my colleagues from Foreign Armies East days, Colonel Gerhard Wessel and Colonel Josef Selmayr, then took command of the intelligence branches established within the new Defense Ministry.

\* \* \*

By this time we had expanded our headquarters at Pullach considerably. From the air it would look like a housing project with tidy green lawns and flower beds surrounding the lace-curtained villas and low administration buildings. But it was a housing project with a difference: the approach roads were guarded with electrically operated steel-mesh gates, and there were sentries and constant guard-dog patrols around the steel-fenced perimeter.

In 1949 I had moved with my family into a villa down a secluded lane near Starnberg. Among my personal papers I still have the results of the security investigation into the character of the village that was to be my home that was carried out on my orders: it named every potential source of trouble and identified the local Communists. But it was no easy matter to emerge from the official limbo in which I had lived since 1945; officially I was an "economic adviser," working somewhere in America. To settle in a village in postwar Germany, I needed papers, and I did not have any. Relations between the CIA and the State Department were so delicately poised that this harmless task proved impossible for them; so I ordered my own "technical section" to produce the documents I needed. And in no time, I was the possessor of a long, folding Red Cross identity document. It was fabricated complete with my real name and photograph and a dozen different border-crossings apparently authentically stamped upon its pages (the visa stamps were the hardest to obtain, but eventually these too were affixed and canceled). The document would probably have passed scrutiny by the KGB, and the local parish authorities certainly never suspected I was not the *"commerçant"* the document made me out to be.

I had to devote considerable attention to my personal safety —not without reason, for in 1953 the windshield of my car was shattered by a projectile which the Munich forensic authorities who investigated the case later established was a bullet. Both I and my government service driver were always armed, and I practiced regularly with my revolver at an American firing range. More than once we observed that my house was being kept under surveillance; on one occasion we returned home at 2:00 A.M. to see one man driving off hurriedly in a Volkswagen van—the police identified him from the registration plate as an undercover Communist from a nearby town. To my neighbors I had to explain somehow how I came to possess a car, and what I lived from; so I invented a one-man firm and had a letterhead printed, "Patent and Idea Applications and Negotiation," a firm which did indeed do occasional business, but of which the "organization" proper was unaware. The camouflage was so good that when our activities were "exposed" by a British journalist in 1952 and I was identified as its head, the local villagers knew better: the general, they told each other, really made his living from his patents company—the intelligence work was just a sideline.

The organization itself was initially structured like a large commercial undertaking, with its national head office at Pullach, and eight "regional head offices" distributed throughout West Germany, each controlling between three and six suboffices; these suboffices supervised the activities of the local branches. Abroad, we established "residents" in the countries which were of interest to us, each controlling its own network. Initially, equipment was so scarce that we had to employ ordinary teleprinters for our communications from Pullach—an Achilles' heel that caused me much anxiety. Gradually we were able to replace them with coded teleprinters and an extensive system of couriers. The old-fashioned "inverter" type of scrambler telephone, which offered no real protection (our own wartime Ministry of Posts had unscrambled and recorded all the transatlantic radio telephone conversations from 1942 to the end of the war, including top-secret conversations between Churchill and Roosevelt), was replaced by a modern communications system with the various government agencies which is absolutely proof against interception. I myself communicated with the outside world mostly by "teleprinter conversations"; or I would dictate messages onto the plastic reels of an Ultravox dictaphone on my desk: depressing one knob erased the whole reel immediately. (We had special machines for erasing ordinary recording tapes, and document shredders for our classified materials.) A constant stream of technical experts from our particularly closely guarded technical laboratories visited my first floor office, bringing me the latest items of equipment for approval. Our investment in scientific research paid off, and I was able to aid many Allied intelligence services in this way.* The overriding security principle was that of the "watertight compartment": members of one network or branch knew nobody outside their immediate unit. Even at Pullach, the compound was physically divided into different zones, and headquarters personnel were allowed access only to certain specified areas. They received their identity permits at the main gate, so they could not be lost or copied outside the compound. To enter a different zone they had to have a special stamp in their permit; only my most trusted senior colleagues had all-embracing permits on a permanent basis.

We kept the identities of our sources our most sacred secret, and in this the physical detachment of the evaluation section from the intelligence procurement section was most important. Within the procurement section, a department called *Sichtung* ("sifting") checked every report the section issued to insure that the source could not be even remotely identified, and decided into what category the source could be placed. Our best agents' reports were given a *B* grade; less reliable sources were given *C;* and untried sources were given *D*. *A* grades were reserved for original documents of whose authenticity there could be no doubt,

---

* Professor Carstens, state-secretary in the Chancellor's Office, emphasized the technical aspects of our achievements in his speech to me upon my resignation: "Scientific progress in electronics, cybernetics, and automation necessitated new means of information procurement: they afforded the enemy new means of safeguarding his secrets. A veritable arsenal of increasingly sophisticated tools and gadgets has been added to the conventional secret service implements of the past. You devoted special interest to the new scientific espionage methods and to complex data-storing and analyzing systems whose introduction could no longer be delayed; you were the first to recognize the importance of this new branch of intelligence activity, and devoted yourself wholeheartedly and successfully to its systematic expansion."

and which the federal chancellor had an automatic right to see. Under considerable pressure from the head of the evaluation section, I did grant him the exclusive right to approach the head of the procurement section in person for verbal information as to the nature of the source—whether the report came from a minister, a secretary, or a cleaning woman. If it came from a regular source of reports, the source's code name would be attached to the report on a slip of paper for the attention of the head of the evaluation section alone. His section would then decide the probability that the report was true on the basis of other material at its disposal, and a code number to that effect would be added to the grade letter.

It was the evaluation section which had to decide whether an apparently genuine report was being deliberately fed to us by the enemy; the evaluators gradually developed a "nose" for this, and in this way we were usually able to detect disaster approaching a particular network a long time in advance, and flash a warning to its members to go underground. We had a particularly brilliant "source adviser" whom we dubbed *der Quellenpapst* ("the pope of the sources"). He had long been an assistant of Baun, and he carried out the same remarkable task at Pullach from 1946 until quite recently, comparing the reports with other sources and with other reports from the same source, and asking himself the all-important question: how could this source come into possession of information like that? It was the kind of job that no electronic computer will ever be able to do, and the Americans showed particular appreciation of his work.

Very few of my staff knew me personally, and if they did deal with me they frequently did not know who I was. To encourage security-mindedness, I allowed my staff to address each other only by their code names, and these are secret even now.

Occasionally the tightness of our security measures produced remarkable results. I remember that on one occasion I entered an express train at Würzburg station, and found two journalists and a third passenger in the same compartment. After a while one of the journalists began talking about the "Gehlen organization," and commented that since its head must sometimes travel by rail or air, it must be possible to come face to face with him. Two days later, I received on my desk a written report on the conversation: the third passenger had been a director of one of my regional offices; since such officials were never allowed near Pullach, he had recognized me as little as had the journalists. Nor had I known him.

\* \* \*

The first phase of the Korean War was fought parallel with these developments in Germany. The war began with a severe reverse for the Americans, and it was only the outstanding leadership of General MacArthur that enabled them to recover their balance after an almost impossible start, in an operation of classic strategy. Just as had the Berlin crisis preceding it, even this remote Korean conflict led to a considerable increase in the demands made on the American and our own intelligence services.

Our efficiency remained unimpaired by the internal changes that were made in anticipation of our eventual transfer to federal control. After meeting Adenauer, I had advised the American liaison team that in the future I intended to keep both him and the leader of the opposition up-to-date on the Gehlen organization by means of regular oral reports to them; and that any information we collected which had a bearing on the internal security of the Federal Republic we would pass on to Dr. Otto John's new office. I went over the technical details of this with John and his superior, State-Secretary von Lex, on December 13, 1950. On the day before, Dr. Globke had confirmed to me that the federal government intended to take us over as soon as its sovereignty was restored and it had the necessary funds. The financial aspect was the real bugbear still: perhaps Bonn was hoping that the Americans, who had so far been the main beneficiaries of our work, would continue to bear part of the financial burden for some time to come. My own view was that with our transfer to federal responsibility United States financial aid should be discontinued, so that there should be no question as to where our loyalties lay. This was one of the several reasons for the delay in our final transfer until 1956.

From the end of 1950 onward, I paid briefing calls on Dr. Globke at the Chancellor's Office every one or two weeks in Bonn. We were de facto serving two masters now, one in Washington, the other in Bonn. We set up a special office at Pullach to process and forward any reports of particular importance and interest to the German government; and in addition, on February 6, 1951, we opened a liaison office at Oberpleis, near Bonn, to establish and maintain contact with the various federal agencies with whom we had to work—the Chancellor's Office, the Foreign Ministry, the Defense Ministry, the Ministry of the Interior, the Finance Ministry, and the BfV. As a first step toward the federal take-over I had ordered that as of January 1, 1950, our accounting system was to be modeled on the practices adopted by the Abwehr. (Until that date we had followed the American system of double bookkeeping.) All nonsecret costs were now accounted for down to the last pfennig, in strict accordance with the old Reich (and now federal) regulations.

It would burden the reader too much were I to list the various stages of negotiations between Bonn and Pullach which paved the way for our transfer to federal control. Globke, who showed particular sympathy for my insistence that the organization be given a free hand and not be throttled by red tape, visited our Pullach headquarters for the first time on May 7, 1951. We showed him the individual sections at work, and he was able to form a clear idea of our structure and the kind of staff we employed. On July 12 there was a further meeting of Schumacher and Ollenhauer with Carlo Schmid, attended this time by the generals Heusinger and Speidel, who were military advisers in the Blank Office and were later to take up key positions in the West German armed forces. The principal object of that meeting was to discuss how the organization would operate in such a way as not to conflict with Germany's defense interests.

Two senior civil servants from the Chancellor's Office, Gumbel and Grau, were particularly frequent visitors to us from 1952 onward. One outcome of these visits and the discussions my colleagues and I attended in Bonn was that on May 16 and again three months later I was able to submit to Adenauer papers on the duties and organization of my agency, on the procedure to be employed during our take-over by the government, and on the various other procedural questions that would arise in the course of the reorganization. They contained roughly the following proposals for the period of transfer:

1. The question of a future federal intelligence service would have to be aired with representatives of the main political parties.
2. As soon as the German Treaty* came into force, General Gehlen and a small staff should be transferred to the government as the "Office of the Federal Intelligence Service," charged with establishing a federal intelligence service from the existing organization and from other agencies and other suitable people, in accordance with directives issued by the Federal Chancellor's Office.
3. At the same time as the Office of the Federal Intelligence Service was set up, special sections should be set up within each ministry concerned to assist in our organization's smooth transfer to government control.
4. The transfer of the Gehlen organization into the Federal Intelligence Service should proceed in such a manner that the flow of intelligence work would continue unimpeded and the continuity of reporting would not be impaired.
5. Simultaneously, any other suitable groups should be merged into ours, and their work taken over by us.

As time passed, of course, these proposals underwent constant modification and refinement until the German Treaty signed in May 1952 finally came into force three years later. But these were the general bases on which we worked. It may have caught the reader's attention that I referred to the need to merge "other suitable groups" into our organization. In this connection Bonn and I

---

* The German Treaty was the convention on relations between the Three Powers and the Federal Republic of Germany of May 26, 1952, by which sovereignty was restored to the West German state.—TRANS.

were referring not to the BfV offices at either federal or provincial level so much as to the small, German-staffed intelligence agencies created and financed by the Western Allies on German soil. When the time for our transfer came, we were duly offered a strange assortment of such agencies. But with the exception of an unusually good group of economic intelligence analysts operated by the British in northern Germany, I did not consider it expedient to accept responsibility for any of these groups.

With the treaty signed, we now began to think in terms of transferring the Gehlen organization to government control beginning on April 1, 1953.

## CHAPTER SEVEN

# Setbacks
# and
# Successes

**M**uch has been written about the determined attempt of the Communist secret services to discredit the Gehlen organization before it could become a federal government agency. An intensive intelligence battle was fought on German soil in the early 1950s, with Berlin as its focal point, affording the newspapers every opportunity for exciting if not sensational reporting. So much intelligence activity was crammed into such a short space of time, with attack and counterattack, that even the most superficially informed writer could hardly fail to distill the requisite quantities of color and drama from those events to come up with a story for his editor.

This was a very damaging climate for a fragile organization to grow in. In our organization's formative years we had tried to steer clear of any kind of publicity, choosing careful camouflage and acting very circumspectly in public. The handful of confidants among the leaders of the democratic political parties in West

Germany kept the secret of our existence as closely as the people I had established contact with during the earliest years of our existence. The Communist secret services—and particularly East Germany's, which was controlled by Wilhelm Zaisser—kept silent about how much they knew in order to expand their knowledge of us as best they could, while at the same time awaiting a suitable opportunity to launch massive attacks on us. From the events that followed it is not difficult to demonstrate that this waiting game played by the Communist secret services had been ordered at the highest political level.

So the East kept its mouth shut, and it remained for a Western journalist to call public attention to my organization. On March 17, 1952, the well-known newspaperman Sefton Delmer published an article in the London *Daily Express* under the headline HITLER'S GENERAL NOW SPIES FOR DOLLARS. This was followed by a deluge of other articles. Delmer was well versed in German affairs; his father, Professor F. Sefton Delmer, had lectured in English at the University of Berlin and he himself had worked as the Berlin correspondent of the *Daily Express* from 1928 to 1933. As a war correspondent in the Spanish civil war, in Poland, and in France, and then broadcasting from the spurious "Soldiers' Radio Calais" later in the war, Sefton Delmer had pumped out vitriolic propaganda against Hitler's Germany. But now his continuing hostility toward Germany had evidently blinded him to the fact that our country had successfully bid for recognition by our former enemies, the three Western powers, and we were now their partner and ally in the fight against the corrosive forces of communism. In "exposing" our organization, as Sefton Delmer must have known, he was attacking one of the few institutions that had been fighting for the free world since long before the 1952 treaty was signed. In his article, Delmer branded the organization a danger for the future of Europe, and in doing so, he unconsciously provided the slogan the press hounds of both East and West were waiting for. He followed up his exposure by alleging that under my control the Gehlen organization had already infiltrated every government agency of the Federal Republic, and that it was trying to enlarge this foothold and exert improper influence on government policy.

He further charged us with methodically and deliberately shielding former Nazis and SS men from prosecution.

Although Delmer offered no proof for his attacks on the organization and no competent or well-informed Western authority associated itself with them, his allegations were given further currency by both German and foreign newspapers. Sometimes blown up into unrecognizable and spiteful proportions, Delmer's "disclosures" were kicked around from one sensation-hunting journalist to the next, each more piqued than the other at the thought that he had failed to scent the existence of the Gehlen organization until then. I retaliated in the way I thought most suitable: I established contact with a number of leading journalists, representative of various political points of view, and did what I could to set the record straight. Out of these early talks emerged a regular policy of the organization (and later of the Federal Intelligence Service) of collaborating with selected representatives of the press and other media. Our organization was the object of much envy because of these connections with the press and was the victim of misunderstandings in this connection as well.

The timing of Delmer's bombshell under the Federal Republic and its future foreign intelligence agency suggested strongly that he was acting—perhaps unwittingly—on someone else's orders.* It has always been the custom of hostile propaganda agencies (and not just intelligence services) to arrange for the publication of either spurious or genuine allegations about inconvenient adversaries or rivals in some third country, and then to follow this up with additional material themselves, referring to the original disclosures. Delmer's actions, which he explained as having been prompted by his private fears about the future, could hardly have tied in better with such Communist designs.

* * *

Despite this unwelcome public attention, preparations for the organization's transfer to federal control pressed ahead. They

---

* The conservative newspaper *Christ und Welt* repeated this suggestion on August 19, 1954: "It may well be that Sefton Delmer is not a Communist, as has repeatedly been claimed. It may not be his intention to play into the hands of the Russians. But that is just what he is doing."

received a great boost from the incorporation of West Germany into the Western alliance under the terms of the German Treaty of May 1952, and by the agreements on the establishment of a European defense community.* This alliance between the German federal government and the Western powers put an end for the time being to Soviet attempts to draw the western part of Germany into the Communist sphere of influence. The demarcation line which had been drawn across Germany at Teheran and Yalta was thus confirmed anew as the front line of defense for the Western Hemisphere.

The Soviet Union recognized that its German policies had collapsed and accelerated the total expropriation of its own zone of occupation. From then on, East Germany became one of the most important elements in the Soviet campaign to dominate Europe. Even though the Soviet-occupied zone was later transformed into a state, the German Democratic Republic, and reached a position second only to the Soviet Union as an economic power, it is its importance as a forward military area that has made it a dominant factor in every intelligence appreciation up to the present day.

Stalin's death on March 5, 1953, occurred at a time when Soviet attempts to mobilize their zone of occupation for the conflict with West Germany were approaching their peak. The sudden demise of this dictator, a man later to be condemned even by Moscow for his actions, raised new hopes throughout the world that Soviet policies of subjugation and suppression would be relaxed. In the Soviet zone of Germany there were numerous signs in those first months after Stalin's death that a political process of liberalization was taking place—but it was impossible to reconcile this process with the unwavering demands made on the zone's economy and labor force. In May 1953 the work norms were suddenly increased. To the populace's growing aspirations for greater personal freedom, there was thus added the resentment of the workers at the continuing deterioration of their working conditions.

---

* For the history of these agreements, the reader's attention is drawn to Konrad Adenauer, *Memoirs, 1945–53* (London: Weidenfeld and Nicolson, 1965), especially Chapter 21.

In the middle of June, Berlin construction workers demonstrated in the streets of the capital, protesting the actions of the "first workers' and peasants' state." On the following morning, June 17, this wave of protest erupted into a general strike. The anti-Ulbricht movement spread like wildfire, with large sections of the population throughout the Soviet zone joining in the uprising. For many hours the fate of the lords of East Berlin seemed sealed; but Russian troops came to their rescue. Soviet tanks crushed the defenseless citizens and saved Ulbricht's skin, while the zone's population fell back from the brief ecstasy of freedom into the gray and lethargic existence of everyday life under Communist dictatorship. Lacking central guidance for the revolt, and searching in vain for signs of assistance from abroad, the East Germans lost all hope on that June 17 of ever seeing Germany reunified.

There are many indications that the national uprising, which is commemorated in West Germany every year, was in fact a spontaneous and elemental act comparable only with the revolutionary movement that swept Hungary three years later. But the Russian authorities immediately attempted to indict the Gehlen organization with having planned and organized the June 17 uprising, and this alone was proof enough that from now on we were to be the main target for a vindictive and persistent Communist smear campaign. Two months before, in April, the East German Foreign Ministry had been blaming the Allied intelligence services for the increased tension in Berlin; now, after June 17, their attacks were directed at my organization. Wilhelm Zaisser was dismissed as chief of the East German state security service (SSD) a few weeks later, and a new man replaced him—Ernst Wollweber. Before this, an even more startling change occurred: Lavrenti Beria, chief of the Soviet MGB, was overthrown and executed in Moscow. (We were the first Western intelligence service to learn of this.)

I still have a number of papers which reflect the disturbance this caused in West Germany. One of my senior colleagues wrote in an internal memorandum,

> Our views on the struggle for power in the Kremlin and the conflict on the new line in foreign policy have been confirmed with unexpected crudeness. The consequences are incalculable.

And he posed the following questions for our agents to investigate:

> On the basis of what internal shifts of power could Beria's over-
> throw have been possible? Did his own security apparatus get
> out of hand? Is the influence of the party machine now greater
> than that of the security apparatus? Did the ultimate decision-
> making force, the Soviet army, back up the provisional victor
> [Malenkov]?

We had to investigate why Beria alone had been kicked out and
not, for example, Molotov, whose political line was not unsimilar.
Was it coincidence that the *Pravda* leader attacking Beria's record
was redolent of Vishinsky's speeches in the purge trials of the thirties?
And above all, we had to find out what the consequences would be
for Soviet occupation policy in the Communist zone and the SSD,
which was at the time still controlled by Zaisser: "Are there signs of
strong disagreements between Zaisser's oganization and the party's
political authorities?" We ordered our agents to report on the relations of the Russian MVD troops and offices and the conventional
armed forces, and to keep watch on the MVD headquarters located
within the forbidden zones in Berlin's Grunau suburb, particularly at
Ragata Strasse and the barracks compounds at Bohndorfer Strasse
and Wuhlheide. Any signs that the Soviet Twenty-fourth Airborne
Army was being put onto full alert were to be reported to us at once.

Before we had time to appreciate the full significance of Beria's
overthrow, we learned that Zaisser had been replaced by Wollweber, who for the next five years was to be my most determined
adversary—a man notorious throughout the world as a
professional revolutionary and expert on sabotage, one of the most
unscrupulous figures in Ulbricht's government. He scorned no
method in his war against my organization, and at one stage he
put a price of a million marks on my head. I never met him; I never
saw him in film or newsreel; and as far as I know I have only seen
one photograph of him—a paunchy figure with dark eyes deep-set
in a fleshy face, beneath thick, black eyebrows. But it was his
campaign against us that delayed our transfer to federal control
for three long years until 1956. Neither his predecessor, Wilhelm
Zaisser, who had distinguished himself by service on the Republi-

can side in the Spanish civil war, nor his successor Erich Mielke came anywhere near matching Wollweber's notoriety. Compared with him, even the current incumbent of that office, General Mielke, who has been known to brag of how he shot down two police captains in Bülow Square, Berlin, pales into insignificance.

Wollweber had waited a long time to emerge from the shadows and climb to this new rank, as Moscow's favorite spy-hunter. He was by no means a mystery to my organization; we had followed his career with interest for a long time. Born in 1898 near Hanover, he had won his spurs as a revolutionary while a sailor on the battleship *Helgoland* in the kaiser's navy, playing a leading part in the mutiny at Kiel in 1918. He joined the German Communist party, later becoming a member of the Prussian assembly and of the Reichstag, prior to Hitler's seizure of power in 1933; meanwhile, in the Soviet Union he was put through an extensive schooling in sabotage work, specializing in the destruction of large merchant ships. He built up an international seamen's union, and used it in the 1930s to organize sabotage attacks on important merchant vessels of various flags: tens of millions of dollars' worth of damage was inflicted on the British, French, American, and German merchant fleets, as their vessels suddenly caught fire in port and burned with their cargos. As chief of the Comintern in Copenhagen, Wollweber continued this campaign; and from Stockholm, after the war broke out, he headed a major espionage and sabotage network until his capture by Swedish authorities in 1940. He was sentenced to three years' imprisonment for illegal entry, but the Soviet Union successfully applied for his extradition and thus recovered their successful saboteur for employment in fresh pastures.

He surfaced again in 1946, as director general of shipping in the Soviet-occupied zone of Germany, with Moscow's recommendation that he be assigned wider duties. Wollweber returned to form, resuming his antishipping sabotage campaign, establishing schools to train scores of saboteurs. British shipping was a special target. On May 1, 1953, he had become state-secretary for shipping; but now, barely two months later, he took over from Zaisser as head of the SSD. His primary task was to destroy our organization and to prevent its transfer to the federal government by fair means or foul. He knew from Zaisser's example—the victim of vitriolic and partisan criticism over his handling of the attack on our organization—what to expect if he should fail. In the first few days after taking office he swept aside his unfortunate predecessor's subtle plans and poured scorn on Zaisser's efforts. To the newcomer it only seemed necessary to round up the people suspected of working for the Gehlen organization in the Soviet zone in one fell swoop, and then splash the results all over the Communist newspapers.

Within barely two months of taking office, he had already mounted his public onslaught on the organization. As the end of 1953 approached he initiated a series of sudden and coordinated raids on what he described as "Western espionage, terrorist, and sabotage groups." Hardly a day passed without fresh raids being announced in the newspapers and radio broadcasts of the Soviet zone. By the end of October ninety-eight arrests—all of alleged members of various Western intelligence agencies—had been reported in this series of "victory communiqués." But from early November 1953 on, Wollweber's spy-hunters were apparently rounding up only "Gehlen agents," because there was no longer mention of any others.

I had done all I could to make my organization watertight and security-conscious. In Germany and abroad I traveled under different names, and in each of the three subsections in West Germany I was known by a different name: in the North it was Dr. Schneider; I had also had an American passport issued in the name of Garner and another identity card in the name of Gross. I felt it better to assume the dignity of "Doctor," since then I could be addressed anonymously as *Herr Doktor*—the less use that was made of any name the better. I knew the overall shape of the organization's structure, and from time to time I would be shown area charts of our operations on the other side of the Iron Curtain; but I took care not to learn too much about identities or the minutiae of the organization's undertakings. Probably nobody knows less of the operational incidents which fill the pages of modern spy books than the director of an intelligence agency; but, conversely, the man in the field knew only what was happening at his immediate level, and could betray few other people if he was caught. I myself could always have been kidnapped, and modern science knows ways of breaking the silence of any man. If one of our agents was caught, we had ways of learning almost immediately; and we took all possible steps to tip off any others who might have been compromised and extract them from the Soviet zone by one or another of our pipelines. The taking out of a cell or the loss of important agents was a tragedy, of course; but I regarded my organization as a living tree—as one branch collapsed or was cut down, another was already growing elsewhere. The tree itself survived.

Wollweber's onslaught against the Gehlen organization reached its climax during November 1953. At an East Berlin press conference on the ninth, a certain Hans-Joachim Geyer was produced to the newsmen and introduced as having worked for us in the Soviet zone since 1952, allegedly as deputy manager of one of our Berlin offices. It is true that Geyer, author of a number of popular detective stories, had volunteered to operate for some months in East Germany as a "collector" of V-men,* but for security reasons he was then relieved of that position and recalled to West Berlin, where unknown to me, at the beginning of 1953, he was given a job as assistant in the one-man bureau of an agent leader. This reemployment contravened a strict embargo I had placed on permitting operatives who had been recovered from the Soviet zone to continue working in certain sensitive jobs. Geyer had indeed become a double agent by the time of his return. At the end of October 1953, his partner asked him to obtain a new female secretary. Geyer interviewed the applicants at a restaurant—he could hardly invite them to the office—and since he could only answer evasively about the nature of his "business," one of the girls became suspicious and reported to the police that Geyer might be engaged in some kind of white-slave trading. The vice squad police called at his apartment in his absence; hearing of this on his return, Geyer

---

* Gehlen's organization distinguished between the V-man (German *V-Mann, Vertrauensmann,* "trusted man"), who worked for idealistic reasons, and the *Agent,* who worked only for money.—TRANS.

feared the police were from the counterespionage and bolted back to East Berlin, no doubt in accordance with SSD instructions.

It was only then that we realized that Geyer had been recruited and turned around by the SSD long before his return to West Berlin —and possibly even before he volunteered to work for our organization in the Soviet zone. At the spectacular press conference on November 9 Geyer described himself untruthfully as "deputy manager of Gehlen's West Berlin branch" and rehearsed a number of statements put into his mouth by his Communist bosses. He had changed sides, he said, because his conscience troubled him, and as a dowry he had taken with him original files and personnel records from the West Berlin bureau.

I need scarcely add that my colleagues and I immediately took every conceivable step to prevent similar mishaps in the future. I issued instructions demanding that my security regulations be observed more stringently, since otherwise there were bound to be disasters in an organization employing as many operatives as we did. We introduced new security precautions as quickly as we could, since we fully expected Wollweber to continue with his campaign. Geyer's treachery had meanwhile unleashed a wave of carefully prepared arrests throughout the Soviet zone. It was later established that the majority of people rounded up in this purge had nothing at all to do with either our organization or any Western intelligence agency. They were just people who had run afoul of the government in other ways, and so they were arrested too. The Ministry of State Security announced the arrest of 546 spies, saboteurs, and terrorists employed by the Gehlen organization—a fantastic figure which should itself have sufficed to convince any neutral observer that this was pure propaganda; it reminded me of the RAF and Luftwaffe claims in the Battle of Britain. Even if our security had been very slack indeed, Geyer could never have picked up information on more than a fraction of the army of agents the other side was now bragging about having captured. The truth was that in his tiny bureau, which was only one among dozens of similar bureaus in West Berlin, he would have been able to put the finger on only a handful of our operatives in the Soviet zone with sufficient detail to insure their identification and arrest.

Just at the peak of our efforts to make the intelligence procure-ment arm of the organization absolutely watertight, a second and this time more painful blow was struck by Wollweber only four nights after the Geyer press conference. On the night of November 13, 1953, the agent leader of one of our other cells, Major Werner Haase, vanished near the border between East and West Berlin. From the clues left behind, it was clear he had been ambushed by an SSD snatch squad on West Berlin territory and hauled into the East. This was very different from the Geyer affair: Geyer's was a cowardly defection exploited to the full on the Communist propaganda stage; in the case of Haase it was the daring of one dedicated officer that resulted in this further injury to the organization.

A particularly reliable and imaginative agent, Haase had been ordered to reconnoiter a possible route for a secret telephone cable across a canal which ran along the sector boundary between East and West Berlin. We had expressly ordered that the actual laying of the cable was not to be risked until explicit instructions to that effect arrived. We planned to maintain contact with our agents in East Berlin by means of this cable, what is now referred to as a telephone sluice. It would obviate the need to rely on the increas-ingly hazardous courier service. Although Haase was aware of the implications of the Geyer incident and of the security precautions I had ordered throughout the organization, he decided to go ahead with the laying of the cable on his own initiative. Under cover of darkness he proposed to feed the cable across the canal using a toy steamboat, helped by an agent from East Berlin on the other side. Only later did we find out that this agent had shortly before responded to the SSD's widely publicized offer to Western agents promising them amnesty if they surrendered to the authorities.

Haase was ambushed and kidnapped, and after a show trial in East Berlin he was sentenced to life imprisonment on December 21, 1953. In numerous interrogations beforehand and under cross-examination during the trial he was forced to make statements on matters we knew he could not possibly have learned in the course of his own limited intelligence work. But he also managed to color his testimony in such a way as to deceive the enemy on many matters, while allowing us to recognize from the trial reports that he had so deceived them. He could have faced the death penalty, a fate meted out to many of my agents in the early years. (Later on, the Communists recognized their mistake, for dead Gehlen agents cannot be "turned around.") After protracted efforts, we finally managed to exchange Haase for a Communist agent early in 1957. I expressed to him the organization's boundless admiration for his intrepid work and for his exemplary courage during his trial.

\* \* \*

At the end of the same month, November 1953, the Soviet zone's Radio Germany and Communist newspapers published what they claimed was the "interrogation report" on a "recently captured Gehlen agent," Wolfgang Höher. We knew that Höher, another of the organization's workers in West Berlin, had disappeared some nine months before; at the time we had camouflaged his defection to the Communists as a kidnapping. According to the version fed to our organization, a stranger had lured him into a well-known West Berlin bar, had laced Höher's drink with some kind of powder, and then dragged the unconscious agent out, explaining that he was intoxicated. It was easily believed, because this sort of thing had actually occurred on more than one occasion. (The Allied public safety officer listed more than 150 instances of political kidnapping in West Berlin during the 1950s in which the Communists resorted to "luring and entrapment." We know, for example, that in April 1954 the Soviet secret service, in concert with the SSD, succeeded in kidnapping Dr. Alexander Trukhnovich, the eminent leader of the Russian émigré organization NTS\* in West Berlin, and conveyed him to the eastern sector, rolled up inside a carpet. But on another occasion, an SSD attempt to lure an important Gehlen organization official across the sector boundary—his wife having been kidnapped by means of a fake telephone message from the Soviet zone—was happily a total failure.)

---

\* Russian *Narodnyi Trudovoy Soyuz,* "National Labor Union"—an anti-Communist organization.

The Höher case was different. We were able to establish almost at once that he had been recalled by the SSD to East Berlin, evidently to prevent his imminent unmasking as a double agent. It was characteristic of Wollweber's methods that he had kept Höher on ice for nine months after his defection before producing him as a "star witness" against the organization. But again Wollweber and his men committed serious blunders which were bound to discredit this kind of sensational revelation, at least in the eyes of intelligence experts. Höher described himself as the organization's expert for espionage operations against France, and claimed that we were shadowing French personalities and were operating a "vast and complex" network of agents in the Saar, all of which was completely untrue.

Ernst Wollweber did not get everything his own way. He needed a steady flow of incidents to feed his publicity campaign against our organization. In mid-November he splashed in considerable detail the story of a number of arrests at the Baltic ports of Rostock and Warnemünde and branded the organization with responsibility for an incident with which it was in reality entirely unconnected. In fact, the arrests had taken place eighteen months earlier. These "fresh arrests" blazoned by Wollweber across the newspapers and radio system of the Communist zone were identical with those made in May 1952—except that at that time the three men now described as "Gehlen agents," caught red-handed installing explosive devices in the port areas, had been described as members of the Battle Group against Inhumanity, an organization from whose methods we had always firmly dissociated ourselves. (The League of Free Jurists was another such idealistic but extremist organization backed by the Americans.) The Battle Group caused us a good deal of trouble: it was German controlled but was furnished with material and financial support by the Americans. We considered the sabotage operations it conducted immoral and futile. Their agents were committed to activities which might have had some point if there was a full-scale war and they were properly coordinated with military operations; but in peacetime these activities injured only our fellow Germans behind the Iron Curtain. Bridges were blown up,

public installations were set on fire, and many agents were caught
and executed. Armed with the reports procured for me by Colonel
Metz's department,* I presented the American authorities with a
constant stream of objections to the Battle Group's operations: I
tried to point out that quite apart from the clumsiness of the planning,
the Communist countermeasures were affecting my own networks
too.

Three years later, after our transfer to West German government
control, the Americans offered us control of these groups; but I
could not sympathize with sabotage operations in peacetime, so I
turned the offer down. These groups did not fight cleanly. All that
we later took over was the personnel card-index of the Battle Group,
but not the people themselves. We did make extensive use of
American commando-training facilities (for their rangers) in Bavaria to teach our agents how to live off the land when parachuted
into hostile territory; we considered this training necessary in case
there was an attack from the East. But again, these were strictly
espionage agents, not sabotage. I resisted all American pressure to
undertake sabotage operations behind the Iron Curtain, and I refused to invite their sabotage agents to carry out spotting missions
on our behalf. The two kinds of operation must always be kept
strictly separate. My own view was that in the long run only he
who fights with a spotless shield will triumph—a legacy of my contacts with Canaris.

Our effective replies to his allegations whipped Wollweber into
a new frenzy of action against us. By the end of November 1953, it
was clear to him that even by employing the entire Soviet propaganda machine for his purposes, and despite the widespread publicity in his favor throughout the other Communist countries in
Eastern Europe, he had failed to convert the individual and local
successes he had admittedly scored in his fight against the Gehlen
organization into anything like the total annihilation he had prom-

---

* Colonel (later Brigadier General) Lothar Metz had served in Foreign Armies
West under von Roenne and had joined my organization on October 22, 1948, on
the counterespionage-intelligence evaluation side (intelligence procurement was
later attached to the same department as far as counterespionage was concerned).
Metz was later attached to our liaison office at Bonn; and until his retirement in
1965, he dealt with our relations with Allied intelligence services, at Pullach.

# Im Namen
## des
# Deutschen Volkes
### befördere ich

den Hauptmann

# Reinhard Gehlen
## mit Wirkung vom 1. März 1939
## zum Major.

Ich vollziehe diese Urkunde in der Erwartung, daß der Genannte getreu seinem Diensteide seine Berufspflichten gewissenhaft erfüllt und das Vertrauen rechtfertigt, das ihm durch diese Beförderung bewiesen wird. Zugleich sichere ich ihm meinen besonderen Schutz zu.

## Berlin, den 28. Februar 1939
# Der Führer und Reichskanzler

*Gehlen's certificate of promotion from captain to major, effective March 1, 1939. The signature is that of the "Führer and Reich Chancellor," Adolf Hitler.*

*Roll-call at Zossen, headquarters of Foreign
Armies East. Colonel Gehlen, left, took
the credit for the excellent state of German
military intelligence on Russia during the war.*

Above: *Colonel Gehlen at pistol practice in East Prussia in 1943; watching is Captain (later Professor) Klaus Ritter, who was to become head of the BND's political section.*
Right: *Gehlen (back to camera) talks with Count Klaus Schenk von Stauffenberg, right, and Colonel Zoelestin von Zitzewitz at the General Staff headquarters in Mauerwald, East Prussia.*
Facing page: *Lieutenant Colonel Heinz Danko Herre in 1942; he remained one of Gehlen's principal assistants until Gehlen retired.*

Above left: *Some of the female staff of Foreign Armies East.*
Above right: *The staff of Foreign Armies East outside their headquarters at Zossen, south of Berlin. Chief was Colonel Gehlen (X). Gerhard Wessel (XX), the present head of the BND, was at the time Gehlen's deputy.*
Right: *Major Reinhard Gehlen during the French campaign of 1940 (as liaison officer to General von Brauchitsch) with his son Christoph.*

X XX

Overleaf: *He wanted to fight Stalin: General A. A. Vlasov with Russian soldiers in German uniform at the troop exercise area at Münsingen.*

Above: *Autumn 1942: Colonel Heinz Danko Herre at Gehlen's headquarters at Vinnitsa, with Tango, Gehlen's favorite horse.*
Right: *General Gehlen, left, reviewing troops of the Russian Liberation Army during World War II.*

Right: *1954 photo of Ernst Wollweber, who was head of the East German SSD (state security service) until the end of October 1957.*
Bottom: *The hydrogen cyanide gun built by the KGB and used by Bogdan Stashinskyi. A pressure on the levers detonated capsules which pumped the contents of the ampules out of the tubes.* Below, from left to right: *Stashinskyi's wife —she persuaded him to confess; Stashinskyi—the "torpedo"; the victim—Stefan Bandera.*

Left: *Ensign Reinhard Gehlen at Munich infantry school in 1923, shortly before his promotion to lieutenant in the Reichswehr.*
Below: *Colonel Reinhard Gehlen in 1944 as head of Foreign Armies East.*

Above: *Gehlen during his presidency of the Federal Intelligence Service.*
Right: *Gehlen after his retirement.*

Above: *Gehlen's Foreign
Armies East headquarters.
near Angerburg in
East Prussia.*
Right: *The Elend Lodge, a
lonely mountain hut in
the Bavarian alps, which was
Gehlen's hideout in 1945
until his surrender to
the Americans.*

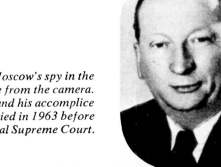

Above: *Heinz Felfe, Moscow's spy in the BND, shields his face from the camera.*
Right: *Felfe* (top photo) *and his accomplice Hans Clemens were tried in 1963 before the German Federal Supreme Court.*

ised. He made his infamous offer of a million deutschmarks for any man who succeeded in handing me over to him, dead or alive. There can be no doubt that such a reward was offered not only for my head but for those of others, too, for my organization was by now well placed to secure accurate details of such internal East German government pronouncements.

For several years, my organization had employed an important agent in Wollweber's very office. At the end of November I considered it time for this man to be extracted to the West, both for his own safety and to damn Wollweber still further. Walter Gramsch, a high-ranking civil servant (*Ministerialrat*), had been an intimate colleague of Wollweber since 1946, when Wollweber himself had been appointed director general of shipping. In Gramsch, Wollweber had seen an outstanding expert on transportation problems, and over the years he relied more and more upon him as a general factotum. Moreover, he had continued to heap praise on him, most recently in a letter dated March 28, 1953, in which he thanked him for his magnificent service on the Central Transport Commission.

Gramsch started by supplying important documents on the whole field of transportation behind the Iron Curtain, and soon he was sending us regular reports on the secret service work of Wollweber as well. For years he had despised Wollweber for his unscrupulous methods, and saw in him the real obstacle to the eventual reunification of Germany; so he passed on everything he could to our organization, convinced that in so doing he was thwarting the Ulbricht regime's plans and serving the cause of the German people. After the June 17 uprising was crushed, the flow of material from Gramsch doubled, and this perhaps illustrates his personal involvement best. We were forced to discontinue "Brutus" when we detected the first signs that people were becoming suspicious of his activities.

*  *  *

But other branches of the tree remained. At the same time as we were extracting Brutus, our organization controlled two female informants of considerable significance. These were women employed in particularly important positions by the Communists, and they showed unparalleled devotion to the free world's cause. One of the two must and always will remain cloaked in secrecy; suffice it to say that she was a senior official in the Soviet zone's Free German Youth (FDJ) movement, an organization primarily devoted to undermining West German youth organizations and securing footholds for penetration of the Federal Republic. The other, Elli Barczatis, was personal secretary to the East German prime minister Otto Grotewohl; the reports from her were given a very high rating, and when they emerged from the procurement section a slip was attached to them for the benefit of Colonel Herre, chief of evaluation, code-naming the source as "Daisy." (For a long time Heere thought the material too good to be true; but when he ordered a thorough debriefing of the secretary, she explained convincingly how she had come into possession of the documents.) It was one of the supreme ironies of the situation that we were receiving top-level documents and information from Daisy at the very same time Wollweber was bragging that he had annihilated the Gehlen organization.

What she and others accepted by way of risk and personal sacrifice may sound incomprehensible nowadays, since working for one's country out of sheer idealism is a matter for contempt rather than for commendation in West Germany now. In recent years the Russians have repeatedly honored their own spies working in non-Communist countries with medals and public eulogies—a manner of public retrospective recognition which may well seem misplaced to some. But I would like here to place on record my gratitude to Daisy, for her devoted and successful work for Germany. She supplied us with carbon copies of cabinet-level documents and, incidentally, with a quantity of material incriminating political figures in the West (of which however we were unable to make any formal use). In the end her overeagerness to help us led to her being caught. She was tried in secret for espionage, and guillotined. I will have cause to refer to her once more, when I describe the conflict between Grotewohl and Wollweber which led to Grotewohl's elimination.

* * *

Another of the informants our organization could rely on at that time was none other than a former deputy prime minister of East Germany, Professor Hermann Kastner. As joint founder and chairman of the Liberal Democratic Party (LDPD), he had been given a high rank in the government to bestow some semblance of bourgeois respectability on it (as had the long-standing chairman of the Liberal Democratic Union in the Soviet Union, Otto Nuschke, who was also a deputy prime minister under Grotewohl, and the foreign minister Lothar Bolz, chairman of the National Democratic Party [NDPD]). These "bourgeois parties" had been created by the Soviet authorities for the sole purpose of simulating some kind of alternative to the principal government party—the Socialist Unity Party (SED)—in the eyes of foreign countries. These sham parties had their government deputies nominated in advance, however, and they never attained a domestic political status comparable with that of the SED.

Kastner placed himself first at the disposal of the Americans and then of our organization, after a series of arguments with Ulbricht and other SED officials had convinced him his own political ambitions would never be fulfilled. He had managed to preserve his excellent contacts with the Soviet occupation authorities—and particularly with the Russian commander in chief in Germany, Chuikov—but not even these could keep him on top in the East German government, though they did keep him alive. They also made him a particularly valuable source of intelligence to our organization. Kastner did not like the cold shoulder he got from Ulbricht; he decided to help first by supplying us with intelligence material, in which his wife was of great aid to us, and later on he agreed to emerge in the public eye as a kind of antipode to Ulbricht—if we could get him out of East Germany. By this time life had become intolerable for the Kastners in the East. Although they possessed two villas, a service car, and a chauffeur, they were constantly shadowed and we learned from our sources that only their Soviet contacts kept them alive. Frau Kastner was almost hysterical with fear. Eventually we decided the risk they were running was too great. I suggested to Dr. Adenauer the idea of promoting Kastner—

if we could get him out—as the most prominent refugee yet to flee
East Germany, and he expressed a strong interest in this. We arranged a date with the Kastners, and told Frau Kastner she would
be able to take only her jewelry with her—she must leave everything else behind. We spirited the professor and his wife out of East
Berlin in a dramatic smuggling operation: one of our agents guided
the couple through two empty buildings into West Berlin, a particularly risky operation with two refugees. We immediately flew the
couple to West Germany.

We wanted to make immediate capital from their escape: we
wanted Kastner to deliver a major speech to the German people,
attacking Ulbricht and his regime. But while one segment of the
press saw Kastner's defection as a serious blow to East Berlin, others
dismissed him as an opportunist who had basked in the limelight of
the Ulbricht regime as long as he could, and who should be treated
as such. We were not able at that time to reveal the extent to which
he had cooperated with our organization while in office. The sniping came mainly from the Free Democratic Party, whose approaches to Kastner's similar party in the Soviet zone had earlier
been rebuffed. His first wife, who lived in Munich, was also less
than enchanted at the prospect of the emergence of Kastner with
his new spouse, and caused us many difficulties.

As the hostile clamor in the newspapers increased, we recognized it might rebound on us; we had to cast Kastner adrift, and
the government decided to drop its plan for Kastner to deliver a
public denunciation of Ulbricht. We would exploit his knowledge
and experience in some other way instead. A few months later
Kastner died of a heart attack in Munich's Central Station.

*  *  *

The increasingly noisy Communist campaign against the Gehlen
organization was inevitably an embarrassment to the authorities in
Bonn. While government spokesmen officially pooh-poohed the campaign and announced on one occasion that the Federal Cabinet had
discussed my organization "for several seconds," in private it was
clear that there were reservations about the early incorporation of

the organization into government service, a plan on which the new state-secretary in the Chancellor's Office, Dr. Hans Globke, was working. On December 10, 1953, I was called on to testify before the EDC* committee of the Federal Parliament, and Fritz Erler, the Socialist deputy chairman of the committee, put a number of distinctly hostile questions to me on the Geyer affair. That enabled me to deliver a lengthy but broadly intelligible speech on the role of the organization and on its structure and methods, and to report in detail on the Geyer case as well. At the end of the three-hour session, Erler congratulated me and encouraged me to carry on the work as we had been doing so far. Several of the other committee members afterward told the press they were "deeply impressed" by what they had heard.†

By this time it had become increasingly plain to us that Wollweber's immediate target was to support the Soviet campaign to disrupt the foreign ministers' conference which had been arranged to take place in Berlin during January. Throughout December the Soviet zone newspapers and radio published a barrage of mostly outdated "revelations" about the organization in an unusually vigorous campaign, which became explicable only when examined in the context of the Soviet political offensive that followed. I should stress here that until Wollweber ordered these disclosures about the organization, it had been an unwritten law common to all intelligence services to keep quiet about anything of importance found out about the enemy's intelligence service, in order to keep him guessing and to prevent him from making running repairs on his organization. The first clue as to the Russian intentions came on December 10, 1953, just as I was addressing the EDC committee in Bonn. The Soviet zone's Radio Germany accused Dr. Adenauer of planning to disrupt the meeting of foreign ministers in Berlin; and at the same time, the Russians tried to

---

* European Defense Community.
† The *Hamburger Abendblatt* of August 15, 1954, reported, "Most of them praise his confident and collected manner, his intelligence and versatility. They gained the impression that Gehlen is an expert and that his organization is kept pure of political influence. He shows no trace of political ambition."—TRANS.

brand the Western intelligence agencies as the permanent enemies of peace.

A few days later, my organization scored an important coup in the fight against the coordinated Russian and East German smear campaigns against us. One of our cells procured from the Soviet embassy in East Berlin an original copy of an unpublished Russian-language "white book." It was a nasty piece of handiwork, listing just about all the lying allegations that had ever been made against the Western intelligence agencies. We found out that it was intended to circulate this white book among the foreign ministers (Molotov, Dulles, Eden, and Bidault) during the conference; the main attack was to be concentrated on the Gehlen organization. We were depicted as a suspect association of former Abwehr officers and ex-Nazis, and our alleged war-mongering activities were described in bloodthirsty detail. Once again we were painted in lurid colors as an organization whose tentacles extended right across Europe, engaged in espionage, sabotage, and all kinds of underground activities which ought to have been quashed long ago by the three Western powers. Patent though the objectives and purpose of this white book were, it was equally implicit in this onslaught that to Moscow the organization over which Wollweber had spoken the last rites so frequently was still very much alive and kicking.

The result of receiving this book was a series of intensive discussions with my closest colleagues at Pullach in the last few days before Christmas. We decided to answer the Soviet litany of allegations with a white book of our own. Like theirs, it would not be intended for general publication, but for confidential distribution to the foreign ministers meeting in Berlin, if need arose. Obviously we would only use such information in our white book as we could justify publishing. The final decision on whether or not to include specific matters was mine. Throughout that Christmas there was feverish activity at Pullach, as page by page the Soviet brochure was translated and analyzed, and page by page I cleared the final text of our reply, "White Book on the Soviet Communist Offensive against the German Federal Republic." In the first part of our narrative we illustrated the enemy's political activity and organization, citing specific instances of propaganda and infiltration. The second part reported on the work of the Communist secret services operating within West Germany. Whereas the Soviet publication took as its theme the alleged espionage and subversion operations of the West, our own reply contained extensive material proving that East Berlin was being used as a base of operations against the Federal Republic. We attached particular importance to exposing the Soviet tactics and techniques with respect to Germany and to exposing their current goal—the fomenting of a popular revolutionary movement in West Germany. All in all, our document would have clearly revealed the subtle interplay of the enemy's secret service operations with his other political activities.

When the Four Power talks began in Berlin on January 21, 1954, the Russians were advised through suitable channels that a reply to their white book had been prepared. They thereupon decided it might be better not to circulate their own confidential brochure. Our organization's document of rebuttal stayed locked in its safe as well—it had served its purpose merely by its existence. The conference itself ended a month later, with the foreign ministers not having made the least headway toward a settlement of the German problem.

* * *

In the mid-1950s we succeeded in doing what was more insult than injury to the Soviet secret service through what was in fact a massive deception operation.

We called it Operation Uranus. It started in the Soviet zone at Aue, in Saxony, at the uranium mine from which our organization received a number of valuable mineral samples from an agent. Later, this agent transferred to East Berlin, where he surrendered to the headquarters of the Soviet secret police in the suburb of Karlshorst. But he did so on our organization's instructions. We provided him with the material to enable him to convince the Russians that he had infiltrated a (wholly fictitious) "main controlling office" of ours in West Berlin. This ostensible double agent persistently warned his Russian controller, the later notorious Colonel Petrov, that there were a large number of "Gehlen agents" functioning throughout Saxony, and so vivid a picture did he paint of their effectiveness that the Russians took hasty steps to smash the spy ring. After strenuous preparations—for the Russians were particularly sensitive about the area around the uranium mine—they sprang their dragnets simultaneously throughout the province, only to find this spurious army of agents evaporate before their eyes. This was one Gehlen network in which there were more holes than net.

In the case of Emil Bahr—no relation of Brandt's state-secretary Egon Bahr—Wollweber burned his fingers even more unpleasantly. Bahr was one of our agents who fell into Wollweber's hands immediately before the Four Power talks in Berlin were due to begin. To the media of the Soviet zone this was a godsend. As a welcome to the Western delegates, Bahr's "revelations" were broadcast by the radio system of the Soviet zone throughout January 24, 1954, the day before the conference began, and they were published in every newspaper there. Since Bahr's supposed confessions included damaging details of "widespread preparations being made by the Gehlen organization to disrupt the conference," there could be no doubt but that the Communists saw Bahr, this self-styled "key Gehlen agent," as a curtain raiser to the distribution of their white book. A witness like Bahr, who could be persuaded to pass himself off as a repentant sinner, willing to expose his former bosses, is obviously worth his weight in gold—at least, so long as he was available. We can readily imagine the discomfiture of the SSD's boss, Wollweber, when Bahr—whose presence in East Berlin had of course been demonstrated to the foreign press—escaped from custody and fled to West Berlin. There, this intersector commuter declared to the world that he had not uttered one word of his supposed confession, and that his "testimony" had been faked from start to finish by the SSD.

During the rest of 1954 it became clear to even the loyalist Communists in East Berlin that Wollweber had not attained one of his objectives. The Gehlen organization had not been crushed—indeed, from his expostulations and statements, my colleagues and I were frequently able to make intelligence deductions as to our weak points. We were able to correct our earlier errors and constantly improve on our security precautions. The morale of our agents in the field remained high: for the greater part they continued working for us, unimpressed by the Communist propaganda campaigns. Wollweber had succeeded neither in annihilating the organization's working substance nor in discrediting us in the eyes of the government in Bonn. Though the transfer of the organization to government control was still shelved for the time being, the very fact that I had addressed the EDC committee during December 1953 marked a further degree of indirect recognition of our organization's existence and capabilities.

Thanks to the early contacts I had established between Pullach and the publishers and editors of selected West German newspapers and magazines,* we had also succeeded in neutralizing a number of press channels which had initially displayed undue hostility toward us as well as an indecent readiness to repeat Communist propaganda. On various occasions we were able to use the friendlier organs to put the truth in its proper context, in reply to the muck raked by these irresponsible journals; and this in time served as a warning to those who might otherwise have felt inclined to publish material emanating from Communist sources without critical judgment.

Ernst Wollweber's attempts to smear the organization in the eyes of Allied and neutral countries of the West also proved a futile exercise. His countless distorted or downright mendacious accusations frequently defeated their own purpose, so exaggerated and sensational was the form in which the "revelations" were publicized. In the end, the SSD had done itself more harm than good, because by their clumsy methods they frequently unmasked agents of their own; and in their show trials they staged proceedings which in the long run could only reflect more on the prosecutors than on the defendants. At the end of this first campaign, *Neues Deutschland* published an item which cannot have pleased Wollweber: on

---

* Among them were *Bayernkurier; Die Welt,* and its Sunday edition; *Der Spiegel; Die Zeit;* and *Deutsche Soldatenzeitung.* All of them respected the confidence we showed toward them, but *Der Spiegel* was later a bitter disappointment.

February 24, 1954, the East German national newspaper reported under the headline GEHLEN TO ENTER BONN'S SERVICE the somewhat premature news:

> ... Meanwhile it has been announced in Bonn that the Gehlen espionage organization, which has hitherto operated under American orders in collusion with the federal government, is to be transferred in its entirety to federal responsibility, in other words to the control of the Adenauer government.

In printing this, the official and principal organ of the Socialist Unity Party admitted that the broadsides the SSD had fired to prevent the federal government from taking over the organization had failed.

## CHAPTER EIGHT

# Transferred to Federal Control

$\mathcal{T}$he transfer of the Gehlen organization to federal control had originally been planned to take place in 1952 or 1953, but this proved impossible. The Communist smear campaign and the events of 1953—mishaps against which no intelligence service can be entirely immune—may well have stirred misgivings in the politically minded West German public, not to mention some members of the Federal Parliament, as to whether the organization would act for the good of the Federal Republic if it were to enter government service. This was hardly surprising in view of the ignorance and skepticism displayed by many Germans as to what work is necessary and vital to the interests of a state.

The principal figures of the Federal Republic—especially Chancellor Adenauer and his State-Secretary Globke, who had succeeded Lenz in October 1953—refused to be deterred by the Communist campaign. They remained convinced, as did the leaders of the opposition parties, that the Gehlen organization would have to be taken over by Bonn as soon as possible. Both my American colleagues and I agreed that the proper time for this would arrive when West Germany's political sovereignty was restored; and this would occur when the occupation statute legalizing the residual rights of the Allies in West Germany was rescinded (with certain exceptions).* This condition was met on May 5, 1955, when West Germany was accepted for membership in NATO and a mutual defense pact was signed with the United States. By then, three years had elapsed since the signing of the German Treaty, and the long period of waiting before the organization was formally taken over was in many respects something of an endurance test, although in retrospect the wait was well worthwhile. I know many of my colleagues, anxious for their futures, would have preferred the transfer to have taken place earlier. As it was, the organization avoided becoming infected with many of the teething troubles which beset the civil service at that time; by 1956, when the date for the formal transfer finally arrived, the necessary maturing process in the federal authorities was largely complete, a circumstance which went a long way toward insuring a smooth transfer to government control.

The Office for the Protection of the Constitution (BfV) chaired by Dr. Otto John, had been under federal control since its inception in 1950, subordinated to the Ministry of the Interior. This federal agency and its provincial subsidiaries were very different in character from my foreign intelligence service. Dr. John's job was to provide a defense against internal dangers such as seditious agitation, espionage, and sabotage. His was purely a reporting function, as his agency had no powers of arrest comparable to those of the Federal Bureau of Investigation in the United States. Where the BfV uncovered the necessary evidence, it was for the regular prosecuting authorities to institute the arrests. Unlike my organization's job, therefore, the Office for the Protection of the Constitution had a purely domestic function, and provided that the functions of the two

---

* After the occupation statute lapsed, the Allies retained certain residual rights in West Germany; e.g., the sole authority to monitor private telephone conversations.

agencies were clearly defined, there should have been only a few exceptional cases where overlapping occurred to any degree.

It is misleading to suggest that my organization at any time wanted to take over the BfV. A foreign intelligence service like mine had only one task—to gather information on other countries, to aid in shaping foreign policy. It is obvious that useful information would be obtained by keeping the activities of the various international Communist organizations under surveillance. This in turn justified our operating on West German soil, as well as abroad. Where the intelligence we obtained through these sources touched on the internal security of the nation, we passed it on to the BfV as the responsible agency. This study of international Communist organizations was of great importance in our analysis of Soviet foreign policy, and this may explain the motives behind the Communist-inspired attempts to discredit my organization for having been involved in "domestic espionage," as they describe it. The main focus of a foreign intelligence service's search for information will always be directed abroad, but domestic sources cannot be entirely ignored. Clearly, I had to insist very definitely that our organization remain impartial, which our first federal chancellor did not always appreciate. I remember Adenauer more than once invited me to put our watchdogs on certain Social Democrat officials.*

I would never have favored a merger of the two organizations: the surveillance of subversive activities in West Germany calls for coordination and cooperation, not for amalgamation. In nearly every country of the world the two organizations do in fact operate independently of each other. The Soviet government in particular carefully guards against any squabbling over jurisdiction between their espionage and security agencies.

Of course relations between my organization and the BfV were put under a severe strain by the tragedy of the Otto John affair. Late on July 20, 1954, under circumstances which are still a matter of controversy, he crossed or was conveyed across the sector bound-

---

* I still have among my papers a report that was drawn up for internal organization purposes: "The Growing Influence of the Communists Within the Social Democrat Party."

ary into East Berlin and participated in a spectacular press conference there in August—to all appearances a defector, a top-level Soviet agent who had been recalled by his paymasters. Some time before, John had made an official visit to the United States; I had sent a private warning to my colleagues there that it would be unwise to show him too much, and this prescience on my part was not considered by the Americans to have been justified. Whatever the actual circumstances of John's border-crossing were, the fact remains that in my organization it would have been impossible for a senior official, let alone its head, to visit West Berlin. Nor is it possible to forgive John for his actions once he was in East Berlin, and it was for *these* that he was later sentenced by our Supreme Court to imprisonment for treason, not for the dubious circumstances of his border-crossing. In East Berlin, John broadcast over the radio the favorite Communist lie that my organization was carrying out espionage against France, and suggested that West Germany was on the threshold of a new Nazi revival. He seems to have regarded me as his great rival for the role of Adenauer's Canaris; unfortunately, Dr. John was inclined to see all his real friends as enemies and—far more dangerously—vice versa.

In mid-December 1955, even as a parliamentary commission of inquiry into the defection was resuming its sittings, Dr. Otto John reappeared in West Berlin. Our organization played no part in retrieving him. Adenauer certainly had no affection to spare for the returning prodigal, and is said to have announced the news to his cabinet colleagues with the words, "I have an item of information which will fill you with mirth. Dr. John has defected." Ollenhauer, the opposition leader, privately described John as a case for psychiatrists rather than for politicians, which is an overharsh assessment in my opinion. I believe Dr. John deserves our sympathy for suffering what was a hideous personal tragedy; his eighteen months in Communist hands must be attributed at most to a temporary breakdown. He has served his sentence, and there I propose to let the matter rest.

* * *

Meanwhile, the problem of restoring West Germany as a military power could no longer be ignored. This was accomplished in several stages: first, General Count Schwerin was appointed military adviser to Adenauer; then a special office was created under Blank, later defense minister, to pave the way for the establishment of the Bundeswehr—the federal armed forces. As the Gehlen organization had not yet come under the government's aegis, Bonn activated within the general framework of the Bundeswehr a modest military intelligence agency with a limited scope for carrying out intelligence evaluation work. This task was taken care of by the Americans as well. With Minister Blank's approval the Chancellor's Office ordered this agency to collaborate as closely as possible with our organization until such time as we were in a position to take on that work too. As a result of his detailed exchanges of ideas with the Chancellor's Office and his regular talks with me, Minister Blank willingly endorsed my concept of a uniform foreign intelligence service; and over the years that followed he made efforts to secure the close collaboration between the Blank Office and our organization. Meanwhile, the man who has twice been my successor, Gerhard Wessel, became the liaison officer between Blank and Pullach, and he later accepted the position of G-2 to the Bundeswehr.

The question of transferring the organization's headquarters from Pullach to Bonn never arose. The selection of Pullach as the site for our headquarters in 1947 had been pure chance; it had happened purely and simply because the location was just what we were looking for and because it could be made available without serious problems, merely by moving out one Allied agency, which was not unimportant at that time. Our geographical separation from the nation's capital—some 350 miles—did not hamper us in our work at all, since there were rail, air, and autobahn connections available. In addition, I saw to it that our liaison office just outside Bonn was well staffed with high-grade, experienced experts who were available for immediate discussions if the need arose. In another sense this remoteness had one great advantage: our organization and its staff were far from the political bustle of the capital, and could attend to their work without distraction.

* * *

The most complicated problems were those connected with the transfer of our staff, of course. Would it be possible to transfer them all to government service? Whose services would we have to terminate?—an unpleasant decision for any superior concerned with the welfare of his men. What would be the status of staff involved in the transfer? Would their earlier employment within the Gehlen organization be credited to them as public service employment, and what would the effect be on them if it was not? Some of the more stubborn questions in this field have remained unresolved to this day.

On the other hand, we had been able to convert our permanent salaried staff to the same scale as that for other public service officials (TOA*) as early as February 1953, so that at least as far as salaries are concerned we were in line with other federal agencies three full years before we were taken over by the government. This conversion to the TOA made it necessary for us to group our staff into the same groupings as laid down in the TOA criteria. Apart from our secretarial staff, drivers, and others employed mainly on technical matters, this was not often easy, and it was here that my colleagues and I were grateful for the advice of the Federal Audit Office (working at that time in their capacity as staff of the federal commissioner for economic efficiency in government) on how to have things our way, without contravening government regulations.

The net result, to our understandable pleasure, was an increase in our incomes, and this was not without its effect on the recruitment of personnel. The consequent increase in our financial requirements, which coincided with a cutback in the funds allocated to us by Washington in November 1953, had to be balanced somehow in our annual budget sheet. But with the help of a rationalization committee, and by taking constant measures to reduce red tape, we managed somehow to surmount our financial problems without impairing our intelligence work.

At the same time we began to restrict our Pullach headquarters to exclusively official purposes: the families of our staff had

---

* *Tarifordnung für Angestellte,* "Salary Classification for Employees."

to move out of the compound, and internal facilities like the kindergarten and school were closed down. These necessary measures brought problems of their own. Homes had to be found, and since the village of Pullach was out of bounds for security reasons, and given the prevailing housing shortage, the new accommodations were frequently some distance away. Local transport connections with Pullach were not ideal, so we had to establish a transportation service. Many of our employees had to resign, and this in turn required us to find replacements.

These innovations were not without psychological consequences. Hitherto we had been, so to speak, one large family—the enforced togetherness by night and day, at work and off duty, had brought us all close to one another. Everybody knew everybody else—though few of my staff knew me. They shared their sorrows and excitements and helped each other out whenever possible. Naturally there was friction too; it is unavoidable in even the smallest family, and it was so much the worse in a large community like ours. But I am happy to be able to record that over all the years, the sunny side of community living far outshone the bickering. But now all this was coming to an end. We were soon to become a government agency. While it would certainly make our daily work more businesslike, it would also mark the disappearance of the indefinable something, the inner warmth and sense of real solidarity that had pervaded the Gehlen organization since its foundation a decade before.

* * *

Since late 1950 the attitude of our American friends toward the future of the Gehlen organization had undergone a remarkable change. The two CIA directors, General Walter Bedell Smith and, from January 1953, Allen Dulles, had come to recognize that my 1945 plan was bound to come to fruition, just as General Sibert had accepted in his gentlemen's agreement with me. They concluded that they should give their utmost support to the transfer of the organization to federal control. Over the following years American representatives had therefore held many conversations with the Chancellor's Office in Bonn in which the technical details of the transfer were thrashed out. By various means they prevailed on their other allies to accept at government level what had formerly been an American-controlled agency. The expectation was that my organization would continue to work in close collaboration with the Western Allies; and the CIA was convinced that this helpfulness on their part would pay for itself later in cementing the future political partnership between Bonn and the Western Allies. In this they were not disappointed.

The lasting comradeship and trust that was born then has since profited everybody concerned. By the early 1950s the advantages that naturally accrue from a properly managed distribution of effort were already becoming apparent: it is always the case that the results of a balanced joint effort between several allied intelligence agencies will far exceed the sum of the component efforts. Besides, given a regular exchange of intelligence, facts can be double-checked, faulty conclusions can be avoided, and the chances of preventing enemy infiltration of one's service reduced to a minimum. Our collaboration with the other NATO agencies shaped up and continually improved between 1953, when Dulles became Director of the CIA, and 1956. In every important crisis, such as the Berlin uprising of 1953, the Suez conflict of July 1956, the Berlin incidents of 1958 (in which Khrushchev demanded the withdrawal of Allied troops), and the Cuban crisis, as indeed during several episodes in Asia, our cooperation with the other Western agencies stood the test.

In the course of my work I met Allen Dulles many times, both in Germany and later in the United States. We would limit ourselves to discussions of top-level policy. He pleased me by his air of wisdom, born of years of experience; he was both fatherly and boisterous, and he became a close personal friend of mine. Once he made me a gift of a small carved wooden statuette—a sinister figure with cloak and dagger, whose nameplate betrayed his American nationality: "Fnu Nmi-Lnu" (the American index-card abbreviations for "first name unknown," "no middle initial," "last name unknown"). This anonymous gentleman still graces my study desk. In all the years of my collaboration with the CIA, I had no personal disputes with Dulles. There were minor problems caused by different concepts and procedures, particularly in financial affairs, but I have no cause to criticize these allies.

Nor was this close collaboration impaired by the transfer measures. It gained in importance from the fact that after 1952 the West German federal government repeatedly channeled to us requests for intelligence work, even though it was by no means entitled to act as our master. These inquiries were not limited to Iron Curtain countries alone, but applied to every country in the world. Eventually, there was not one country in which we did not have our sources. I regarded the growing federal interest in us as a token of recognition of the work we had done so far, and I took good care that these inquiries were answered as promptly as could be arranged.

The Gehlen organization was increasingly called upon to furnish material as a basis for foreign policy appreciations at times when Bonn faced important discussions. I admit we had to overcome certain misgivings from professional diplomatic quarters in the beginning. Given their unhappy experiences with some representatives of the Abwehr and of the Reich Main Security Office (RSHA) during the war years, they showed a marked reserve at first which was only natural. Nonetheless, the principal figures in the Foreign Ministry set great store by our reports; and they repeatedly encouraged us, especially after our transfer in 1956, to draft summaries analyzing certain specific themes.

The initial misgivings did on occasions lead to grotesque situations: for example, a German ambassador once asked one of his foreign colleagues about an intelligence report which had been supplied by us to the Foreign Ministry and passed on to him for his information. The report concerned some exceptionally secret activities in which the foreigner was engaged. Of course the latter—who, incidentally, was himself a former member of his country's intelligence service—indignantly denied the accuracy of the report, whereupon the German ambassador reproached the Foreign Ministry with this and told them not to bother him with such nonsense in future. (A frantic search for our organization's source immediately began in the country concerned.) The facts our man had provided were incidentally probably the most valuable we could have hoped for. About two months after this episode his report was confirmed in every respect by history.

Bonn's demands on our organization multiplied, so I had to set up special sections to work almost exclusively for the Federal Republic from as early as 1952. From 1954 onward, the volume of work that they handled increased.

Parallel to our discussions with the various government departments, including the BfV, which had been directed by the former attorney general Hubert Schrübbers since the Otto John affair, we made a point of establishing contact with the provincial (*Land*) governments, and building on these contacts where we could. For various reasons the Americans had built up these contacts in their occupation zone during the early years of the organization's existence. In the French and British zones the links were rudimentary at best, and in Berlin they were channeled through the Allied garrison headquarters. Due to a number of tactless actions, there had frequently occurred some unpleasant friction, mainly as a result of the psychological climate of those years. The Americans were therefore happy to see me begin to pay visits to the prime ministers of the various provinces, with the blessing of the state-secretary in the Chancellor's Office as well. I briefed these local dignitaries on the Gehlen organization and on my plans for a federal intelligence service in the future, and I outlined to them how the provinces could best help us. It was in these meetings that the groundwork was done for the appointment over the next three years of "liaison experts" between my service and the provincial governments, an arrangement which was to prove exceptionally useful. I well recall my visit to the prime minister of Hesse, Herr Zinn, and his minister of the interior Schneider on February 20, 1953: they displayed a powerful interest in the work of the organization, particularly since various careless slips by our American friends had repeatedly caused them offense in their own province. They listened avidly to all I told them, and in later years we received considerable support from them. We established outstandingly good contacts with both

Prime Minister Ehard of Bavaria and his successor, Högner; without their support we could scarcely have been able to overcome the obstacles that confronted us during the construction of our organization.

\* \* \*

On May 5, 1955, West Germany was accepted by NATO as a member with equal rights, and on the same day her sovereignty was restored to her. Thus the last formal obstacle to the organization's transfer to federal responsibility was removed. We could hasten our preparations and get to work on the main problems that were left.

The transfer could have been effected in two different ways: a law could have been passed, or the transfer could simply have been ordained by the government under the powers granted it by Article 86 of German Basic Law. The two possibilities were debated within the government, and the parliamentary committees concerned discussed them with my colleagues and myself. In the end, a simple cabinet decision was resorted to. It is true that passing a special law would have anchored the future intelligence service firmly in the structure of the government and that it would have obviated a lot of the ambiguity and vagueness that later surrounded it. But on the other hand it would have cramped both the government and the service in their dealings with each other. The service would immediately have become an inflexible body, virtually incapable of change, because any structural alterations could be sanctioned only by passing new laws—unless the original law was left so general that all actual discretion was left to the federal chancellor. Such a law would be but an empty shell, and the later process of legislation unnecessarily time-consuming. With opposition approval—an important requisite in my view—the government opted for the second alternative. On February 21, it was decided that a new agency should be set up, with the title "Federal Intelligence Service,"\* and attached—not subordinated—to the Chan-

---

\* *Bundesnachrichtendienst* (BND).

cellor's Office. Adenauer directed that the formal transfer of the Gehlen organization into this new service should begin on April 1, 1956, the beginning of the new fiscal year.

Opting for the second alternative did not preclude the government from reverting to the first one at some later date and formalizing the new service's position by statute. As it was, the simple cabinet decision left the government and the service's directors flexible in their approach, while enabling us to make our operational decisions without red tape, keeping within the broad directives issued to us. Our attachment to the Chancellor's Office gave us something of the status of a central government agency like the Federal Press Office; had we been subordinated to the Chancellor's Office, its head would have become de facto the responsible superior of the Federal Intelligence Service, and he would have had to take the enormous responsibility for all our actions and omissions.

Most countries grant their intelligence services wide discretion to perform their duties, so long as they remain within the broad framework of the cabinet directives issued to them. The requirements of security are one obvious reason for this; another is that it would be illusory to hope that such services could be adequately supervised by lay civil servants. But the operations of intelligence services can yield embarrassing situations which can even place a burden on the government's relations with foreign countries— the kind of incident which even great circumspection can never entirely prevent. (One has only to consider the U-2 affair in 1960, which Khrushchev swiftly exploited to torpedo the Paris summit conference in which he had lost interest. At the time, President Eisenhower stood up for his secret service chief Allen Dulles— there could be no better witness to the soldierly bearing of that outstanding president. But it was not typical of the common practice in such cases, and even in America it attracted strong domestic criticism. The British and French governments would have acted very differently.)

It is an occupational hazard for every intelligence service chief and his senior colleagues that in such incidents they have to go it alone. Raison d'état demands that they cannot expect either public support or approbation for their actions. Every government will publicly dissociate itself from incidents where an intelligence service has "exceeded its discretion." Such political considerations motivated the solution of attaching rather than subordinating us to the Chancellor's Office; in effect, I was personally responsible to the chief of that office, and hence to Chancellor Adenauer himself. An added blessing was that I could discuss matters directly with various federal departments or with provincial governments without intermediate bureaucratic stages (although the Chancellor's Office was kept fully informed of such negotiations, of course). This direct line of communication with other departments proved absolutely vital for the rapid evaluation of the information we obtained. Had we been subordinated to the Chancellor's Office, it would have placed a considerable burden on its administrative staff. As it was, it proved sufficient to appoint one liaison officer, with duties similar to those appointed by the various federal ministries to the Chancellor's Office.

Finally, the "attachment" process also made it possible for the Federal Intelligence Service to be used—as were the services of other countries—as a channel for putting out unofficial feelers before resorting to the diplomatic service itself. This method, in which a service may be able to exploit its links with other friendly services, has the advantage that the government can explore delicate matters in advance without official commitment. It was the method Adenauer used when he first explored the possibility of a rapprochement with France; even before our transfer to federal control, my organization was employed to approach our French opposite numbers to prepare the basis for an entente, long before the respective Foreign Ministries were engaged. The advantage is that such feelers can be broken off by either side at any time with no consequent loss of prestige. Adenauer made use of these channels more than once.

On only two occasions did I become involved in intelligence contacts with the Russian secret service. In about 1953 we established contact with a KGB officer in a Mediterranean country and turned him around; it was through him that we received the first news that Lavrenti Beria, head of the Soviet secret service, had been liquidated—news so incredible that at first we did not know whether to treat him seriously. We prepared to exploit this officer as a direct channel of political contact with Moscow, but his superiors must have smelled a rat, for after a year of working for us he vanished without a trace before we were able to put our ideas into operation. Although the III F (counterespionage) part of this case was known at Pullach, our attempts to use him as a link were known only to Adenauer and myself; the whole affair was of such sensitivity that I personally destroyed all papers relating to it.

On the second occasion, contact was definitely established. A former panzer colonel, Bogislaw von Bonin, who had been chief of the German Army's operations branch after 1944, called to see me late in 1955 and informed me that he had been invited by the Russians to discuss the political future of the two Germanys in a meeting at their headquarters in East Berlin. Bonin inquired whether he ought to admit that he was a personal acquaintance of mine (though not in any sense a member of my organization). I advised him to tell the Russians that, and that our organization was aware of his invitation to Berlin and the nature of the proposed unofficial talks. Nothing came of this approach—the talks merely confirmed that the gulf between the Eastern and Western standpoints on Germany was as wide as ever. For eleven years after that, the Russians kept the secret of these unofficial talks before disclosing it in characteristic fashion in an attempt to discredit me in the eyes of our government.* This item of "disinformation" failed, however. I had taken the precaution of recording my conversations when Bonin visited me and had immediately sent the tapes to the attorney general at that time.

*  *  *

The organization's staff was transferred to federal service not en bloc but individually. The whole transfer took about two years to

---

* A retired colonel in the Soviet secret service, Vladimir Karpov, summoned *Der Spiegel*'s Moscow correspondent and revealed the story early in 1966.

complete, and we took the opportunity of screening every member of the staff once more with respect to his ability, security record, and character.

At the time, the question of the Nazi past of some of the staff was also of some importance. During the postwar years we had of course recruited nobody who had not passed the proper denazification procedures, but in some cases where staff had been members of certain Nazi party formations we considered it appropriate to vet them once again. In following years we repeated the vetting process several times, particularly with respect to the few former SS members employed by the organization. We had sent certain former members of the SS on special missions overseas, insofar as they had clean political records; this was done with the full approval of the American authorities. For example, we found the Arab countries particularly willing to embrace Germans with an ostensibly "Nazi" past. There were not many of them in our organization. The accusations that have been mouthed against us, of employing large numbers of former SS officers, are false. Most of these allegations emanated from East Germany, and occasionally they were echoed by the less informed sections of the Western press. This was a matter that was also repeatedly raised in the special parliamentary committee responsible for liaison with the Federal Intelligence Service.

It was I who had proposed that a small parliamentary committee be set up to look after our affairs. This was probably in State-Secretary Globke's mind as well, for the aftermath of the 1953 Geyer affair and the length at which it was debated by the EDC committee that December* indicated that above all my organization needed to gain the confidence of the parliamentary deputies. The result was the birth of the Confidential Committee in 1956, a committee consisting of the leaders of the parliamentary parties, who in due course displayed the utmost understanding and readiness to assist the service.

And so on April 1, 1956, the Stars and Stripes were hauled down for the last time outside our Pullach headquarters, and the

---

* See p. 183.

black, red, and gold federal flag was hoisted. All of us knew that the most exacting phase of our existence had begun: now we would find out whether the organization was adequate in structure and concept for its new role as an official German government agency. Looking at the empty flagpole, it occurred to me that it might be a pleasant idea for the flag of Bavaria to be flown at Pullach too; I telephoned Prime Minister Högner in Munich, and the Bavarian government sent a blue and white flag soon after. It was dedicated at a small ceremony in Högner's presence, and it has flown ever since next to the federal flag. It was wholly improper from the federal point of view, of course; but then there is much that happens in an intelligence service that is not strictly by the book.

# Part Three

# In Service of West Germany

Knowledge of the future cannot be acquired from the gods or demons; nor can it be obtained by comparisons or measurements or calculations. Knowledge of the enemy is acquired only by human agencies.

The kinds of spies that are used are five in number: there are the native spies, and there are the spies within; there are the spies that return from the other side; there are the spies of death and the spies of life.

If all five kinds of spies are employed, then nobody will ever learn their secret ways; that is what we call a divine secret. It is the most priceless possession of the lord and master.

The lord and master must control his spies' work in person. The spies that return are those that render the best knowledge of the enemy, so show particular nobleness unto them.

—SUN-TSE, *Treatise on the Art of War*

CHAPTER NINE

# The
# Intelligence
# Service

propose to preface this part, which is to be an account of the
work of the Federal Intelligence Service, with a chapter on the
general character of such services; and at its head I have set a
quotation from Sun-tse's *Treatise on the Art of War*.* This
Chinese philosopher lived from 550 to 470 B.C., and his treatise is
the oldest surviving complete theoretical work on war; it is some
130 years older than Xenophon's *Anabasis* and was written at about
the time of the battle of Thermopylae, a struggle which was decided
in the Persians' favor by an act of treachery—the antithesis of espionage. Sun-tse's treatise has found countless commentators, and
their writings, together with the original teachings of the master
himself, can serve even today as a comprehensive and timeless set of
guiding principles for the organization of a foreign intelligence
service.

---

* Published by the East German Ministry of National Defense, 1957 (translated
from the Old Chinese into Russian, and thence into German).

One thing common to all the old legends and narratives of "scouts" and "explorers" is that intelligence procurement is regarded as a necessary and natural occupation. It has attracted an unjustified notoriety in the public mind through its association with treachery: treachery, of course, has always been regarded as a despicable act, customarily punished by death. High treason, on the other hand, was not necessarily so; both crime and punishment were almost honorable. Treachery and espionage, however, are regarded as indictable offenses and are subject to severe punishment in every country. Among our own ranks we unearthed individual instances of treachery, and insofar as this lay in our hands (for example in the Felfe case*) I did all I conceivably could to investigate and prevent a repetition.

The man convicted of treason can expect as little clemency from his judges as can the captured spy. He must accept responsibility for his actions in court regardless of whether they were motivated by idealism or by greed. In my own life and chosen profession I have learned not to be too hasty with moral condemnation of such cases. Particularly in view of the recent past, I have come to believe that each act—including espionage and treason—must be weighed morally against the motives that inspired it, and these are completely independent of what legalistic minds may later decide about them.

One such case of an agent acting from idealism was that of Alfred Frenzel, a Social Democrat member of Parliament who was arrested for treachery in 1960. Born in Czechoslovakia, he emigrated to Britain in 1938 and eventually joined the RAF. He entered the Parliament in Bonn in 1953 and sat on such committees as the committee investigating the Otto John affair, the party's internal security committee, and the parliamentary defense committee. For four and a half years he supplied the Czech intelligence service with top secret West German defense plans and documents. My own view was that he had been recruited by the Czechs long before he entered Parliament. But I find it ethically difficult to condemn such acts, born as they are of deep-rooted convictions, and this is a dictum

---

* The Felfe case is discussed on pp. 245–52.

which holds regardless of whether the acts are committed in the interests of the enemy or ourselves and regardless of their consequences.

It is obvious that Oleg Penkovsky and other agents sentenced to harsh penalties in Communist countries for working for the West are not alone in deserving our admiration and sympathy. We must reassess in this light the acts of Soviet spies like Klaus Fuchs, the Rosenbergs, Richard Sorge, and many others, applying standards other than the purely legalistic ones by which they were condemned. These agents also knew that their acts exposed them to prosecution, but they still committed them, motivated so far as can be known purely by their Communist convictions. I have always regarded communism as a deadly danger to us all and totally reject its ideology; but nonetheless we must differentiate between the agent who risks his life out of a sense of idealism and conviction and the man who is motivated purely by lust and greed. The former are the more deadly adversaries—the ones that can be unmasked and captured only after years of painstaking work. Having said all this, I must also make it plain that such an abstract and purely ethical approach should under no circumstances be allowed to interfere with the due processes of law in punishing all traitors, whatever their motives.

The purpose of these remarks is to attempt to dismantle some of the general prejudices against secret service work. Not all services work with bribery, blackmail, and drug addiction; and above all they need human material of the highest caliber. Some intelligence services distribute large amounts of cash and expect to obtain results; but we always preferred to rely on V-men, the kind of agent who works for nothing more tangible than his expenses. It will suffice to say that many such people came forward, willing to risk their freedom, their health, and their lives to work on behalf of West Germany, acting out of a sense of duty toward their country and out of hatred for the totalitarian system of the Communists.

* * *

It has been claimed that until comparatively recent years secret services fulfilled a primarily military purpose. In my view this claim is erroneous. Apart from Byzantium after the decline of the Roman Empire in the sixth century, for almost 900 years there were no standing armies of any kind against which espionage could have been carried out; there were only brief periods of crisis in which conscription was introduced. Such espionage as was conducted in those centuries must have been for political ends. Of course it was not a rigidly disciplined espionage, but it was centrally controlled—controlled in fact by the chancelleries of the kings and monarchs, precisely as Sun-tse recommended.

Thus we know that Louis XI of France (reign: 1461–83), who smashed the tyranny of the French nobility and was the first continental European monarch to maintain a small standing army (of Scottish bowmen), deployed a large, permanent network of agents in the principal cities of Europe. These agents served two purposes: they culled information from various sources, and at the same time they had instructions to influence public opinion in France's favor. So even the "influencers" favored by the Russians and British now are by no means a modern invention. One of these agents, "Le Mauvais," of Ghent, rose to the rank of king's privy secretary; his life and works were dramatized, though not without exaggeration of his historical importance, in a best-selling novel of the 1920s, *Der Teufel* ("The Devil") by Robert Neumann.

Other monarchs, notably the British kings, acted similarly to Louis XI of France. Frederick the Great employed among his official emissaries to the European courts a number of secret service agents, with orders to keep an eye on the situation independently of the accredited ambassadors. From the Middle Ages until the beginning of modern times, the two Italian city-states Venice and Genoa ran regular political intelligence organizations of a covert nature. As the secret reports filed by the diplomatic representatives and other emissaries of these states show, these were in every respect the forerunners of modern secret intelligence services, even using codes and secret inks. After the Italian city-states, the British have the intelligence service with the longest tradition—its roots go back some 600 years. As an island nation, Britain was cut off from the general flow of events and the intelligence bound up in them, and this may well have obliged the British crown to lay its hands on additional firsthand information by whatever means it could. To this end the British service employed people of high social standing and with access to the notables—and hence to the primary sources of intelligence—of the countries concerned.

As in many other fields of activity in Britain, there is an unbroken tradition in their secret service too. This is why in my view the British intelligence service—which may not be the biggest in the Western Hemisphere—is certainly one of the most efficient; indeed, only those now run by the United States and by Israel come anywhere near the British in effectiveness. The British get by with a minimum of red tape, but at the same time their SIS (Secret Intelligence Service) is endowed with a high degree of confidence by both government and Parliament. It is treated with the utmost discretion —not even the name of its head may be referred to. This discretion is of course observed by the entire British press, regardless of whether it is a mass circulation daily or a serious magazine, and regardless of whether the newspaper inclines to Labour or Conservative opinions. Their so-called D-notice system deserves particular attention: confidential standing instructions are circulated for the advice of editors on matters which the government of the day requests them not to publicize. The British press observes this agreement without exception. Would that such a system were workable in West Germany too!

* * *

Various authors have put their hands to writing histories of the German secret service, including Colonel Walter Nicolai, the head of the service during World War I,* and, more recently, Dr. Gert Buchheit.† Its history differs little from that of the other European services except that, unlike them, the German service had to struggle constantly against the tendency to be ignored and neglected. In this respect it can be compared roughly with similar agencies in the United States in the interwar years.

---

* Colonel Walter Nicolai, *Der Nachrichtendienst* [The Intelligence Service] (Berlin, 1920).
† Dr. Gert Buchheit, *Der deutsche Geheimdienst* [The German Secret Service] (Munich, 1966).

In an age in which war is a paramount activity of man, with the total annihilation of the enemy as its primary aim, or (if we express it in the language of Clausewitz) with military objectives elevated to the status of political ends, the gathering of secret intelligence is more important than it has ever been. By World War I, it was no longer enough to scout around for largely military secrets; the rapid procurement of information on the enemy's foreign policy, his economic potential, and his morale, as well as on other political factors, attracted greater attention than before. It is true that in the Franco-Prussian war of 1870–71 the head of the enemy intelligence section of our Grand General Staff, Lieutenant Colonel von Verdy du Vernois, had already instituted a thorough examination of the powers of resistance of the French people, in particular of the population of Paris; but this was the exception.

Just how crucial such intelligence could have been is shown by an instance from World War I. We now know that our High Command was unaware of the depths to which French morale had sunk after the failure of their Nivelle offensive in 1917. Had this crisis been recognized to its full extent, it might have encouraged an offensive against the main French front, instead of our attacking in a minor theater of war, namely Italy, and transporting Lenin back to Russia. Thus France gained the breathing space she desperately needed. On the other hand, the Allies were far better informed on the level of public morale in Germany: they succeeded in gauging exactly the rate at which the German will to resist was ebbing, a process heralded by the big munition workers' strike and the first of the naval mutinies. They were thus enabled to reject the various peace feelers extended to them in 1917 with an easier conscience than if they had been wholly ignorant of Germany's precarious internal situation.

At any rate, World War I taught us how vital it was for all of one's intelligence agencies to work in close coordination—assuming it was not possible to bring them together under one roof. That was how it had always been in Britain; and in France the Deuxième Bureau of the General Staff had always performed this duty. But by the Treaty of Versailles of 1919 Germany had been expressly forbidden to establish or maintain an independent intelligence service; so we did what we could by means of expanding the Abwehr organization into a highly efficient intelligence service under its successive heads—Gemp, Patzig, and Canaris.

The interwar years and World War II confirmed the lessons of World War I, and these in turn were amplified by the lessons we and the Allies later learned in the fight against the Russians— namely that sabotage and counterespionage operations also rightfully belong within the ambit of secret service duties. Since 1945 it has become universally accepted that only a uniformly controlled foreign intelligence service has any prospect of justifying the expectations held for it. This service must transmit to the political leaders every item of secret information (in digested form of course) that they may need for the formation of policy or for the security of the nation. The information must improve or modify the existing premises on which the government bases its decisions; but it must never be used as the sole basis for decisions—only as one source of special and often new accents, which may in certain circumstances be sufficient to tilt the balance one way or the other.

The intelligence service's digests must be strictly nonpartisan and objective. I am reminded of an episode in 1959, when Fritz Erler, the Socialist politician, who was by no means a complaisant critic, paid a visit to Pullach in his role of parliamentary watchdog. During this visit he expressed his doubts about the objectivity of our weekly digest; this digest was a continuing series of weekly summaries of the political situation. Its main section, "Soviet Foreign Policy," was always read with great respect in Bonn, as it was the only such condensed but easily comprehended account of its kind at that time. But Erler thought this digest reflected the subjective opinions of whoever was its author, and doubted that its contents were based solely on intelligence sources at our disposal. "If that is so," he told me, "then it is clear you are attempting to bring subjective pressures to bear on Bonn." I was convinced of the objectivity of my official's analysis, but it was equally clear that I now had to prove it beyond reasonable doubt to Erler. I sent for the official, but Erler repeated his skepticism; so my man invited the politician to select any of the countless weekly digests and undertook to provide the complete file of documentary sources used for each digest within half an hour (of which he would need ten minutes to get back to his office and another ten minutes to return). He was as good as his word. Erler was visibly impressed by the balanced and cautious picture the digests presented when he compared them with the documents on which they had been based. I subsequently learned that from that moment on he always based his own political judgment on the weekly digest and defended it against other skeptics.

A Western intelligence service will report to its government on the plans, prospects, and events of the country under observation and on current and future trends in politics, arms technology, and military planning; it will also report on that country's morale. It will supply facts on anything from new weapons to production statistics, military transport movements, the utterances of top officials, and the like. It will procure secret documents like reports of conferences and organization plans, and it will prepare assessments on the fighting quality of the country's armed forces. In forwarding such information, every service is accepting a considerable responsibility; that is why a detailed background knowledge of every factor involved, including the national character and ideology, is indispensable. How far are the actions of governments conditioned by their ideology? To what extent is ideology only a smoke screen? What part do international party ties play in a country's foreign policy?—for example, what part do the various international Communist parties play in Soviet foreign policy? Above all, an intelligence service's operatives must never apply their own values in formulating their conjectures of what the enemy may do, for this will lead to false conclusions more frequently than not.

Of course, the government will always want to be briefed as comprehensively as possible on events with which it may have to contend; it may ask for the exact date and time when a certain event predicted by the service concerned may occur. Remonstrances that this or that service has "let us down again" are usually sparked by developments which have taken the public—if not the government or its intelligence service—by surprise.* But secret intelligence on political and to a certain extent military affairs is largely a matter of prediction. That something may occur does not necessarily mean that it will.

This is because every political or military action can be split up into three parts: first, the decision to act; second, the preparation of that action; and third, its commission. A secret service can usually detect only the second of these stages, the preparatory stage, and from its further observations it will detect what progress is being made and finally the completion of preparations. Of course, there are occasionally great coups in which a service pulls off a master stroke and ascertains the actual decision or even the date set for an operation to commence. For example, our Federal Intelligence Service was in a position to report to the government that Khrushchev had decided to break up the Paris summit conference of 1960. But instances like these are the purest good fortune in every sense of the word. They have nothing to do with the quality of an intelligence service; this can be judged only by the consistency and regularity of its reporting.

Nor, I might add, is the value of a prediction to be judged solely on the basis of whether that prediction comes true. It is perfectly possible for certain intentions to exist in the enemy's mind at a time an intelligence report is made, only to be revoked later on because, for example, they are known to have been compromised. For instance, on January 10, 1940, documents revealing that Hitler planned to attack the Western powers, including neutral Belgium, fell into Belgian hands just a few days before the seventeenth, the date set for the attack. Hitler had no option but to cancel the operation on the thirteenth. What the Belgian intelligence service reported at the time was true, even though it was not borne out by subsequent events. Unfortunately, the opposite situation is more often the case. Reports forwarded by an intelligence service are frequently dismissed as irresponsible by their political recipients if

---

* The erection of the Berlin Wall was a case in point. See pp. 238–40.

they do not dovetail neatly into their own view of the situation, which is all too often shaped by wishful thinking. I write of this with some feeling in view of my own wartime experiences in connection with the November 1942 Russian offensive, which resulted in the encirclement of the Sixth Army in Stalingrad and the thwarting of our Operation Citadel the following summer.

\* \* \*

A major headache in the organization of a secret service lies in the modern controversy over effectiveness versus accountability. It should hardly be necessary for me to emphasize that intelligence work is essentially a secret pursuit. This is why it is necessary to scrap the attitude prevailing in the rest of government, including the armed forces, which requires the accountability (*Transparenz\**) of public bodies for themselves and their activities. The basic principle should be this: whereas every other sound organization must be transparently open and frank and everyone must know precisely what his function is, in an intelligence service exactly the opposite applies. The organization must be as opaque and confusing as possible to outsiders, yet nevertheless everyone must still know what is expected of him. Security considerations demand that the internal structure contain so many watertight compartments that certain problems can occasionally be kept under scrutiny by two separate sections, acting entirely independently and in ignorance of each other, so as to reduce possible error. If the organization of the service is an open secret, it will not be long before the enemy has found his way in.

For similar reasons, experience has shown that the organization in the field should not be entrusted to a few large networks; it is far better to work with numerous small cells of up to ten men as the tactical unit. Large networks lack the necessary flexibility; and the smaller and more versatile the unit the better its security will be. Such units force the enemy to disperse his counterespionage activ-

---

\* *Transparenz* was the catchword under which Professor Horst Ehmke, minister in charge of Brandt's Chancellor's Office, pressed the reorganization of the Federal Intelligence Service.—TRANS.

ities, and from the purely budgetary standpoint they are more economical to run. Their transport, security, and so forth are cheaper. Moreover, the service's structure must constantly undergo a process of methodical, gradual change, so that anything the enemy's counterespionage may have learned yesterday will be obsolete and useless by tomorrow. The "industrial" camouflage of my organization, with its head office at Pullach and its local branches, regional head offices, and "representatives," was discarded years ago. Obviously this constant change adds to the expenses, but security and camouflage can never be purchased for nothing. For similar reasons, the intelligence headquarters must never make direct contact with its operatives in the field. None of our real agents ever saw the inside of Pullach; they were met at distant rendezvous, often hundreds of miles away.

In its final perfect form, each cog in the secret service machine must mesh so perfectly with the next that no one unit can function entirely independently of the others. If an individual unit is being manipulated by the enemy, the whole machine will sense it after a while, and in this way errors and security lapses are automatically brought to the surface.

In short, if the governments of our allies give their secret service heads a free hand to organize their machines and do their jobs as they see fit, they do so with good cause. The best example of this is the way the Americans have run their secret service over the years. Until World War II, American intelligence had led only a skeleton existence, consisting of separate agencies for each branch of the armed forces—Army Intelligence, the Office of Naval Intelligence (ONI), and the State Department's Bureau of Intelligence and Research; each of these employed only a small number of officers, civil servants, and other employees. But during the war, with the active assistance of their British allies, the Office of Strategic Services (OSS) was founded, under General William J. Donovan; and by 1945 this office employed some 12,000 people and embraced the work of the other agencies referred to. It was Allen Dulles who headed the OSS European section in Switzerland. To the OSS must go the credit for having recognized at an early date the importance of science and technology for modern intelligence work.

Before the end of 1945 the OSS was disbanded; but the need soon arose to coordinate the various other agencies, including the FBI, to prevent overlapping the efforts and getting in each other's way. This was achieved by the passage of the National Security Act in 1947, which set up the Central Intelligence Agency (CIA). The act established the National Security Council, headed by the president himself, which was to advise him on all matters of external and internal security. In his absence, the president is represented by a chairman he himself nominates; the National Security Council consists of the president, the vice-president, the secretary of state, the secretary of defense, chairman of the National Security Resources Board, and the director of Central Intelligence, who is a nonvoting member of the council, together with a number of representatives appointed by other departments.

The 1947 act created the CIA as a foreign intelligence service for the United States. Its director is nominated by the president, with Senate approval, from among officers of the armed forces or leading civilian figures. In his capacity as a member of the Security Council, the director has the task of coordinating all agencies working in the intelligence field or processing intelligence information. He is permitted to hire and fire CIA officials, alter its organization and structure as he sees fit, and fix staff salaries (bound by the sole proviso that he may not raise any salary to a level higher than his own). The CIA is supervised by its own internal inspecting authorities. As a consequence, the director of the CIA has all the freedom of decision in personnel, financial, administrative, and organizational matters that is vital to the efficient running of an intelligence agency. In Britain and America, however outstanding a senior civil servant may be, he will be incapable of taking over a high-ranking position in an intelligence service if he does not have years of solid experience in intelligence work, among other qualifications. In Germany this has been overlooked: after my retirement the position of vice-president of the Federal Intelligence Service was handed to an outsider who had distinguished himself in the management of the Hamburg office of the Social Democratic party, Dieter Blötz; and the obvious misgivings that such an appointment must provoke have unhappily been borne out.

The freedom of the CIA from political interference has been insured by an act of Congress, so its effectiveness is guaranteed. Perhaps the CIA will even succeed in outstripping the performance of the British SIS, which sets an example for the entire Western Hemisphere. In particular, the director of the CIA is ultimately responsible to the government for all intelligence operations, and particularly those of his own agency, and this fact explains his unusual privileges and prerogatives. Where the safety or protection of his sources is at stake, it is proper that he should not be held to the regulations binding the rest of the public service. In all major intelligence services of the world—except the West German since its reorganization by the Brandt government—these matters are settled in a similar manner, with but minor differences.

\* \* \*

Internal security is probably the most thankless task of an intelligence service. If it can be said of secret services in general that they work behind closed doors and can expect no public recognition for their achievements, this is true in far greater degree for their internal security sections. This section gets all the blame when there are lapses in security—for example, when a double agent is unmasked. Paradoxically, when they score a success like this, it is at the same time an admission of defeat, for it establishes that up to that moment of unmasking the man had gone about his errands undetected. On the other hand, a good security section enhances the efficiency of the entire service. Its influence is felt throughout the machine; it affects the further development of the organization's structure; and it plays a major part in the welfare and recruitment of internal staff.

\* \* \*

I have concentrated on a few prerequisites for a modern intelligence service. Even if these are ignored, the resulting service may still outwardly resemble a hard-working and efficient machine for some time. But even if the enemy does not succeed in penetrating it, its output will deteriorate little by little until instead of providing adequate intelligence digests, it will derive information that is superficial and inadequate to justify the man-hours and funds expended on the service. This, at any rate, is the conviction I acquired in twenty-six years of working in intelligence.

Elsewhere in the West, the major foreign intelligence services are large high-grade machines answerable only to the head of state or prime minister. They are absolutely independent of party politics. To obviate the need for a reshuffle at the top each time the government changes, they are separate from the agencies concerned with national security, which can never free themselves entirely from the maelstrom of domestic politics. In any foreign intelligence service it is obvious that a constant chopping and changing of higher officials must be reflected in diminished efficiency for long periods at a time, and this will particularly be so when civil servants are appointed to senior positions from outside the service. Experience in other branches of the civil service cannot be considered adequate qualification for positions of authority in a secret intelligence service.

A foreign intelligence service is to a certain extent comparable with a costly scientific instrument: it must be operated by scientific specialists of the highest order if it is to obtain the information needed to permit a sound assessment of an enemy's potential (or, for that matter, of an important ally). I know for a fact that when one Western prime minister took office in 1964 virtually his first act in office was to spend a whole day with his foreign intelligence service in order to obtain a briefing on the world situation as they saw it. This is one example—and there have been many others—of the exceptional importance attached by other governments to their services; but not, unfortunately, by the heirs of Konrad Adenauer.

Countless other countries employ their intelligence services to supplement the operations of their diplomatic services. There is an internationally accepted tacit understanding that the covert work of the former can be officially disowned at any time by the government concerned. In these countries, an operation like the (to me, uncanny) mission of Egon Bahr* to Moscow in February 1970 would have been preceded by a visit from a suitable official of the intelligence service hand-picked by the government. Indiscretions such as we have seen would then have been quite impossible. Of course, for this to be made possible, the intelligence service must be accorded its proper place in the state, its head must be afforded the necessary personal discretion of action, and its staff must be capable of performing what is asked of them; this kind of function cannot be performed by a service demoted to second place, and dictated to by a clique of ignoramuses. In short, an intelligence service should receive broad *political* directives from its superior minister or prime minister (who will of course inevitably lack the necessary specialized knowledge); but the expert direction of the service from that point onward must be recognized to belong solely in the hands of its chief.

---

* Bahr, as state-secretary in the Chancellor's Office, conducted exploratory talks on a treaty between Germany and the Soviet Union. See also pp. 356–58.

## CHAPTER TEN

# Zones of Permanent Crisis

*I* have hesitated a long time before deciding to include in this book any chapters on the work of the Federal Intelligence Service (BND, *Bundesnachrichtendienst*) itself. For twenty-six years I occupied a senior position in Germany's various intelligence services, and for the last twenty-two years I was head of the Gehlen organization and of the BND that succeeded it. Many world events left their mark on the twelve years in which I headed Germany's foreign intelligence service. Both these events and the work of our organization have remained indelible in my memory; so it has not been easy to make a selection from the superabundance of impressions, from the ups and downs of many dramatic years.

One feature distinguishes me from the small number of authors who have written about my organization: I know the true facts in all their details. For that reason many readers will expect me to narrate certain well-known episodes in far greater detail than they have learned from published sources so far; they expect me to correct previous versions of incidents which have been by design or ignorance wrongly reported hitherto, with a consequent public controversy and loss of confidence in the service.

While respecting the proper limits on what I may reveal, I will narrate a few particularly important events as they occurred and the part played in them by my service. Nearly all the episodes I will describe belong, as is only natural, to the grand conflict between communism and the free world. Virtually all of them have as their backdrop areas which I—regarding them from a purely intelligence viewpoint—term "permanent crisis zones": central Europe, with the special conditions created by the division of Germany and the isolation of Berlin; Eastern Europe, its recent history scarred by bloody uprisings in the name of national liberation and the brutal Russian measures of repression; the Middle East, a theater of latent tensions which has twice forced the world to hold its breath, in 1956 and at the beginning of the 1970s; Asia, where the Vietnam War has followed that in Korea, and where Red China has steadily increased in influence; and Central America, where, in Cuba, the Communists have succeeded in establishing a base from which to subvert the whole of Latin America, and which can be expanded into a military bridgehead from which to launch an assault on the United States at any time the political situation may call for it. And, meanwhile, there are indications of new sources of unrest in South America, among which must be counted the steady conversion of Chile into a base for Soviet foreign policy.

* * *

Prior to the transfer of our service to the Federal Republic in 1956, my directives to our intelligence procurement section were that it should concentrate mainly on espionage in and observation of the Communist empire—its military strength and the important developments and changes it was undergoing. After our transfer to federal control, however, our frame of reference was enlarged to include the activities of international communism in the crisis zones I listed. This significant expansion was executed stage by stage, until by 1960 it was complete; eventually, I had agents watching the Communist movement in virtually every country of the world. Only in the United States did we refrain from establishing a network of our own, for the FBI functioned perfectly and we needed only to address our inquiries to it to learn all we needed. I attached particular importance to establishing contacts in even the remotest regions, to insure that we had some opportunity of gleaning information independently of our allies. It was in these remote regions, where intensive espionage would have proved very costly (and even then incomplete, in view of the vast areas involved), that the work of our analytic section came into its own. Our evaluators pieced together their reports from scraps of information until the mosaic was complete.

I tried to put to good effect all the latest technical aids in expanding the basis of our intelligence work. I took a personal interest in investigating and testing the modern processes and equipment. I was fascinated by some of the items involved—the codes, chemicals, and inks. I made a point of reading all the scientific journals and visiting the laboratories where special devices were developed and tested, both in West Germany and the United States. We carried out advanced electronic research, so that our workers in the field would be properly equipped; and a computer was installed at Pullach, not only to aid our code-breakers but as a data bank (at the time of my retirement, however, we had still not solved all the problems connected with computerized data processing). I also had experts studying possible applications of specialized fields like medicine and psychology in intelligence work; I had in mind the possibility of compiling psychological studies of leading enemy figures, as the British SIS did with notable accuracy in the case of Khrushchev, for example.

All our most important intelligence reports were transmitted by coded Telex to Bonn, either to the Foreign Ministry or to the federal chancellor. Globke later told me Adenauer was an avid reader of all our reports, reading up to ten pages of them every day and taking them home to study in further detail as well. About once a week I would drive to Bonn and report in person to Globke or Adenauer. Sometimes we at Pullach would receive an intelligence report which we considered wrong; but if it was important, we were bound to forward it just the same, making clear in the accompanying obligatory commentary the reasons why we discounted it. If Adenauer went abroad he consulted us rather than the Foreign Ministry for details about the country he was visiting.

There is one thing I must however make quite clear about our espionage activity. The German press has repeatedly claimed that we carried out intensive domestic espionage on West German political figures, although our legitimate duty is purely foreign espionage. It is absurd to believe I would be so foolhardy as to risk the future of the BND by getting mixed up in internal political espionage, which is purely the duty of the various offices for the protection of the constitution. Obviously, before there was a federal government and before the BfV was established, we kept the Communist party in West Germany under surveillance, but we discontinued this as soon as the proper authorities began to function. Moreover, every report which emanated from Pullach was filtered through a special section attached to my own office which had strict instructions to insure that the content of the reports was nonpartisan and impartial. I believe it did its job magnificently, and I am convinced that not one report containing BND material on domestic political affairs was forwarded to Bonn during my tenure of office.

Of course, I am only too well aware that the Communist countries have repeatedly alleged that we were engaged in internal activities in the hope of injuring the service thereby. They have employed the most diverse channels to air these allegations—supported by what appear to be actual examples—in West German political and newspaper circles. The latter have then frequently followed up these claims in good faith and given them publicity. We certainly never shadowed Ollenhauer, as has recently been suggested, a man whose absolute integrity was conceded even by his staunchest political opponents. On the other hand, in the years prior to the establishment of the BfV we had naturally kept an index of all known Communists in West Germany at our headquarters in Pullach. We would have been falling down on our job if we had not.

* * *

Fortunately, our preparations for the period of transfer to federal control and the associated reconstitution of the organization as the BND were to stand us in good stead—the new Federal Intelligence Service was able to flex its muscles that same year.

In two different theaters a hot and arid summer heralded the storm that was to come later in 1956. In the Soviet-dominated part of Europe, the signs multiplied first in Poland and then in Hungary that there would be manifestations of the same yearnings for liberty as were crushed by Russian tanks in East Germany barely three years before. While the Communist security forces succeeded in localizing the unrest that flared up in Poland, in October 1956 the floodgates of revolution burst in Hungary. As we had secretly predicted in intelligence appreciations some time before, the people suddenly arose in a violent insurrection and seized power in the first days of the uprising. But the Russians moved swiftly, threw several divisions of troops into the unhappy country, and subjugated it for their satraps to rule again.

A flood of Hungarian refugees descended on Austria and Bavaria, and with them they brought the real possibility that the Russian tanks might not halt at the Hungarian frontier but—under the pretext of stamping out the rebels' nests abroad—continue to steamroll westward into the free half of Europe. This was the agonizing question the federal government asked us to find an answer to. We had a wealth of intelligence material relating to this and were able to follow the precise course of the Russian military movements and operations and see how they fit in with Soviet power politics. I became convinced that the Russians were solely concerned with demonstrating their military might in order to quiet down their restless satellite empire (just as they had done in 1953, in Germany, and again in 1968, when they invaded Czechoslovakia). We were, accordingly, able to advise the government that there was no reason to fear that Soviet military operations would spill over into Austria and Bavaria.

The Hungarian tragedy, of course, occurred in the very heart of our intelligence area. The growing Middle East crisis, however, brought the first extension of our intelligence effort to a non-

European area, strategically placed between Europe, Asia, and Africa. Almost simultaneously with the Hungarian uprising, the Israelis attacked Egypt. And when it seemed likely that the fighting on the Suez front, which was complicated by the intervention of the British and the French, might spread to a military conflict on an international scale, our service was in a position to report rapidly and accurately from the very focal point of those events, with newly acquired contacts dramatically proving their worth to us. For several days Bulganin issued ultimatums which culminated in his threat to subject London and Paris to rocket attack; a constant exchange of ideas between the Allied intelligence agencies and ourselves proved necessary. In these discussions I recognized with considerable pleasure that our service's "launching" into the Middle East had been a complete success. While many contacts built up there by our allies in one of their traditional hunting grounds had been hampered and sometimes completely "grounded" by the watch kept on their diplomatic missions (the British came off better than the Americans), our own agents, working with unorthodox methods, were able to preserve their constant and unrestricted freedom of movement.

I chanced to meet my American colleague and partner Allen Dulles at the height of this Suez crisis. His assessment of the overall situation was perhaps somewhat more pessimistic than my own, but we both agreed the Soviet rocket bombardment threats should be regarded simply as saber-rattling bluster, and we were both convinced Moscow was a long way from actually putting her finger on the button.

* * *

Thus, the events in Hungary and on the Suez Canal were the first real tests for the new Federal Intelligence Service. I have therefore related them before an event which, more than any other, decided the international flavor of the 1950s. This was the ceremonial launching of the dangerous Russian policy of "peaceful coexistence," which began to make itself felt during that crisis year of 1956.

Ours was the first, and so far as I know only, intelligence service to obtain a complete transcript of Nikita Khrushchev's secret speech to the Twentieth Party Congress on February 25, 1956. In it, the Communist party leader announced what he described as a new policy toward the Soviet empire and her neighbors. According to him, peaceful coexistence would lead not only to a relaxation of the permanent confrontation between the power blocs of East and West but would also guarantee a future in which they could live together without fear of strife. It was not long before it became clear that all these promising noises were nothing more than the familiar Soviet ploy of embracing the enemy and softening him up for the final kill, as Lenin had always advocated. While outwardly the Russians continued to propagate this principle of "unity of nations," at the same time they rearmed their forces for the resumption of the conflict between the world's power systems— but using other methods and other means. Thus, they were absolutely honest when they ruled that peaceful coexistence could not be extended to the ideological plane; and they made no attempt to conceal that the purpose of this new policy was to set suspicious minds at rest and make the public in non-Communist countries more receptive to Soviet propaganda than it had been so far.

The whole complex Communist machine throughout the world was called on to support Soviet foreign policy under this new slogan of "peaceful coexistence." It was hardly surprising that there were governments, as well as individuals, that accepted the new Moscow message at its face value and put their faith in it. The Russians seemed to be achieving their first aims almost without effort. But Khrushchev's speech was immediately subjected to detailed analysis by the Soviet experts we employed, and they concluded that the danger to the free world was now greater than ever. I warned many of our correspondents abroad of the results of our analysis and of the grim consequences of accepting Khrushchev's slogans. The experts among them had already reached the same conclusion themselves, but in West Germany there were many people who were reluctant to heed our warnings. They regarded us all as incorrigible "cold-warriors." Many were as entranced by this Soviet slogan of peaceful coexistence as a rabbit that has been hypnotized by a snake.

It was only when the Russians eight months later smashed the Hungarian uprising with brute force that it became plain to even the most die-hard optimist that contrary to Khrushchev's promises the Russians were not prepared to extend their much publicized "peaceful coexistence" to their own sphere of influence. Seldom has a lie been so swiftly exposed. It is incomprehensible that most people have managed to obliterate these tragic events from their memories so quickly—just as they have already virtually forgotten the Soviet invasion of Czechoslovakia in 1968.

* * *

If 1956 had barely allowed the new service respite to consolidate itself as a government agency, the following year was marked by a calm that bordered on the monotonous. In the field of grand diplomacy the troubles of the previous autumn had subsided, and in West Germany the political parties and the public began to get accustomed to the idea of a Federal Intelligence Service.

Early in 1957, however, the BND was once again the target of an East German smear campaign. *Neues Deutschland,* the principal organ of the Socialist Unity Party in East Berlin, fired the first shots on January 27, with an article headlined, GEHLEN AIDED THE COUNTERREVOLUTION IN HUNGARY. This was wholly untrue; promoting insurrections is the kind of makeshift which achieves nothing except to expose the bankruptcy of one's own policies. This did not prevent them from printing purely fictitious evidence to suggest that the service had sent agents into Hungary to support antigovernment forces in their insurrection, just as we had allegedly done prior to the uprising of June 17, 1953, in East Germany.

The new smear campaign was reminiscent of Wollweber's earlier assault on the Gehlen organization by the mass media of the Communist bloc, aided by the Communist and fellow-traveling publications in the West. At the beginning of his campaign, Wollweber had frequently exploited isolated arrests of our agents to make the most fantastic allegations against us; as this flow of "suspects" had dried up, he had satisfied himself with inventing wholly fictitious fresh sins we had committed. He had even begun to snipe against the prime minister, Otto Grotewohl. Initially, Grotewohl had been able to restrain his ambitious and unscrupulous rival, but he suffered a severe setback when Wollweber was able to produce the affair of Elli Barczatis against him as a trump card (she was, it will be remembered, in our employ while serving as Grotewohl's personal secretary). When she fell into Wollweber's hands and was liquidated, the secret service chief had Grotewohl just where he wanted him.

By the end of 1957, however, Ernst Wollweber, the professional revolutionary and sabotage expert of the 1940s, had come to the end of the road: on November 1 he was demoted from the Central Committee of the Socialist Unity Party, his espionage organization in ruins as a result of his barren and unimaginative management. In February of the following year Grotewohl and the two top functionaries Schirdewan and Oelssner lost their positions in the Socialist Unity Party's politburo and sank without trace. For Grotewohl the overthrow of Wollweber was sweet revenge, but he himself was already a broken man, with only the semblance of his former power and authority. He had been the leading member of the postwar Socialist party in East Germany, which had merged with the Communist party to form the Socialist Unity Party, and it was he who had long tried to keep senior members of the "bourgeois" parties in his cabinet to shore up its reputation. Grotewohl had tried to steer a relatively moderate course and had sent out numerous feelers to the West German government; but he never managed to build a bridge that was quite strong enough to enable him to bail out as did his deputy prime minister Professor Hermann Kastner.*

As for Wollweber, it is one of the most remarkable episodes in the history of East Germany that the minister who for years had been built up as our great adversary finally attempted to apply his revolutionary experience to bringing about the downfall of his own comrades. There can be no doubt that he was planning to dispose of

---

* The Kastner affair is discussed on pp. 181–82.

Walter Ulbricht, according to the information reaching us. That his last actions before dismissal have been cloaked by the East German government in an almost impenetrable darkness is something that can be understood only too well.

\* \* \*

In the autumn of 1958 the world's attention was once again focused on Berlin. On October 27, Ulbricht announced that "all Berlin" was "the sovereign territory of the German Democratic Republic." This claim was at first regarded by most of our politicians in Bonn as little more than a one-man *coup de théâtre,* but shortly afterward it was followed up by equally aggressive posturing by the Soviet party leader Khrushchev; on November 10 he called for the "repeal of Berlin's Four Power status," and two weeks later he repeated this demand in a note. In East Germany these claims were clearly recognized for the hidden threat they were; scores of refugees arrived in the West, and anxiety and fear spread throughout the country as so often on earlier occasions. There were differing anxiety reactions in the various official circles in Bonn. But the government was able to counter these with its own sober appreciation, which had been formulated with the help of the intelligence we supplied. From the facts which reached us we recognized this as a clearly coordinated action on the part of Moscow and East Berlin and as a renewed attempt to exploit Berlin's "lever effect," which they had put to such impressive use earlier in the 1950s. The city has retained its importance as a pivot of Soviet foreign policy ever since. During those autumn weeks of 1958 the Federal Intelligence Service was repeatedly pressed to give its opinion. We replied that while Khrushchev and Ulbricht would push the Berlin crisis as far as they could, they would not take it to the point of violence.

In January 1959 it became clear from the Soviet proposals for a German peace treaty that the Russian leaders regarded their campaign for a settlement of the German and Berlin problems as by no means over. They seized their next opportunity to act during the Four Power foreign ministers' conference at Geneva, which was to last for almost three months that summer. But despite unsubtle

Soviet threats to sign a separate peace treaty with their puppet government in East Germany if the Western powers continued to oppose them, the Geneva talks ended without profit for Ulbricht. From the reports which reached Pullach, it was clear that the disappointment in East Berlin was keen. All the greater was the effort they now invested in the celebration of the tenth anniversary of the foundation of the German Democratic Republic, to attempt to secure its de facto recognition by Western countries.

Ulbricht personally took charge. He dispatched his emissaries not only to the capitals of the Communist bloc countries, but to London and Paris as well to persuade their most noteworthy politicians to attend the celebrations in East Berlin. One of the most important of these emissaries, E——, had already volunteered years before to work for the Gehlen organization, and through him we now learned every detail of the preparations: the first acceptances of former French premiers and of well-known British parliamentarians soon arrived; by their presence as guests of honor, it seemed, they would show the world that Ulbricht's was a regime worthy of international recognition.

Seldom have I had to make a harder decision as head of the service. This man was one of our most valuable sources, with exceptional opportunities for access to secret material in East Berlin. Ought I now to discontinue him and extract him to the West to prevent the appearance of the prominent French and British politicians in East Berlin? I put the whole matter to the federal chancellor, Dr. Adenauer, and secured his approval before I decided after considerable thought on the appropriate countermove: we would evacuate E—— with his family to the West and dispatch him immediately in secret to Paris and London again, this time with the job of persuading those he had so recently invited to East Berlin to cancel their acceptances. The coup was successful: East Berlin had to celebrate the coming-of-age without any prominent visitors from London or Paris. As for E—— himself, he now lives in the West, a free man.

\* \* \*

While for West Germany and its intelligence service these two years had been overshadowed by the international dispute over the German problem, by the beginning of 1960 we observed the first dim outlines of a far graver confrontation looming up over the Soviet Union. An increasing volume of intelligence flowed in, confirming what had at first been little more than vague prophecies by politicians about a growing aggravation of the relationship between the Soviet Union and Red China. I will refer in more detail to this greatly overestimated conflict elsewhere; it will suffice to say here that for many years to come it was to destroy the united front of international communism, and for a time even jeopardized the supremacy of the Soviet Union. Here again our organization was the first Western intelligence service to report in detail on the coming rift with Red China, but I was always at some pains to keep it in perspective. I recall how Globke once told me after Adenauer returned from his visit to Moscow that the Russian leaders had assured the chancellor their real problem was with China; it took some effort on my part afterward to persuade the chancellor that this was not really so.

We at Pullach recorded our opinions on this power struggle in numerous analyses. At first some of the most experienced observers we employed doubted there really would be any split between the two Communist superpowers. After all, the supreme maxim of international communism, which they had observed most recently in the Korean War, was that the ultimate defeat of capitalism could only be obtained through the combined efforts of Communist movements throughout the world. These early doubts seemed confirmed by indications we received of "voices of reason" speaking out among the top Communist hierarchy, urging immediate steps to seal the widening gap between Moscow and Peking. But we soon received unshakable documentary evidence that the conflict was intensifying and we learned many details of the hatred felt by each side for the other. The BND was unable to sit on the fence any longer. We concluded in our reports that the dispute would be a long one, but that a major armed conflict between the Soviet Union and Red China was out of the question, for we believed China hadn't the slightest prospect of overcoming her crippling backwardness in arms technology and economic potential in the foreseeable future.*

This was an opportunity the Western world should have grasped. In my view it was of the utmost importance to put out feelers to Peking with the aim of securing a détente in Russia's rear. If we were to strengthen our hand in dealing with the Russians, then we had to come to terms with their potential enemies. It was a mystery and disappointment to me that the West hesitated for too long. The consequence has been, in my opinion, that this split between the giants of the Communist camp—which was hitherto something inconceivable—has been only inadequately and marginally exploited.

Seen against this awkward background, it is easier to understand what a godsend the U-2 incident of 1960 was to Khrushchev, a brilliant opportunity for him to distract attention from his own difficulties with Red China. The American intelligence service had been flying photographic reconnaissance missions over the Soviet Union since 1952, using very high-altitude U-2 aircraft; the results wholly justified the high political risk involved in such an unusual operation. (Of course, the BND was too exposed an intelligence service to have been supplied with regular prints of the photographs obtained.) Unfortunately, a U-2 piloted by one Francis Gary Powers was shot down over Soviet territory on May 1, 1960. He was put on trial and imprisoned, and two years later exchanged for the KGB "resident" arrested in the United States, Colonel Rudolf Abel. For a long while it remained a matter for speculation whether the aircraft had been downed by a chance shot of some Soviet anti-aircraft missile system or whether it had been planned in advance and executed at a particularly opportune time. Suffice it to say that at Pullach we received enough information to indicate that the shooting down occurred at a moment which was not exactly inconvenient for the Russians. Khrushchev used the incident as an excuse to break off first the summit meeting in Paris sixteen days later and

---

* See pp. 366–67.

then the Geneva disarmament talks shortly afterward. It is quite obvious that his almost orgiastic outburst in Paris was caused by more than mere indignation at the incursion of an enemy reconnaissance plane.

\* \* \*

East Berlin continued throughout 1960 to prosecute its smear campaign against my intelligence service with undiminished vigor. Whereas at the beginning of the year the defamation had been purveyed in single items, in November a book was published in which were concentrated all the attacks that had ever been made on us. This book, *The Gray Hand: Squaring Accounts with Bonn's Secret Service* (published by Kongress Verlag, East Berlin), was authored by the notorious Dr. Julius Mader.

When I was asked about this standard textbook of defamation, I limited myself to a statement that it was evidently primarily intended to discredit the BND as a whole and myself as its head in particular in foreign eyes and to undermine our allies' and colleagues' confidence in us. (This was clearly the purpose of the "evidence" that was served up of our espionage work in Western countries.) Of equal importance was the aim of bringing the service into disrepute in West Germany itself. We were depicted as a state within a state, "politically ambitious," dominated by adventurers of dubious past who were recklessly sacrificing their agents' lives behind the Iron Curtain. It speaks well of the responsibility of the larger part of the West German press that it saw through these transparent claims and recognized the real purpose of East Berlin's agitprop experts. For the Communists the consequence was an embarrassing failure, and *The Gray Hand,* which they had distributed with such tumultuous publicity, was totally disregarded in the West.

\* \* \*

An incident whose effects were to be felt in full only later was the collapse early in 1961 of the invasion of Cuba launched by Cuban exiles bent on overthrowing Castro. After the debacle there was powerful public criticism in the West of the American intelligence service, not all of which was unjustified. Allen Dulles's CIA was accused of having failed completely and of having neglected to provide sufficient aid for the anti-Castro elements that had launched the operation. There have been claims that the overoptimistic reports supplied by many "native informants" to the effect that the population would rise in support of the invaders were palpably untrue. There have been allegations that the CIA originally promised large-scale military aid for the invasion, and that this was not forthcoming; but there has been no absolute proof one way or the other so far. One is entitled to assume that the exiles mounting the invasion would hardly have hazarded their lives unless the United States had promised them some such support.

One thing is beyond dispute, however: had the United States made the decision to act the world would have been spared the real Cuba crisis of eighteen months later. The truth is that there were certain overriding reasons why the United States deemed it appropriate not to react as the Russians would certainly have reacted under similar circumstances. Moreover, it is not improbable that Washington underestimated the significance of this island nation, and that this played a contributory part: the belief that though Cuba might be right on its "doorstep," it was too diminutive a nation ever to cause real trouble.

As we read the incoming cables at Pullach at the time, I remember telling my colleagues that it was incomprehensible to me why the United States fumbled this unique chance of intervening militarily to eliminate Castro. My opinion was founded on our own in-depth analysis of the future role Cuba might be expected to play on the international scene. Oddly enough, I suspect that the Americans were themselves largely to blame for Castro's overthrow of the dictator Batista, a leader who was certainly not as black as the international press depicted him at the time. It is clear that the Americans did nothing to aid Batista, while in Castro, who was known to have had a devout Jesuit schooling, they believed they would see a leader emerge who would restore democracy. But by mid-1961, his Cuba had become a grave danger to world peace in two respects. Like the Czechoslovakia of Beneš in 1938, the Russians could equip her as a kind of outsized "aircraft carrier"; they could base not only their aircraft, but their missiles and submarines on Cuba and operate them against the United States at point-blank range. And secondly, she could be used as a base for the Communist subversion of Latin America.

After the Bay of Pigs fiasco of April 17, 1961, only eighteen months passed before the United States was forced to the brink of war to halt the emplacement of Soviet missiles on Cuban soil. I will return to this when I discuss that crisis separately.* Since then the presence of Russian military advisers in Cuba has become an accepted fact of life. And the realization that young East Germans are being trained in Cuba for covert Communist infiltration work in West Germany has meanwhile been brought home to the German public with sufficient emphasis. Thus Cuba represents a latent military threat to North America, and a real psycho-political threat to the South; her tentacles have penetrated so densely into the countries of Latin America that it is only a matter of time before she secures impregnable bases on the mainland there. At Pullach I issued the necessary orders for this Communist activity emanating from Cuba to be placed under surveillance; we intensified the efforts of our espionage network against the spread of world communism in South America, particularly in Chile, and reported the results in our regular analysis of Soviet strategy in the West.

* * *

The most vociferous criticism of our service occurred whenever sudden actions by East Berlin were allowed to succeed apparently without resistance. I repeatedly had to calm down my colleagues, who often reacted with great bitterness to the public's lack of understanding and to its often downright unjust criticisms. There were times when I would dearly have liked to contradict publicly the falsehoods published about our work.

The gravest of these criticisms, a criticism with which some

---

* The Cuban missile crisis is discussed on pp. 256–57.

politicians identified themselves, was that we failed to provide
warning of the Communist plans to build the Berlin Wall on
August 13, 1961. The truth is that in countless individual reports
before that date we indicated that the situation at the authorized
crossing points in Berlin was worsening, and that East Berlin would
have to stem the mass flight of labor, which was costing them far
too many of their skilled workers and specialists; otherwise, the
Ulbricht regime would face a catastrophe. Many items of information showed it would not be long before the Communists had to
take rigorous steps to constrict this flow; then we learned from a
reliable source that the Russians had given Ulbricht a free hand, so
only the date was left open to conjecture. We reported to Bonn that
a *totale Absperrung,* or total shutdown, was imminent. We received
more reports of an imminent hermetic sealing of the sector boundary, particularly within Berlin itself, and of the stockpiling of light
materials suitable for the construction of barriers. (Later it was to
be claimed that our agents did not detect the stockpiling of the
necessary heavy building materials—steel girders, stone slabs, and
concrete—that were used to construct the wall in its final form.
This claim ignores the fact that the wall was erected in its solid form
only at the end of an operation lasting about a year, the success of
which was only a matter of some doubt at its beginning. In the
beginning, the barrier was a light and temporary structure, which
could have been withdrawn at the least sign of force from the three
Western powers.)

   We could not predict the actual date they would start; it was
known, we later found out, only to a handful of top party officials.
When the day dawned, only barbed wire barriers were put up at
first. It was only when they saw that the tanks of the protecting
powers in West Berlin (Britain, America, and France) made no
move to flatten these barricades that more permanent material was
unloaded; and even then the barrier that was constructed was nothing like the Berlin Wall we know today—with its tank traps, mine-
fields, watchtowers, and other permanent defenses.

   In view of the criticism that was voiced against us, I ordered
a complete file drawn up later that year to document the case. This

established that the service had more than performed its duty in warning the authorities in Bonn in good time. The leader of our parliamentary assembly, Dr. Eugen Gerstenmaier, and many other politicians who were permitted access to the file, all vindicated us of the allegations leveled against us.

* * *

A few days before the first barbed wire barrier went up, a KGB agent, Bogdan Stashinskyi, turned himself over to the West Berlin police and confessed he had murdered two well-known exiled Ukrainian politicians. He had killed the politician Lev Rebet on October 12, 1957, in Munich, and Stefan Bandera, a former Allied agent and leader of the anti-Communist group OUN,* which Stashinskyi had infiltrated four years before, on October 15, 1959, in the same city. He claimed he had carried out both assassinations on the direct orders of the Soviet KGB. He had shadowed both these "targets" for a long time in Munich on the orders of the KGB chief Aleksandr Nikolayevich Shelyepin (about whom we shall be hearing more) and then finally disposed of them with a specially designed poison-dart pistol provided to him by Moscow. This was a silent gas pistol which fired a capsule of hydrogen cyanide into the victim's face, poisoning him immediately; Stashinskyi himself had been given a pill to swallow beforehand, as an antidote to any cyanide fumes he might himself inhale. After perfunctory medical examination, both deaths had been ascribed to heart failure. Shelyepin had personally bestowed the Order of the Red Banner on Stashinskyi for these deeds.

The whole affair was so monstrous that after the first cries of public outrage that such crimes could have been committed in the heart of Munich, there were numerous skeptical newspaper reports. The consensus was that the peace-loving Soviet Union could not have been responsible. The deaths of Bandera and Rebet were now believed to have been unnatural ones, but they were comfortably labeled the obvious outcome of "internal power struggles within the émigré organizations," as in a similar case in which the

* Organization of Ukrainian Nationalists.

exiled politician Czermak had opened a parcel addressed to him at a Munich post office and been blown up by the bomb it contained. We knew that, like Bandera, Czermak was one of our men, so we were in no doubt as to who had mailed this present to him. Two days after the West German authorities made public the news of Stashinskyi's confession, the Communists called a press conference in East Berlin, complete with the familiar, contrite "ex–Gehlen agent," and announced that the orders for the elimination of Bandera and Rebet had been issued not from Moscow, but from Pullach, and this hint was taken up by a number of Western publications.

But Bogdan Stashinskyi, who had been persuaded by his German-born wife Inge to confess the crimes and take the load off his troubled conscience, stuck resolutely to his statements. His testimony convinced the investigating authorities. He reconstructed the crimes precisely as they had happened, revisiting the crumbling business premises at the Stachus, in the heart of Munich, where Lev Rebet had entered the office of a Ukrainian exile newspaper, his suitcase in his hand. And he showed them how the hydrogen cyanide capsule had exploded in Rebet's face and how he had left him slumped over the rickety staircase. The case before the federal court began on October 8, 1962, and world interest in the incident was revived. Passing sentence eleven days later, the court identified Stashinskyi's unscrupulous employer Shelyepin as the person principally responsible for the hideous murders, and the defendant— who had given a highly credible account of the extreme pressure applied to him by the KGB to act as he did—received a comparatively mild sentence. He served most of it and was then released. Today the KGB's "torpedo" is living as a free man somewhere in the world he chose that day in the summer of 1961, a few days before the wall was erected across Berlin.

CHAPTER ELEVEN

# Moscow Calling Heinz Felfe

𝒯he Stashinskyi affair taught us many lessons. We were able, thanks to his confession and his cooperative behavior, to establish beyond all doubt in the eyes of the world that two political assassinations had been planned and executed in the West for which the head of the KGB, Shelyepin, was alone responsible. We concluded from the careful planning and the perfection of the means employed that similar methods and devices must have been used to eliminate other inconvenient anti-Communists as well. Several political assassinations in the West which had remained unexplained or whose perpetrators had been allowed to escape for reasons of expedience could now be explained without much difficulty. They were "special operations" by the Soviet secret service or those of satellite Communist countries.

It was no novelty for our intelligence service to be blamed by Communist propaganda for having liquidated these prominent émigrés ourselves; we were repeatedly accused of using the most brutal forms of sabotage, intimidation, and murder. I wish to emphasize that every one of the intelligence organizations I ever controlled always dissociated itself from any kind of violence, and nobody has ever produced a shred of evidence to the contrary.

The political dialogues and events of the past are swiftly forgotten. This is inevitable, for many an episode of recent history would otherwise be bound to have a retarding influence on the events of today. Many contemporary politicians would like to be able to eradicate all memory of the murders of Bandera and Rebet in Munich from their minds. How else could they even contemplate inviting Shelyepin—the man identified by the German supreme court as having commissioned the assassinations, but now promoted to leader of the All-Union Council of Trade Unions—as an honored guest to West Germany? Not all of us can boast of consciences as easy as the politicians'; they figure to themselves, Why bother about the past?—we have got to learn to live with the Russians, and life must go on. With regard to the Stashinskyi affair, to display such an attitude was not only immoral and an offense against public propriety, it was downright incomprehensible as well.

It was equally unintelligible to me that our government did not utter the smallest squeak of protest to Moscow about the murders committed on its soil. Bonn has no sense of sovereignty. This was brought home to me with even greater force a year later when a leading French opponent of de Gaulle, the OAS* Colonel Antoine Argoud, was kidnapped in the heart of Munich and left the next day in a van parked outside a police prefecture in Paris; in France he was a wanted man, having been sentenced to death in absentia for political offenses. (Our service had had tenuous contacts with the FLN movement† in Algeria, and de Gaulle's government had made use of these channels in its early dealings with them.) We had no doubt that de Gaulle himself had sanctioned Argoud's abduction, but we waited in vain for Bonn to register a formal protest at this violation of our sovereignty. So the BND raised its own complaint

---

* *Organisation de l'Armée Secrète,* the secret, counterrevolutionary organization comprised of key French army officers whose purpose was to crush the Algerian independence movement.
† *Front de Libération Nationale,* the Algerian National Liberation Front.

through secret service channels. I had our colonel—who was attached to the embassy in Paris—lodge a stiff protest with my opposite number in France. In the interval we had learned that an independent French secret service group was responsible, and we had no hesitation in identifying them sufficiently in our protest to compromise the French minister concerned. If a formal protest is properly made, and clearly justified, then it need not affect one's long-term relations with a neighbor, and our own cooperation with the French SDECE* remained exceptionally close. Its head, General Grossin, used to visit us about twice a year in Pullach.

* * *

By this time I was faced with a far more vexing problem, one of the most regrettable and damaging episodes in the history of the Federal Intelligence Service. This was the affair of Heinz Felfe, a top Soviet agent who we discovered had been working for ten years in the headquarters of the BND at Pullach. For week after week the affair continued to hold the newspaper headlines: his character, his Nazi past, and his subsequent treachery were grist for their mill, resulting in increasingly exaggerated reports about us and, not infrequently, in astringent criticism as well.

There can be no doubt that Felfe was an extremely adroit and intelligent worker; he was mobile, slight in build, and active. His complexion always seemed pasty, as though he suffered from some chronic internal disorder. He was a man of few friends but had no enemies either; the type constantly—but unsuccessfully—seeking contact with his fellow men, who instinctively brushed him off without bothering to explain to themselves why. He was married and lived at first in a small apartment in a residential part of Munich. At the time of his arrest, Felfe was working as an assistant adviser in our section, handling counterespionage work against Communist networks in the West. He had risen to the modest civil service rank of a probationary *Regierungsrat* and was known internally only by his code name, Friesen. He had been set up and

---

* *Service de Documentation Extérieure et de Contre-Espionage,* the French foreign intelligence service.

controlled as a KGB agent in a manner characteristic of their un-scrupulousness. Whereas other Soviet double agents arrested in West Germany had been fed with "bait material" of only very limited value to us, on Shelyepin's orders Felfe had been given secrets to feed to us which were unique in the history of the intelli-gence war between East and West. This was their way of insuring that he would be rapidly promoted within the Gehlen organization and subsequently the BND. After he in turn won the confidence of his Communist employers by furnishing them with important docu-ments and other "deliveries" from Pullach, Felfe was kept well sup-plied with priceless political intelligence to feed to us. These reports sometimes contained important state secrets of the East German government; the Russians sacrificed their satellite government's secrets for one purpose alone—to build up this traitor's prestige within the BND and to give the impression that he was one of our most dependable intelligence procurers. It will demonstrate the ruthlessness of the KGB if I reveal that at one stage, to speed up his promotion still further and to enhance his access to classified ma-terial, the KGB sacrificed one of its own political agents in West Germany without the slightest compunction, a step rare even for the Soviet secret service. Through Felfe, they fed us in cleverly regulated doses the clues that led to the arrest and conviction of C. A. Weber, the editor of the magazine *Die deutsche Woche*. He was an agent who acted for the Russians out of mistaken idealism and had long been under observation. Thus, the agent who was of the greater value to Moscow was permitted to deliver his less im-portant colleague to the sword.

For many years Felfe had been able to work without attracting serious suspicion. It is one of the most difficult tasks for the officer processing incoming intelligence reports to detect well-prepared "bait" material of genuine content for what it really is. But if the flow of reports is on balance too good to be true, it can bring about the downfall of the officer who procures them. Broadly speaking, this was where Felfe first went wrong. During 1960, one of the analysts working in our counterespionage section tipped us off that something about Felfe's work was wrong. We then put Felfe under the microscope without his being aware of it. Nothing the Russians could do on his behalf could block the painstaking internal security investigation which was undertaken by our small security section. The secret was known to myself and five others from start to finish—neither my vice-president, Hans-Heinrich Worgitzky, nor my personal assistant was aware of it at this early stage. Under my direct supervision the security section began a screening process which was to last many months until the evidence was complete.

We learned that Felfe had purchased an expensive house and grounds at Oberaudorf and had begun boasting of the financial transactions with which he had raised the funds for this; but to our chagrin, we learned that he had indeed taken the precaution of financing the purchase with a regular home loan (although he had undoubtedly received large sums of money from the Russians). Our first inclination then was to send our experts in to search the house in Felfe's absence—in other words, to break in without leaving any signs of having done so; this might provide us with the confirmatory evidence—a photographic laboratory or radio transmitter—that we needed to pull him in. But our legal experts explained that this would be illegal, and that any evidence found by such means would have no legal standing in a trial.

Thus our hands were tied for many months by our quaint West German laws. We could not act against the man, although we were convinced he was an agent for the other side. The strain of working with this senior colleague can be readily imagined. As the security section's file of circumstantial evidence grew thicker, I had to find some means of restricting Felfe's freedom of movement within the compound without arousing his suspicions. I instructed his immediate superior to pick an argument with him and see that Felfe was given no new cases to deal with for the time being. Felfe should attribute his "shelving" to the bad odor the row had provoked. All my instincts suggested we should find some pretext to dismiss him forthwith, despite his civil service status. The fact that he had concealed his Nazi past from us would have been grounds enough, and Globke could have done the rest. Only Moscow and the KGB would benefit from a public scandal involving the BND. But as the investigation revealed the extent of his treachery, it became clear his arrest and trial were inevitable. There was no attempt to sweep the affair under the carpet as has been claimed.*

For several months prior to his arrest, we deliberately fed certain material to him in the knowledge that this would be taken as authentic in Moscow, so we did not entirely take a loss on the affair. Felfe continued to suspect nothing. Indeed, he approached the personnel section and pointed out that his three years' probation as a *Regierungsrat* was over; and he asked for a permanent civil service grade and applied for a transfer to the post of security officer in our ComInt section (communications intelligence)—our most sensitive area. I was able to block this; and I prevented his being awarded a gold medal for ten years' service to which he was formally entitled.

By the end of October 1961, the evidence was almost complete. We had even intercepted radio messages from the KGB to its agent at Pullach (whom we now of course believed we had identified), asking for advice on how to handle the propaganda campaign against the Stashinskyi confessions. We set the normal legal procedures in motion, and without any hesitation I ordered the affair brought to its distasteful conclusion. At the attorney general's request, neither I nor my deputy was present when Felfe was summoned to the office of General Wolfgang Lankau, head of our strategic intelligence section, and arrested. In his possession as he was arrested were a number of microfilms of our classified documents and a miniature recording tape. Two accomplices, one of whom was not a BND employee, were arrested soon after. I have always held that such black sheep will be found in the best of families, and the Allied intelligence agencies certainly recognized that none of us was proof against such affairs, however rigorous the security precautions we might take. One Allied service cabled us, "Congratulations. We are still looking for the Felfe in our own

---

* Recent publications have claimed that there was an "anti-Felfe front" at Pullach which insisted on formally warning me that Felfe was a traitor and that my private secretary took written notes of their warnings; and it is further claimed that after Felfe was arrested, I arranged for the destruction of these notes. This is completely untrue. Moreover, my secretary has confirmed to me that there was no such "front" and no such notes.

ranks." It would be uncharitable for me to say which service signed it.

The federal investigators then revealed the full extent of Felfe's treachery and its probable consequences. In the interrogations, it was disclosed that he had been recruited by a fellow ex–SS officer called Hans Clemens, who had been persuaded by a KGB officer to work for the Soviet secret service during a visit to East Germany, where his wife lived. As a courier, they had made use of one Erwin Tiebel, who like them had been born in Dresden and had served in the SS. These were the three who had been arrested. Clemens stated he had agreed to serve the Communists out of his hatred of the Americans and to avenge the Allied bombing of Dresden in 1945; Felfe gave the same reason, adding that he had been brutally treated in England in prison camps. Throughout the years of his service Felfe had secretly supplied the Russians with regular copies of the BND's weekly digests* and the monthly reports of the BfV on its campaign against Communist agents in West Germany. He admitted supplying some 15,000 frames of microfilmed documents and 20 reels of tape recordings, and he confessed to receiving more than 310,000 deutschmarks. Since Felfe proved to be an incorrigible liar, the real extent of his treachery will probably never be known.

It may well have been less than he claimed. I understand that shortly a volume of memoirs will be published under Felfe's name, for which purpose the Soviet KGB has released material. From what I know of the facts, I can only state that I have reason to believe he did not work as successfully as Moscow had hoped and as no doubt the book will suggest. The "watertight bulkhead" system I had introduced between the various sections of our headquarters had severely restricted his field of view at Pullach. That he was an incurable braggart was shown by his claim at his trial to have been one of Schellenberg's top agents in Switzerland during the war, and to have secured information on the Teheran and Yalta conferences "out of the mouth of Allen Dulles," which had then been confirmed by Cicero's reports (Cicero ceased sending reports in

---

* The weekly digests were not as sensitive as their name might imply; they were relatively unimportant summaries I circulated for psychological reasons so that their recipients might believe they were in the know. The really important digests were distributed to only about eight recipients, and these Felfe did not have access to.

January 1944, a full year before the Yalta conference). Of course, the West German mass media had a field day when Felfe and his two accomplices were put on trial in July 1963. After a brief initial session *in camera,* the rest was unfortunately conducted in open court, causing just the kind of public damage to the BND that our Soviet adversaries would have wished.

The main public interest centered not on the traitor Felfe and what he had perpetrated—the court found that he had betrayed the names and characteristics of no fewer than ninety-five BND agents to the Russians—so much as on what was described as the "misguided personnel policy" operated by the service. The Social Democrats described it as a "scandal without parallel" and attacked us for our "lax standards" in recruiting staff. The press made a great deal of Felfe's Nazi past (which he had concealed from us); a large number of articles appeared in which the BND was simply but thoughtlessly labeled a "collecting point" for ex-Nazis. The fact was that Felfe had allegedly worked for two or three years after the war in the British intelligence service in West Germany, and this implied a certain clearance in our view. In addition, he was recommended to us by an official of the Ministry for All-German Affairs (who was now, of course, himself the object of our curiosity, although we were never able to prove anything against him). State-Secretary Globke courageously defended the BND when it came under fire over this affair, and made it a matter of public record that fewer than one percent of our staff had ever worked for the SS (we had started the Gehlen organization with only seven such officials).*

Felfe was sentenced to fourteen years' imprisonment and a severe financial penalty; Clemens, the more truthful of the two, received a lesser sentence. When Gustav Heinemann became the Socialist minister of justice in the Grand Coalition of 1966, he exchanged the other traitor, Alfred Frenzel, for a prisoner held by the Czechs. And he moved heaven and earth to try to arrange an

---

* During my time the rule was that, apart from the Waffen-SS, no SS members were permitted to work at headquarters in Pullach unless they were special cases given clearance by checking the files at the Berlin Document Center or at Ludwigsburg. There were grounds for believing that the BDC file on Felfe had been doctored by the Soviet authorities who turned it over to the Allies.

early release for Felfe "for humane reasons" too. He asked me to come and discuss with him the question of exchanging this prisoner for somebody from the East, but I would not hear of it and refused to see him; I sent him a written memorandum explaining why. Nonetheless, in the summer of 1968, Felfe was exchanged by Heinemann for a number of people, including three students who had had nothing whatever to do with the BND but had been recruited by the Americans to spy in Russia, and a number of prisoners of the East Germans, of whom only one was ours. Clemens, who sincerely regretted his deeds, was not exchanged. He preferred to remain in West Germany.

\* \* \*

In West Germany our hands have always been tied when it comes to tracking down Soviet agents. I have often said we make things too easy for them—Soviet espionage work in the Federal Republic is practically a sinecure. It had taken us a year from the first hints of suspicion to gather enough evidence to pull Felfe in for questioning. In Britain, for example, it would have been much easier. He could have been grilled for three days until he broke down and confessed. I am a great admirer of the British Official Secrets Act—it is worded in a way which really guarantees national security. I had a copy of it translated into German, and I put it to our minister of the interior as a model for a German law, but there was no response at all to my proposal.

With a staff of four to five thousand working for the BND, security was a constant problem. We did try lie detectors on the staff, but this was done strictly on an experimental basis and we made it a rule that all subjects had to volunteer. The machine was really quite remarkable: in one case we applied the test to an agent who had some time before on our instructions joined the Socialist Unity Party in East Germany (we had to extricate him prematurely for security reasons). The fact that he had been a member of the party was kept secret even at Pullach, although it was on his secret personnel file. When he took the polygraph test, I instructed him to answer negatively the standard question he would be asked as to whether he had ever belonged to the party. The result was a mighty leap in the detector reading—a result which deeply impressed us.

On the other hand, when we applied the test to another man we suspected might have a guilty conscience, the results were completely haywire. A secret committee of specialists examined this improbable result for some time; the medical members considered it possible he had imbibed some tranquilizer or narcotic before the test was run. The evidence of lie detectors is not accepted by German courts of law—but to a security branch it can under special circumstances be regarded as an indicator.

At the conclusion of the Felfe affair, we circulated a comprehensive report of our findings to all our allied intelligence services in the West so that they could learn from our experience—I will not say from our mistakes. After my retirement my successor prepared a popular history of the Felfe affair, which was to be published in West Germany under the title *Moscow Calling Heinz Felfe*. Horst Ehmke, Brandt's minister in charge of the Chancellor's Office, prohibited publication of the book after it had already been set into proof at the publishers; the government paid compensation to the publisher, and a proof copy reached *Der Spiegel*.

\* \* \*

Scarcely any event cast a more turbid and suspicious light on the Federal Intelligence Service than its apparent involvement in the controversial *Der Spiegel* affair. Eight years earlier, in 1954, the publication of my photograph on that magazine's front cover had been a tip-off that there were ties of some kind between Pullach and the Hamburg news magazine, as well as with certain other organs of the press. It has always been my view that it is perfectly legitimate for a secret service to establish contacts with the press in the national interest. We had established this particular link shortly after the SSD campaign against us began, since the West German press had begun to accept Ernst Wollweber's fantastic claims about his successes in hunting down my agents. At that time I thought quite highly of Detlev Becker, the publisher of *Der Spiegel*. Obviously, any such links with the press and other mass media have to be handled very gingerly if there are not to be any popular misunderstandings. This is a risk that will always have to be taken where the press attempts to satisfy a public curiosity for facts and information that can only be procured by using secret service channels.

There have been numerous versions of the *Der Spiegel* affair published in the press and in books. Colorful and overdramatized though they are, they could hardly have gone further in their innuendos, imputations, and speculations. It was almost as though there was some hidden hand at work, bent on obscuring the facts and discrediting the BND, and that is why I feel it necessary to break my silence on the affair.

At some stage in 1962 the magazine decided to publish a major assault on the defense minister, Franz Josef Strauss. It has been claimed that my relations with Strauss were strained, but in fact I always thought very highly of him. He had a remarkable memory and an impressive grasp of the essence of affairs; I consider him one of the most capable and active politicians we have. *Der Spiegel* had first attacked him over alleged irregularities concerning a commercial concern, Fibag, at a time when, to my knowledge, Strauss was completely unaware of the existence of such a company. What I did not realize at the time was that the magazine had evidently intended to deliver the coup de grace in such a way as to implicate the BND as well, thus killing two birds with one stone. The "stone" was to be a mammoth article on the recent Bundeswehr maneuvers, Fallex '62, about which top secret documents had been fed into their hands by Strauss's opponents in Bonn, and in particular one Colonel Martin. The article, which was written by Conrad Ahlers, was designed to expose alleged fallacies in Strauss's atomic weapons policies.

The manner in which the magazine sought to implicate the BND was this: they put to our Hamburg representative, Colonel Adolf Wicht, a list of ten detailed questions a number of weeks before the planned publication date of their controversial article. I was away from Pullach at the time this list of ten questions arrived. They were handled in accordance with standard BND policy by my press liaison officer, Winterstein. He checked which of the questions could be answered at all without violating defense secrets. *Der Spiegel* had informed us that the questions were being asked in connection with an article they were planning on the subject of General Foertsch, who was at that time inspector general of the Bundeswehr. At no time did they tell us the answers would be used in an article based largely on top-secret maneuver documents of a particularly high classification (documents which did not, however, emanate from the Federal Intelligence Service). In any event, the questions were answered from published material which the magazine could by diligent research have turned up itself anyway. It is now clear to me that the sole intention in approaching the BND was to establish a "lightning conductor" for when the authorities took their revenge over the publication of the article.

The article was published in *Der Spiegel* on October 8, 1962. I was uneasy about the part the BND had played. When Winterstein showed me the list of questions and his harmless reply, I said that frankly I thought things might yet go wrong. Strictly speaking, such questions should have been referred to Strauss's Defense Ministry for reply. Shortly afterward, I happened to be with Strauss, and he angrily informed me that he had turned the affair over to his legal experts and was informing the chancellor and the attorney general that in his view the magazine ought to be prosecuted. Since the horse had already bolted, I saw little point in trying to lock the stable door and thought no more of the matter until a few days later when the magazine's offices were raided, on the evening of October 26, and its top editors were pulled in on treason charges. The publisher, Augstein, and several others, including Detlev Becker, were arrested in Germany on the attorney general's instructions. Ahlers was in Spain, which brought his arrest into the ambit of the Defense Ministry. Strauss himself telephoned the military attaché in Madrid, and the Spanish police were called in.

All at once our Colonel Wicht was also arrested. Among Becker's papers the police had found a note which appeared to indicate that Wicht had tipped off *Der Spiegel* about the imminent raid by the attorney general. I do not know why it appeared expedient to the defendants, and acceptable to the prosecutors, to drag the BND into the position of an accomplice. With Wicht's arrest, rumors swept the country, fed by people who claimed to know of my alleged antipathy toward Strauss. *Newsweek* magazine wrote, "Most Germans are convinced Wicht acted on Gehlen's orders." To those of us who knew the full story, the accusation was absurd. Why should I have tipped off a magazine I was increasingly coming to recognize as a hostile instrument? But evidently this view of the matter was taken seriously in Bonn. The truth is that the BND was unaware of the article's contents in their entirety; and the allegation that we sanctioned its publication was designed to divert attention from the political figure who evidently *did* carry out the vetting of the article before it was printed.

It was not until I called on Adenauer for one of my regular briefing sessions a few days after the arrests that I learned of the suspicions being voiced against us. Strauss had evidently deduced from the note among Becker's papers that after my lively conversation with him, I had immediately acted through Wicht to tip off the magazine. I was kept waiting in an anteroom for some time, and I was then called in to see Adenauer (Globke himself was away—I believe he was ill that day). Adenauer had just seen Strauss, and he left me in no doubt as to his displeasure. It was clear he had been led to believe that the BND had played a dubious role—that we had supplied both the material for the articles and, through Wicht, tipped off the magazine as to the arrests. In fact, the arrests had come as a complete surprise to me. I stood my ground and demanded that a federal attorney hold an inquiry into the affair. Adenauer agreed to this, and while he got on the telephone to Karlsruhe I contacted my deputy, Worgitzky, at Pullach and told him to catch the next train to Bonn and to bring Horst Wendland and Winterstein with him. They arrived the next morning.

The federal attorney Kuhn, who usually dealt with the BND's affairs, personally investigated the involvement of the BND.* He interrogated my three colleagues in the security office of the Crim-

---

* Clearly, had the federal attorney general thought there was any substance in the charges he would have investigated the matter himself and not delegated the inquiry to Kuhn.

inal Police headquarters in Bonn, and then myself. The whole inquiry was conducted in an atmosphere of goodwill. We were found to be absolutely blameless in the affair, and Wicht was also subsequently acquitted. We were able to show that at the time he was alleged to have tipped off Detlev Becker about the coming arrests, nobody at Pullach had had the slightest inkling about them, which made it improbable that Wicht could have uttered such a warning. We concluded that the document had been providently left lying around by Becker in order to conceal the identity of the prominent defense ministry figure who was the real culprit—the official who had supplied the secret documents. As the initiators of this cover-up calculated, we would hardly be able to reveal publicly the true identity of this personality in Bonn.

The affair unfortunately caused considerable bad feeling within the service. While Wicht was still remanded in custody, Worgitzky—who had once held Wicht's office in Hamburg himself, and knew him well—demanded I make a public statement in defense of Wicht. I refused, since this would have been construed as interference with the due processes of law, whereupon Worgitzky himself published such a declaration. Wicht was subsequently released without a stain on his name; afterward, I was interested to learn, he was engaged by Detlev Becker for a large monthly salary, under contract as a journalist.

Unhappily, after this unpleasant affair, Konrad Adenauer changed his attitude toward us for some time.

* * *

In October 1962, as the *Der Spiegel* controversy was occupying the front pages of West Germany's newspapers, the United States was dragged by Cuba into one of the most dangerous crises of the postwar years. Now, it was forcibly brought home to President Kennedy that he had let slip more than just a minor guerilla victory in allowing the invasion of the Bay of Pigs to fail. For now the Russians were blatantly preparing to exploit the situation by setting up missile bases in Cuba, within point-blank range of the East coast. The CIA succeeded in detecting the early stages of construction work in

Cuba by aerial reconnaissance, and there was still time to prevent the arrival by sea of most of the Soviet missiles. A number of transport vessels disguised as harmless merchantmen were already on their way to Cuba when Kennedy took his experts' advice and imposed a sea blockade on Cuba. Khrushchev was forced to back down. Confronted with this show of determination, which was coupled with an impressive demonstration of U.S. naval strength, the merchantmen delivering the missiles turned back (although I still suspect that part of the batch of missiles is still in Cuba). The malevolent cargos were returned to the Soviet Union. Many people who watched with admiration this new-found resolution of the United States to defend its liberty in those October days of 1962 probably asked themselves whether the first barriers erected across Berlin in August the year before would have stayed up long had the Western powers displayed a similar determination then. But this was Kennedy's basic weakness: he was a man of half measures; a president who wanted only the best, and frequently saw things in their real light, but was afraid to commit himself to the full to realize his aims.

We learned just how seriously the Americans viewed the situation from statements of the director of the CIA at that time, John A. McCone, who described the crisis as one which "could have sparked off a war, perhaps even a nuclear war." We at Pullach were proud of the part our agents played in Cuba: they investigated the extent of the construction work there and supplied the resulting reports to the CIA, who fitted them into the overall picture. I have always considered the CIA's intelligence success on this occasion to have been one of its biggest accomplishments in postwar years.

* * *

The new year brought us the rapprochement we had long worked for with France. No longer our arch enemy, she now became our partner and ally for all time. In my eyes it was one of Adenauer's most spectacular triumphs that he had succeeded in winning General de Gaulle's faith in the new Germany. With the ceremonial signing of the Franco-German Agreement on January 22, 1963, in Paris, Adenauer had crowned his lifetime's work.

From our own service, this historic event meant a formalization of our long-standing and friendly relations with the French foreign intelligence service, the SDECE; long before our transfer to federal control, we had entered into informal agreements with our counterparts in France for collaboration in intelligence affairs and the exchange of material. For a long time we had supplied the French with our Gehlen organization reports in exchange for nothing more than goodwill, to build up West Germany's diplomatic status in French eyes. And using these reports as a quid pro quo, we had gradually persuaded our French colleagues to discontinue their degrading practice of hiring leading German personalities in political life to report on internal German trends. Although the respective roles of the SDECE and the BND were not identical, there still remained many areas where we could usefully cooperate. I was always grateful that this relationship between the services was never affected by the strains which were occasionally placed on relations at the higher diplomatic levels. Regardless of the barometer reading on Franco-German relations as such, relations between the two intelligence services remained constant and cordial.

If I made it my particular concern to cultivate our intelligence relations with Britain, America, and France, this should not be read as detracting in any way from the value of the many other ties we established. But the fact that these three powers had accepted responsibility for the protection of Western Germany was one reason to me why they had a right to our support wherever it was possible. A further reason of no less validity was that I had the highest professional and personal regard for the directors of these Allied services. I knew and dealt with all of them personally on my visits to Washington, Paris, or London. With the CIA's representatives what impressed me was the clear, sober, and practical manner in which they tackled and overcame even the toughest intelligence obstacles; with Britain's SIS it was the self-assured, almost superior manner of their extremely competent intelligence officers—men who had been brought up in an almost legendary tradition, in short, anything but the James Bond type. I had many private meetings with Brigadier Menzies, the first head of the SIS, and his successor. They invited me to their clubs in St. James's, and I remember thinking that history might have been different had Germany had institutions like the Travellers' Club or the Reform. In the representatives of the French service one sensed something that I can only loosely characterize as patriotism. Whereas we Germans can scarcely whisper the word *Vaterland* without risk of serious misunderstanding, a member of the French state service is and always will be an upright and willing "servant of the state," with all that that implies, and is proud of it. This nationalism displayed by my French counterparts impressed me more than once. As a French colleague once pointed out to me, "The only person who will ever make a good European is one who started off as a good Frenchman, or a good Briton, or a good Italian, or a good German, and is proud of his country's traditions."

While the trial of Heinz Felfe firmly occupied the center of the newspaper stage, we at Pullach were more concerned with the important political events of the time. In Germany the chronic Berlin crisis was stepped up on June 21, 1963, by the erection of a new barrier around West Berlin to supplement the wall already existing between the two halves of the city and to prevent further escape attempts. The Crossing Permit Agreement signed six months later afforded only the weakest ray of hope in these years of blackmail. And hopes that this would lead to any easing of the tension were soon disappointed.

\* \* \*

Particularly in the Mediterranean, the year 1963 brought a number of changes in key government positions. In Greece the resignation of Prime Minister Karamanlis on June 11 touched off a chain of events which has disturbed that country—strategically so important for NATO's southern flank—ever since. As far as I could see, the Greek intelligence service paid no attention to the changes in the government and continued to perform its difficult task with its customary devotion and skill. Anyone concerned about Europe's future must hope as I do that this ancient land of culture will once again recapture something of the importance of its magnificent past, as a bulwark of the West and of peace. Whatever may be said of political trends in Greece, one fact cannot be denied—that today Greece would be a Communist country if its forces had not gathered in defense in time and warded off that fate.

A few days after Karamanlis' resignation, Israel's grand old man David Ben-Gurion stepped down from the political stage as Israeli prime minister; he was succeeded by Levi Eshkol. Ben-Gurion's great service to history was that he paved the way for the vital reconciliation between the Germans and the Jews in his meeting with Dr. Adenauer. I have always regarded it as something of a tragedy that West Germany was inevitably dragged into an alliance with the state of Israel against the Arab countries. The struggle seemed to me so purposeless. I recall a leading Arab personality telling me in 1953 that he knew only too well that the Arabs had to reach some kind of agreement with Israel—that they ought to talk things over with Ben-Gurion, "But I would not dare to discuss such an idea even with my closest confidants, because if I did I would have no guarantee that I would survive another day." The Arabs have always been too headstrong in their policies. I always regarded their traditional friendship for Germany as of immense value for our national reconstruction. And at the request of Allen Dulles and the CIA, we at Pullach did our best to inject life and expertise into the Egyptian secret service, supplying them with the former SS officers I have mentioned. But, equally, I recognized the political debt Germany owed to the Jews; we had to do what we could to contribute to the survival of Israel.

Leading figures of both camps did their utmost to build up and improve their bonds with the federal government and, accordingly, with me as well. After the Sinai campaign of 1956, we began to take a more professional interest in the Israelis. We gave them expert advice on the development of their small but powerful secret service; we made facilities available to them and aided them in placing key agents in the Arab countries, especially since Nasser was becoming increasingly involved with Moscow, and we recognized that Israel was as much an outpost of the free world as West Berlin. In the end, the concatenation of political and military events, culminating in the renewed trial of strength in June 1967, obliged the Federal Republic to take up an unambiguous attitude in favor of Israel. We maintained our espionage contacts in Egypt, while in Israel we had no agents; we communicated our information to each other through normal diplomatic channels. I was allowed to send experts from Pullach to inspect the Israeli military installations; we were particularly interested in observing their forces' fighting strength and morale.

* * *

Later in 1963 there were far-reaching changes in the West German government. On October 15 Dr. Adenauer resigned as federal chancellor, and was succeeded by Professor Ludwig Erhard.

More skilled pens than mine have written their appraisals of Adenauer's service to history. I can only add that a head of an intelligence service will seldom have the good fortune to work under a head of government possessed of such an understanding for the uses of intelligence and of such a sound judgment springing from perusing secret materials. It is not meant in any way as a detraction from this if I add that Adenauer possessed in his state-secretary Dr. Globke an aide who was an incomparable and indispensable mediator. Globke was replaced by a new state-secretary, Westrick, following Adenauer's resignation. I found no cause to amend my appraisal of Adenauer, even when he had momentarily adopted a critical and skeptical attitude toward the BND and myself over the *Der Spiegel* affair one year earlier.

With this changing of the guard at Bonn, a postwar era came to an end not only for the West German government but for us at Pullach too. I deeply respected Professor Erhard as an economics expert, but he could not find the same active sympathy for the BND as had his illustrious predecessor. He did not recognize in it one of the basic props of government; an intelligence service?—it was anathema to his personal disposition and beliefs. I could sense a certain hostility toward us among the civil servants at the Chancellor's Office.

To quench the public's thirst for knowledge of our activities, I decided, with the government's approval, to authorize the first major documentary film about our work. I was visited by two television producers, Günther Müggenburg and Rudolf Rohlinger, and I subsequently issued instructions that they were to be given access to anything they asked within obvious limits of national security. I need hardly add that there was no lack of warnings at the time: our security section was particularly concerned about the scores of shots that would have to be filmed at Pullach. We had the filming done on weekends so that our staff members' faces would not appear. (It may seem naive, but "rogues galleries" of faces play an important part in espionage work: we unmasked the director of Soviet atomic espionage solely with the aid of one photograph. This man, Sergei Kudriavtsev, is now Soviet ambassador in Cambodia.) The two producers were as fair in their work as they were critical, and this confirmed the view I had always held that a responsible journalist will always respect and repay the trust that is displayed to him when it comes to treating sensitive subjects in a discreet way. The film, entitled "From the Gehlen Organization to the BND," was shown on West German television on June 26. It had a huge audience and went down far better than we had dared to hope.

Our main purpose in authorizing this television documentary was to forestall a number of books and articles of dubious origins and doubtful tendencies that had already been advertised in advance. It was a further example of the kind of public relations work in which we had to indulge. What I particularly wanted to get away from was the image created by modern espionage thrillers; I wanted to have the BND seen in its proper light as a modern and efficient foreign intelligence service, a far cry from the Hollywood image. Whereas in earlier years it had been the spicy sexual element that had pervaded the spy films, during the 1960s we were witnessing the new wave of sadistic strong-arm types. This was what the layman imagined now when he visualized the world of espionage. It may have been good for the box office, but it did extensive damage to the BND's reputation. The staid television documentary went a long way toward eliminating these prejudices and bringing home to the public the real nature of our work.

This is not to suggest that the real face of the Soviet KGB had changed since the early 1950s or the days of the assassinations it had carried out in Munich. One Sunday early in September 1964, Horst Schwirkmann, a technician attached to the West German embassy in Moscow, had been with a party of other diplomats visiting Sagorsk monastery, forty-five miles outside Moscow; as he kneeled in prayer at the monastery, he felt something pressed against his leg, and seconds later a damp patch appeared on his trousers. When he looked up, his neighbor had vanished. By the time the party returned to the embassy he was a very ill man, in severe pain and suffering from a sense of weariness. An American doctor in Moscow found skin burns caused by some kind of chemical poisoning. The Russians tried to detain Schwirkmann in one of their hospitals, but we managed to fly him out to a hospital in Bonn; medical experts there ascertained that the burns had been caused by a sudden spray of mustard gas at short range—a poison of a special type that could kill within a few days without leaving a trace of the cause.

Schwirkmann had been due to return home two days later, on September 8, anyway; since Khrushchev was due to pay an official visit to Germany in the near future, the incident caused acute anxiety in Bonn, where Prime Minister Erhard called a meeting of the party leaders on the eleventh. Eventually the government made a formal protest to Moscow, since the evidence was as clear as it had been in the Stashinskyi affair. After thirteen days the Russian government rejected the protest and claimed that "certain circles" in West Germany were trying to hinder any improvement in Soviet-German relations. At Pullach we were in no doubt as to the identity of the would-be murderers: Schwirkmann was one of our specialists whom we had trained to ferret out the hidden microphones planted by the KGB in our diplomatic buildings around the world. They had tried to eliminate him because he was on the threshold of unearthing their installation in our embassy in Moscow (we later found over thirty microphones concealed in the building).

## CHAPTER TWELVE

# The Final
# Years

𝕴n our reports from Pullach we always made it absolutely plain
that it was only American intervention in Vietnam that prevented the loss of all Indochina to the Communists. I lent all my
personal authority in support of the American decision to hold on to
Vietnam whatever the cost, but I could never understand the planning and methods applied by Washington out of ill-conceived regard for world and domestic public opinion. On the other hand, I
wonder which other nation would have been willing to sustain such
sacrifices in the cause of preserving freedom.

To an officer fighting the Communists in the field since 1941,
the military strategy of the Americans is inexplicable. Right from
the start they have done everything in Vietnam by half measures.
They began with a force of 30,000, and when this was not enough
they gradually escalated to 500,000. In other words, they have been
trying to win a war by the one method every German staff officer
would recognize as an impossibility, and which not even Hitler was

able to make work.* In staff college we were always taught: *"Nicht kleckern, sondern klotzen!"*—"don't fiddle with the food, make a meal of it!" With our wartime experience on the eastern and southeastern fronts, we would have moved heaven and earth to avoid provoking partisan war, even if we had had to launch a massive airborne assault on the North Vietnamese headquarters to do so.

Under the adverse conditions their political leaders have created, the achievements of the American ground forces in Vietnam have been really remarkable. Many a German military commander was confronted by a hopeless situation in World War II, but few were caught in such a difficult situation as the generals in Vietnam. At the American commanders' disposal were every means for conducting military actions on the heaviest scale; behind them they had the entire resources of the United States, the mightiest nuclear power on earth. But these commanders could apply their military means only to a limited extent and in ineffective doses. Company after company of servicemen was swallowed up in merciless jungle warfare, fighting an ephemeral enemy who merged with jungle or civilian population at a moment's notice, and who could change his tactics with a speed that would be totally impossible for a democratic and bureaucratic power. Given the circumstances it is difficult to comprehend why the Americans tried to adopt a mode of warfare which was bound to be rich in casualties instead of thoroughly exploiting the technical weapons at their disposal—helicopter units, modern artillery, tanks, and rockets. Our own blitz campaign against France in 1940 taught us that a massive and crushing use of force always costs fewer casualties (on both sides) than a gradual escalation such as we later tried in the Russian campaign.

The trouble is that we predicted all this so clearly. The Americans started by leaving the French in the lurch in Indochina. When the French withdrew, the Americans had to foot the bill. Early in November 1963, the Americans encouraged the overthrow of the Diem regime by a military junta. Diem's assassination was followed by a rapid succession of military revolts and changes of government,

---

* We always used to say that Hitler could have done with a year or two at staff college.

which crippled the government's authority to act and weakened the army. The expansion of the Vietnam conflict to full-scale civil war was the outcome. In the same month, November 1963, Kennedy was assassinated; and the BND had to remain in particularly close contact with our American colleagues, ready to take immediate steps in case the Russians were tempted to exploit the emotional turmoil the assassination sparked in the West. The Vietnam conflict continued to smolder until the "incident" in the Gulf of Tonkin ignited the powder keg. As 1965 began, it seemed possible that the world was on the brink of a new world war.

This was the possibility that we had to investigate. The new war in Vietnam involved directly or indirectly the United States, Communist China, and the Soviet Union. Remote though this new theater of events was insofar as the BND was concerned, we had to do what we could to put the fighting in Indochina into its larger world context and investigate what its effects on other areas of the globe might be. (Right up to the present day there has in fact been a most interesting interaction between the events of Southeast Asia and those in Europe.) We could only speculate whether the Russians, who had the greater influence on North Vietnam, would have permitted Red Chinese aggression which would have led to the occupation of the whole of Indochina, including Thailand. From numerous reliable reports which reached us, we knew that at that time the Red Chinese leaders regarded the occupation of the areas of Indochina and Burma bordering on southern China as merely the first stage in their expansionist strategy. In a second phase, they were planning to eliminate the "troublesome border positions" of South Korea and Taiwan (Nationalist China). The Chinese assumed that once they had effected these two stages, the acquisition of the strategically vital island federation of Indonesia would automatically follow. In Indonesia there were over 2,500,000 organized Communists waiting for the hour of their "liberation."

As far as Vietnam is concerned, only the future will show whether the United States, with its years of bloody engagement in the south, will at least have accomplished one thing—the reconstitution and fortification of South Vietnam so that she will be capable of defending herself even after all the American troops have been withdrawn. According to my present information, I cannot believe that this will be so, taking the long view. Once Red China has overcome her internal troubles, she will resume her expansionist ambitions, unless, of course, the entire political situation is somehow changed. The recent rapprochement between the United States and Communist China may lead to an initial self-limitation of this expansionism for the time being; and Washington's wooing of Peking, which has aroused alarm in Moscow, may also have a retarding effect on the Southeast Asian interests of the Soviet Union.

Thus my own assessment is that if Nixon succeeds in his political ambitions toward China, he may yet achieve a termination of the American involvement in Vietnam which would be in the interests of the West.

\* \* \*

In 1964 the Soviet leadership had to contend with internal difficulties of its own which were to culminate in the overthrow of the most powerful man in the Communist camp. On October 14, 1964, Nikita Khrushchev, last of the line of absolute Soviet dictators, went into political oblivion—stripped of his power under circumstances that the most hardened Kremlin observer would not previously have thought possible. Even the most influential Soviet officials doubted right up to the last moment whether the coup would succeed when the dictator was summoned to answer their imprecations and accusations. But Khrushchev did vanish unceremoniously from the political scene after those few dramatic hours in the Kremlin, leaving party leaders in the Communist countries as unprepared and nonplussed as the Western governments. As usual, there was no lack of reproach for the Western intelligence services, including the BND, that we had not clearly predicted Khrushchev's overthrow; for that was the impression that the public had gained.

In fact, we at Pullach had continually reported that there were growing differences of opinion at top levels in the Kremlin. Our information tallied in its essential details with what the other Western intelligence services found out. According to our sources, major disputes had arisen during 1964 out of what had originally been minor differences of opinion. The younger members of the government had accused Khrushchev of responsibility for just about everything that had gone wrong with their plans outside Europe—the growing internecine conflict with Red China, the "humiliating backdown" over the Cuban missiles, and certain mishaps they had suffered with premature operations in Africa. In internal debates, the policy of "peaceful coexistence" was labeled a complete failure, and Khrushchev the hapless promoter of that policy.

Numerous reports identified as his possible successor a leading member of this younger generation, none other than Alexandr N. Shelyepin, former boss of the KGB; but his hour had still not come. The old guard of Kremlin officials denied their younger colleague their allegiance. The final outcome was equally unexpected for the renowned Kremlinologists of the West. Khrushchev was succeeded by a troika, a triumvirate of leaders whose long survival has proven an almost greater surprise than the fact that such a compromise was adopted in the first place. In numerous BND summaries I stressed that the troika was in reality a three-horse team in which one would always have the most pulling to do; and that it was with this one that the West would always have to bargain. This primus inter pares was the dynamic party leader Leonid Brezhnev. As the strongest man, he could formally take over absolute power in this leadership collective any time he so desired; but as long as his two colleagues, the jovial State President Podgorny and the adroit Prime Minister Kosygin, continue to play their parts in the troika as they have done up to now, Brezhnev has no need to use his elbows.

Two days after Khrushchev's downfall, the Chinese exploded their first atomic bomb and thus joined the nuclear powers—a development which in no way took the Western governments by surprise.

The Western intelligence services had been concerned about the problem of the Chinese bomb for some time and had tried to establish how powerful it was. As individual facts were hard to come by, intelligence analysts had to work overtime to complete their calculations accurately and rapidly. At the time, we predicted quite correctly that without the assistance of Moscow, Red China would never succeed in catching up with the two big nuclear powers, and this prediction has been borne out by subsequent events. One glimmer of hope remains for Peking as a second-rate nuclear power—that the major powers will tie their hands with a nonproliferation treaty and weaken themselves in so doing. It is obvious that under the existing circumstances Red China is not going to sign any treaty limiting the development of nuclear weapons.

*  *  *

Early in 1965, the West German government's attention reverted from the Moscow-Peking axis to the situation in the Middle East. The Bonn government, which had hitherto kept firmly on the fence, was forced by the long-feared sharpening of German-Arab relations to come out into the open and make decisions which ruled out all prospect of a compromise solution.

There had long been a division of opinion in West Germany over the expediency of exporting arms to Israel. These exports provoked violent controversy and minatory reactions from the Arab states, and ignited a dangerous fanaticism which can only be explained by the Arab mentality. It is true that Bonn discontinued its support for the Jewish state in February 1965 insofar as it discontinued its arms deliveries, but by then the train of events that had been set in motion could no longer be halted.

On February 24, Walter Ulbricht, the East German leader, arrived in Cairo for a week's visit to add fuel to the fire. The Communist leader was welcomed as an honored visitor and lauded at every stopping point of his extended tour as the antithesis of the "imperialist West German government, the promoters of Israel's power politics." But behind the glittering facade erected by Cairo for the East German visit, a natural product of the Arabs' traditional hospitality, it was clear from many reports reaching Pullach that Nasser had suffered many disappointments, principally because East Germany was in a far less satisfactory economic position than the West, and was therefore by no means able to satisfy all the Egyptian requirements. Nasser showed frequent embarrassment at having to deal with the East Germans—not so much with the prim and lifeless Ulbricht as with the numerous Communist functionaries who came hawking their wares around Cairo as the years passed.

But by 1965 it was realpolitik alone that mattered. This was no time for the Arabs to be guided by personal dislikes, contemptuous though Cairo may have been of the East German officials. Professor Erhard's government had decided to announce its establishment of diplomatic relations with Israel in May that year; Cairo had no alternative. I could have told Erhard that the Egyptians had an intelligence team that knew precisely what weapons had been supplied to Israel, and that they would certainly not be satisfied with less themselves. We had repeatedly reported to Bonn that granting diplomatic recognition to Israel would result in the majority of the Arab states retaliating immediately by breaking off relations with Bonn. There could be no doubt whatsoever that this would happen, however much certain politicians believed such an outcome could be staved off.

On May 13, 1965, formal diplomatic relations were established between Bonn and Israel. An important element of the foreign policy formulated by Adenauer had been brought to its completion; but at the same time West Germany lost many traditional friends of long standing in the Arab world, and these ties have remained broken to this day.

* * *

The West German government was harshly reminded of its own domestic problems that spring. We received several reports that the East Germans and the Russians were planning to disrupt the German parliamentary sessions scheduled to take place in West Berlin early in April, and at the same time Berlin and Bonn were swamped with Communist-inspired rumors designed to spread panic among the West German population. The resulting hectic activity in the political parties and government agencies created an atmosphere in which it is remarkable that we were able to produce any level-headed analysis at all.

We adhered to our old assessment of the Berlin situation in our analyses from Pullach, and this convinced the Federal Parliament and other political authorities that they should ignore the clumsy Communist attempts at intimidation and proceed with their sessions in West Berlin. From the intelligence reports we had, we deduced that whatever Moscow and East Berlin might think up by way of propaganda and agitation, they would stop short of the actual use of military force or anything that might make a confrontation with the Western powers inevitable. Their sole purpose was to force Bonn and West Berlin to cancel the scheduled sessions and thereby concede indirectly that the Federal Republic had no business to be in West Berlin. The climax of this coercion campaign was reached on April 4, with the blocking of the access corridors across East Germany, and particularly the autobahn from Helmstedt to West Berlin. While the military traffic of the Western powers was allowed to pass unhindered, the West German parliamentary deputies had to fly (as most of them had already planned). There were fears that a civil airliner laden with these deputies would be forced down at the East Berlin airport of Schönefeld, but these proved unfounded. The only other incident was when *Russian* fighter aircraft buzzed the assembly hall at low level, which was not without its effect on world opinion.

Both the Berliners and the parliamentary deputies kept their nerve. What East Berlin had hoped might lead to the banishment of the West German Parliament forever from Berlin had the opposite effect: the steadfastness and solidarity of city and Federal Republic were demonstrated for all the world to see.

\* \* \*

Not many months after the level of hostilities in Vietnam had been stepped up, we saw indications that widespread preparations were being made for a Communist insurrection in Indonesia. Most remarkable for us was the complicity in this of the president himself, Sukarno. This irresolute leader had held on to power for several years by playing off the growing Communist party of Indonesia against his army officers. But now, with his tacit approval the party had established powerful cells all over the country with the job of murdering the army's principal generals so as to remove it as a pillar of the state and tilt the balance of power in the party's favor. For a long time we had received indications that Sukarno was secretly making common cause with the Chinese Communists who were behind these preparations. He felt deceived by the powerful military clique, and the Communists had offered him the leadership of an Indonesian "People's Republic" if the coup succeeded. (In reality they were planning to eliminate Sukarno too, and to transfer power to the leader of the Indonesian Communist party, Aidit.)

The insurrection began after dark on September 30, 1965, when Communist squads murdered a number of the most important army officers in a particularly bestial fashion. But the coup as such was a failure, because the other key assassinations were prevented. The popular military commander in chief General Nasution and the present Indonesian head of state General Suharto crushed the uprising with the help of loyal troops. Among the senior officers whom the Communists had managed to murder were two particular friends of Germany, the army's commander in chief General Yani and the former military attaché in Bonn, Brigadier General Pandyaitan. We in Pullach were in the fortunate position of being able to furnish the Bonn government with prompt and detailed reports from Indonesia, thanks to one particularly reliable source there; it was he who had advised us much earlier of the deteriorating situation. No words of mine will do justice to the importance of the Indonesian army's subsequent success in eliminating the Communist party in its entirety; the liquidation of the Communists, including Aidit himself, who was executed, was carried out with a harshness and thoroughness typical of the Asian mentality.

* * *

I have refrained so far from discussing either the development of the BND's organization and staff or its changeable relations with the federal government after Adenauer's retirement. The attentive reader may well have guessed that this relationship was not always devoid of misunderstandings, and on occasion it underwent what might be called a degree of strain. It is in the nature of an intelligence service that it must receive encouragement and support from the government of the day; if the government lacks interest in or expert understanding for its intelligence service, not even the best service will succeed in overcoming external prejudices against it. Accountability (*Transparenz*) and image-building may perhaps be constructive concepts when applied to other government departments, but they will not benefit the BND if the government's leaders lack unconditional confidence in the reliability and loyalty of the service.

The real controversy over the future of the BND started in 1966, the last year of Professor Erhard's office. A number of newspapers published articles debating the future structure of what they misleadingly referred to as "the three intelligence services"—meaning the BND, the BfV, and the MAD.* A number of qualified writers discussed the situation, but there were also unqualified journalists who claimed that there were "catastrophic conditions" in the three services and put forward suggestions of their own. In the news media several self-proclaimed experts on the secret service fired broadsides at us, offering us their advice. To the uninitiated it must have appeared that there had never been any coordination between the three services, and that we were all at each other's throats, concerned only with expanding our private empires at the expense of the others.

At the time, I regretted that the government did little to counter these usually baseless allegations. This official silence encouraged the publication of even wilder conjectures about us. Eventually, in many journals, including some of considerable standing, the old proposal was aired that the three services should be merged. Often the proposals were so vague that it was difficult to determine whether they merely advocated bringing the organizations together under some superior coordinating authority or whether they were thinking in terms of the complete amalgamation of the three agencies into one "super service."

---

* *Militärischer Abschirmdienst,* "Military Screening Service," the military intelligence agency controlled by the Defense Ministry.

My own view was that the existing degree of loose collaboration was ideal and that it would have been impossible for them to be brought together under one person. The three services had such clearly separated fields of operation that an amalgamation would not have served any purpose whatsoever, particularly from the political point of view. The BND, as a foreign espionage organization operating outside West Germany, was obliged to remain absolutely nonpolitical and objective; but the BfV and MAD are security organizations, exercising counterespionage and defensive functions in the civilian and military planes respectively, and as such they are necessarily more political in character. The clear distinction between their duties ought to be apparent even to the layman.

Moreover, since each of the three services is responsible to a different government department—the BND to the Chancellor's Office, the BfV to the Ministry of the Interior, and MAD to the Defense Ministry—it was highly unlikely that they could be brought together under one coordinating authority. Such a solution would mean that each of the three superior departments would have to agree to relinquish its control of the service concerned. It goes without saying that a new ministry set up to control the three services would be exceptionally prone to attack: not even the most upright minister (and at the time the one most frequently hinted at in this connection was the minister without portfolio, Krone, who enjoyed the esteem of all the political parties) could have avoided incurring the stigma of being the "all-powerful secret service supremo."

This sort of irritating speculation continued during the Erhard administration, but with the formation of the Grand Coalition under Kurt Kiesinger in December 1966, the situation changed. Quite apart from the fact that the Chancellor's Office kept as tight a grip on "its" intelligence service as did the other two ministries on theirs, the very nature of the Grand Coalition was such as to evoke little enthusiasm for a "ministry of state security."

Thus, the clear division of duties and the existing organizational links between the BND as the foreign intelligence service and the two security agencies (BfV and MAD) in West Germany will continue.

* * *

My last complete year of office, 1967, brought the BND one more triumph—one which has been frequently referred to since then at home and abroad. We predicted the Israeli attack on Egypt down to the very day. A few days before hostilities broke out in the Middle East, I had committed myself in a written intelligence appreciation to the view that an Israeli preventive attack on Egypt was to be expected in early June. My colleagues and I were so convinced of the inevitability of this that we briefed a group of parliamentary deputies who just happened to be visiting Pullach on the threat (they have regarded themselves as "eyewitnesses" to our warnings ever since). During the week preceding the attack, I had to attend one of the regular parliamentary budget committee hearings on the BND, and one of the deputies there also asked me whether there would be war in the Middle East. I replied that I thought the Israelis would attack "next Monday."

We were right, even though—as an angry American journalist pointed out on Werner Höfer's television program long afterward—at the time of my prediction the Israelis themselves had not made the decision. Our prediction was a typical example of what can be achieved by close collaboration between espionage and military and economic analysis experts. In this particular case the analysts were able to draw upon a large number of individual reports from our Middle Eastern sources. Even so, it was a bold prophecy, as is evidenced by the fact that there was a complete lack of confirmation from the other Western intelligence services. Even the CIA, which had far and away the best contacts with the Israeli secret service, was convinced right up to the last minute that the United States had succeeded in preventing the outbreak of a war. Unfortunately, our prediction fell on deaf ears: the deputies to whom we made it admitted at the time that they believed it was just another instance of undue intelligence service pessimism.

We had first observed the gathering signs of Egypt's preparation for war with Israel through our intelligence channels after Gromyko's four-day visit to Cairo ended on April 1. Our sources clearly indicated that he had made no attempt to subdue the belligerence of his Arab friends; on the contrary, we received pointers that in his discussions with Nasser, Gromyko had deliberately withheld the latest Soviet secret service estimate of the relative military strengths of the two opposing countries. The Russians were privately convinced that the Arabs would never manage to catch up with the (numerically inferior) Israeli armed forces insofar as quality superiority was concerned. We can only speculate why Gromyko actually encouraged the Arabs to fight in such a hopeless situation.

The Israeli intelligence service Shin Beth—which had become one of the most efficient in the world in the two decades of its existence—lived up to its reputation. It was able to follow the war preparations of its Arab neighbors with extreme accuracy, as was shown by later investigations, and it provided the Israeli military authorities with all the information they needed. In view of the numerical superiority of the Egyptian air force, they had to tilt the balance as early as possible, so they used their own magnificently equipped air force to deliver a preemptive strike on the Egyptians in lieu of a declaration of war. These were the same tactics as Hitler had used in Poland, France, and Yugoslavia. This forestalled the Arab air assault, which would otherwise have proved fatal to the little country. The Israelis were able to strike at the most important Egyptian air bases with surprise air attacks launched from the Mediterranean, and the majority of the Egyptians' operational aircraft were wiped out on the ground. Concentrated tank attacks followed hard on this initial victory, and the Arabs' fate was sealed. In a blitzkrieg lasting only six days, the Israelis seized victory with a rapidity that had previously seemed possible only with the use of atomic warheads.

The major powers then intervened and hostilities ceased. Since then, Israel has hung on to the Arab territories she occupied during the war, and is holding them in pawn for a later peace settlement. But the Russians have undertaken not only to replenish the material losses of the Arab countries, but to guarantee them superiority in modern weapons too. This lays bare Soviet aims in all their refinement. By means of these arms deliveries (which the Western intelligence services have been keeping close check on) Moscow has secured for itself an increasing influence on Egypt, just as Gromyko planned. It looks like a brutal rationalization of Soviet scheming: the Arabs, once defeated, would be forced to give up all aspirations to independence—thus, no matter who won the armed conflict, the Soviet Union was bound to emerge the victor in an Arab-Israeli conflict in 1967.

In the wake of the Arab defeat, Soviet aid to Egypt has multiplied. Over the last three years thousands of Soviet advisers and technicians have flooded into the country. There can, however, be no doubt that while the proud and patriotic Arabs welcome the Russians as helpers, they will never welcome them as friends. Between the foreign instructors—despised for their arrogance—and their "trainees," there has recently been friction that has led to blows. To Nasser and his senior officials the defeat was a disgrace, which Soviet patronage only served to prolong.

* * *

In the five and a half years between Adenauer's retirement and my own, my presidency of the BND came under increasingly heavy fire. While I was rewarded with the esteem of Adenauer's successors —Professor Erhard and then Kurt Kiesinger—as well as of their state-secretaries, my work at Pullach was burdened in an increasingly unpleasant manner by the sniping of a number of senior civil servants. Ignorant of the ways of an intelligence service, they persisted in entangling us in red tape and ill-informed criticisms. I repeatedly found that when I tried to settle important problems I had the responsible parliamentary subcommittees and the all-powerful chairman of the audit committee on my side but the ignorant bureaucracy of the civil service firmly up in arms against me.

It was at about this time that Professor Erhard resigned, and on December 1, 1966, the Grand Coalition was formed in Bonn under Kiesinger. I had anticipated that with the dawning of coalition government the Federal Intelligence Service might become an object of political controversy; so in my very first conference with Kiesinger after he became federal chancellor, I recommended to him that since I would reach normal retirement age in 1967, I ought not to remain more than one year beyond that, since otherwise the question of my successor would have to be settled in the hectic atmosphere of an election year (scheduled for 1969). When the time came for deciding on my successor, the choice fell on Gerhard Wessel.

\* \* \*

Wessel* succeeded me as president of the Federal Intelligence Service on May 1, 1968. In a short ceremony attended by some sixty officers and men, Professor Carstens delivered a farewell speech and introduced my successor to the senior members of the service. Wessel spoke a few words, followed by myself, and then it was all over. The warmth of the words delivered by Carstens on behalf of Kiesinger and the federal government and the award some days earlier of the highest medal the West German republic can bestow went some way toward compensating me for the last years of intrigue by the civil servants of both political parties. "Obviously you have had to swallow disappointments and suffer setbacks," Carstens said. "But taken as a whole, we can only regard your achievement as exceptional and vital for the future of our country; it was an achievement that had to be accomplished behind closed doors. I can only quote the words of President Kennedy as he took leave of his former secret service chief Allen Dulles at the end of November 1961, and handed the office of director of the CIA over to my old friend John Alex McCone. He remarked, 'Your triumphs remain unsung, while your mistakes are trumpeted to the skies.' " About that, I myself have no complaint: the head of a secret service must learn to take criticism in silence.

My going and the new appointments that were made to the BND brought tragedy in their wake. General Wendland, who had been in the service since its beginning, and who had been my chief of staff and then my acting deputy, learned that he was to be by-passed by a politician for the post of vice-president (eventually

---

* Lieutenant General Gerhard Wessel, my successor, was born on Christmas eve, 1913; he joined the General Staff in 1941 and served under me in Foreign Armies East from 1942 until the end of the war, succeeding me as its chief in April 1945. He joined the Gehlen organization in 1946, transferred to the embryo Bundeswehr, and supervised the setting up of the MAD.

the Socialists appointed their party manager in Hamburg, Dieter Blötz, to the post). Perhaps the years of stress under which all the BND senior staff had labored in the cause of Germany had proved too much for him or perhaps it was his general ill health, but when I spoke to him before flying to Istanbul to take leave of my old colleagues in the Turkish intelligence service, I thought he seemed depressed. In Istanbul I received a telegram that Wendland had shot himself in his office at our headquarters on October 9, 1968.

# Part Four

# The Future of the West

## CHAPTER THIRTEEN

# Soviet
# Foreign Policy
# and the
# Communist Ideology

𝕴 n previous chapters I have described the origins of the service and how it developed, but in doing so I have tried to keep one thing clearly in view—the red streak that extends from one end of the story to the other. Virtually all of the incidents I have described have been conditioned in some way by the great conflict existing between the free world and the Communist world. This struggle has already influenced our lives for many decades, and I have no doubt it will continue to affect the future of our country for years to come. It is this that compels me to devote the concluding chapters of this book to something more than just an amplification and rounding off of the narrative I have written about my own experiences; it must be a clear personal credo, a statement of my own beliefs about the future.

The political contradictions between East and West are coupled with an unceasing conflict of ideologies from which nobody has either the right or the means to escape; sometimes the conflict

[ 283

is conducted silently, but frequently it is fought out in full view of world opinion. It is prosecuted at every level of human life, and in every field of activity. On our own side we still have the support of a massive phalanx, the democratic West, resolute and determined to fight for the maintenance of liberty, although in West Germany the will has grown somewhat weaker recently. The guardians of all we hold dear and sacred are fighting with weapons of the mind to defend us against the destructive influences of the Communist ideology, especially in those breeding grounds where communism is marching toward new objectives. May none of those called upon to fight in defense of peace and freedom ever tire of admonishing the irresolute and exhorting the discouraged, the deceived, and the besotted.

The theoretical and ideological premises of communism are unchanged: they are as fundamental in deciding practical political actions as they ever have been. I will try to describe the various interrelated factors and features of the international Communist goal, which is to bring about "world revolution," or to "bestow the blessings of socialism on mankind," as the Communists put it. I will then end by putting in perspective the achievements of Soviet power politics during the latter twenty years of my office, from 1948 to 1968, and by analyzing the present world situation. Let a quotation from Heinrich Heine introduce these final chapters. Heine, a poet who can certainly not be accused of being reactionary, wrote of communism,

> Communism is the secret name of a terrible antagonist who is going to throw the rule of the proletariat (with all that that implies) into battle with the modern bourgeois regiments. It will be a bitter struggle. How will it end? Only the gods and goddesses privy to the secrets of the future can tell. But one thing is certain: "Communism" may be alien to our tongues as yet; he may loaf idly in his murky attics, lolling on his miserable mattresses of straw; but without a doubt a heroic role has been assigned him in the modern tragedy, and he is but waiting for the cue to step on stage. Let us therefore never lose sight of this actor; from time to time we must report on the secret rehearsals he is holding in preparation for his grand

debut. Intimations of these may well prove more important than all the reports of election scandals, party bickering, and cabinet intrigues together.*

At the time Heine wrote these prophetic words he would have known nothing of Karl Marx. He could not suspect that eighty-five years later a revolutionary called Lenin would introduce communism into czarist Russia—hardly a country for which either Marx or Engels had known any sympathy. All the more remarkable was Heine's vision, insofar as the clandestine factions that called themselves "Communists" possessed such little significance at the time of his writing.

A century later Stalin was fighting for absolute power within the Soviet Union, and by 1945 the red dictator had secured his position and had vanquished Germany in alliance with the Western powers. He stood on the river Elbe, and with the solitary exception of the Straits of Constantinople he had realized not only the wildest ambitions of the czars but virtually all the dreams of Pan-Slavism as well. The "conversion" of all the countries in eastern and southeastern Europe that had fallen under Soviet rule was the inevitable consequence. By 1949 the process was complete.

Over the years that followed, we could clearly see that Soviet power politics remained completely unchanged. For myself and my colleagues, the situation emerging at the end of the forties—which coincided with the foundation of the Federal Republic of Germany —brought with it new and important responsibilities. Until then we had been concentrating our attention and analysis on the military planning and potential of the Russians and their satellite territories. Our mission now embraced the surveillance and scrutiny of Soviet power politics in all its aspects, including short-term operations, medium- and long-term planning, and broad-based preparations of a strategic and geopolitical character. On top of this, we had to devote attention to the domestic situation within the Soviet frontiers as well as to the expansionist policies of the Russians beyond them.

The consequences of Yalta had already indicated that terror

---

* Heinrich Heine, *Französische Zustände* (1833).

and destruction would probably accompany the spread of communism. Within a few years we had final proof that this would indeed be one of the results of Soviet foreign policy: this episode was the violent overthrow of Beneš, whereby Czechoslovakia was converted to a Communist "people's democracy" in June 1948. Twenty years later, as my years of office drew to an end, the Czechs and Slovaks were prevented by the Russians from going their "own way toward socialism" and choosing freedom if they wished. It was a convincing and irrefutable confirmation that Soviet policies have remained the same. Both the beginning and the end of my directorship of our foreign intelligence organization were distinguished by violent coups against a virtually defenseless country.

What has happened to the Czechs and Slovaks, to the Hungarians, the Poles, and our own countrymen in East Germany, has evoked a degree of lasting condemnation in the West (particularly in our own country) that should have brought people to their senses. But today, barely three years after the dramatic military invasion of Czechoslovakia in August 1968, it has been all but forgotten. What was the undisguised use of brute force at the time is now dressed up by skillful propaganda as a measure which was urgently necessary to preserve Communist interests in the Eastern bloc.

Starting from nothing, it was not easy to trace the initiatives and directives emanating from the Soviet bloc or to piece together a complete picture of its most important political developments. Our potential enemy controlled a gigantic machine, a political apparatus affording an unlimited selection of operations and an inexhaustible arsenal of weapons and tactics with which to put them into effect. In the following chapter I propose to examine these tactics more closely and the basic vehicles employed by the Russians to promote their policies at home and abroad.

* * *

Convincing and conclusive though our service's analyses were, they were not always to the liking or taste of every political personality in West Germany. We detected virtually every significant trend in the Soviet bloc quite early, often months or years in advance; and in most cases we correctly estimated the consequences as well. But we were forced to realize again and again that any foreign intelligence service that reports unfavorable facts, even if only occasionally, rapidly attracts a reputation for being narrow-minded, if not downright pessimistic. More than once I felt cast in the role of a Cassandra when I warned that the facts did not support certain illusions and unsound judgments entertained by Bonn. This was particularly true of the late 1960s, as more and more of our country's politicians rediscovered Russia's "love of peace," attractively packaged in the Soviet offerings of "coexistence and détente." It fell to our lot at Pullach to be labeled "cold-war–mongers." I confidently leave it to future generations to judge whether we promoted the cold war or not.

The purposefulness of Soviet foreign policy has frequently escaped notice. One astounding feature we confronted was the opinion of many leading politicians and senior government officials that Soviet policies were inscrutable and, indeed, irrational in some aspects. I could never understand how anybody could have such an opinion. I have always maintained that Communist policies in general and Soviet foreign policy in particular are distinguished by their almost fascinating consistency and unparalleled single-mindedness. A further factor is that Communist statesmen are often so convinced of the rectitude of their beliefs that they announce their aims and intentions with almost brutal frankness. It is a curious feature they have in common with Adolf Hitler, who also made no secret of his aims.* These unofficial and official announcements are seldom taken seriously by our side, or they are robbed of their value by the fact that people who are all too unfamiliar with the subject matter select only those passages that tie in with their own opinions, which are sometimes controversial to say the least. The Communist bloc speeches and publications reaching us are skillfully dosed and doctored, and lack of perception and insufficient judgment prevent such people from drawing the proper conclusions from them.

---

* National socialism and communism always did overlap at their extremes. I once suggested we adopt as our slogan, "Fight the Red fascism," but found little support.

The dominant role played by the Soviet ideology is largely forgotten or disbelieved. I am convinced that only a broad and accurate knowledge of the enemy can protect us from faulty decisions —knowledge without which any political conflict with communism and the world power that promotes it is simply quite hopeless. What is needed is a knowledge of the mentality of the Soviet peoples and their allies, and a knowledge of the doctrines of Marxism and Leninism, which the Communists see as a means not only of explaining the world about us but of changing it as well. However violently this may be disputed by many "experts" of today, the Communist ideology is still the basis on which all important decisions in the Communist empire are made. It is and always will be the manual on which all their actions are based.

The following argument will make this clear. In the West, many political analysts maintain that the "age of ideologies" is over; that in consequence the virulence of world revolution is on the decline as well, if not already extinct; that as a result all Communist foreign policy (although not domestic policy as yet) is independent of Communist ideology; that this makes it unnecessary for us to impute to our Communist political opponents an "ideological" strain in their deliberations and planning (i.e., the goal of world revolution) when we do our foreign affairs "arithmetic"; and, finally, that this permits us to conclude that our relations with the Communist states, and above all with the Soviet Union, may yet be "normalized." By this we are to understand that in these foreign relations the interests of the state, or raison d'état, will come increasingly to the fore in Communist countries, while ideological factors—the elements of weltanschauung—will lose the influence on foreign policy they have exercised up to now. This argument clearly depends on the conviction expressed by a host of Western Sovietologists that the two heterogeneous social systems are converging; and it gainsays the virulence of the Marxist and Leninist teachings of world revolution as a factor in Soviet foreign policy.

The Communists, on the other hand, maintain that the highly developed capitalist countries have reached a significant stage in their development process and that this process is leading to the emergence of a new kind of capitalism. This new capitalism is characterized by the accumulation of capital, and hence power, in the hands of the state and major industrial corporations—the capitalism of old has become a capitalism of state monopolies. They believe that this new capitalism harbors the same malignancies as before and is therefore doomed to destruction despite its highly developed ability to master social and economic crises. Furthermore, the Communists argue, this capitalism of state monopolies is capable of raising the living standards and improving the working conditions of the working classes by methodically encouraging scientific research and by social reform. But while this will admittedly improve the absolute position of the working classes it will not halt their progressive relative pauperization. This new kind of capitalism is not just a consequence of the technological revolution, it has been brought about by pressure exercised by the Socialist camp on the world's social order too. Hence, every reform movement in the modern capitalist social structure must be seen as a predictable phase in the continuing process of world revolution. Finally, the capitalism of state monopolies is what Lenin himself predicted would occur as the "important preliminary development phase" in the transition from capitalism to socialism—the Communist version of the theory of convergence. These conclusions depend on the conviction that the process of world revolution conforms precisely to the laws of Marxism-Leninism—a conviction shared by Communist parties throughout the world. Naturally, the agreement between the Western theory of convergence and political fact is denied by the Communists.

In recent years there has been a growing public controversy as to whether Soviet foreign policy is still rooted in ideology or whether it primarily serves the imperialist and nationalist interests of the Soviet Union. In my view this controversy is barren and pointless since Soviet foreign policy serves both interests equally. If we class the ideological objectives as a facet of political strategy— as the Communists do themselves, until they take over power within a country—all the apparent contradictions vanish. At any rate it would scarcely be possible to find any evidence of an action or "development phase" in the relations between Communist and non-Communist countries which does not conform with Communist ideologies; the (at present unratified) treaty concluded between Moscow and Bonn on August 12, 1970 is a case in point. Nor does the Soviet Union's spectacular support for the United Arab Republic (specifically, Egypt) conflict in any way with the long-term, ideologically aligned plans of Moscow, even though in Egypt the Communist party is still prohibited and its members, at least at the time of Nasser, have been persecuted. The waxing influence of Moscow in the Middle East, with its principal focus in Egypt, will—as the Soviet leaders argue—convert Arab-style "socialism" to the pure version represented by Moscow more rapidly than if the United Arab Republic were left to its own fate as a penalty for suppressing Communists in its own territories.

\* \* \*

Before I turn to the policies of communism in general (and Soviet policies and their consequences in particular) and before I deal with their implementing organs and their most important weapons and tactics, I feel that a few basic comments on the relationship between Communist theory and practice are called for. Better brains than mine have already examined this theme from every angle, frequently without finding the audience they deserve. I therefore intend to limit this discussion to those matters in which the relationship between Communist theory—in other words, Communist ideology—and practice, as represented in politically significant events, can be identified beyond all doubt.

If any government policy is to be successful it must be both purposeful and resolute; this is particularly true of foreign policy. The force, intensity, and ultimate results of such policies depend on the government's capabilities—its military, economic, technical, and psycho-political potential—and on external conditioning factors like the overall situation and the intentions of its allies and enemies.

The first thing to recognize is that in a given situation the active politician frequently sums up the relationship between policy and objective in a subjective way. He investigates whether and how the desired objective can be achieved, and from a number of potential solutions he identifies those which he believes will serve that purpose best. But the intelligence analyst—the officer responsible for assessing the enemy's situation—must in general take his own side's situation and intentions into account only as secondary factors. Therefore, in appraising the enemy's situation he will frequently display a greater degree of objectivity than the politician, assuming that he is capable of penetrating the enemy's mind. The politician who properly realizes this and does not act as Hitler did— accepting only what jibed with his own ideas—and who weighs his own capabilities against the "enemy situation" dispassionately and with clarity of vision will make the right decisions, free of all illusions.

Politics takes certain fundamental values as its premises, foundations which at the same time embrace the ultimate objectives in view. These premises consist in part of constitutional edicts like our Basic Law, international law, and conventions like the United Nations Charter; but they also derive, although we are not always conscious of them, from religious convictions and from our weltanschauung and ideologies.

So long as all the actors on the stage of international politics are following the same ideological premises and rules, these latter limitations assume a lesser importance—in the free interplay of forces the same norms and laws hold for everybody. In this situation, politics are attuned only to the desired profit: they have become "de-ideologized," to use one of the fashionable terms of the late 1960s. In my view, this was the state of affairs that prevailed in the eighteenth century and, with certain limitations (I am thinking of the influences emanating from the great French Revolution), in the nineteenth century as well.

But once the premises and values conditioning political acts had become as diverse as they were by the time of the Russian Revolution in October 1917, then this parity of interests that I have postulated was bound to disappear. Ever since then, the leading politicians of a country have had to adjust their actions to accord not only with the ultimate profit that they seek, but also with the norms and values currently approved by their own country, while at the same time judging the actions of the adversary by the different norms valid for that country. In doing so, they repeatedly recognize that the enemy's tactics and actions conflict with their own norms. Were this not so, our own politicians would not continually have to appeal to our highest values (liberty and democracy, for example) to justify our actions and prove the validity of our demands, or to expose the baseness of the enemy's arguments.

It is obvious that the values conditioning political decisions in East and West are different. And as long as Communist parties, whether in or out of power, adhere to the Communist dogma, politics will continue to be significantly beset by the ideological element. It would be a good thing if we could all come to terms with this harsh fact, just as all Communists are convinced that the struggle with "imperialism" is inevitable. Certain trends in West Germany like the outlandish behavior of the Young Socialists* and the increasingly virulent radical strain ought to cause us to see the role of ideology in political practice in a more realistic and responsible light than we have so far.

We can find the ultimate values and objectives which serve as the polestar for the Soviet Union, its satellite countries, and every Communist party in what is claimed to be the scientifically based weltanschauung of Marxism-Leninism. It is there for all the world to see—in the institutions of learning, in written constitutions, in party programs and statutes, as well as in countless basic documents which, I can only keep emphasizing, represent the Soviet manual of attack.

\* \* \*

The information collected by the major Western intelligence services over the years establishes that Soviet offensive aims have remained constant. I am not blind to the many objections that will probably be raised to such a viewpoint. The same people who have learned

---

\* The radical left wing of the Social Democratic Party in West Germany.

nothing from even the most recent Communist "lessons" (over the German and Berlin problems, for example) never tire, it seems, of pointing out that within the Soviet bloc there have been developments over the past few years which have restricted the practicable segments of Marxism-Leninism to an ever smaller area. These changes were there for all the world to see, they say, it was just that certain "pessimists" refused to accept the evidence. Of course, I fully recognize that modern Marxism-Leninism is as remote from the classical teachings of Marx and Lenin as modern Christianity is from the teachings of Our Lord. This does not alter the fact that in countries where communism is in power, it insists immutably on the predominant role of the party, and "splinter groups" are brought back into the fold with considerable severity. The all-powerful party in turn fashions the more important elements of its doctrines to meet in advance every objection that may be made by its adversaries. That is how the nonruling Communist parties in France and Italy can call for the conversion of their countries into "Socialist" societies, without, of course, altering their true programs one iota. Nor has communism given up its claim to exclusiveness any more than it has altered the "Socialist" characteristics of its economic programs, ineffectual though they have proved to be in many instances.

Until such time as the opposite is proved true—and this can only consist of some country organized hitherto on socialist principles adopting on its own initiative, and unimpeded by its allies, some other form of government and society—we must assume that Communist ideology will continue to be the dominant factor conditioning Communist policies. Therefore any discussion of Soviet policies is bound to take as its starting point the fact that political and social concepts are understood differently by Communists and non-Communists.

My own experience suggests that these ambiguities have been deliberately created by the Communists. In any event, they certainly work to our disadvantage in everyday diplomatic dealings between the Western countries and the Soviet bloc. Highly trained dialecticians as they are, the Russians exploit these difficulties to maximum effect. Moreover, the necessity for a rapid flow of information through the various media in our open society in the West leaves little time or inclination for precise explanations of the divergencies between Soviet and Western interpretations of the same word. It is not surprising that this produces a dangerous disorientation in the public's political awareness in the West.

There seems to be a distinct reluctance to face the consequences of this, so it seems vital to me to go into the semantic distinctions at this point. Unless these distinctions can be made intelligible to everybody, the Russians will always hold all the cards; while the Westerner, confused by the use of identical words to refer to different and sometimes mutually exclusive concepts, will fall victim to the mind-bending campaign of his Soviet adversary.

At the heart of the Soviet conception of foreign policy are two terms whose interpretation is indispensable for an understanding of the practical politics of the Soviet state: *ideology* and *coexistence*. The word *ideology* has undergone many metamorphoses in its long history. Originally it was a word of purely philosophical content. Presently, however, it is used to refer to a complex of inseparable and obscure theoretical, pragmatic, ideological, and praxeological propositions. Since the Russian Revolution of 1917 and the emergence of the Soviet Union, the political history of the world has been overshadowed by the conflict of two opposing systems of government, society, and economy, founded on two divergent sets of values. The governmental, social, and economic structure of the Soviet Union is based on the ideology of Marxism-Leninism, whose content can be summarized as follows: an ideology is a false conviction when it consists of idealistic or bourgeois notions; it is a true conviction when it echoes the notions of dialectical materialism and the proletariat. Two criteria distinguish a true way of thinking from a false one: a philosophical element (the distinction between materialism and idealism) and a class element (or class distinction). In this sense, Marxism-Leninism draws a distinction between scientific and unscientific ideologies and temporarily deprives us of the chance of referring to positive experience as the distinguishing criterion between truth and falsehood. All learning that is politically neutral with respect to society is rejected as ideologically false, as it is claimed to be capable of grasping only the surface of reality.

Similarly, the definition of *coexistence* as understood by the Soviet government and the Eastern bloc countries is different from the interpretation preferred by the non-Communist world. The Communist version of coexistence can be summarized as being a transitory state somewhere along the road toward the establishment of a Socialist society. It is characterized by "peaceful" competition in every sphere between the two great camps, while avoiding any actual military confrontation. Seen in this light, it is wholly understandable that Moscow continues to pay lip service to the theory of the avoidability of nuclear war, even if it no longer suggests it is actually impossible, as Khrushchev once did. But peaceful coexistence precludes the Russians neither from supporting violent revolutions, nor from intervening in certain circumstances which may actually lead to conventional war—what we refer to as "localized wars" and the Russians, "national wars of liberation." The conclusion to be drawn from all this with respect to Soviet foreign policy—and it is a conclusion we always drew in our own appreciations—is that the Russians will always avoid a direct confrontation with the United States where they can, and they will take good care that localized wars such as that in the Middle East do not get out of hand.

At the purely ideological level, however, which delineates the intellectual area of conflict, there can be no coexistence, and the Communists have made no secret of this fact. It is a fact that has been emphasized as recently as December 1970, in a policy article published in East Germany by *Neues Deutschland*.

The Soviet understanding of the word *coexistence* as I have described it is fundamentally different from what the non-Communist world understands by the word. We regard coexistence, as its name implies, as a permanent state of living together in harmony. We do not regard it as a state of Communist political aggression, using clandestine methods of subversion from behind a smokescreen of ostensibly peaceful cohabitation.

Despite its basically competitive nature, coexistence is a state of affairs particularly desired by the Communists. It enables them to overcome the natural barriers of anxiety and fear, and, in conjunction with open and covert propaganda methods, it enhances their prospects of penetrating the minds of the working classes as well as of the intellectuals within the capitalist countries. In the Communist sense of the word, therefore, coexistence is nothing less than a prerequisite for the gradual ripening of revolutionary conditions. This has been confirmed not only by Khrushchev, but quite recently by other leading Communists as well. And in my view it is of particular importance. It shows that contrary to popular opinion in the West, the Russians themselves understand the word *coexistence* in a purely offensive sense, and it should not be equated with what the West means when it speaks of attempts at détente. A typical example of the conversion of a country to a Socialist (that is, Communist) system by peaceful means can be seen in the recent developments in Chile, where a Marxist government has been democratically elected to power—the first great triumph of the Russians in South America.

* * *

It is one of the most important themes of Marxism-Leninism that the conflict between capitalism and socialism (that is, communism) is an antagonistic conflict and is therefore incapable of being called off; and that this conflict must and will end sooner or later in the suffocation or destruction of capitalism. Capitalism is of course already weakened, and conditions are thus favorable for the final triumph, it is said; but this is precisely why capitalism is now deadlier and more aggressive than ever before. That, at least, is how it was set out in the Karlovy Vary Declaration of April 1967, in the Moscow policy memorandum of June 1969, and in the various theses published on the occasion of Lenin's centenary. We can read and hear similar pronouncements almost daily in the mass media of the Soviet bloc.

To many, it will probably come as a surprise that for the Communists the word *détente* has quite a different meaning from what we understand by it in the West, just as in the case of *co-existence*. The dictum I just mentioned about an antagonistic conflict leads us to conclude that détente—a tension-free state of affairs—is understood by the Communists to be a purely relative concept, or at least one of only limited duration. The détente—and this fact is of particular importance in light of the détente euphoria in which our country is wallowing—will last only so long as it serves the Communists' interests. The harsh reality of this is frequently brought home to us by the persistence and, indeed, the intensification of the ideological conflict and its associated agitation and propaganda campaigns. The West understands *détente* as an element and objective of political strategy. But in the Communist meaning of the word it is a weapon of political tactics—one which can be exploited to one's own profit just like its heavier-caliber brother, *coexistence*. Among its many possibilities, like improving the prospects of a popular front or expanding trade relations, détente also creates a better climate for an offensive approach to the problem of "penetrating the minds" of the capitalist peoples. In this context it is not uninteresting to observe that in the more important basic documents, the Communists speak to the peoples as such, and not their respective governments. This well-considered distinction derives from the expectation that when their minds have been aroused to what "peace, progress, and socialism" can offer, the people themselves will ultimately force their governments to accede to the Communist demands.

Soviet foreign policy is conducted at two distinct levels. The Communists draw on both their agencies of national government and the organizations and machinery of the international Communist movement for effecting their foreign policies; but in so doing they keep the two levels of activity as separate as possible. While the former operates strictly within the limits and concepts of international law—although here too the terms are differently interpreted by the Communists—the spider's web of links between the international Communist parties makes it possible for them to influence the domestic policies and the political minds of other countries in various covert ways without the foreign Communist governments themselves being called to account for them. In this connection it is worth noting that every Communist party organization maintains a bureau solely concerned with liaison with other Communist parties.

This two-tiered system has been worked up to a fine art by the ruling Communist parties. In my opinion too little attention is paid to it in the free world. At best, if at all, it is regarded as a matter concerning only the agencies for internal security in the countries concerned. This state of affairs comes to public attention only from time to time, such as when the Soviet ambassador to West Germany (at present, Zarapkin) does not attend the official Karl Marx centenary celebrations but prefers to honor the local German Communist party ceremony a few blocks away.

This duality of political behavior is only part of the potential permanently available to the Communist bloc. Intercourse with foreign states—foreign affairs—was formerly exclusively a matter for diplomats; and other kinds of intercourse beyond the frontiers, such as trade or cultural exchanges, were regarded as nonpolitical activities. Diplomacy offered assistance where necessary, but was otherwise happy to leave things well alone. The recent pronouncement of our Federal Chancellor Brandt in connection with some projects in underdeveloped countries that insofar as possible politics must be kept out of trade, was wholly in accordance with this attitude, which is still widely held.

The Communists put a completely different interpretation on things: for them there is no area or activity free of ideology. It follows from this that there are, equally, no areas or activities free of politics. If we were to try to demonstrate this from Communist teachings, we would only have to refer to Lenin's dictum that all actions must be "partisan," and to his flat condemnation of any attempt to act positivistically, let alone neutrally. Nonetheless, I must mention here that the scholars of the Communist bloc are constantly casting about for nonideological fields in which to work, much to the distress of their parties.

The philosophy that every human activity and action must have an ideological and political content produces an astonishing multiplicity of means and methods open to the Communists in their relations with other countries, and these they apply with consummate skill. On the one hand, they use conventional diplomacy, as they always have and always will; on the other, they also regard economic, trade, cultural, and psycho-political relations—the latter being the dissemination of information, agitation, and propaganda —as legitimate means to an end in foreign policy.

It is the duty of diplomacy to make contacts and to maintain and extend them; in general, this work will be done statically rather than dynamically, for in the interests of the contacts, this diplomacy must appear to "advance the cause of peace." The other means of foreign policy are regarded as offensive means, and they are to be applied with versatility and vigor. An example may make this a little clearer: while the Soviet Union undertakes constant attempts to keep up the diplomatic dialogue with the United States, at the same time it continues without abatement its cam-paign of hatred against this bastion of the West. After all, the "addressees" are quite different people: the diplomats deal with the foreign ministries of the other side, while the "unorthodox" methods are aimed at the man in the street—to receptive social groups like the "friends of peace" and other fellow travelers, as well as to the broad fields of economics, learning, technology, and culture, by-passing the government as far as possible. The favorite targets for this kind of campaign are parliamentary deputies and public per-sonalities in the widest sense—people whose interest is roused and whose sense of personal importance (particularly in West Ger-many) is appealed to, frequently with great subtlety.

\* \* \*

An important part is played on the Soviet and Communist side in this continuing struggle by psycho-politics and *desinformatsiya,* or "disinformation"—a targeted stream of information deliberately designed to influence the recipient in a certain, predetermined man-ner. By means of the two-tier approach I have described, the Soviet Union tries to secure both an immediate political profit—like, for example, the political dependence of other countries by virtue of the economic aid or technological and military assistance they receive from her—and an indirect political gain from the penetration of the enemy mind. It was Marx who stated that the idea becomes a political force as soon as it penetrates the mind of the masses. If we accept the Communist theory of the absolute interdependence of all that happens, it follows that (in terms of current political practice) every political action carries within it the means of penetrating the mind: conversely, every mind-penetrating action both can and should lead to political consequences.

The most glaring example of this kind of politics is the monotonous Soviet call for "total disarmament." Of course, the Russians and their fellow travelers understand full well that this demand can never be realized. Nor, moreover, would they ever like to see it realized, for this would jeopardize the security of their own power system and rob the Russians of the ability to nourish the fires of conflict in every corner of the globe by their arms supplies. But this loud and insistent demand has first and foremost the consequence that there can be no alternative to this extreme political objective—because such an alternative could only be "total rearmament." The sheer effrontery of the demand, with its apparently humanitarian overtones, puts the West in the awkward position of having to reject it as impracticable. In response the West can only produce counterproposals which must inevitably seem feeble in comparison with the Soviet "offer" and, at least in the eyes of neutrals, point up an apparent lack of goodwill. It casts the Communist bloc in the role of "peace lovers," while the Western powers can be pilloried as warmongers and aggressors. Without doubt, the persistent Soviet references to the "warmongering and belligerent" role of the United States have found their mark in the Western Hemisphere. This is all the more to be regretted since we do not have the opportunities we should to counter the Soviet claim that they and their allies act solely to protect their own proper interests on those occasions when they are "forced" to intervene in another country's affairs.

The false alternative of coexistence or war is yet another example of this dangerously successful *desinformatsiya*. (Of course, the true alternative to war is peace, not coexistence.) I could list many more examples of the systematic and deliberate psychopolitical methods applied by the Russians, where we in the service repeatedly warned of the deeper connotations, which were frequently anything but easy to perceive. The burning question of

Berlin is an example which will serve here to speak for many others. My own impression—which is founded on my knowledge of a mass of reliable intelligence reports—is that the Russians are trying (and largely succeeding) to build up West Berlin in the public mind as an independent political entity. In doing so, the Russians are proceeding step by step, making alternate and frequent use of the elements of blandishment and bluster, and allowing neither the ideas of the East German Communist functionaries (which do not always conform with their own) nor the countless protests from our own government to disturb them. Laudable though the frequent interventions by famous politicians of every party in West Germany on behalf of the former German capital may be, there is not the slightest prospect that these alone will dissuade the Russians from their long-term plan of attack.

It is clear that the Russians can already consider it a substantial victory that although many of our country's politicians now talk of the "accepted fact" that Berlin belongs to West Germany, the Federal Parliament has not been convened in Berlin for several years now. Apparently many politicians on this side of the Iron Curtain (and on the other) have forgotten that according to Article 23 of our Basic Law, which was drawn up by the Four Powers, Greater Berlin (which, of course, includes East Berlin) has been part of the area subject to the Basic Law from the very outset—in other words, part of the Federal Republic. Perhaps they were eager to overlook this fact in order to present as accommodating a face to the Russians as possible. The fact remains that according to Basic Law, Berlin has been an integral part of the Federal Republic since 1949, with the well-known reservation that the relationship of Berlin to the Federal Republic is subject (under Paragraph 2 of Article 144) to certain limitations by virtue of the continued validity of the occupation statute and the primary responsibility of the three protecting powers for the security of West Berlin.

I have never ceased to regret that the West German government—out of deference to our public allergy toward anything which might smack of the methods of the Nazi Propaganda Ministry—has refrained from reacting vigorously and purposefully to the Communist smear campaigns, and has failed to reply in the same vernacular, propagating our own sets of values and making our intentions clear beyond all doubt. It is incomprehensible to me that we do not even employ the extensive facilities of our Radio Germany (*Deutschlandfunk*) or the German Wavelength (*Deutsche Welle*) or the Goethe Houses, of which foreign countries speak so highly, to disseminate our own ideas abroad with adequate emphasis and in an unequivocal tone instead of the deliberately circumspect opinions voiced at present, which the Russians just regard as feebleness on our part.

I am perfectly aware that our constitution in particular and the democratic social system in general circumscribe the extent to which we are able to conduct a methodical and purposeful propaganda campaign. The vital freedom of opinion and freedom of the press anchored in our Basic Law prevent us from harnessing the mass media to the same extent as they are harnessed by the Communist bloc. Nonetheless, it could have been possible, as a few particularly successful acts of initiative have shown, for us to put a stop to a lot that has happened by using relatively modest means. We could for example have prevented the distortion of the popular attitude toward Berlin, and we could have challenged the ready acceptance of the incorporation of East Berlin into the East German state, a move which even Ulbricht long hesitated to make.

*  *  *

Before I attempt to summarize what I have argued so far, I want to make a few suggestions as to how we could improve our position in this field—which will be one of the decisive factors for our future—while taking account of the present situation. Neither we in West Germany nor our allies possess as does the Soviet Union a network of active, remote-controlled political parties and organizations abroad, capable of carrying out propaganda and agitation campaigns parallel to the existing mass media. So we must help ourselves. I would consider it useful, if not absolutely vital, for our news dissemination agencies (and particularly the Federal Press and Information Office) to have seconded to them experts capable of providing analytical, evaluatory, and advisory assistance on any problem that arises. Obviously there will be little point to employing such experts unless our government not only makes the fullest possible use of them but also issues with their help detailed and *immediate* replies to allegations, accusations, and innuendoes broadcast by the enemy with the object of injuring our country's interests. If it should be suggested that there are already more than enough such experts on hand, then I can only respond that we have not heard very much from them so far; or alternatively that they are doomed to the same fate as the Cassandras of the intelligence service—that nobody will listen to them. I would also suggest to the central committees of our political parties that they do all they can to make use of qualified advisers before passing judgment on particular incidents and developments in the Communist bloc countries which may rebound on our own country either now or in the future. At any rate, neither the federal government nor the party leaders ought leave any stone unturned to avoid basing their decisions on inaccurate or premature judgments. Intuition, skillful improvisation, and imagination are not enough; there is no shortcut to careful, conscientious, and responsible analysis. I need scarcely mention just how important is the work of the special sections of the other Western intelligence services operating in this field, which are no longer at the disposal of the West German intelligence service. One of the first actions of the Socialist government was to disband the service's world communism section, which Colonel Herre had founded in the early fifties and fostered ever since; it had been staffed with highly skilled German specialists (most of whom had originally been connected with the Vlasov project) and worked in collaboration with identical sections in most other Western intelligence services. Ehmke's argument was that this field was none of the service's concern.* The work of the Eastern experts of the

---

* Among this section's principal members were General Hermann Foertsch (brother of the inspector general of the Bundeswehr) and Theodor Krause, formerly of the OKW's cryptanalysis branch. This section maintained contact, for example, with the Russian intelligentsia dissatisfied with Soviet rule; one of our experts, Nicolaus von Grote, recently published a book on the Russian underground, *Stimmen aus dem Sowjetischen Untergrund* [Voices from the Soviet underground] (Osnabrück: Verlag A. Fromm, 1971).

other government agencies remains classified and is hence withheld from public scrutiny, not of course that their reports are any less valuable for the federal government and party leaders as an aid in their decision-making processes.

My aim in writing these last pages has been to refute the widespread contention that there have been substantial changes in the aims the Communists have set themselves. Whatever changes there may have been in the methods they employ in pursuit of those aims, there can be no denying that communism itself is as dangerous as ever. Communism still menaces the free world—it still wants to bring our countries into its domain, to win our peoples, and to incorporate us into its own power system. There is not the slightest indication that these ambitions will change one iota in the foreseeable future.

While the Soviet leaders have long recognized the dangers inherent in a worldwide military conflict, they are seeking (and finding) their successes by using "other means." This obvious fact is confirmed again and again by the evidence that these means are being resorted to anew with every day that dawns. It was the purpose of this chapter to point to at least a few of these successful Communist methods of influencing and undermining other peoples. Thus the concepts of ideology and coexistence—as the Soviet mind understands them—of normalization of relations, and of the struggle for peace, and demands for détente and for total disarmament all stand arrayed against us, doing their bit for the "creative further development" in the "continued struggle." The mind-boggling variety of these concepts is matched only by the variety and quantity of the organizations and agencies established throughout the world with the sole task of putting these Communist theories into practice, and it is these, the vehicles of world communism, that I now propose to consider.

## CHAPTER FOURTEEN

# World Communist Operations and Infiltration

The confusing variety of associations and organizations, agencies and bases, at the disposal of international communism as vehicles for its operations at home and overseas suggests that it will be both useful and necessary to examine them in their various categories. I have decided to tabulate them in a way which avoids the schematic pitfalls found in various other surveys, while at the same time showing that the spider's web spun by the Communists over the whole globe is a very serious threat. The tabulation must take account of all the links established by these organizations and of their capacity for becoming mutually entwined and meshed. I need scarcely add that this interweaving by the instruments and tools employed by the agents of international communism is precisely what makes it so difficult for both politicians and citizens to scrutinize particular operations or to appreciate the enormity of the danger looming over the non-Communist world.

The following associations and organizations are controlled

and coordinated directly from Moscow and operate as part and parcel of the grand Communist design: the eleven international "front" organizations, to which I shall refer in detail later; various national organizations of a covert and auxiliary nature, operating either in conjunction with the international organizations mentioned or independently of them, and sometimes only for a limited time during which they fulfill a specific purpose; and the legal and illegal Communist party organizations.

These associations and organizations are served by various foreign agencies acting as undercover bases and control points. Almost without exception, these groups are capable of undertaking operations on their own and of carrying out political actions. Among them I count principally the following categories: Communist diplomatic missions and other "official" bodies such as trade missions and agencies, as well as groups of technical advisers; "quasi-official" establishments such as schools and hospitals which are maintained abroad by government funds provided by Communist countries; and legal or illegal "residences" and organs of the Communist secret services, whose "classical" espionage work is often only a small part of their effort.

In carrying out their campaigns and operations these associations, organizations, and agencies resort largely to methods and tactics whose very application allows the initiated to recognize or at least guess what the long-term objectives are. In every case they are designed to subvert the administrative and social order of the non-Communist countries and to weaken or destroy their national potential. Propaganda and agitation, infiltration and diversion, subversion and sabotage, are the methods which they hope will see the operations of international communism through to victory. All too often these methods have succeeded.

Before I turn to a detailed examination of the individual vehicles of international Communist activity, it will be necessary for me to comment on the consequences of the profound tensions existing between Moscow and Peking—the headquarters of the largest and most powerful Communist parties. Peking has tried to challenge the Soviet predominance and to construct a second stronghold of world communism which, in the Chinese view, is not only the equal of but vastly superior to and more progressive than the Soviet Union. All the exertions of Red China in this direction can be regarded as having come to naught so far. Whatever local and temporary successes Peking may have scored, never has her strength or national potential (which is in several areas distinctly restricted) proved sufficient to secure and hold on to important strongpoints in other parts of the world. This is without doubt a consequence of events within Communist China. The clash between the Communist superpowers has moreover resulted in internal problems throughout the structure of international communism, penetrating right down to the individual organizations and to the Communist parties in particular. For example, unlike the other European Communist parties, the Albanian party owes fierce allegiance to Peking. This strain was compounded on the one hand by simultaneous mishaps within the Soviet empire in Europe—culminating in the invasion of Czechoslovakia—and on the other, by the insistence with which Red Chinese leaders lay claim to being the sole apostles of the "true" communism, surpassing even the Russians with their promises and demands. In the next chapter, I will examine in detail the political-power aspect of the conflict between Moscow and Peking; but it is important to emphasize here that while we in the service never underestimated the effects of this dispute on the worldwide Communist program, at the same time we never regarded it as a threat to Soviet leadership in the Communist world either. In saying so, I do not exclude the possibility that in the future we shall see a Red China freed of internal strife and fully recovered emerging to inject new impulses into the body of international communism, defining fresh objectives, and spreading its teachings particularly throughout the expanses of Asia. Whereas Peking failed in Indonesia in 1965, she may yet succeed in some other Far East country, with a resulting extension of the Red Chinese empire.

Although the cracks appearing between Moscow and Peking—which some experts go so far as to call schisms—figure most prominently in many current analyses of international communism and the stagnation and impaired efficiency threatening to afflict it, I am inclined to see greater dangers to Moscow in other developments. Above all, there is the bitter fight Moscow is having to wage against separatist trends and the increasing tendency of "deviators" to go their own way in the European empire.

The principal evidence of a gradual decay within the Communist camp is that since the dissolution of Comintern in 1943 and Cominform in 1956, there has been no institutionalized central control of the world movement. Many events of recent years, and indeed certain terms used in the formulation of Communist policy documents, indicate moreover that Moscow's claim to the predominant role is being increasingly challenged.

In the opinion of the Yugoslav Communist Milovan Djilas there are centrifugal tendencies in international communism. This seems a very valid point to me; but it is important not to succumb to wishful thinking. My own view is that at some time in the future, instead of the one, uniting world movement there will be a number of "national communisms." Then, the Communist countries—if I may misquote Stalin here—will be Communist in form but nationalist in essence. But this development will take decades, if not a century; at present, nobody can predict where it will end, so we cannot take it into account in our political calculations. Obviously, it is the duty of every intelligence service and every planning branch to bear the possibility of such a development constantly in mind; and it seems equally obvious that they ought to keep a constant lookout for ways in which the free world can encourage such tendencies. This is quite different from launching an offensive anti-Communist crusade; it is a matter of whether the West is capable of surviving the present crucial conflict with the East and whether we can preserve our peace and freedom for posterity. To achieve these ends, we must be willing to employ all possible means, including psychological measures, to maintain our position.

We cannot exclude the possibility that over the next few years we shall see a fresh (even if temporary) rapprochement between Moscow and Peking. Specifically, this might occur after the present generation of leaders in the East retires. Younger forces that believe worldwide victory can be achieved only if all Communist forces pull together may then be able to prevail. I know that even Tito is grimly aware that after his demise Moscow may succeed in pulling Yugoslavia firmly into its grip again, for this would be an important move toward the solidarity of the orthodox Communist front.

At the beginning of the seventies, it is at any rate Moscow's brand of communism that represents the real challenge to us; this is the force with which we must do intellectual and political battle in the widest sense. Moscow is, and will be for some time, the leader of the majority of Communist parties and organizations abroad, and it is capable of maintaining this predominance by virtue of its heavy expenditure of funds and by exploiting its numerous agencies and bases abroad.

* * *

Among the most controversial of the vehicles and supports of Moscow's worldwide activities are the eleven international front organizations which are largely controlled and financed as instruments for carrying out large-scale operations under subtle camouflage. This system of well-concealed mass organizations is supplemented by numerous active associations like the Organization of Afro-Asian Solidarity, for example. The eleven international associations embrace hundreds of millions of people and are divided into the most diverse kinds of organizations and subgroups. The Russians have repeatedly drawn on their services on a broad front to bring out particular aspects of the Communist propaganda campaign; but they are also used to perpetuate smear campaigns initiated in connection with various incidents in the West. The large number of organizations in this worldwide network enables the Soviet leaders to switch from one campaign to another with great rapidity.

Diverse though the eleven associations may be in their functions, objectives, and modi operandi, they do display a number of common features. I intend to discuss below the role that the International Federation of Resistance Fighters (see the table on p. 310) has played in West Germany. With the exception of this federation, which was founded in 1951, and of the headquarters of the World Peace Council, which was founded in 1949, all these organizations were products of the immediate postwar years. Under the subtle and

### THE VEHICLES OF INTERNATIONAL COMMUNISM

|  | Headquarters | Membership |
|---|---|---|
| World Federation of Trade Unions | Prague | 138 million in 56 countries |
| World Peace Council | Helsinki | over 100 peace committees at national level |
| World Federation of Democratic Youth | Budapest | 100 million in 180 youth organizations |
| International Union of Students | Prague | 4 million in 87 organizations |
| Women's International Democratic Federation | East Berlin | 200 million claimed in 90 countries |
| World Federation of Teachers' Unions | Prague | 7.65 million in 25 countries |
| International Organization of Journalists | Prague | 140,000 in over 100 countries |
| International Radio and Television Organization | Prague | subgroups in 19 countries |
| International Association of Democratic Lawyers | Brussels | approximately 50 branches and subgroups |
| World Federation of Scientific Workers | London | 300,000 in 51 countries |
| International Federation of Resistance Fighters | Vienna | 4 million in 470 organizations in 20 countries |

circumspect direction of Moscow, they came into being during 1945 and 1946 from the merging of local associations and leagues in each country, among which of course there were also a number of non–Communist-aligned organizations at that time. I have no doubt that in many cases these groups had the highest and most respectable motives and that their campaigns were not only logical but necessary from the point of view of the countries concerned; but equally, there can be no doubt that the Communists made very refined overtures to them, that these newly founded national associations rapidly became their playthings, and that once they had become wholly affiliated to Moscow their policies were purposefully channeled in the right direction. Again and again, my colleagues and I in the early organization could see this happening: by means of these "bourgeois" groups, the Communists rapidly succeeded in penetrating the entire "bourgeois camp" of their target countries. From what the Russians referred to as the "useful idiots" of the 1950s, whose ineptness not infrequently accelerated the process of decay desired by their Communist puppet masters, there has emerged a new generation of conscious helpers and deliberate sympathizers of the 1970s, who are certainly far more useful to the Communists in their undercover work today. At any rate, it was the myriad of small groups that mushroomed throughout the world twenty-five years ago that gave the international associations the impressive start they got.

Many of these small national groups were disillusioned by the fact that the influential key posts in the international headquarters were in Communist hands or were taken over by the Russians within a short period of time. The positions left over for the "national" groups were at best honorary positions, whose meager importance was obvious from the outset. While for these and other reasons numerous groups and associations went into liquidation, new ones emerged to take their place, and these frequently developed independent policies. A number of these newly established associations in the free world merged with other like-minded groups to form international federations that were distinctly anti-Communist in alignment. But during this phase of the political development, the only organization that emerged as a real adversary to the worldwide Communist organizations was the International Confederation of Free Trade Unions; it rapidly gained in strength until, by the second half of the 1960s, it was absolutely comparable to its Communist adversary in terms of attracting-power and influence.

The Kremlin gave its world organizations every possible support to guarantee the continued existence of these "superunions." The dispute which broke out after 1960 with Peking led to difficulties and incidents, with the Red Chinese representatives disrupting the world organizations' congresses and conventions by their constant procedural interruptions and bickering; but these disruptions were slapped down so massively by the member organizations from the Third World, and in particular from Africa, that the Red Chinese and their Albanian satellite withdrew from the central committees of the international organizations and discontinued their subsidies to them. In contrast to Yugoslavia, it is worth noting, neither country has withdrawn its membership, however; it may seem a Communist curiosity that the appropriate seats are kept vacant on the central committees for both Communist China and her European satellite, but even this would not be done were it not for the ulterior motive of showing that a rapprochement between the Soviet Union and Red China is still in the cards.

For those of us who were studying the developing tension between Moscow and Peking and writing regular intelligence summaries on it, these Communist Chinese setbacks in the world organizations were of considerable importance. They were highlighted by the failure of the continuing attempts to destroy the big parent organizations from within by means of Chinese-controlled member organizations. Later, I will describe how the Chinese failure to amputate powerful branches with millions of members from the main Moscow party stems was of considerable moment to us in our analysis.* One consequence of our analysis and summation of these developments was that we issued frequent warnings against overestimating the effects of the Sino-Soviet conflict on the situation in Europe.

---

* See pp. 322–23.

* * *

In my table of the eleven world organizations I have listed the most active organizations first. This reveals a feature which may seem surprising: nearly all of the most active organizations—and these are the ones that are the most dangerous for the free world—have their seats in Prague (no fewer than five of the eleven). This geographical concentration, to which far too little attention has been paid in the West, can be regarded as a headquarters not unlike the old Cominform; it makes Czechoslovakia look like a kind of junior partner of the Soviet Union in the administration of these big organizations. It scarcely needs to be stressed that in occupying the country by force in 1968 the Russians were concerned at least in part with keeping this stronghold of international communism in their grasp.

Moreover, it will be observed that one of the most important organizations, the World Peace Council, has its central headquarters in Helsinki. With its virtually inexhaustible potentialities, the council is thus based in a country which may not belong de jure to the Communist empire but is dependent as is no other on the Russians. The fact that two international organizations have managed to maintain their headquarters in countries which are members of NATO gives me a chance to draw attention to Communist measures of concealment and deception which, I suggest, ought to have been doomed to failure long ago. That they still flourish demonstrates not only the lack of education of the public in those countries but also the ignorance of countless politicians in the West as to the true nature of a Communist machine which has been designed and is operated for only one reason—to launch a ruthless attack on the Western mind from behind a cover of harmless activity, and thereby bring about the decline and fall of Western society.

Prima facie, the Communist world organizations can still claim to be impartial parent organizations. They will point out that non-Communists in positions of apparent influence are in the majority. It is also true that numerous groups belong to these world organizations—particularly those from Africa and the rest of the Third World—that really do represent common interests and really do keep their national concerns constantly in mind and represent them with great vigor and determination. Their interest in the Communist parent organizations is solely a function of the assistance they receive, which is, above all, in the form of training facilities for future leaders.

But it is here, in my view, that we must see one of the greatest dangers represented by these world organizations. The future leaders of the underdeveloped countries are being trained predominantly in the Communist countries, after being recruited to a considerable extent by the extensive facilities of the big international organizations. The training is carried out mainly in the Soviet Union and in East Germany; Czechoslovakia, with its magnificent, large training centers at Prague and Zlin, has been permitted to rejoin this training program only little by little since the events of 1968. There are numerous indications that this special training is carried out with exceptional subtlety of method and teaching psychology. Since a number of disappointments over attempts at direct indoctrination were experienced in earlier years, no particular importance is attached to this now. The benefits now are indirect, embedded in the political content of the texts used for language instruction, for example, and the conclusions the guests will draw from their observations of the Socialist system in the flesh. Students from the underdeveloped countries usually have no other basis for comparison than their native lands, so they usually leave their Communist host country some years later with the impression that in "socialism" (that is, communism) they have discovered an extremely effective system for modern planning and control. They have become fully trained fighters for the Communist cause. Back in their native countries, they become the "progressive" forces in government or in other organizations—and can at a later time be rapidly called upon to support unrest and revolution.

The second danger inherent in these world organizations is the permanent influence they have on their members. In their twenty-five years of existence only the Soviet occupation of Czechoslovakia resulted in any protests, and these were principally from the organizations based in Prague. Aside from this special case, all the organizations have supported all the Soviet policies throughout the years, without exception or reservation; and they have demonstrated this support by resolutions, by fund raising, by political gatherings and campaigns. Their influencing of public attitudes seldom makes use of "direct" methods. They prefer to work indirectly and usually almost imperceptibly; and it is this that makes them so effective in the long run.

We always found these world organizations were well worth close scrutiny and surveillance because the content of their agitation and propaganda campaigns frequently pointed to shifts in emphasis of long-term Communist policies. Further clues as to the geographical shift of focus of Soviet foreign policy can frequently be gleaned from the extensive traveling diplomacy of the world organizations, but these clues are for the most part only inadequately heeded by the West.

As it is impossible for me to deal individually with all the world organizations and their work within the scope of this book, I must restrict myself to a very few cases. I have always considered the World Federation of Trade Unions to be the most rigidly controlled and the most dynamic. In overall effectiveness, however, the World Peace Council seems to be even more dangerous, even if the Communist "peace movement" does not publish exact data on its membership (it prefers to operate with fictitious numbers of fellow travelers and sympathizers not far short of the billion mark). Regarding the World Peace Council—and the Christian Peace Conference and the International Peace Institute, which are linked to this parent organization—the most important aspect is that the objectives they proclaim are absolutely irreproachable. It is hardly surprising therefore that these vehicles of world Communist activity can point to the cooperation of countless personalities who are clearly not Communists. These personalities include many of fame and standing, who obviously sincerely believe that coexistence is practicable.

According to information at my disposal, the Christian Peace Conference has become a relic of the past. It was set up by Czech theologians in 1958 with the approval of the Czech State Office for

Religious Affairs. The father of the idea was a Protestant professor
of theology, Hromadka, who died in 1969; the intention was, "in
the interests of generations born and as yet unborn," to set up a
Christian world congress to "condemn all arms manufacture and
all weapons of mass destruction," and to "urge the need for peace."
Leading members of the Christian churches, regardless of nationality or creed, were to be called upon by the Czech Ecumenical
Council to meet during 1958 to elaborate the necessary plans for
the proposed world congress. The Christian Peace Conference set
up national committees in a large number of countries. The high
points were the All-Christian Peace Assemblies.

Professor Hromadka had believed that in the long run communism could reach accord with Christianity. Christianity must
hold itself in readiness for that moment, he once said, when the
"vacuum" in the minds of the Communist masses would demand to
be "replenished with fresh Christian sustenance." The Soviet occupation of Czechoslovakia destroyed this illusion. It destroyed
Hromadka's work as well, for when he fearlessly protested the
rape of his mother country, he was strongly censured by the head
of the Russian Orthodox Church for his pains. Hromadka died a
resigned and disappointed man.

\* \* \*

According to information published in the East German handbook
of international organizations in 1969, the World Peace Council
employed in that year 475 individuals delegated to it by the world
associations and other organizations. The council was founded on
April 21, 1949, and operates in conjunction with national peace
committees in about 100 countries. To characterize the World
Peace Council I can do no better than quote from the East German
handbook. It provides the clearest example of how behind an impressive, inviting, and glossy facade there often beats a crude and
dedicated Soviet heart:

> The work of the World Peace Council is supported by the
> national peace organizations existing in most countries of the
> world and by various international and national bodies which

are interested in preserving peace but do not belong organizationally to the world peace movement. The World Peace Council contributes to the expansion of the peace movement, and does what it can to insure that this movement attracts into its ranks representatives of every class, regardless of their political affiliations or religious creeds.

Thus far, it is a program in which perhaps only the grating repetition of the word "peace" might give cause for suspicion. But the handbook continues:

> From December 16 to 19, 1961, a conference was held by the World Peace Council in Stockholm which was one of the most important and representative of its history. The resolutions passed at the Stockholm conference were an important contribution to mobilizing large circles of the public in every country and uniting them in the fight against the danger of a nuclear world war. The conference stated that world peace is seriously endangered by the lack of a final German peace treaty and by the rebirth of militarism and revisionism in West Germany. It called for the mobilization of large sections of world opinion in the fight for talks on the settlement of a German peace treaty.

This is a different tone altogether. As soon as they touch upon the German problem, the element of subversion becomes painfully clear; here the "peaceful" World Peace Council joins the ranks of the other agencies spreading the worldwide smear campaign against the "militarist and revisionist Adenauer Germany" of the 1950s and 1960s.

> From July 10 to 15, 1965, the World Congress on Peace, National Independence, and General Disarmament took place at Helsinki. The congress assembled in a complex international situation—escalation of the imperialist aggression in Vietnam; occupation of Santo Domingo by American troops; increasingly impudent demands by Bonn's generals for nuclear weapons for West Germany; the struggle of patriotic forces in Angola, Mozambique, the Arabian Peninsula, and so on—and they were thus conscious of a special responsibility in passing their resolutions. In contrast with earlier meetings of these warriors for peace, this Helsinki congress

was remarkable for the exceptional breadth of movements and organizations represented there. The peace groups united in the World Peace Council were joined by participants from many autonomous international groups who sometimes brought their own distinct religious or pacifist ideas with them. Altogether 1,470 representatives of national organizations from ninety-eight countries and every continent, and from eighteen international organizations attended the conference. Although some of the problems touched on raised strong arguments at the congress, all the participants voted unanimously for the final documents (the Vietnam Resolution and the General Declaration), thereby giving living witness to the fact that faced with the serious tension caused by the aggression of imperialist forces, all those who are concerned with the preservation of peace can put the task of mobilizing their fellow citizens for the struggle against the warmongers above all other interests, and close their ranks to this end.

This extract shows how the marshaled "friends of peace" are encouraged to see international problems in the light the Russians want them to.

The theme of the Congress on Peace, National Independence, and General Disarmament is to emphasize the unity and conformity of all the democratic mainstream movements of the present day whose common objective is the unimpeded advance of mankind. In this context, great importance is to be attached to the General Declaration, in which it is demonstrated that it is the imperialists who are responsible for the present international tension, with their attempts to suppress the peoples' national struggles for liberation, with their stepping-up of the arms race, and with their preparations for a new world war. The congress discussed problems of the national liberation movements and their interrelationship with the struggle for peace among all nations.

The example of the World Peace Council shows particularly clearly how the Communists were able to succeed in overcoming their postwar isolation during the 1960s, and how personalities often motivated by the best of intentions unconsciously and unwittingly afforded them "covering fire"—if I may be permitted to emulate the incongruously martial vocabulary used to describe the peace movement's campaign. Sincere pacifists have joined forces with devout Christians and others deeply concerned with improving social conditions throughout the world to work within the World Peace Council or in the national committees affiliated with it; and they do not face up to the fact that they are not thereby serving the cause of peace, but are indirectly lending their support to the revolutionary transformation of the world.

In this connection, it is worth recalling that neutral Austria attached importance to dissociating itself from the World Peace Council and closed down its headquarters there on February 2, 1957, after it had already been ejected from France in 1951, two years after its official founding, for activities incompatible with the interests of France. This attitude on the part of our neighbors speaks well for their political instinct. It shows they possess a determination to defend their interests which is unhappily not always matched here in the West.

*  *  *

As with the World Peace Council, the World Federation of Democratic Youth puts forth slogans in its publicity and campaigns whose innocuous terms are designed to mask its role in the struggle of international communism. A case in point was the Ninth World Youth Festival of Sport, held from July 28 to August 6, 1968, in Sofia, the capital of Bulgaria. The two halves of Germany each entered delegations, of which the one entered by the West German Federal Youth League by all accounts put up a stout fight. (It is because they took part that I have chosen this particular case.)

In the advance publicity there occurred certain terms and phrases—for example, "the political, economic, social, and cultural rights of youth"; "the rights of youth and students to active participation in political life"; the rights to "work and professional training" and to "education and the democratization of education"— which could only be regarded as "progressive" in the pejorative sense of the word. These slogans were bound to arouse the suspicions of the cognoscenti. As many readers may still recall, there occurred violent debates and arguments throughout the festival. The result was that neither the Bulgarian hosts nor the real (if camouflaged) foster organizations, the World Federation of Democratic Youth and the International Union of Students, managed to attain the objectives they had set themselves—namely, getting all the resolutions they had prepared in advance carried. For my former colleagues in the service and for myself as a lay observer (for at that time I had just retired), the event was remarkable in two respects. On the one hand it proved yet again the significance attached by the Communist movement to political penetration of the mind, even in fields that we have been accustomed to regard as free of politics; but on the other hand it also showed that just as during the earlier games held in Vienna in 1959 and in Helsinki in 1962, our own youth has no cause to shrink from public conflict with the Communists, provided we have prepared them in advance even moderately well for the conflict.

* * *

The International Federation of Resistance Fighters is, admittedly, not one of the most important Communist organizations; but as I have already indicated, it proved a particular thorn in our flesh, perpetrating a nonstop series of smear campaigns against the West German government, which lasted until the mid-1960s. These campaigns were aimed both at our country as a whole, which was described as "militarist, revisionist, and neofascist," and at segments of the population such as officers, judges, and other public servants; they were also aimed at specific individuals, who were blackened by every conceivable means. Though this era of defamation campaigns is now a thing of the past, I look back on it as a period in which my service did some of its most successful work in the fight against international communism on this particular front. By procuring secret intelligence, by carefully analyzing the information flooding out of the international Communist front organizations, and by tipping off the people and personalities likely to be affected, we were able to make a contribution to our own country

and to other Western European countries which did not pass un-
noticed. In conjunction with other agencies, we were able to expose
forgeries circulated as part of these uninterrupted campaigns, and
thereby deprive the people masterminding them of their most dangerous weapons.

*  *  *

Having discussed the work of the international Communist organizations, I will outline some of the features of the second major group
of vehicles of international communism, the parties themselves.

In the previous chapter I touched on the role of the legal
Communist parties—and in particular of the ruling, or government, parties—in connection with their function as supporters and
exponents of the official foreign policy of the Communist countries,
but this is only one aspect of the functions and opportunities open
to the legal and illegal Communist parties. Whatever the country
they operate in, and diverse though the effects of their work may
be, one thing unites all the Communist parties—their constant, exact, and unchanging mission. The first phase of this mission is to
subvert and divert, and to recruit the people who will make future
leaders; the second is to bring influence to bear on every sector of
public life; the third is to put pressure on the government until the
Communists are allowed a share of the power; and the final phase
is that in which the Communists take over all power themselves.

Given this progression, it will be seen that Communist parties
in many countries have proved incapable of sufficiently overcoming
the resistance of freedom-loving and conservative citizens to complete even the first phase of their mission. As a case in
point, in the course of our inquiries before the parliamentary
elections in West Germany in 1953—the last in which the
German Communist party took part, as it was banned not long
after—we detected attempts by the authorities in Moscow and East
Berlin to put their weight behind a certain pro-Communist party
wholly separate from the official German Communist party, and
hiding behind bourgeois colors. They pumped a considerable

amount of money into this party, the League of Germans. Their plan was to penetrate the bourgeois camp by using prominent individuals—a former Reich chancellor, Dr. Joseph Wirth; a former lord mayor of Berlin, Wilhelm Elfes; and a retired officer, Colonel Joseph Weber—to provide the window-dressing in the key positions. For this purpose, according to intelligence reports we received from East Berlin, the League of Germans made an election alliance with the All-German People's Party, a neutralist party launched in November 1952 by Gustav Heinemann (the present federal president and a convinced opponent of West German rearmament) and Helene Wessel. The League of Germans was officially branded a Communist front organization by our security agency, the Office for the Protection of the Constitution, but the All-German People's Party ignored all the warnings and submitted a joint list of candidates together with the league. The parliamentary elections were duly held on September 6, 1953. Neither the Communist party nor the new tandem party presided over by Wirth, Helene Wessel, and Gustav Heinemann came even within sniffing distance of the obligatory five percent of the electorate needed to qualify for seats. So the pecuniary mésalliance collapsed, and with it the illusion of a "bourgeois alternative" to the German Communist party.

In other countries of the free world the party's influence has already made considerable progress, however; in other words, the second phase of the Communist progression has already been reached. The real vanguard are the Communists in some countries where they have succeeded in establishing popular front governments, the transitional stage before the final phase in which the Communists take over all power and smooth the way for their country's ingestion into the Communist empire.

In 1970 there were 49,800,000 card-carrying members of about 200 Communist parties and splinter groups of party status; but of these, 46,700,000 belonged to the so-called ruling parties, and only 3,100,000 belonged to Communist parties in the eighty-five countries of the rest of the world. If we distinguish between the Moscow and Peking versions of communism, we can describe 22,600,000 as being "loyal to Moscow" (of which 13,500,000 are party members in Soviet Russia) and 21,400,000 as being "pro-Chinese." Of the latter, it must be added, no fewer than 21,000,000 are residents of Red China itself. From this compilation, it can be seen that 5,800,000 Communist party members are "floaters." In other words, they neither bow to Moscow nor scrape to Peking.

It is possible to draw many conclusions from these kinds of data, and the figures tempt even the experts to try their hand at number juggling. I have no intention of joining in this numbers game, but I can state without hesitation that Peking's attempt to influence Communist parties outside her sprawling empire has unquestionably failed for the time being; and in Western Europe, in particular, we have seen Chinese attempts of recent years to form splinter groups within the existing Communist parties gradually dwindle to insignificance. In my view, only the three huge, overstaffed Red Chinese missions maintained at The Hague, Paris, and Berne are worth any note as outposts of Communist China in Western Europe. They are distinguished from their Soviet competitors by their more subtle methods, I might add.

Of the Soviet-aligned Communist parties in western Europe, the Italian and French parties are particularly conspicuous by virtue of their large membership—1,500,000 and 300,000, respectively. They therefore represent a factor to be considered in the domestic policies of these countries.

The improvement of West Germany's relations with France, which I both welcomed and encouraged in every respect, obliged us to pay somewhat closer attention to the role of the French Communist party. Through the operatives that we infiltrated into that party, we were able to keep track of the influence it wielded over domestic affairs in France (the declared aim of the French Communist party is and always has been the setting up of a popular front) and also to obtain advance notice of the smear tactics used by the French Communists to try to disrupt the Franco-German rapprochement. We were able to watch their collaboration with the German Communists in this campaign as well. From our own standpoint—and no doubt my French colleagues shared this view as well—it took a great load off our minds that the French Communist party was driven by internal dissension as to whether the military intervention of Russian and satellite troops in Czechoslovakia in the summer of 1968 was justifiable or not. The French Communists lost a number of their best-known intellectuals, and the party itself lost much of the ground it had gained in its progress toward a popular front. Only the next few years will tell whether the palpable transition from their previously flexible approach to a new dogmatic, rigid, and unwavering party line will benefit the French Communists or not.

By way of contrast, the Italian Communist party must be regarded as the most dynamic Communist party in Europe at the present time. It is working very purposefully toward its goal of setting up a popular front in Italy, but at the same time, it manages to reconcile local problems and conditions with a rigid loyalty toward the broad party line laid down by Moscow. Numerous reports clearly showed that the occupation of Czechoslovakia shook the Italian Communist party no less violently than the French—indeed, the Russians' brutal invasion pulled the rug out from beneath those powerful elements within the Italian party that had begun to propagate a Dubcek-type communism for their own country; after this grave setback, the Italian Communists criticized their comrades in the Soviet Union so shrilly that there was considerable speculation in other Western European countries. But at the time, I was convinced, even when the noises of protest grew quite insistent, that the Italian Communist party leaders would under no circumstances allow this to cause an open split between them and their headquarters in Moscow.

Every Communist party in Western Europe is confronted—and will continue to be so confronted for the foreseeable future, I confidently predict—by something of a dilemma. For the time being, they can scarcely expect to come to power legally or under their own steam; but they cannot see much promise in effecting their ideals by means of violent revolution, nor will this situation alter much for a long time to come. This is why the Communist parties in virtually every country of Western Europe see themselves obliged to establish cells in the most diverse sectors of public life and to engage in intensified propaganda and subversive activities. In other words, if they are to promote their Communist ideals phase by phase, they are still dealing with the preliminary stages. The most instructive example here is the numerically small Communist party in Great Britain, which numbered only some 32,000 members in 1970. The party is not officially represented in the House of Commons. It concentrates its efforts, not without success, on the infiltration of the leadership of the various trade unions; as the unions are the props of the Labour party and moreover the principal source of that party's finances, the Communist foothold in the unions affords them powerful opportunities of influencing Labour party policy.

In other Western countries it is not only the unions, with their vast memberships, but the management of the economy and of social organizations that provide excellent scope for Communist infiltration. I can see a number of highly dangerous developments of this nature in the next few years; we have not tried to stamp out these cancers at their roots with the necessary determination. As the 1971 steel-industry strike showed, there is absolutely no doubt that West Germany is one of the key areas under attack in Europe. Whatever the reasons certain people may have for playing down the current importance of the Communist party in West Germany, the fact remains that its fighting power is multiplied by such a plethora of auxiliary organs and agencies, such as the Communist-inspired League of Conscientious Objectors, that it is only a matter of time before the party begins its final assault on every section of the public mind. In West German industry, voices have already been raised in alarm, and these must not be ignored; they call for an intensification and coordination of measures for the protection of factories and buildings against Communist-inspired attacks, and a campaign to thwart further attempts at infiltration. My own impression is that the steps that have been taken so far in this direction are wholly insufficient.

\* \* \*

The reader will recall that I have already referred to the two-tiered nature of the diplomatic missions maintained by Communist countries abroad: they are both organs for the dissemination and propagation of official foreign policy and vehicles for local or international Communist campaigns. This dual role of Communist diplomatic missions is worth studying more closely, particularly since it is wholly incompatible with the conventional status of diplomacy. As a base and catalyst for subversive activity, the diplomatic mission of a Communist country is often called upon—indeed, forced—to undergo risks whose magnitude and possible consequences are a function of the circumstances in the host country concerned. There are countries in which even the Russians would not dream of entrusting senior members of their missions with duties beyond the pale of strictly "classical" diplomacy; in these cases, the subversive operations or other covert missions are performed by the lesser staff of the mission, such as chauffeurs or junior clerical staff. In other capitals, the Russians have not hesitated to employ even the senior members of their embassies on this kind of work. Thus, there have been numerous incidents in various countries, including West Germany, in which counselors of embassy (that is, the next senior official to the ambassador himself) have been required to perform acts which have caused their host countries the gravest injury. There are even individual cases known to me in which the heads of mission themselves managed to couple their functions as senior diplomatic representatives with those of undercover agents. In this connection, I am thinking in particular of the Soviet ambassador Solod, who overstepped the mark so far in Guinea at the beginning of the 1960s that even the "progressive" head of state Sékou Touré was obliged to declare him persona non grata on account of his infiltration work and subversive activities. Taking advantage of his position as a diplomat, Solod had tried to subvert the Guinea National Youth and to establish Communist cells throughout the country. More recent events show that Sékou Touré unfortunately learned nothing from his experience. After a lengthy period of pronounced neutrality, which had a beneficial effect on Guinea's relations with West Germany as well, Sékou

Touré finally succumbed to massive Communist pressure; and this head of state, who appears to be as ambitious as he is flexible, has now prescribed an extreme form of socialism for his country which is not all that remote from Solod's brand of communism.

In addition to the diplomatic missions, whose advantages as camouflage and supply bases have never been lost on the Russians, the other official and unofficial Communist missions and agencies abroad can also be exploited to cover illegal activities. The "doctor" working in a Soviet-financed hospital gratefully accepted by some African country, or the Czech "teacher" operating from some school in an Arab capital, can function as effectively as the agent based in a diplomatic mission. These tactics can be easily adapted to the circumstances that obtain in the particular theater of operations, and especially to the security situation there. A primary requirement for this is that there be a continual supply of suitable Communist agents of both sexes, people who have been given a thorough training and have been specially prepared in their native Communist lands for operations based in missions and agencies in the target countries. Even though these highly trained specialists ultimately surface at their destination groomed as "diplomats," their training has little in common with the training for an orthodox diplomatic career. It is true that knowledge of the country concerned, its mentality, and its languages is common to both careers; but the most important part of the preparatory work of these people consists of mastering certain illegal arts and approaches. In many cases, the specialists sent out to conduct subversive activities and infiltration operations in a country work closely with the "residents" or other members of the Communist secret services based there.

* * *

This book has no chapter on the Soviet secret service as such. It is true that its operations and tactics are a basic element of many of the affairs I have described, but they can play only a minor part in a study which has as its main subject the West German intelligence service and its work. The things my colleagues and I witnessed and experienced in our fight against the KGB would fill a book; and perhaps one day it can all be told. It would inevitably be very different from anything that has ever been written in Germany or elsewhere about the Soviet secret service and the intelligence services of other Communist countries. As far as I can see, the bulk of serious histories so far published deal with the more distant past, while for security reasons there have not been any notable and perceptive accounts of more recent years.

At least forty percent of the staff of the embassies, trade missions, and other agencies of the Communist countries belong to the KGB or the other secret services of the Communist countries concerned. Scarcely a week passes in which members of these staffs are not requested to leave Western countries as personae non gratae; sometimes a public fuss is made, sometimes it is not. In most cases which occurred over the last few years in West Germany, the most that the public learned was that another Soviet "diplomat" had been obliged to pack his bags and leave without ceremony, having been caught spying; there is unlikely to be any change in this in the future, since it is obvious that higher interests are at stake here.

For example, I recall that during my own period of office more than 100 espionage incidents were revealed from January 1957 to autumn 1963, involving Soviet diplomatic missions in thirty-six countries. Some of these diplomats were kept under observation, and no further direct action was taken; in the other cases about 160 Soviet intelligence agents were unmasked, declared personae non gratae, and ordered out of the country. Some of them preferred not to await being told to leave, and got out while the going was good.

During my time, for example, the deputy head of the Czech trade mission at Frankfurt-am-Main was, as we in the service were well aware, a member of the Czech secret service. Again, when the traveling exhibition "Fifty Years of the Soviet Union" was held in West Germany in 1967 and 1968, its deputy director, Mme Bassova, was also a member of the KGB. Among the members of every delegation put together in the Soviet Union for trips to the West there are always two or three members of the Soviet intelligence or security services, partly to keep an eye on their colleagues and partly to pursue their own inquiries. These may be interesting sidelights for the reader, but they are commonplace, so to speak, in the intelligence and security agencies of those countries.

* * *

Communist influencers and other specialists are very seldom required to leave a country; in most cases they are not even recognized for what they are. Chameleonlike, they adapt their tactics and approaches to the opportunities afforded them. The experts infiltrated into a country to disseminate *desinformatsiya* are the ones particularly worth watching. They do not operate through official information media like newspapers, radio, and television—these are scrutinized and manipulated by the press, radio, and television commissions and by the Soviet Committee for Cultural Relations Abroad. While the coordination of the information program is in the hands of a subdivision of the Secretariat of the Communist Party's Central Committee—the agitation and propaganda division—the KGB has established for its active *desinformatsiya* operations a vast and magnificently equipped department so that it can master its many different jobs and keep control of the influencers. By "influencer" the KGB understands people who, by virtue of their position, can multiply the impact of the information fed to them and give it the widest possible distribution.

A specific and curious example of disinformation was a book published by a French author* on the *Rote Kapelle* ("Red Orchestra") Communist espionage network; here the object was to suggest that what the Germans referred to as Rote Kapelle was merely a resistance group of patriots based primarily in Nazi-occupied Europe. In reality, it was merely one of the many arms of an octopus existing long before the war in Germany, Britain, Scandinavia (where Ernst Wollweber was the resident, succeeded by Herbert Wehner), and many other European countries. Only the anti-Nazi arm was destroyed, the other arms survived to continue the fight against the Allies after the war. The British SIS defector Philby was probably recruited by the British arm. His postdefection "memoirs," supplied by Moscow with the object of discrediting the British SIS and pur-

---

* Gilles Perrault, *L'Orchestre Rouge*, 2nd ed. (Paris: Fayard, 1968).

chased by the gullible British newspapers, were an unusually inept piece of disinformation. Nor are British newspapers the only targets. About a decade ago, we recruited an SSD agent in East Germany to work for us as a double agent; of course, he had to carry out his East German missions in our country as before, and one of these, he duly reported to us, was to supply certain documents to *Der Spiegel* from East Berlin.

Often the influencers do not realize that they are merely playing a game to rules drawn up by the KGB. One of the most notorious of them all was without doubt Alger Hiss. Mr. Cyrus B. Eaton, the respected, gullible, and philanthropic founder of the Pugwash conferences, and his friends are probably regarded by the Russians as influencers, too, without their knowing it. In many cases, the work of the influencers is not even punishable; it is this feature, and their completely unsuspecting character, that makes it impossible even to estimate how many influencers there are, let alone pinpoint and neutralize them. In West Germany, it has not proved possible to identify more than a few isolated cases, and these influencers have been prevented from doing further harm. But the conditions in West Germany are so favorable for the Communist intelligence services— as indeed they are in a number of other West European countries— that it is clear that there must be many hundreds of these Communist influencers at work in our country, in addition to the thousands of regular Communist espionage agents.

How welcome it must be for their Communist controllers to find that their own training and subtlety are actually aided by our guilelessness (which verges on downright rashness) and political ineptitude. Many of the politicians concerned with our current *Ostpolitik* (to whom must be added a host of industrialists and economic experts and journalists) seem to have an insatiable thirst for contacts with Communist diplomats. Their conversation partners, as Communist officials, benefit from years of training on security matters, so it is hardly surprising that the West Germans, who are largely unversed in security considerations, readily fall for what appear to be provocative or flattering remarks. Germans are very naive in this respect; while the British and Americans, as well as the French and Italians, are fully awake to the fact that a cleverly programmed "verbal reconnaissance" aimed at a sufficiently broad base of people can yield exceptionally valuable and instructive intelligence information. Our adversaries show a real genius in their application of this tactic to friend and foe alike. I need scarcely add the obvious rider that if these founts that otherwise have a natural tendency to gush and splutter are to be effectively dammed, both enlightenment and discipline are necessary, and this goes for the unwitting underlings who time and time again turn out to help the enemy as well.

I will conclude this chapter with an extract from the "Rules for Political and Psychological Subversion" laid down by the Chinese Sun-tse about five hundred years before Christ:

> There is no art higher than that of destroying the enemy's re-sistance without a fight on the battlefield. The direct tactic of war is necessary only on the battlefield; but only the indirect tactic can lead to a real and lasting victory.
>
> Subvert anything of value in the enemy's country. Im-plicate the emissaries of the major powers in criminal under-takings; undermine their position and destroy their reputation in other ways as well, and expose them to the public ridicule of their fellow citizens.
>
> Do not shun the aid of even the lowest and most despic-able people. Disrupt the work of their government with every means you can.
>
> Spread disunity and dispute among the citizens of the enemy's country. Turn the young against the old. Use every means to destroy their arms, their supplies, and the discipline of the enemy's forces. Debase old traditions and accepted gods. Be generous with promises and rewards to purchase in-telligence and accomplices. Send out your secret agents in all directions. Do not skimp with money or with promises, for they yield a high return.*

If we divest these sentences of the peculiarities of their age, the rules laid down by the Chinese philosopher can be seen as a set of principles which in my view still hold good, virtually without change or reservation, for every one of the aspects I have mentioned of world Communist activity and subversion.

---

* Quoted in *Encyclopédie Française,* 1959.

CHAPTER FIFTEEN

# Twenty-five Years of Soviet Power Politics

In this final chapter I propose to show the most important consequences of Soviet power politics since the end of World War II, thus concluding my general analysis of Soviet policy, Chapter 13 having dealt with basic premises, and Chapter 14 with the more important instruments of that policy. In doing so I will consider primarily Soviet policies toward Germany and deal in some detail with the present state of Soviet-German relations in light of the West German government's new *Ostpolitik*. I propose to lay bare the unaltered nucleus of Soviet power politics, a driving force which is too often camouflaged. I want to show the iceberg in all its immensity, and not just the minute tip that shows above the surface. Finally, I will end with a prognosis of the future consequences of Soviet policy both for the near future and for the long run.

Communist policies can at present be seen in their most perfect form in the Soviet version; they are absolute policies which embrace and envelop all human activity, employ every conceivable

[ 333

means to an end, and exploit every type of person. As I have tried to show, they are policies which even today must be studied in the narrow context of the Communist ideology. There is much truth in the dictum that what is of benefit to the Soviet Union cannot be of harm to the Communist movement and, conversely, that the triumph of communism in any corner of the globe must also benefit the interests of the Soviet Union as an imperialist world power.

The goal is the revolutionary transformation of the world into a utopian Communist "ultimate society." It is unlikely to be realized in the foreseeable future; but this "ultimate society" is, and will continue to be, the strategic goal nonetheless. As far as the short- and medium-term policies of the Soviet Union and her allies are concerned—whether these latter are the Communist countries or the nonruling Communist parties—this adherence to the strategic goal of a Communist society is by no means an outdated and inconvenient ballast which (as many people in the West seem to think) the Communists are going to unload at the first opportunity in order to enhance their freedom of action. This opinion is all we can expect from the almost naive judgment displayed by many Western observers, including some respected Kremlinologists. Despite all historical experience to the contrary, they apparently feel compelled to view the development and formulation of Soviet policies purely in terms of Western values.

Errors of judgment on this decisive point could only lead to the most fateful and incalculable consequences for an intelligence service. That is why my colleagues and I regarded it as a matter of common sense to take regular soundings on the status of ideology in Communist foreign policy.

One urgent instance of such misjudgment occurred when the former Eastern affairs adviser of President Johnson, the normally wise and highly qualified Zbigniew Brzezinski, proclaimed to anybody who would listen that the era of "de-ideologization" had finally dawned. This pronouncement of a widely acknowledged expert (who has since revised his opinion) could have had untold effects on American foreign policy and hence on our own, quite apart from whether his judgment was sound or not. He turned out to be wrong, a clear fact which our own conscientious inquiries confirmed time and again.

I have always regarded Soviet policies as a uniform whole, and they must be judged as a whole if dangerous and damaging errors are not to arise. I have never been able to understand why —for reasons which often seem to be deliberately played down— individual segments of Soviet foreign policy have been treated with a respect wholly out of keeping with both the objectives and the general trend of Soviet policies. However much others may dispute this, agreements and treaties signed by the Soviet Union, whatever the area they cover, should never be regarded as being divorced from the principal trend of the Communists' main strategic policies. They must not be misjudged by the West. That is why it is absurd in our own particular case to evaluate the Moscow agreement between the Soviet Union and West Germany in isolation. This treaty cannot be regarded in any other light than as a contractually settled political chess move which has to be viewed in the context of the enemy's overall objectives. In stating this, I have no intention of detracting from the significance of the German-Soviet treaty; quite the contrary, I wish its *true* significance to be seen. The fact that it has been designed to dovetail neatly into an overall plan must be recognized as a threat to our liberty.

I accept the fact that the Communists do not form a monolithic bloc in any way. There are signs of tensions and there are divergent theories within the Communist system. There are errors of judgment, mishaps, and setbacks, so that the Communist world movement sometimes appears as disunited and crisis-prone as the Atlantic alliance. Communist politicians are also human beings; they are fallible and they show it. Moreover, the Communist bloc houses a quantity of dry tinder, and if this were ever to be ignited, it could bring disaster for Moscow and her satellites. Later in this chapter I will indicate where such prospects might be sought. One thing is certain, it is as wrong to ignore them altogether as it would be to overestimate their explosive force.

\* \* \*

As a result of World War II, the Soviets realized nearly all of the czars' dreams of expansion. They reincorporated the Baltic states, and Finland came de facto within their sway. In the Far East, the Soviet Union occupied part of the Kuril Islands, thereby avenging the losses suffered in the Russo-Japanese War of 1905. To the triumph of Soviet arms was added—contrary to the terms agreed on at Teheran and Yalta—the transformation of the eastern and southeastern European countries into "socialist societies." Via Yugoslavia and Albania, which had also been made into "people's democracies," the Russians secured routes of access to the Adriatic and thus to the Mediterranean. Germany, which, *pace* Lenin, was the key to world revolution, was now half within the Communist grasp; and the prospects seem auspicious for the triumph of communism in West Germany as well.

The Communist parties in Italy and France survived their years of repression remarkably well; within a short period of time they were again operational and had won a hand in the government of their countries. The turmoil of the war also exacerbated the social tensions in Latin America. In the rest of the world, the British and French colonial systems were creaking at the joints. As a result of the aid afforded them by the United States—more for a mixture of philanthropic and moral reasons than out of political farsightedness—it would only be a matter of time before the inevitable chaos stirred up by the independence movements paved the way for communism. Finally, it was also clear that the days of Chiang Kai-shek's Nationalist China were numbered, and that Mao Tse-tung was certain to succeed him. The triumph of communism on a worldwide scale seemed just around the corner.

Scarcely any of my readers will disagree that this colossal increase in the power of the Soviet Union ought to have alarmed every person concerned with the future of the non-Communist free world. But the truth was that the warning voices went unheeded by almost every government. This is certainly not explicable merely in terms of the postwar difficulties and moral burdens shared by the former allies who had joined the Soviet Union in the war against Germany. The neglect is, rather, a glaring example of how a potential adversary and his plans and objectives failed to be identified in time. While the Soviet Union restocked Hitler's depleted munitions dumps in eastern Europe, the Western Allies destroyed the arms factories and industrial installations in their zones of Germany. The United States demobilized her armies posthaste, thereby inflicting on herself a military weakness which was to cost her dearly in Korea a few years later.

As was only to be expected, given their offensive policies, the Soviets at once set about enlarging the powerful position they had attained by the ruthless use of the Communist parties, fifth column organizations, and other minions. But favorable though the beginning was, the Soviet Union proved incapable in the early postwar years of accomplishing the strategic objectives she had set in many countries. Just as Lenin had deceived himself between 1918 and 1920, now Stalin, too, found that the "decadent, imperialist capitalism" still had astounding fighting power. When China fell to the Communists in 1949 there arose out of this predictable development not only a crippling economic burden for Stalin but also a major rival for the leadership and domination of the Communist world.

In Czechoslovakia, too, the Communists managed to seize power in 1948; but for the time being, the other attempts to expand the Communist power base were frustrated. The Russians failed in their attempts to put pressure on Turkey to open the straits to their naval vessels; moreover, the Russians had to relinquish the northern provinces of Iran they had occupied. The Communist revolution in Greece collapsed. In Malaysia it became apparent that the local Communist strength was insufficient to open the territory up as a base for the Soviet Union in Southeast Asia. Nor did the Communists succeed in taking over power in those countries which regained their independence or were now tasting it for the first time. The way things went in the industrial countries of western Europe was a particularly bitter disappointment for Stalin. Everywhere, the Communist parties were squeezed out of the governments, and in several cases they lost all their parliamentary seats as well. In West Germany, the Western Allies prevented the Russians from exerting any kind of influence on the restoration of political and economic life. The historic service rendered by Dr. Kurt Schumacher, the first postwar German Socialist leader, in preventing the formation of a West German "Socialist unity" party deserves special recognition; and the attitude of the Western powers at the time of the Russian blockade of Berlin proved, moreover, that they were resolved to prevent the Communist movement from scoring any further successes in Europe.

Later, when I discuss current developments, I will turn again to the Berlin problem—the cold war *cause célèbre* that Dean Acheson, the U.S. secretary of state from 1948 to 1952, termed the "most vital problem of the present day." But here I will try to recall that first climax of the permanent Berlin crisis as it really was. When Stalin ordered the blockade of West Berlin, he did not do so just because of Lenin's dictum that he who holds Berlin is lord of Europe and, thus, of the world. He wanted to force the West to give up West Berlin as a forward position behind the Iron Curtain and to permit its incorporation into East Germany as a preliminary to the eventual inclusion of the whole of Germany into the Soviet empire. Without doubt, the occupation of *all* Germany has always been one of the cardinal objects of Soviet policy in Europe. It was only when his blockade failed to weaken West Berlin, and when, years later, the intensive Communist attempts to take over West Germany from within proved equally fruitless, that Stalin resigned himself to an interim period in which the partition of Germany would be maintained. His new concern was then to confront the West German Federal Republic that had meanwhile emerged with a powerful and stable East German state in order to make a fusion of the two halves of Germany impossible without Soviet acquiescence. I remember that we received reports of several remarks by Khrushchev in which he stated quite bluntly that even if West Germany were to become wholly Communist, Moscow would still keep the two German states apart in the interest of Soviet security. This principle has been echoed by Khrushchev's successors.

I am not sure what impressed Stalin more at the time of the

Berlin airlift: the determination the Western powers displayed in direct confrontation with the Soviet Union in establishing the airlift to supply a besieged West Berlin or the steadfastness and magnificent morale of the city's population under the most daunting physical and moral pressure.

The collapse of the Berlin blockade and the failure of the Communist advance into South Korea signaled the end of an epoch in which the political strategy and tactics of the entire Communist movement were devoted to the aggressive expansion of its empire. Stalin drew radical conclusions from all this, and these were observed by his successors, from Khrushchev down to Brezhnev. He immediately adjourned the strategic offensive and began to consolidate and strengthen his own empire. Since the beginning of the 1950s, we have seen the development of general Communist policies which are characterized by the attempts of the nonruling Communist parties finally to overcome their isolation and to achieve a degree of cooperation with the "progressive" forces. Their aim is a new popular front whereby the United States will be inched out of Europe and isolated on a worldwide scale, while all risks are carefully avoided. As far as her own empire is concerned, the Soviet Union's primary aim is to improve the political and ideological climate by completing the assimilation of her satellites and the attendant world organizations, and to promote with all possible speed the political solidarity of the masses by means of an accelerated program of social, political, and ideological education.

Naturally, the course of this does not always run true or smooth. There have been and will continue to be disruptions and setbacks in the Eastern bloc such as June 17, 1953, in East Germany, the uprisings in Hungary and Poland in 1956, and the Czechoslovakian crisis of 1968.

The efforts of the nonruling Communist parties to prove they were capable of government were vitiated for the duration of the cold war (that is, until 1955). The historical incidents I have mentioned, like the Communist seizure of power in Czechoslovakia at the end of the 1940s and similar coups in the early 1950s, can hardly have acted as an inducement to other parties to allow the Communists a share of the government elsewhere. Nothing better illustrates the strategically offensive nature of the policy of peaceful coexistence than the fact that it is only since its introduction in 1955 that nonruling Communist parties could hope for any success in their dialogues with the "progressive forces," as they regard the leftist parties. This new brand of popular front was achieved in a somewhat diluted form in Finland some years ago, and it has recently been accomplished with a much more Marxist flavor in Chile as well. The new popular front is distinguished from that of the 1930s by the fact that it permits the collaboration of non-Marxist elements such as Christian organizations and groups. In permitting this, the Communists are satisfied that as time passes they will take over all the power themselves by virtue of their superior organization. The example of Cuba, where Castro regarded himself at first merely as a social reformer, until he ultimately slithered further and further toward total dependence on the Communists, appears to lend substance to these Soviet hopes. That is why we must pay the closest possible attention to the worrying developments in Chile and in other countries where the Communists already have, or soon will have, a hand on the reins of government.

It is clear that the position of the nonruling Communist parties is in large measure dependent on whether and how far the Communists can make their policies of coexistence, peace, and détente seem credible. As a particular example of this kind of détente policy the Russians repeatedly refer to the Cuba crisis of 1961. Here, I only intend to point out the new shades of meaning that—in light of the events in Cuba—must be attached to the policy of peaceful coexistence. The Cuba conflict has been regarded by many in the West as proof that crises in which both superpowers are in direct confrontation need not necessarily lead to war. This belief was confirmed by Khrushchev's dismantling the Soviet missile bases in Cuba, thereby demonstrating that he preferred a political defeat to a war which might have ended with total annihilation. It has long seemed obvious to me that this inference—which is somewhat typical of Western thought—needs urgent correction. What we are being asked to regard as a Soviet defeat has in fact left the Russians with an unrivaled opportunity for exploiting Cuba as an all-purpose base for international Communist activity. At any rate, the West was wrong to conclude from the Cuba crisis that it could be possible to achieve a détente which was something more than mere coexistence.

Attempts at détente (which have at times bordered on the frantic) have characterized the Western political posture since then. The Russians respond to these attempts in their own way. In the various world councils they debate the possibilities for détente from every angle, and although their plans are mostly predestined to fail since they refuse to allow inspection of their own military potential, they are nonetheless psychologically extremely effective, for they focus public attention on the apparent "peaceability" of the Socialist camp. Of these plans—apart from the demand for total disarmament and the two nuclear test-ban treaties —the Russians have, in particular, been capitalizing for many years on the Rapacki Plan as a propaganda ploy. Adam Rapacki, a foreign minister in postwar Poland, called for a neutral zone, free of atomic weapons, extending across northern and eastern central Europe, as a buffer between the Soviet Union and the West. To the naive, it was probably a very attractive proposition; it was a plan which was very difficult to oppose without knowledge of the background and of the objectives the Russians were pursuing with the plan.

The modern variation of this general line was the doctrine decided on at the Rumanian Communist party's congress on July 4, 1966, and announced by Brezhnev. This plan proposes a European security system consisting of only the European powers and calls for the dissolution of the two military alliances, NATO and the Warsaw Pact. If accepted, the outcome would be a withdrawal of all United States forces from Europe, while Soviet forces could still mass at will along the Russo-Polish frontier—hardly an attractive proposition for Western Europe. This doctrine has been repeated in all the important declarations of the Communist countries and parties since then, most recently at the summit meeting of party leaders and heads of government of the Warsaw Pact countries in East Berlin on December 2, 1970. I think it worth noticing that the East Berlin declaration refers expressly to the Budapest resolution of March 1966 and withdraws the concessions hinted at on that occasion (that there would be no Communist objection to the United States and Canada participating in the security conference and no demand for previous recognition of the German Democratic Republic).

* * *

It is natural that the aggressive nature of the Russian policies of "peaceful coexistence and détente" must primarily affect their relations with the most powerful nation in the free world, the United States. This was demonstrated most explicitly by their injured disruption of the Paris summit conference of May 16 and 17, 1960, after the U-2 incident.*

The ambition of Soviet policy is the isolation of the United States and, in the long run, its withdrawal from Europe; this has always implied for the Russians that the United States must remain permanently embroiled in crisis situations outside Europe, but also that, for the time being, any direct confrontation with the major Western powers must be avoided. There will definitely be no change in this policy so long as the potential of the United States remains superior or equivalent to that of the Soviet Union. This simple fact alone, which was confirmed by countless intelligence reports prior to my retirement from the service, shows that the Soviet Union cannot have the least interest in releasing the United States from her involvement in Vietnam by putting pressure on the North Vietnamese to end the war.

Of course, the Russians could bring pressure to bear on North Vietnam any time they wish, but they will do so only if the United States decides to abandon South Vietnam to its fate. Such a surrender, while not imminent given the prevailing political climate, cannot be excluded altogether from our long-term calculations.

---

* See pp. 235–36.

Such a step might bring a turn of the tide for the whole of Asia. Not only would Washington have lost face forever in Asia, but the Soviet Union would at one bound come within sight of its objective of isolating and eliminating the United States. The credibility of the United States would, moreover, be jeopardized throughout the whole of Latin America, Africa, and last but not least in Western Europe as well.

If he plays his political cards right, President Nixon's wise attempt to normalize his country's diplomatic relations with Red China may open up the path to a solution of the Vietnam problem. While it would undoubtedly not be a completely satisfactory one, it would at least be tolerable, while avoiding the unpleasant repercussions I have described. But actually, the North Vietnamese will to resist and the material capabilities on which this fighting spirit depends are nine-tenths nourished by the Soviet Union and her satellites, and only marginally by Red China.

One of the principal American errors leading to the present situation in Vietnam was to support the liquidation of President Diem of South Vietnam. Quite apart from the moral objections to political assassinations which I have already voiced, his removal plunged South Vietnam into a domestic conflict and gravely weakened it at a time when the country was fighting for its very existence. The political climate was so cleverly manipulated by the Soviet and Chinese secret services that the Americans obviously lacked an accurate or complete picture of the internal situation. Admittedly, Diem was—at that time, at least—no great champion of democracy; but to try to introduce democracy to a people of that backwardness in the middle of a war would have been a completely unjustifiable hazard. This was a view, I might add, that I already held at the time when the first intelligence reports of an approaching crisis in South Vietnam began to come in.

It would be foolish to cherish the illusion that the Kremlin will not try to serve up fresh "Vietnams" for the United States wherever it can. That is, it will force the United States to become involved in further conflicts which require no very great exertion on the part of the Russians to exploit them to the fullest disadvantage of Washington—the kind of conflict which can be extensively exploited for its propaganda value in the eyes of the rest of the world.

* * *

As with Vietnam, the Soviet Union is not directly involved in the other most dangerous crisis existing at the beginning of the 1970s —the crisis in the Middle East. But unlike the remote fringe conflict in Vietnam, the Middle East dispute is seated in one of the most important world zones as far as we Germans are concerned, and it is endowed with a significance far transcending the simple dispute between the state of Israel and the Arab countries. This is a region of vast importance for Europe. Both bridge and pivot, it confronts the southern flank of NATO and borders on the Mediterranean, the domination of which has always been one of the great Soviet ambitions. Here are Europe's vital oil reserves, without which we cannot survive for any length of time. I have already referred more than once to the fatal dangers inherent in any underestimation of the developments in the Middle East.

For the Soviet Union, the Arab region is not merely a conglomeration of countries that have passed the phase of national revolution and are already well on the way to becoming Socialist societies. The Russians see the Arabian subcontinent geographically as a springboard for the assault on Africa. Moreover, unlike the major Western powers, the Russians require the Suez Canal for their sea routes to Southeast Asia.

The growing interest of the Russians in the Arab world has been apparent to us since the mid-1950s; that was why, as I have indicated, we decided to establish a network of contacts there for the service in order to provide a continuous flow of intelligence reports. As they still do today, the Russians centered most of their interest and their operations on the United Arab Republic (UAR). Egypt soon topped the list of all the countries receiving material aid from the Soviet Union, followed by Syria and then Iraq. From the Soviet standpoint the other countries merited particular attention only if their social transformation was sufficiently far advanced or they displayed a willingness to provide bases for the Soviet navy or air force. Their purpose is to contribute to the network of air bases and anchorages built up by the Russians over the eastern end of the Mediterranean, where the Soviet naval squadron is already a dangerous adversary for the long unchallenged and formidable American Sixth Fleet.

The Middle East fulfills a double role in Soviet grand strategy. It is a geopolitical base of the first order, tying down the United States by means of the Arab-Israeli conflict, just as in Vietnam, and challenging the NATO alliance on its strategically particularly vulnerable southern flank. Unlike Vietnam, however, there is always the possibility that should the conflict again flare up, the Soviet Union may be forced to intervene actively to prevent an even more forceful defeat of the Arabs than they suffered in 1967. The explosive situation is particularly exacerbated by the presence of thousands of Soviet technical advisers in Egypt, and by the stationing there of Soviet aircraft, which are flown by Soviet pilots and are maintained on a constant stand-by basis to compensate for the chronic weakness of the Egyptian air force. The Soviet military presence obliges Moscow to keep the situation permanently under close watch to prevent the glowing embers from blazing up into a full-scale conflagration. This degree of control is particularly important in view of the fact that the senior Soviet advisers, headed by the Middle East specialist, Ambassador Vinogradov, have so far apparently failed to couple the considerable arms deliveries with the necessary safeguards to protect the Russian position under every eventuality.

Nor do the long-term treaties the Russians have signed alter this uncomfortable situation. From my own detailed knowledge of the Arab mentality, I believe the Russians will find it extremely difficult to convert their enormous military and economic aid into political currency; they will not get a share in the government. Despite every public assurance to the contrary, I am inclined to regard President Sadat's vigorous steps against his opponents, among whom were the most outspoken supporters of Moscow, as being proof that he has taken up the sword dashed from Nasser's hand and is continuing the unremitting, secret fight against every kind of Communist activity in his country.

Given these multiple Moscow aims—of tying down the United States and NATO while maintaining and increasing the dependence of the Arab countries on the Soviet Union—it is clear that there is little hope that the Palestine conflict will see an early or final solution in the foreseeable future. Even if the coming years see a peace settlement, which under present conditions can be reached only at Israel's expense, the Middle East will remain the world's most crucial crisis area for a long time to come. The United States and Western Europe would do well to grow accustomed to this fact.

* * *

The danger of a direct confrontation between the United States and the Soviet Union is obviously greatest in Europe; by Europe, I mean Germany, and that in turn means Berlin. This is why Moscow is doing all it possibly can to prize Europe out of the arms of the United States. Coexistence and détente, which the Russians are now offering in the form of the European security system, are the means by which this risk of confrontation will be dismantled piecemeal by the Europeans themselves, and the withdrawal of the United States force from Europe will ultimately remove the danger altogether—or so the Russian doctrine would have us believe.

As I know from my discussions with French colleagues at the time, the late French President de Gaulle saw all this coming in 1961 and 1962. At that time, de Gaulle assumed that, voluntarily or involuntarily, the Americans would sooner or later have to withdraw from Europe, and he foresaw with mounting foreboding the day when a disunited Europe would have to withstand Soviet imperialism on its own. This was the situation that would arise, or so de Gaulle believed, in the latter part of the 1970s; the important thing was to prepare for it while there was still time. De Gaulle saw the new Paris-Bonn axis in that event as the bulwark of an independent—and in his language that meant "self-defensible"—Europe. While de Gaulle certainly assessed the menace of Soviet power to Europe correctly, he was inclined until 1968 to underestimate the contagious effects of the Marxist ideology and the Russian campaign of subversion. But this shortcoming in no way diminishes my respect for the general's great farsightedness.

In this connection I am reminded of a conversation I had with General Ollié, a close confidant of de Gaulle and a former commander in chief of the French forces; he visited me early in October 1962 at the general's request and adumbrated to me the latter's innermost thoughts for unofficial forwarding to the federal chancellor, Dr. Adenauer. The chancellor told me he believed that the general's ideas were right in every aspect, but for various reasons he was unable to adopt them in their entirety as exclusively as the French president had perhaps expected. Whatever other considerations there were, the special character of Germany's position and our heavy reliance on the United States for defense resulting from it had to be considered above anything else.

* * *

I have referred in various contexts to the unchanging and consistently pursued aims of Soviet foreign policy and to their policies toward Germany, in particular. As I do not consider we are anywhere near reaching a turning point in German-Soviet relations, let alone actually arriving at one, I consider it my duty to identify briefly the principal milestones in Soviet policy toward Germany, which have exerted such a powerful influence on domestic German politics since the end of the war and which will probably continue to do so to an ever greater degree.

From Stalin's original postwar dream of incorporating all of Germany into the empire he had built up in eastern Europe, right up to the present Soviet-German treaty of August 12, 1970, Soviet policy has traveled a long and tedious road. It may at times have changed its methods and its tactics so frequently as to seem to have lost all sense of purpose and direction, but the objectives have always remained the same. This is why I flatly refuse to regard as "solutions" the threats and blandishments, the

acts of violence and the moderately termed proposals. And I refuse, too, to see them as "missed opportunities" which (as some
politicians still opine to this day), properly grasped, could have
preserved our country from this permanent confrontation with the
forces of an active and frequently aggressive communism. I emphatically reject the notion that we missed the opportunity of
creating a unified Germany as a neutral state on the Austrian
model; that belongs in the realms of Utopia. Nor could there ever
be any doubt in my mind, in view of the intelligence we received,*
that the Soviet Union would ever contemplate a reunified Germany
unless it became a Communist Germany, withdrawn from the
Western fold, enveloped in the Communist empire, and its liberty
lost forever; if even then.

Soviet policies toward Germany since 1945 have been defined
in countless conferences and consultations, and scarred by many
crises. Any survey of these policies must take as its starting point
the fact that the Soviet Union has always justified its campaigns
and actions by reference to the Potsdam Agreement of August
1945. Even though "political reality," an argument of which the
Russians have on other occasions made frequent use, has long
guaranteed West Germany its rightful place at the side of the
free nations of the Western world, our intelligence repeatedly
showed that the dismemberment and disarming of Germany resolved at the Potsdam Conference continue to overshadow Soviet
policies toward us; accordingly, the Russians have never tired of
interfering in all German affairs, using the flimsiest of arguments
and the most unlikely of pretexts.

In the early postwar years, Stalin hoped—in the first phase
of his German policy—to secure a direct voice in deciding the
affairs of western Germany, without at the same time conceding
to the West the slightest opportunity of influencing affairs in the
Soviet-occupied zone of Germany. On the one hand, the Soviet
Union tried to entrench its influence over the three Western zones
by means of the Control Council, the Reparations Commissions,
and the other Four Power bodies; on the other, they hoped that

* See p. 338.

the destruction of every last shred of resistance and the widespread pauperization of the German people would catapult the newly launched German Communist party and its affiliated organizations into positions of authority. On this reckoning, the transformation of West Germany into a Socialist society would be but a matter of time.

It was at this stage that the Russians committed an act of brute force, the grave consequences of which I have already discussed—the blockade of Berlin. Stalin perpetrated this not only as an attempt to grab West Berlin but as an attempt to intimidate the West German public into supporting the German Communist party and its subsidiaries; this latter ambition went very wide of the mark indeed. Succored by the airlift of the Western powers, the Berliners displayed a stoicism in adversity which was by its example to influence many other events. In the first provincial and local elections that were held afterward the German Communist party proved to be a totally insignificant factor in domestic politics, despite all the circumstances which had favored them at the beginning. The West German public remained as impermeable to the cajolery and threats of the Russians as the West Berliners, particularly since the visual evidence offered of life in the Soviet-occupied zone could hardly have anything but a deterrent effect on them.

No less notable was the reaction of the peoples of the free world: they marveled at Berlin, and it became a symbol of freedom to them from that moment on. The Western allies acknowledged more dramatically than ever before their responsibility for the future preservation of that freedom. The Russians drew what conclusions they could, and realistically reappraised their position. Their original plan to assimilate the western zones of Germany into the Soviet sphere of influence had clearly failed; so they altered their tactics, without changing their strategic objectives. They retained their object of extending Soviet influence to the whole of Germany; but as a preliminary stage, they planned to isolate the Federal Republic, detach it from the Western system of alliances, and neutralize it both militarily and politically.

Within this general framework, Moscow and East Berlin

continued to propagate the need for German reunification under the supervision of the victorious Four Powers, making constant reference to the terms of the Potsdam Agreement and the following conferences. At the same time, the conversion of East Germany into a Bolshevist state was purposefully and unwaveringly pressed ahead. For several years the Kremlin felt it important to appear to champion German reunification; but our intensive espionage and intelligence operations and analyses pointed repeatedly to the conclusion that this Soviet initiative on the German issue served only one purpose, namely to delay the development and consolidation of the Federal Republic while at the same time using domestic German emotions as a psychological weapon to impede, if not prevent altogether, the process of integration with the West.

In this connection, the events of 1952 are particularly interesting. In order to disrupt the negotiations over the Paris treaties, the Russians interpolated proposals which are still the subject of passionate debate in Germany today, under the heading of "missed opportunities." The Soviet demarches of 1952 were, it will be remembered, introduced by a note dated March 10 containing the draft of a proposed peace treaty with Germany; this first note was followed by further documents until, altogether, four notes had been exchanged by the Russians and the West. In them, Moscow proposed the "restoration of Germany as a united country," but they left open the actual procedure whereby an all-German government would be formed and also the question of free elections, a condition the Western powers adamantly refused to withdraw throughout the subsequent negotiations.

In the course of this exchange of notes, it became clear that the Soviets intended to encourage certain groups and organizations in the Federal Republic, notably those that came closest to the Communist idea of "democratic organizations," while any organization alleged to be hostile to "democracy" and to the "cause of peace" was to be proscribed on German soil. In their much quoted proposal of March 10, 1952, they also called for the withdrawal of all armed forces of the occupying powers not later than one year after the peace treaty had come into force in Germany. It need scarcely be added that as numerous intelligence reports confirmed, this section of the proposals was designed to strip the Western powers of their ability to guarantee the uninterrupted progress of political development in West Germany. It was claimed to be a particular token of the Soviet willingness to make concessions that West Germany was to be permitted such national armed forces as were necessary for the defense of their country; but this concession—which was received with evident surprise by many politicians within West Germany—clearly served only one purpose: to throw a hefty wrench into the negotiations on the setting up of a European defense community.

In short, one can state in retrospect that the texts of the Soviet notes, taken together with all our own intelligence reports of that time, clearly indicated what the Russians had in mind when they spoke of a "peace-loving, democratic Germany": a mirror image of their German Democratic Republic set up in the East, a West Germany in which the "democratic mass organizations" were to have a direct say in, for example, the composition of lists of parliamentary candidates—something quite unthinkable under our own constitution. The episode ended with an Allied note of September 23, 1952, to which Moscow never replied—presumably because by that time the Paris treaties were almost an accomplished fact.

I have dealt with the texts of these notes in some detail because politicians who were in opposition in 1952 now form part of our coalition government in Bonn, but still voice criticism along the following lines:*

> The West should not have insisted on "free elections first," but should have reached some kind of agreement with the Russians first on the military status of a reunited Germany; it was clear at the time that Moscow was prepared to agree to a reunification with free elections only if the military status had been clarified first.

---

* These criticisms are summarized in, for example, the journal *Die politische Meinung,* no. 90, p. 45.

The Soviet notes were directed against the European Defense Community, which was torpedoed in the end by the French veto anyway; and today the Federal Republic disposes of her own army, which was denied her at the time by the Western powers.

It is a distortion of the facts to dismiss the Soviet notes as a "return to Potsdam," because a return to Potsdam would also have restored full Four Power responsibility for Germany, from which the Western powers continue to derive their prerogatives since the German Treaty.

Apart from the recognition of the Oder-Neisse line and of the nonaffiliation of a reunified Germany to one or other of the power blocs, Moscow attached no further strings to reunification.

In my view these criticisms—which are as much a criticism of the Western powers as of the Federal Republic of the time— ignore the facts. It is a fatal error to assume that in insisting on a "united, independent, and democratic Germany" the Russians were ever thinking in terms of anything different from the state they have developed and molded in their own occupation zone.

* * *

During the Khrushchev era, from 1953 to 1964, Soviet policy toward Germany by no means lay dormant. While according to many reports reaching us the domestic tensions and uncertainties persisted in the Soviet Union and in its eastern European empire even after Stalin's death, the doctrine of "peaceful coexistence" already mapped out the new path that was to be followed. Tempered since then in numerous conferences and dialogues, there emerged from this basic principle and policy an important new weapon that from that time on proved as useful a tool in bargaining as it was a weapon in actual operational practice. In this phase we can see the East German uprising of June 17, 1953, the Geneva conference of 1955, the second Berlin crisis provoked by Khrushchev in November 1958, the collapse of the Paris summit conference in May 1960, and the erection of the Berlin Wall starting on August 13, 1961, as milestones in a European tragedy about which much has already been written.

Khrushchev's dramatic overthrow on October 14, 1964, brought little improvement in the situation of the Federal Republic, particularly as his alleged arbitrary attitude toward the German problem was one of the sharpest accusations raised against him by his critics. In fact, in his last two years of office Khrushchev had developed a policy toward Germany which simply could not be dismissed as a flexible interpretation of the doctrine of "peaceful coexistence." While Khrushchev, the last of the Kremlin dictators so far, continued on the one hand to pay lip service to the Moscow hard line and announced that the Berlin Wall was the legal frontier of the "de facto German Democratic Republic state," at the same time he endeavored to awaken hopes in Bonn. Once more the plan for a confederation of the German states was touched upon in conversations, with Khrushchev's son-in-law Adzhubei as the apostle of this policy of rapprochement. Adzhubei's mission foundered on the lively mistrust of East Berlin, and the final torpedoes were launched by Khrushchev's opponents within the Kremlin who were later to prove Khrushchev's own undoing. With Khrushchev's departure from the scene, there went a dynamic and unstereotyped party leader who had given much cause for hope in the West and, above all, in the Federal Republic. On the other hand, I hope it will justify our consistent reporting during the Khrushchev epoch if I now state that, however often we were criticized and rebuked for this, we never allowed ourselves to be taken in by the "man-of-his-word" aura with which Khrushchev was occasionally pleased to surround himself.

While during the Stalin and Khrushchev periods Soviet policy toward Germany was marked by constant change—albeit the Soviet ambitions remained the same—it rigidified after Khrushchev's political demise into the policy so familiar to us now. The determining factor in all this was that in twenty years, the Russians had not been able to detach the Federal Republic from the West's grip. The new collective leadership in the Kremlin found it was necessary to rethink their policy toward Germany. Besides, there were now other considerations—events within the Soviet empire which had disclosed unmistakably centrifugal tendencies among the people's republics in eastern Europe.

The Kremlin intensified its propaganda against the Federal Republic, labeling her "the only serious disturber of the peace" and trotting out all the familiar slogans about neo-Nazis, revisionists, and militarists. So long as Adenauer, Erhard, and Kiesinger were in power, the Soviet attitude toward Germany congealed into one of laying down so-called minimal requirements, whose acceptance would have been tantamount to recognition of the German Democratic Republic and renunciation of the reunification of Germany, as a prelude to the remodeling of West Germany's social structure along Soviet lines.

The increasing shrillness of this Soviet campaign of defamation against the West German government led, however, not to its political isolation, but to an even closer drawing together of the NATO partners. All the more formidable was the obstacle, in Soviet eyes, that West Germany presented to the creation of a European security system, which they hoped would be the subject of a security conference as soon as possible.

\* \* \*

The 1969 change of government in Bonn, with the emergence of a Socialist coalition government under Willy Brandt as chancellor, was exploited by the Soviet Union as an ideal opportunity to modify their methods in Germany, while retaining their long-term aims. The new government launched immediate and almost insistent attempts to break the logjam in its *Ostpolitik;* and in view of these overtures, which soon became public knowledge, the Kremlin hastened to tie down the West German government to a treaty which was designed from the outset to be nothing less than a formal confirmation of the partition of Germany. The treaty concluded in Moscow in August 1970 reflected the West German acceptance of the two-state theory, all ceremonially and legally documented just as the Soviet government would have wished, but without the explicit renunciation of Articles 53 and

107—the intervention articles—of the United Nations charter. Thus, the solution of the German problem that the Russians had contended for in vain for so long had been thrust into their startled laps.

At the time of writing, the Soviet-German treaty is still the subject of powerful controversy and awaiting ratification. While its supporters—predominantly Brandt's government and the majority of his coalition's deputies—lauded this as a "settlement at last" and an event of historic importance, its opponents not only called attention to its disadvantages and harsher stipulations but questioned the very essence of such treaty documents. The federal government then went further and amplified the Moscow treaty, with its confirmation of the partition of Germany, by an agreement with Poland, signed in Warsaw on December 7, 1970. This agreement put the seal of law on the final surrender of Germany's ancient territories to the east of the Oder and Neisse rivers and thus formally acquiesced to the Communist policies of aggrandizement in central and eastern Europe.

Moreover, the opponents of this treaty hold the view—a view which I share—that the Russians never have and never will sign a treaty in which their own interests do not come first and foremost; nor, so far as I am aware, has there been any historical instance of the Russians' attaching any importance whatever to establishing a genuine, let alone permanent, rapport with a neighboring country of any international significance. (This is not the same as "peaceful coexistence," as I have already pointed out, which is nothing but a political battle cry developed by the Communists.) I would refer those who still doubt this to the memoirs of the former American ambassador in Moscow, George F. Kennan, who warned most urgently against falling for any Soviet proposals or offers of treaties without first making sure of the necessary safeguards for one's own position; and never should Soviet offers be considered without consulting friendly governments in advance.

I believe that the view repeatedly expressed by the West German government that there is no alternative to the *Ostpolitik* of the Socialist and Liberal coalition is a mistaken one. It may well be that the Soviet Union itself will force us sooner or later to swallow an alternative. The hardening line expressed by the Communist press during 1971 and the unambiguous statements of loudmouthed generals and leading Communist officials—particularly those in the East German government and Communist party —underline this possibility, as does the increasing frequency with which they demand the absolute recognition of the German Democratic Republic.

An exceptionally undesirable consequence of these treaties with the Communist governments is the present widespread distrust of the Federal Republic in the Western world. The Communists have learned that the West German republic's nuisance value as a lever in Soviet strategy in Europe is as effective as ever. This Western mistrust has been aroused and expressed in so many different ways that neither the official words of encouragement and commendation mouthed by Western statesmen—which are beginning to look as hollow as they sound—nor the soothing assurances of the West German government and its spokesmen can camouflage this regrettable aspect. As an example of this mistrust, I understand that Western intelligence services with whom I always enjoyed the utmost cooperation are now reluctant to exchange their more secret information with the present Federal Intelligence Service.

The treaty negotiations between Moscow and Bonn would not have been conceivable had there not been a series of preliminary conversations conducted by close confidants of Willy Brandt (who was at the time foreign minister) in Rome long before he formed his Socialist-Liberal coalition government in the late autumn of 1969. The ice had been broken by the editor of the Italian Communist newspaper *Unità* in a visit to a number of left-wing German journalists in Bonn in September 1967, among whom was Brandt's friend and chief ideological adviser Leo Bauer (a former editor of the magazine *Der Stern*). After this discussion on the two Germanies, Bauer—about whose political background I had had cause to ask the FBI to institute certain inquiries

many years before—traveled to Rome and met the secretary of the leader of the Italian Communist party, Luigi Longo,
and late that November a three-man delegation from Willy Brandt's
Social Democratic party arrived in Rome for unpublicized meetings with leading Communist officials in the Hotel Cavalieri Hil-
ton.* Secret knowledge of these exploratory talks by Brandt's
minions placed the Federal Intelligence Service in an awkward
position for some time; we were still attached to Chancellor Kiesinger's office and I was directly responsible to him. When our
sources in Italy—who kept the Communist party there under surveillance with the knowledge of the leading Italians—sent us their
reports, we forwarded them to Chancellor Kiesinger.

Some details of these 1967 talks between Brandt's SPD officials and leading Italian Communists subsequently leaked out to
the public; but it is apparently not in the interests of the present
West German government for the fog which has continued to
envelop the prehistory of the Moscow treaty to be dispelled. One
thing is certain: it was in these Italian conversations that the foundations were laid for the "new *Ostpolitik*" the Federal Government
was to adopt after Willy Brandt came to power in 1969.

Meanwhile, the talks continued under particularly close secrecy by Egon Bahr, state-secretary in the Foreign Ministry, and
Leo Bauer. A few weeks before my retirement Bahr paid an official visit to us at Pullach. He showed a keen interest in everything
we showed him, politely accused us of being "cold-warriors," and
drove back to Munich. I have reason to know that in
Munich Bahr had kept a secret tryst with a senior Italian Communist official (I presume his trip to Pullach was a blind to distract attention). The rest of this story was to be read between the
lines of the West German newspapers in the weeks that followed.
Franz-Josef Strauss's newspaper *Bayernkurier* reported Bahr's
meeting with the Communists in Munich's hotel Bayerischer Hof.
In April, the Christian Democratic party's foreign affairs spokes-
man, Ernest Majonica, reported that Kiesinger had received a

---

* A full account of these meetings was given in the Italian weekly journal *Vie Nuove*
in November 1970.

secret protocol of recent talks between Willy Brandt and the Italian Communist leader in the latter's home, and *Die Welt* reported American alarm at Brandt's actions as follows: "There are indications that the American secret service received rapid information on the dialogue between the German Social Democrats and the Italian Communists, a dialogue which began in Rome and was continued in Munich." This new road, therefore, which will be beset by advance demands on the one side and by compromise on the other, started out in Rome. We can only ask, Where will it all end?

The profit to the Communists in finally gaining acceptance for their theory of two or, rather, three German states (if Berlin is included) lies mainly in the psychological effect this will have on the East German population. I cannot emphasize this too much. These people have remained far closer to our own country, through all the vicissitudes of humiliation and disappointment, than many would now like to believe. Now they are forced to recognize that their present status is going to remain with them forever and that they have been irrevocably sacrificed to the Communists. And what is true for the psychological effect on the East Germans is equally true, mutatus mutandis, for the people of the other Communist satellite countries, who are just as unsympathetic toward communism as the East Germans. It will have a psychological effect on their powers of resistance, too, since these peoples have largely overcome their resentment toward Germany and have to a certain extent regarded the fact that the German problem was still unsolved as a guarantee that their own fate might not be entirely permanent. In my view, the Kremlin can thus expect to reap a further reward—the consolidation of its satellite empire that it has always striven to achieve. Now the process of bolshevization there can really begin.

Finally, the Russians certainly attach no less importance to the psychological impact of the Soviet-German treaty on the West German population. They are not the only ones to anticipate that there will be an increase in those voices in the Federal Republic that would like to see this new-found modus vivendi with the

Soviet Union built upon and expanded. Thus, the internal stability of NATO will be subjected to new strain in spite of all the pious resolutions adopted at Brussels in December 1970 or at Lisbon the following May. And, moreover, the Kremlin will secure an added (and, once again, unilateral) advantage in its campaign to undermine the West, and its prospects for establishing the security system that the Soviet Union desires will be enhanced.

It always was Khrushchev's opinion that the policy of peaceful coexistence would create particularly favorable conditions for the Communists to attain their objectives. In our own case, we must never forget that for the Communists the bolshevization of all Germany will always be the first proviso for a successful Communist conversion of Europe. The undermining of the Western alliance (exploiting to that end every international political dispute in the countries concerned) and the subversion of the Federal Republic along with its separation from the Western system of alliances—which are facilitated by the two- and three-state concepts —must therefore be recognized as two complementary aspects of a uniform and strategically offensive Soviet policy. Every statement from the Communist camp proves again and again that the Kremlin is interested only in the destruction of the free world's system of alliances. Soviet efforts will become increasingly vigorous as the solution of the German problem desired by the Kremlin comes closer within their grasp. The solution aspired to by Moscow and broadly sanctioned by the present federal government is not, therefore, a defensive measure on the part of the Russians, but the indispensable prerequisite for further diplomatic and psychological operations, camouflaged by the language of peaceful coexistence and the slogans of collective security.

* * *

These remarks on the objectives, methods, and results of Soviet policies toward Germany would be incomplete without an examination of the role of Berlin in this connection. I have repeatedly stressed Berlin's importance as a touchstone for the steadfastness of the West; today, our former capital can be regarded as a test case for the Soviet willingness to make concessions, of which the federal government continues to make so much. Berlin will always be one of the few geographical locations where the moral prestige of the West—its political interests quite apart— will always be at stake, and where it will never be possible to yield one inch to the Communists. The erection of the Berlin Wall on August 13, 1961, was the limit of what the West could tolerate in this regard, as the rights of the Western powers were not overtly infringed. I have already described the intelligence work of our service in connection with the wall's erection.* Here I will add only that, in my view at the time, Ulbricht and the Soviet leaders backing him would have backed down had the three Western powers reacted with determined and immediate countermeasures that day; on the other hand, the Communists would certainly have found other methods of applying the tourniquet.

With the failure of their blockade, called off on July 29, 1949, the Soviet Union could have had no doubts that any further tampering with the three basic requirements of the Western powers— a military presence in West Berlin, unimpeded access to the city, and a guarantee of its economic survival—would inevitably result in a direct confrontation. We accordingly judged the various Berlin crises that followed to be purely momentary exercises to test the resolution of the Western powers. My colleagues and I repeatedly advised that the Russians would never allow things to go too far, provided they were sure the West would stand firm. So now they are trying to achieve by negotiation and dialogue with the Western powers and the Brandt government what they previously failed to gain by force: a loosening of the ties between Berlin and West Germany, and a final declaration that Berlin is a third and autonomous German political entity.

Today, I am more puzzled than ever before as to what kind of normalization the West envisages with respect to West Berlin. Not even the internalization of the road and rail corridors linking Berlin with the West and the elimination of East German controls

---

* See pp. 238–40.

this would permit—neither of which the Russians nor the East Germans will ever accept—could make the exposed position of West Berlin as an outpost of the free world any easier. Every concession that may be made by the Communists, such as easier access for West Berliners to East Berlin and East Germany, can be canceled without a moment's notice—they will always be able to find reason enough. So the crossing of East Germany to West Berlin will remain as prone to disruption as it is today.

If the West and the Federal Republic do not remain constantly on guard, all these piecemeal Berlin settlements will only make the divided city's long-term position more hopeless than it is. In any case, Berlin's usefulness as a political lever will not be done away with by any manner of agreement; it will remain as a bludgeon in the arsenal of the Russians and East Germans, to be produced from time to time to test the nerve of the Western powers and the Federal Republic.

This is no time for the initiated to stop their warnings, for it is not only I who can scent the Brandt government's irresistible urge to make concessions over West Berlin. We must not cease to give voice to our justified anxiety if we are to prevent still further concessions from being made without equivalent returns and gestures by the other side. During World War II and in the postwar years, our country suffered great damage and made great sacrifices in the fight for German interests, German possessions, and German values, and above all in the struggle for the future of our former capital, Berlin. May the politicians now responsible for Germany's new *Ostpolitik* always remember that their first and greatest commandment must always be to avert still greater damage in the future.

\* \* \*

The basically aggressive character of Soviet strategy, which I have demonstrated in some detail using their policy toward Germany as an example, also entails some problems and risks for the Communist empire which the Russians themselves are unable to ignore. The relatively new policies of détente and "security" inevitably pierce holes through the hermetic seal which has hitherto separated the Communist countries from the West. As they seek to expand their trade, technical, and cultural exchanges, there results an intensified contact, both official and personal, between the citizens of East and West under conditions where it is difficult to supervise them. The satellite countries have displayed a tendency to reap what rewards they can from the "golden West" on their own initiative, and this will almost inevitably increase. For this reason, the Russians are obliged to play down the policy they have purposefully adhered to since 1966, namely, that of calling for a European security system within their own Communist empire.

Moscow's easiest task was to stake her claim to the leadership of the Communist world organizations. I have already referred to the problems resulting from the conflict with Peking, so it will suffice for me to state that since Moscow controls the purse strings, and thanks to the self-interests pursued by the Latin American and African member organizations, a split has been avoided so far. Since 1966, Moscow's leadership has passed unchallenged, and even the brief crisis that followed the Russian occupation of Czechoslovakia has not altered that. We are safe, therefore, in assuming that for the foreseeable future the world organizations will continue to toe the Soviet party line.

The same holds true for the Warsaw Pact as well, although as I have indicated more than once, the circumstances are in its case demonstrably more complicated. Here, too, there is no foreseeable danger that the member-countries of the alliance will give up their political allegiance to Moscow. The Brezhnev doctrine can leave none of them in any doubt that Moscow is determined to prevent any repetition of events like those in Poland and Hungary in 1956 or any signs of a Communist reformation like that attempted by Alexander Dubcek in Czechoslovakia. Western journalists ascribed the invasion almost entirely to military considerations—in other words, to factors of power politics. Clearly, such considerations played their part in the decisions that were made, but far weightier than these was the realization that Dubcek was in danger of losing control of the situation and that a landslide might result which would end in a new brand of communism or even in some kind of social democratic order.

Nobody will forget how Dubcek was forced to capitulate. When he could not live up to his promises, the Russians took the necessary steps. The invasion itself was an offensive tactical operation which was designed not only to preserve the Soviet empire but to safeguard the European policies the Russians intended to continue pursuing. In Czechoslovakia that August every hope of attaining a modest degree of national sovereignty, of intellectual freedom, and an improved standard of living was ruthlessly crushed. Once the natural flood tide of a sense of liberty had ebbed, there remained only a residue of resignation and apathy. The passive fatalism of the eastern European population, which is manifested in their unsatisfactory morale, remains meanwhile for the Russians and their lackeys the main problem in pursuing their policies of détente. Strongly though individual eastern European citizens may identify with the Communist leaders in pursuing their own national interests, I remain absolutely convinced that the Communist system is flatly rejected by the broad mass of Polish, Hungarian, and—definitely—Czech populations, although they will obviously not openly admit it.

In the Soviet Union, too, the process of national image building, which saw the emergence of uniform "Soviet citizens" from the numerous Russian ethnic groups, has ground to a halt, choked with indigestible intelligentsia; and now the process actually seems to be operating in reverse. As far as East Germany is concerned, it is known from reliable reports and surveys right up to the present date that among its citizens there is still no real sense of belonging to the German Democratic Republic, apart of course from the narrow circles of party officials and beneficiaries of the system. This in no way detracts from their justifiable pride in their hard-won accomplishments as a new industrial nation; but the bulk of the population will always be indifferent toward communism. They are satisfied with arranging their lives as well as can be expected, without in any way approving of the system. But, at the same time, they have no desire to see certain circumstances in West Germany which are largely incomprehensible to them inflicted on them in the East. Just how phony the public facade of support for the East German regime really is was demonstrated only too clearly when our Federal Chancellor Willy Brandt visited Erfurt in East Germany for talks in March 1970. The chancellor got a huge reception from the East German populace, after which many people were arrested. Neither I nor my former colleagues were in the least surprised that this feeling of solidarity with the West was given such conspicuous and audible expression at Erfurt. The feelings are there, and they will be spontaneously kindled each time the occasion arises.

It should be the irrevocable duty for every West German government to respect this deep-seated emotion in East Germany, and to refrain from committing any action which might serve to perpetuate the partition of Germany either de facto or under international law. The incidents at Erfurt also show, moreover, that no Communist government—least of all that in East Berlin—can afford to introduce measures of liberalization, or to agree to relieve human anguish in connection with the interzonal traffic. To do so would be to jeopardize their very existence, which is based on the unhampered and unchallenged rule of force. Any suggestion that such measures can be encouraged by concessions by the West are pipe dreams, and nothing else.

\* \* \*

Monolithic though the Communist empire established by the Russians in eastern Europe may be, Moscow is troubled by the continuing disunity on the broader Communist front. I have already touched upon the major deviators—Red China and Yugoslavia—in examining the ideological differences between them and the Soviet Union.\* Albania, however, is not a significant factor in all this.

As far as Moscow's East European satellites are concerned, of which three (Hungary, Rumania, and Bulgaria) have common frontiers with the recalcitrant Yugoslavia, the country Tito rules remains the missing link in a chain which—as the Russians see it—must be closed one day. By including Yugoslavia in the Warsaw Pact system they would gain more vital bases on the Mediter-

---

\* See pp. 306–09; 312; 322–23.

ranean and build a further important element into the permanent threat to NATO's southern flank. From many sources we know that the Soviet leaders do not see any possibility of change so long as Yugoslavia's head of state is in any position to decide the fate of his country. So the Soviet Union has its eye on the period immediately following Tito's departure. His going would, the Russians anticipate, release the forces of dyed-in-the-wool Communists who have been pining for closer contact with Moscow and at the same time create opportunities to force this strategically important Adriatic territory under Moscow's sway. The Soviet intelligence service has already begun, under careful cover, to set up the necessary conditions for this in Yugoslavia, and the separatist disturbances in Croatia, late in 1971, are probably to be interpreted in this light.

\* \* \*

Of far greater importance to the entire Communist camp is, of course, the squabble with Red China. Since their objectives of world revolution are identical, it is their ideological differences that first meet the eye. But most likely the real tension is primarily built up by conflicts in power politics and by clashes which have considerably worsened the original differences. While I have no intention of minimizing the bitterness of this conflict—or the "depth of the gulf," as it is sometimes called—I do suggest that the rivalry between the two Communist superpowers has been accorded an exaggerated significance, and that while it is not as yet possible to fathom the political motive underlying this exaggeration, it is clearly influenced by subtle Russian psycho-political propaganda. I see that a study entitled "New Trends in Kremlin Policy," recently published by a European and American joint study group, takes the same view.

I am as reluctant now as I was over ten years ago to regard the split between Moscow and Peking as irrevocable and final— after all, what is "final" in politics? In any case, the Communist and Socialist movements have shown nothing but schisms in their 125 years of history, without having suffered undue injury in them.

I might add that the conflict originally arose over what was basically a procedural dispute over the course to be followed to final victory, and it was then kindled by two of the world movement's documents, namely the Moscow declarations of 1957 and 1960. Even today, the conflict is still expressed in largely ideological arguments, and it boils down to each side accusing the other of having betrayed the world revolution. If we bear in mind that for the Communists ideologies are directives for actions, we can easily see the significance of this theoretical bickering as far as practical politics is concerned.

I have never been able to share the hopes of my Western friends that this dispute might yet force the Soviet Union to come to terms with the West and obtain our support. Nor am I much convinced by the claim that there has been an increase in strife between the Communist blocs as a result of the Russian interest in the European security conference. It is obvious that the dispute with Peking is a nuisance for the Russians; but it does not put them to any serious risk at present, nor will it in the foreseeable future. Given the immense Soviet military superiority, outright war between the two powers is improbable for several years. It would be bound to end in defeat for Peking; while at the same time, the necessary provisioning and administration of the conquered territories would place an almost intolerable burden on Moscow. Nor do the Ussuri River incidents of March 1969 alter this judgment in any way: they were purely local in character, and they were deliberately played up by both sides.

Should I be wrong in my analysis, and should it in fact turn out that the Russians really do wish to secure their rear in the West for fear of Red China, then I can only hope that we and our allies will refuse to grant them any support so long as the Kremlin continues to deny its satellites their independence and forces 17 million Germans to subsist under Communist rule.

As in the case of Yugoslavia—though under wholly different conditions and circumstances—the Russian leaders who are still fighting for a global Communist movement are counting on sweeping changes in Red China once the Chinese dictator Mao Tse-tung has gone. But while I am inclined to put the Soviet chances of assimilating and perhaps even annexing Yugoslavia quite high once Tito goes, I judge the Soviet prospects in China after Mao's death very much less favorably. Neither Prime Minister Chou En-lai nor his defense minister will offer the Russians any hope that China will submit to the unchallenged hegemony of Moscow. But, on the other hand, neither they nor the People's Liberation Army, the major power factor in the country, which stands behind them, will prove either willing or able to carry on the almost godlike cult of personality surrounding Mao. Both are probably realistic enough to try first to restore to their country the interior stability that is vital for an effective foreign policy. A stable and consolidated China will then be able to play its hand in international affairs very differently from the giant nation at present, emasculated as it is by domestic disorders.

In stating my belief that in the long run we are more likely to see a rapprochement between Russia and China than a continuation—let alone an aggravation—of the present conflict, it has of course been necessary to take the state of the Soviet leadership into account as well. It seems probable that future changes in the Soviet command will be of greater significance in all this than is generally accepted. In Khrushchev, the legendary figure of Stalin —utterly intransigent and obsessed with the politics of power— was succeeded by a glittering personality whose sudden tactical whims frequently provoked acute dismay among his own entourage. In Brezhnev and Kosygin we have seen Khrushchev in turn replaced by pragmatic and hard-bitten politicians, wielding power with Podgorny in a triumvirate which was widely believed to have a very short life expectancy.

At the time of writing, there were recurring press reports presenting Leonid Ilyich Brezhnev, the sixty-five-year-old secretary general of the Soviet Union's Communist party, as the "new Stalin." Brezhnev has certainly pronounced that "where we stand is our undisputed empire," and this may well have been taken by many observers to be proof of a reversion to Stalinism in domestic and foreign policy. Nevertheless, I cannot believe that Brezhnev will one day manage to outwit his partners and climb the last rungs alone to absolute dictatorship. This is a mantle that will fall to one of his successors. In this connection, I take the view of many prominent experts on the Soviet Union that one particular personality will attain absolute power in the Kremlin in the not too distant future and that he will then mastermind both the struggle for dominion within the Communist empire and the external conflict with the Western world with extremes of resolution and ruthlessness. Of all the top level Soviet officials we have seen over the last few years, one man has stood head and shoulders above the rest—Alexandr Shelyepin, whose work in the secret service, in the youth movement, and currently as leader of the All-Union Council of Unions has guaranteed him a following of incomparable breadth. Should Shelyepin succeed in improving his relations with the military commanders and Soviet marshals, he may well become the "new Stalin." He has been defeated once already by the resistance of the old-guard officials; but he is shrewd enough to wait until the moment is ripe. Of one thing there can be no doubt: his supporters credit him with all the necessary ambition and ability to reach for the mantle of absolute power.

\* \* \*

Important though this analysis of the future conduct of Soviet power politics may be, it is not the end of the story. Many readers will probably be interested in learning my views on the likely trends these politics will follow over the next few years and decades. With twenty-six years' experience in analyzing the Soviet estate, I would be inclined to predict the Soviet objectives for the 1970s as follows: The Soviets will try—by force, if necessary—to consolidate and secure their empire in Europe, including all their wartime and postwar conquests. This is the Brezhnev doctrine, an example of which was the occupation of Czechoslovakia, to which I would add that in my opinion the Soviet Union will not hesitate to intervene with the same ruthlessness in Poland or Rumania, for example, should the need arise. The Russians will intensify their attempts to dissolve the Western system of alliances in Europe and replace it by a "European peace settlement" (as the Russians understand the concept of peace). The focus of these efforts will remain West Germany, which they will try to undermine, isolate, and intimidate as a preliminary to transferring her to the Soviet sphere of influence.

The Soviet Union will also establish strongpoints in the Mediterranean, in the Arab world, and in the Indian Ocean. They will extend their influence in Scandinavia from Finland to the Barents Sea. They will expand their base on Cuba as a base for the ultimate war with the United States that may later come— although during the 1970s the Russian policy toward the United States will probably be one of delay, while at the same time they consolidate their footholds. Meanwhile, negotiations with the United States, coupled with certain concessions on the Soviet part, will be pursued only where overwhelmingly favorable results will accrue from them for the Russians. Finally, the Russians will make provision for the inclusion of Red China in a Communist world empire under Soviet hegemony once Mao Tse-tung has gone, without resort to armed conflict if possible.

If the West continues to play its present passive political role, the 1980s will probably see an exceptional worsening of the international situation once the present generations of leaders in Moscow and Peking have been replaced. The question of who will take over power within the Kremlin is of particular importance in this connection. During the 1980s, the world will then probably see the elimination of Red China as a contender for the dominant role in world communism by force of Soviet arms, should it have proved impossible to draw her into the fold by means short of war by then. The Communists will then intensify their activity in the key areas of Western Europe and the Mediterranean, coupled with an attempt to draw Western Europe itself and the countries bordering on the southern Soviet Union into the Communist empire, using all the well-tried methods of revolutionary struggle and subversion they have perfected. And the Communists will then make their final dispositions for the ultimate clash with the United States of America.

Given these political objectives, the West's chance of survival will depend on whether we succeed in confronting the Soviet Union with a concerted strategy born of the knowledge I have tried to set out in these pages. Of course, there are numerous experts, even in the United States, who see these dangers in just the same light as I do. But the vast majority of the public has still to recognize the dangers; and above all, they still fail to grasp that the West can fight this virus coming from the East only by a strategy of *political offense*. In every Western country, the public, who naturally cherishes world peace as the most vital chattel of the West, has been blinded by the many devious propaganda ploys adopted by the Soviet Union, and it fails to see the light.

If we ask, has the Soviet Union become less dangerous, I can only reply emphatically that it has not. The Soviet Union is not a static power, solely concerned with defensive affairs and the maintenance of its possessions, it is, rather, a politically dynamic and aggressive world power which will stop at nothing to reach its objectives and secure its aims. There is no basis whatsoever for the numerous hints dropped in recent months about a "genuine change" in Soviet policies. This is the purest speculation. The methods and tactics of Soviet campaigning have been refined; but the will to attack everything we hold most dear, and particularly our freedom of thought and action, remains unchanged.

We should not refuse to deal with the East, but we should be willing to pursue and protract the negotiations over a long period of time, completely devoid of any illusions and without proposing any concessions on our own part. The Soviet mentality will never understand any treaty dealings in which we fail to formulate clear counterdemands against them: such dealings will always be regarded with the utmost mistrust. The correct way to negotiate is always to start off listing the maximum demands, while at the same time bearing constantly in mind what are the minimum demands—that is, the demands whose nonacceptance must be followed by breaking off the negotiations.

We must hope that these facts will come to be accepted, for there is only one way for the free world as we know it to survive

—and that is only if the whole of the West can put its separate, parochial interests in second place and recognize that now the supreme need is for all Western countries to unite into one political entity, capable of combatting on their own terms the aggressive Soviet "peace policies." That is why the most vital step now is the earliest possible coalition of the whole of free Europe, including Spain, to a concerted political unit capable of withstanding the eroding tides of Soviet power and communism. This is also why we must recognize that the repeated Soviet proposals for a European security conference serve only one end—to hinder the unification of Western Europe into such an entity.

Even more important than the unification of Europe is the Atlantic alliance. Here, too, ways must be found of establishing a rigid community of purpose between this reborn Europe and the American continent. While there are obviously many conflicting issues that divide Europe and America, a noble settlement of these differences must nonetheless be reached. One step must be taken immediately: NATO's southeastern hinge in the eastern Mediterranean must be given the massive political and military attention it deserves if this flank is to be defended. There ought to be far closer collaboration between the NATO countries and Turkey and Greece, and if possible the diminutive but politically and militarily virile Israel should be included too. There is no time to lose.

As for the intelligence services of the free world, they must work in close unison and with the greatest possible energy to defeat the Communists' intentions. In doing so they will have played their part in securing a future for the free world, and for our own freedom and security.

## APPENDIX

---

# Memorandum
# on a
# Future Intelligence Service
### May 21, 1952

## 1. *The Need for a Federal Intelligence Service*

One of a sovereign nation's most important sources of the materials on which its political actions are based is its intelligence service. It will be seen that this embraces two distinct kinds of work, which are different in both their objects and their tasks, and it will be most practical for these to be kept organizationally separate as well.

(a) As far as internal affairs are concerned, the German Federal Republic already possesses in the Office for the Protection of the Constitution the intelligence organization it needs for obtaining data on the domestic political scene.

(b) Hitherto, there has existed no intelligence organization for obtaining data on the external scene in the political, economic, military, and counterespionage sectors. With the establishment of the German Federal Republic's autonomy a need arises for the creation of such an organization—i.e., a Federal Intelligence Service which will work beyond the Federal Republic's frontiers, and oper-

[ 373

ate within the Federal Republic only where necessary for the setting up of control points for its work abroad and for the protection of its own intelligence communications.

It will be necessary for these two distinct state agencies to cooperate closely with one another, as the Office for the Protection of the Constitution will have the best opportunities for frustrating the enemy's attack on the inland establishments of the Federal Intelligence Service, and the Federal Intelligence Service for its part will be well placed to detect the enemy's points abroad for launching attacks on our domestic government institutions.

## 2. *Duties and Organization of the Federal Intelligence Service*

In laying down the duties and organizational structure of the Federal Intelligence Service the guiding principle must be to avoid at all costs the errors and shortcomings of the past. So it is not a matter of resuscitating the old Abwehr, but of creating something basically new, bearing the following points in mind:

(a) Unified control of all German intelligence work beyond federal frontiers in the sectors of foreign policy and of economic, military, and counterespionage. Thus, the role of the Federal Intelligence Service will be total intelligence-data procurement of every kind abroad. As in Britain and the United States, the procurement of intelligence and other data must be run on wholly nonpartisan lines, in the national interest alone. It will be an institution working with scientific methods, and in general it will have nothing in common with the picture of the intelligence worker found in cheap popular literature or suggested by the dubious activities of the Kemritz case.

Unified control will enable the Federal Intelligence Service to function economically, because frequently the same agents and the same controllers will be able to operate in several diverse sectors; it will also obviate the risk of duplicated or conflicting efforts such as we have witnessed at Germany's expense in the past. Every other non-German country of any importance is in the process of reorganizing its services along these lines.

(b) It will be found most practical for the unified Federal Intelligence Service, which is ultimately a matter of common interest to all the other government bodies, to be directly subordinated to the head of government (a solution adopted by postwar France and the United States).

Without prejudice to this direct subordination to the federal chancellor, the unified Federal Intelligence Service must also be firmly anchored in the various requisitioning authorities (the Foreign Ministry, the Economics Ministry, the Defense Ministry, the Ministry for All-German Affairs, and other federal agencies with an interest in the intelligence data obtained), to enable the Federal Intelligence Service to accomplish to the full the tasks asked of it by these requisitioning authorities.

To insure this, it will be necessary for each of the ministries concerned to appoint a "special adviser" (*Sonderreferent*) to the minister; he will be the plenipotentiary of the minister in all intelligence matters. He will simultaneously be the liaison officer to the Federal Intelligence Service and will formulate his minister's intelligence requirements to the Federal Intelligence Service. At the same time, he will receive on behalf of his minister the analyses and reports of the Federal Intelligence Service relating to that particular ministry's field, and within the ministry's sector he will insure that the work of the Federal Intelligence Service is given all possible support.

The terms of service of the head of the Federal Intelligence Service must be such as to exclude any encroachment on the right of the minister to express to the federal chancellor opinions on intelligence data produced by his own department. Equally, the head of the Federal Intelligence Service must be enabled to refer to the views of the minister concerned in formulating his own overall analysis of the situation.

(c) All German groups already operating on their own initiative in this field—insofar as they are not operating impermissibly under foreign control—must be embodied in suitable form in the Federal Intelligence Service to be set up.

## 3. *The Setting Up Process*

Experience suggests that to set up an intelligence service and overcome all its teething troubles takes at least five years before it becomes a fully operational and efficient instrument. During the postwar era, an intelligence organization staffed and controlled entirely by Germans has been built up on the initiative of General Gehlen, founded on the idealistic concept of defending the Western way of life and Christian culture against communism. This "Gehlen agency" (*Dienststelle Gehlen*) operates in every intelligence field against the Eastern bloc countries. Hitherto, it has been financed by the Americans on the basis of a "gentlemen's agreement" reached by General Gehlen, in which the purely German character of the service is formally recognized and he is expressly conceded the right to owe allegiance exclusively to the German authorities concerned. In consequence, General Gehlen took up contact with the federal chancellor after the federal government was set up and asked him to authorize the continuation of this work. As the expert opinion was that this is an organization whose achievements are of international standing, it is proposed to use this organization as the matrix for the construction of the Federal Intelligence Service.

Over the last few months, there has therefore been a minute investigation of the organization by the federal chancellor's representatives, as to its political, personnel, administrative, and capability aspects. This investigation has shown that it would be desirable to exploit this organization in setting up the Federal Intelligence Service, especially since the Americans, in the interests of strengthening the Federal Republic's defensive capability against communism, are prepared to transfer to the government the technical equipment available to the organization, including approximately 200 vehicles, and to continue with a financial subsidy in return for the provision of the Eastern intelligence data obtained. There is no danger of any unhealthy dependence on a foreign country inherent in the personnel of this organization, and General Gehlen has moreover stated his intention of disbanding the organization should the federal government not take it over.

It is proposed that the Federal Intelligence Service be set up in the following stages:

(a) Clarification of the issue of a future Federal Intelligence Service with the representatives of the major parties.

(b) After the German Treaty takes effect, the transfer of General Gehlen with a small staff to government status, as "Office for the Federal Intelligence Service," with the task of creating the Federal Intelligence Service from the existing organization and other groups and suitable persons, according to general directives to be laid down by the Chancellor's Office.

(c) Simultaneous with the setting up of the Office for the Federal Intelligence Service, the appointment of the special ministerial advisers in all the ministries concerned.

(d) Programmed transfer into the Federal Intelligence Service of the existing organization according to the procedural rules to be laid down and to the existing German civil service regulations, in such a manner as will not interrupt the flow or quality of the current intelligence reporting.

(e) Simultaneous with (d), incorporation of otherwise suitable groups into the service, or the coordination of their activities.

# Milestones
# in My Career

| | |
|---|---|
| April 3, 1902 | Born in Erfurt, Germany. Parents: Lieutenant Colonel (ret.) Walther Gehlen, publisher, of Breslau, and Katharina Margarete, *née* von Vaernewyck. |
| April 1, 1920 | Completed secondary education. |
| April 20, 1920 | Joined the provisional Reichswehr. |
| Summer 1921 | Officer candidate, Third Artillery Regiment. |
| Autumn 1922 | Ensign. |
| Autumn 1923 | Ensign first class. |
| December 1, 1923 | Promoted to lieutenant. |
| February 1, 1928 | First lieutenant; until early 1933, adjutant of First Detachment, Third Artillery Regiment. |
| October 1, 1933 | Staff college until 1935. |
| May 1, 1934 | Promoted to captain. |
| July 1935 | Posted to General Staff. Served in various positions, including adjutant to deputy chief of staff and simultaneously in the operations branch and in the fortifications branch of the General Staff. |

| | |
|---|---|
| November 10, 1938 | Commander, Eighth Battery, Eighteenth Artillery Regiment. |
| March 1, 1939 | Promoted to major. |
| September 1, 1939 | Upon outbreak of war, operations officer (Ia) of 213th Infantry Division, until October 6, 1939. |
| October 10, 1939 | Chief of Fortifications Group of War Department, until May 1940. |
| May 1940 | In succession, liaison officer to Commander in Chief Brauchitsch of the Sixteenth Army, to General Hoth's panzer group, and to General Guderian's panzer group, until the end of the campaign in France, June 1940. |
| July 1, 1940 | Adjutant of General Halder, chief of the General Staff, until October 1940. |
| October 7, 1940 | Chief of Eastern Group of General Staff's operations branch. |
| July 1, 1941 | Promoted to lieutenant colonel (GS). |
| April 1, 1942 | Appointed head of General Staff's branch, Foreign Armies East. |
| December 1, 1942 | Promoted to colonel (GS). |
| December 1, 1944 | Promoted to brigadier general. |
| April 9, 1945 | Dismissed as head of Foreign Armies East. |
| May 22, 1945 | Surrendered with my principal colleagues to American forces at Fischhausen, on Lake Schliersee. |
| August 26, 1945 | Flown to United States with four of my colleagues. |
| July 1, 1946 | Departure from United States for Europe. |
| July 12, 1946 | Discharged from prisoner of war status. Formal birth of the Gehlen organization. |
| April 1, 1956 | Transfer of Gehlen organization to West German government; birth of Federal Intelligence Service (Bundesnachrichtendienst). Promoted to lieutenant general of reserve in the Bundeswehr. President of the BND. |
| April 30, 1968 | Retirement from Federal Intelligence Service. |

---

| | |
|---|---|
| September 10, 1931 | Married to Herta Gehlen, *née* von Seydlitz-Kurzbach. |

# GLOSSARY

| | |
|---|---|
| Abwehr | The intelligence service controlled by the German OKW (q.v.) until 1944, when it was disbanded. |
| BfV | *Bundesamt für Verfassungsschutz,* "Federal Office for the Protection of the Constitution," the approximate equivalent of the FBI or of the Special Branch in Britain. Founded in 1950, it is the investigatory agency handling West German counterespionage and countersubversion activities—without, however, any executive powers (i.e., of arrest). It is subordinated to the Ministry of the Interior. |
| Blank Office | *Amt Blank,* the West German government agency set up in 1950 as the forerunner of the Ministry of Defense. |
| BND | *Bundesnachrichtendienst,* "Federal Intelligence Service," the successor to the Gehlen organization, which it absorbed upon its creation in April 1956. It was headed by Reinhard Gehlen from then until |

April 1968 and thereafter by General Gerhard Wessel.

Bundesrat
The upper house of the West German Federal Parliament.

Bundestag
The lower house of the West German Federal Parliament—the elected parliamentary assembly.

Bundeswehr
Official title of the West German armed forces.

CIA
Central Intelligence Agency, established in the United States by the National Security Act of 1947, replacing the Office of Strategic Services (q.v.).

CIC
The U.S. Army Counter Intelligence Corps.

Cominform
Communist Information Bureau, established by the Soviet Communist party in 1947 as an organization embracing all of the Communist parties of the world. It was dissolved in 1956.

EDC
European Defense Community, the Western European defense organization proposed in the European Defense Community Treaty signed on May 27, 1952. The plan—which provided for the rearmament of West Germany under the aegis of a European army —effectively fell through when the French National Assembly voted against French participation on August 30, 1954.

FBI
Federal Bureau of Investigation. A branch of the U.S. Department of Justice, it is responsible for internal security matters and for the investigation of federal law violations.

FDJ
*Freie Deutsche Jugend,* "Free German Youth," the official Communist youth organization in the Soviet zone of Germany.

FHO
*Fremde Heere Ost,* "Foreign Armies East," Branch 12 of the German army's General Staff, controlling intelligence activities on the eastern front before and during World War II.

FLN
*Front de Libération Nationale,* the leftist Algerian nationalist political organization—founded on No-

vember 1, 1954—which fought for and won Algerian independence from France.

G-2     Originally U.S. Army Intelligence, the second section of the army's General Staff. Since World War II, the abbreviation has been adopted by other Western powers as a general synonym for military intelligence.

Gestapo     *Geheime Staatspolizei,* "Secret State Police." Organized in 1933 by Goering, it was ultimately controlled by the SS and Heinrich Himmler.

GPU     *Gosudarstvennoye Politicheskoye Upravlenye,* the Soviet office of political security, espionage, and counterespionage which, in 1922, succeeded the infamous Cheka. Later called the OGPU, its functions were assumed by the NKVD (q.v.) in 1934.

Ia     Staff officer, operations.

Ic     Staff officer, intelligence.

Ic/AO     *Ic/Abwehroffizier,* joint military intelligence and counterespionage officer.

KGB     *Komitat Gosudarstvennoy Bezopasnosti,* "Committee for State Security," the Soviet secret police agency; established in 1953, it was the successor of the MVD (q.v.).

LDPD     *Liberal-Demokratische Partei Deutschlands,* the East German Liberal Democratic Party.

MAD     *Militärischer Abschirmdienst,* "Military Screening Service," a West German agency comparable in function with the U.S. Army's CIC, protecting the Bundeswehr units from espionage and subversive activities.

MI6     Military Intelligence, Branch 6, the British intelligence agency linked to the Foreign Office. It is formally known as the Secret Intelligence Service (q.v.).

Ministerialrat     Ranks within the German civil service (in ascending
Ministerialdirigent     order of seniority).
Ministerialdirektor

MVD     *Ministerstvo Vniutrennikh Dyel,* "Ministry of Internal Affairs," a Soviet state security service headed by Lavrenti P. Beria until his liquidation in 1953; its functions were subsequently assumed by the KGB (q.v.).

| | |
|---|---|
| NATO | North Atlantic Treaty Organization, founded in 1949. |
| NDPD | *National-Demokratisches Partei Deutschlands,* the East German National Democratic Party. |
| *Neues Deutschland* | Official organ of the Socialist Unity Party—East Germany's Communist Party. |
| NKVD | *Narodnyi Kommissariat Vniutrennikh Dyel,* "People's Commissariat of Internal Affairs," the Soviet secret police agency that preceded the MVD (q.v.). |
| NTS | *Narodnyi Trudovoy Soyuz,* "National Labor Union," an anti-Communist Russian exile organization, whose initials were sometimes taken to stand for "We bring death to the tyrants." |
| OAS | *Organisation de l'Armée Secrète,* a secret counter-revolutionary organization comprised of key French army officers whose purpose was to crush the Algerian independence movement. It was formed in 1961 and headed by General Raoul Salan. |
| OKH | *Oberkommando des Heeres,* "High Command of the Army." |
| OKW | *Oberkommando der Wehrmacht,* "High Command of the Armed Forces," originally organized as a controlling authority for the German armed forces; during the war it became preoccupied with the conduct of military operations on all fronts except the eastern. |
| ONI | Office of Naval Intelligence, the intelligence agency of the U.S. Navy. |
| OSS | Office of Strategic Services, wartime American intelligence agency, disbanded in 1945. |
| OUN | *Organizatsia Ukrainiskikh Nationalistiv,* "Organization of Ukrainian Nationalists," a resistance group in the Ukraine, first organized against German oc- |

cupation forces in 1941 and then expanded into a nationalist political organization which met the returning Soviets in February 1943 with both open and guerilla resistance. It is reported that the organization yet survives, despite the efforts of the KGB.

| | |
|---|---|
| Reichswehr | Literally, "Reich Defense," the official armed forces of the Second Reich permitted by the Treaty of Versailles of 1919; forerunner of the Wehrmacht and Bundeswehr. |
| RSHA | *Reichssicherheitshauptamt,* "Reich Main Security Office," formed in 1939, comprising the Gestapo, the criminal police, and the SD; ultimately controlled by Heinrich Himmler and the SS. |
| SD | *Sicherheitsdienst,* "Security Service," the intelligence and espionage arm of the SS. |
| SDECE | *Service de Documentation Extérieure et de Contre-Espionage,* the French foreign intelligence service. |
| SED | *Sozialistische Einheitspartei Deutschlands,* "Socialist Unity Party of Germany," the East German Communist party. |
| SFIO | *Section Française de l'Internationale Ouvrière,* the French section of the Worker's International, a Communist organization. |
| SIS | Secret Intelligence Service, the formal name for MI6 (q.v.)—the only British agency authorized to conduct espionage operations overseas and to collect information by illegal means. |
| SPD | *Socialistische Demokratische Partei Deutschlands,* the German Social Democratic Party—suppressed under the Hitler regime, it is currently the leading opposition party in West Germany. |
| SS | *Schutzstaffel,* "Defense Echelon," Himmler's powerful paramilitary organization created in 1929 and expanded ultimately into a fourth armed service. |
| SSD | *Staatssicherheitsdienst,* "State Security Service," the East German political police. |

| | |
|---|---|
| State-Secretary | *Staatssekretär*—the highest rank in the German civil service, akin to the British permanent undersecretary, except that it is not permanent but an essentially political appointment. |
| USFET | United States Forces, European Theater. |
| V-Man | *V-Mann* (*Vertrauensmann*), "trusted man," an especially trustworthy and idealistically motivated intelligence agent. |
| Wehrmacht | German armed forces of all three services from 1933 to 1945. |

Russia's vital raw materials reserves.

The military situation shortly before the conclusion
of the 1942 winter campaign.